Applied Machine Learning II

Applied Machine Learning II

Editor

Grzegorz Dudek

Basel • Beijing • Wuhan • Barcelona • Belgrade • Novi Sad • Cluj • Manchester

Editor
Grzegorz Dudek
Faculty of Electrical
Engineering, Czestochowa
University of Technology
Czestochowa
Poland

Editorial Office
MDPI
St. Alban-Anlage 66
4052 Basel, Switzerland

This is a reprint of articles from the Special Issue published online in the open access journal *Applied Sciences* (ISSN 2076-3417) (available at: https://www.mdpi.com/journal/applsci/special_issues/Machine_Learning_II).

For citation purposes, cite each article independently as indicated on the article page online and as indicated below:

Lastname, A.A.; Lastname, B.B. Article Title. *Journal Name* **Year**, *Volume Number*, Page Range.

ISBN 978-3-7258-0073-5 (Hbk)
ISBN 978-3-7258-0074-2 (PDF)
doi.org/10.3390/books978-3-7258-0074-2

© 2024 by the authors. Articles in this book are Open Access and distributed under the Creative Commons Attribution (CC BY) license. The book as a whole is distributed by MDPI under the terms and conditions of the Creative Commons Attribution-NonCommercial-NoDerivs (CC BY-NC-ND) license.

Contents

About the Editor vii

Grzegorz Dudek
Applied Machine Learning: New Methods, Applications, and Achievements
Reprinted from: *Applied Sciences* **2023**, *13*, 10845, doi:10.3390/app131910845 1

Nora Alhammad and Hmood Al-Dossari
Dynamic Segmentation for Physical Activity Recognition Using a Single Wearable Sensor
Reprinted from: *Applied Sciences* **2021**, *11*, 2633, doi:10.3390/app11062633 7

Jaeun Choi and Yongsung Kim
A Heterogeneous Learning Framework for Over-the-Top Consumer Analysis Reflecting the Actual Market Environment
Reprinted from: *Applied Sciences* **2021**, *11*, 4783, doi:10.3390/app11114783 23

Jože M. Rožanec, Blaž Kažič, Maja Škrjanc, Blaž Fortuna and Dunja Mladenić
Automotive OEM Demand Forecasting: A Comparative Study of Forecasting Algorithms and Strategies
Reprinted from: *Applied Sciences* **2021**, *11*, 6787, doi:10.3390/app11156787 39

Carlos Villaseñor, Alberto A. Gallegos, Gehova Lopez-Gonzalez, Javier Gomez-Avila, Jesus Hernandez-Barragan and Nancy Arana-Daniel
Ellipsoidal Path Planning for Unmanned Aerial Vehicles
Reprinted from: *Applied Sciences* **2021**, *11*, 7997, doi:10.3390/app11177997 58

Julian Webber, Abolfazl Mehbodniya, Rui Teng, Ahmed Arafa and Ahmed Alwakeel
Finger-Gesture Recognition for Visible Light Communication Systems Using Machine Learning
Reprinted from: *Applied Sciences* **2021**, *11*, 11582, doi:10.3390/app112411582 75

Tebogo Bokaba, Wesley Doorsamy and Babu Sena Paul
Comparative Study of Machine Learning Classifiers for Modelling Road Traffic Accidents
Reprinted from: *Applied Sciences* **2022**, *12*, 828, doi:10.3390/app12020828 91

Zhishuo Zhang, Manting Luo, Zhaoting Hu and Huayong Niu
Textual Emotional Tone and Financial Crisis Identification in Chinese Companies: A Multi-Source Data Analysis Based on Machine Learning
Reprinted from: *Applied Sciences* **2022**, *12*, 6662, doi:10.3390/app12136662 109

Sebastian Sakowski, Jacek Waldmajer, Ireneusz Majsterek and Tomasz Poplawski
DNA Computing: Concepts for Medical Applications
Reprinted from: *Applied Sciences* **2022**, *12*, 6928, doi:10.3390/app12146928 133

Evandro Carvalho de Andrade, Plácido Rogerio Pinheiro, Ana Luiza Bessa de Paula Barros, Luciano Comin Nunes, Luana Ibiapina C. C. Pinheiro, Pedro Gabriel Calíope Dantas Pinheiro, et al.
Towards Machine Learning Algorithms in Predicting the Clinical Evolution of Patients Diagnosed with COVID-19
Reprinted from: *Applied Sciences* **2022**, *12*, 8939, doi:10.3390/app12188939 152

Toby R. F. Phillips, Claire E. Heaney, Ellyess Benmoufok, Qingyang Li, Lily Hua, Alexandra E. Porter, et al.
Multi-Output Regression with Generative Adversarial Networks (MOR-GANs)
Reprinted from: *Applied Sciences* **2022**, *12*, 9209, doi:10.3390/app12189209 171

Shahriar Shakir Sumit, Dayang Rohaya Awang Rambli, Seyedali Mirjalili, Muammad Mudassir Ejaz and M. Saef Ullah Miah
ReSTiNet: On Improving the Performance of Tiny-YOLO-Based CNN Architecture for Applications in Human Detection
Reprinted from: *Applied Sciences* **2022**, *12*, 9331, doi:10.3390/app12189331 . . . . **195**

Irfan Khan Tanoli, Imran Amin, Faraz Junejo, and Nukman Yusoff
Systematic Machine Translation of Social Network Data Privacy Policies
Reprinted from: *Applied Sciences* **2022**, *12*, 10499, doi:10.3390/app122010499 . . . . **215**

About the Editor

Grzegorz Dudek

Grzegorz Dudek is Professor of Information and Communication Technology. He received his PhD in electrical engineering from Czestochowa University of Technology (CUT), Poland, in 2003, and his habilitation in computer science from Łódź University of Technology, Poland, in 2013. Currently, he is a professor at the Department of Electrical Engineering, CUT, and the Department of Mathematics and Computer Science, University of Łódź. He is the author of four books on the subject of machine learning for forecasting and evolutionary algorithms for unit commitment in addition to over 120 scientific papers. His research interests include machine learning and artificial intelligence and their application to practical classification, regression, forecasting, and optimization problems.

 applied sciences

Editorial

Applied Machine Learning: New Methods, Applications, and Achievements

Grzegorz Dudek

Department of Electrical Engineering, Częstochowa University of Technology, 42-201 Częstochowa, Poland; grzegorz.dudek@pcz.pl

Citation: Dudek, G. Applied Machine Learning: New Methods, Applications, and Achievements. *Appl. Sci.* **2023**, *13*, 10845. https://doi.org/10.3390/app131910845

Received: 13 September 2023
Accepted: 28 September 2023
Published: 29 September 2023

Copyright: © 2023 by the author. Licensee MDPI, Basel, Switzerland. This article is an open access article distributed under the terms and conditions of the Creative Commons Attribution (CC BY) license (https:// creativecommons.org/licenses/by/ 4.0/).

1. Introduction

The realm of machine learning (ML) is one of the most dynamic and compelling domains within the computing landscape today. Over the past few decades, ML has firmly embedded itself in our daily lives, offering effective solutions to real-world challenges. The scope of ML's applications spans a multitude of sectors, encompassing engineering, industry, business, finance, medicine, and beyond. ML's comprehensive spectrum of techniques embraces traditional algorithms such as linear regression, k-nearest neighbors, decision trees, support vector machines, and neural networks, while also incorporating cutting-edge innovations such as deep learning and boosted tree models.

Finding the optimal architecture and parameters for ML models presents a substantial challenge, but is essential for attaining strong performances in both learning and generalization. Furthermore, as ML is practically applied, it encounters the complexities of managing extensive, incomplete, distorted, and uncertain data. A key requirement for ML methods is interpretability, ensuring a clear understanding of how these models function and fostering confidence in their outcomes.

Based on the reviewers' feedback, as well as the evaluations of the editor, 12 papers from 26 submissions have been selected for this Special Issue. These papers examine the conceptualization of problems, data representation, feature engineering, ML models employed, discerning comparisons against existing techniques, and the lucid interpretation of results. This Special Issue strives to not only showcase the prolific applications of ML, but to also provide insights into the methodologies and interpretations that underpin these advancements. The 12 papers, which cover a broad range of topics, are introduced briefly below.

2. Summary of the Contributions

Paper [1] addresses the challenge of recognizing physical activity in individuals with spinal cord injuries (SCI) using sensor-based approaches. SCI patients often experience health complications like obesity and muscle weakness, necessitating effective rehabilitation. Existing methods, relying on patient surveys, may not accurately capture actual activity levels. The advent of physical activity recognition systems presents a more reliable solution. The paper compares vision-based and sensor-based approaches, favoring wearable sensors for their affordability and ease of use. Sensor placement is crucial, with lower-limb sensors suited for locomotion and upper-limb activity requiring wrist and upper-arm sensors. This paper explores various applications of activity recognition, particularly in rehabilitation monitoring.

Segmenting continuous raw data before classification is a key challenge. While the sliding window approach is common, selecting an appropriate window size is vital to ensuring accuracy. Short windows may truncate activities, while long windows can merge them. Adaptive window techniques have been proposed to address this issue. The paper introduces a novel segmentation method tailored to dynamic activities in rehabilitation. An experiment compares this approach to the fixed sliding window method, demonstrating its effectiveness in boosting recognition accuracy.

This study, which employs wrist-worn accelerometers, reveals an accuracy improvement of over 5%, enhancing model robustness and successfully classifying similar activities. The method achieves recognition rates exceeding 91% with various ML classifiers, particularly the support vector machine. Wearable sensors, such as accelerometers, prove invaluable in rehabilitation assessment. The study acknowledges the potential limitations, while also highlighting the method's potential for segmenting and recognizing physical activities, especially in rehabilitation scenarios.

In [2], a framework for analyzing consumer behavior in the rapidly growing over-the-top (OTT) media consumption market was introduced, considering factors such as pricing, service delivery, and infrastructure investments. This paper addresses the challenge of an imbalanced consumer distribution within the OTT market, and the need for accurate analysis reflecting changing market conditions due to factors like the COVID-19 pandemic. This paper highlights the rapid growth of the OTT market, driven by the availability of digital media content via the internet and IP-based paths. Platforms like YouTube, Netflix, and Amazon Prime are transforming the media landscape, threatening traditional markets. With a projected market value of over a trillion dollars by 2027, various service providers and telecom carriers are competing fiercely in this domain. The COVID-19 pandemic has further accelerated the growth of OTT consumption, making it vital to analyze consumer behavior effectively.

The proposed framework combines a conditional probability-based approach with machine learning techniques, such as support vector machines, k-nearest neighbors, and decision trees. This approach enhances classification performance, particularly for imbalanced consumer groups. The framework also adapts to changing consumer trends by dynamically retraining with incoming OTT consumer data. It yields improved classification accuracy, particularly for lower-number classes, showing a recall-based improvement of 5.3% to 19.2%. Unlike conventional methods, the proposed framework maintains consistently high performance, even as the OTT market environment changes. The study underscores the practical significance of the framework for companies participating in the OTT market, offering a stable performance in a dynamic environment.

Paper [3] investigates demand forecasting for the automotive original equipment manufacturer (OEM) sector, assessing 21 baseline, statistical, and ML algorithms. Utilizing real-world data from a European OEM, the study highlights the superiority of global ML models over local ones. The paper introduces a comprehensive set of metrics for evaluating demand forecasting models, emphasizing their practicality. The research demonstrates the effectiveness of pooling product data based on historical demand magnitude to mitigate forecast errors in global models.

The authors present two data pooling strategies for building global time series models. A novel approach is introduced to control forecast errors in global models. The integration of complementary data sources, such as world GDP, unemployment rates, and fuel prices, is discussed. The findings indicate that grouping products based on demand patterns and magnitude improves the performance of the ML models. The research reveals that certain models, such as SVR, voting ensemble, and random forest, outperform others, particularly when trained on product data of the same demand type. A comparison of batch and streaming ML models highlights the robustness of batch models. The potential of digital twins for accurate forecasts and scenario estimation is explored. The study identifies avenues for future research, focusing on refining error bounding strategies, addressing anomalous forecasts in global models, and enhancing model explainability for user trust. This paper concludes by providing insights into the potential applications of ML in demand forecasting for the automotive OEM sector.

In [4], a novel flight path planning algorithm for unmanned aerial vehicles (UAVs), based on ellipsoidal mapping, is introduced. The paper discusses the use of spheres and ellipsoids for geometric representations and mapping, emphasizing their advantages over other methods. The research addresses the challenge of efficiently calculating distances between ellipsoidal objects by a neural network. The algorithm utilizes teaching–learning based optimization (TLBO) and takes advantage of ellipsoidal representations of obstacles for UAV navigation. The method aims to provide collision-free, smooth flight paths, accommodating various environments, including indoor and outdoor settings.

The methodology used to calculate distances between ellipsoids using a neural network involves generating a training dataset and implementing a novel normalization method. The proposed fitness function for flight path planning considers several factors, including ensuring safe distances between the obstacle ellipsoids and the UAV ellipsoid to prevent collisions, minimizing the overall proximity range of the UAV throughout its entire flight path and other desired features. Results are presented, comparing the algorithm's performance with other evolutionary algorithms and rapidly exploring random tree star algorithm (RRT*). While evolutionary techniques with the proposed fitness function generally outperformed RRT*, the latter demonstrated a better performance in terms of time. Future work is outlined, including developing a cost function for comparing different flight path planning algorithms, replacing the greedy strategy with reinforcement learning, and designing an intelligent low-level control algorithm for UAV navigation.

Paper [5] proposes a gesture recognition system integrated into visible light communication (VLC) systems for human–computer interaction applications. The GR technique utilizes light transitions between fingers, which are detected via a low-cost light-emitting diode (LED) and a photo-diode sensor at the receiver side. The system employs a long short-term memory (LSTM) neural network to classify finger movements based on interruptions in direct light transmission, making it suitable for high-speed communication. The accuracy of the proposed system in identifying gestures reaches 88%.

The authors present a solution that involves minimal additional cost, as it is integrated into a VLC-capable system. The LSTM-based approach offers effective gesture recognition with low computational complexity compared to traditional video processing techniques. The system's performance is robust, achieving accurate recognition even under natural conditions with varying speeds and lighting conditions. Key contributions include the development of a practical gesture recognition methodology for VLC, utilizing off-the-shelf components, and demonstrating the effectiveness of a single photo-diode receiver setup. The system's accuracy and efficiency are notable, allowing for gesture recognition within a communications-based VLC system. Possible future directions involve increasing the number of recognizable gestures, exploring gesture recognition from different aspects of sunlight and placements, and incorporating the system into automated VLC setups for more versatile applications. The study's results highlight the potential of this approach for various domains such as healthcare, commerce, and home automation.

Paper [6] focuses on analyzing and modeling road traffic accidents (RTAs) using ML classifiers. The aim is to assist transportation authorities and policymakers by developing predictive models for RTAs. The research utilizes a real-life RTA dataset from Gauteng, South Africa, and evaluates the performance of various ML classifiers including naïve Bayes, logistic regression, k-nearest neighbor, AdaBoost, support vector machine, and random forest. The study also includes dimensionality reduction techniques and multiple missing data methods.

The findings of the study show that a random forest (RF) classifier combined with multiple imputations by chained equations (MICE) for handling missing data achieves the best overall performance. RF consistently outperformed other classifiers in terms of accuracy, precision, recall, and AUC. Additionally, the study found promising results with linear discriminant analysis (LDA) for dimensionality reduction. The study acknowledges its limitations, such as the use of a dataset from a specific region and the exclusion of certain features. Future work could involve hyperparameter tuning for specific classifiers, testing other ML algorithms like artificial neural networks and deep learning, and expanding the analysis to different datasets or regions.

In [7], a robust financial crisis early warning model for Chinese listed companies is proposed. The study's premise stems from the economic challenges and risks that these companies face, driving the need for effective risk prediction and mitigation strategies. The authors propose a unique approach by incorporating textual data analysis, specifically the sentiment and tone analysis of financial news texts and the management discussion and analysis (MD&A) sections in annual reports. By leveraging web crawling and textual analysis techniques, the emotional tones of these texts are extracted. These tones serve as supplementary indicators alongside traditional financial indicators, providing insights into internal and external aspects of listed companies. The study includes 1082 Chinese A-share listed companies from 2012 to 2021 as its sample.

This research systematically evaluates the impact of emotional tone indicators on the accuracy of financial crisis early warning models. Thirteen ML models are employed to predict financial crises, and their performance is assessed using various evaluation metrics. The findings highlight several key points, such as textual data as indicators, model comparisons, external vs. internal information, and implications and future directions. The findings underscore the potential of emotional tone analysis of financial news in improving early warning models. This approach helps mitigate risks and increases the accuracy of predictions for listed companies. Furthermore, the study suggests avenues for future research, such as exploring the impact of linguistic features beyond emotional tone and developing specialized comprehensive emotional dictionaries for financial texts.

Paper [8] explores the field of DNA-based informatics, focusing on the construction and operation of computers using DNA as both hardware and software. This concept involves the utilization of DNA computers for intelligent and personalized diagnostics, particularly in the context of medical treatment. A new approach to designing diagnostic biochips that combines ML methods with the concept of biomolecular queue automata is introduced. This enables the scheduling of computational tasks at the molecular level by manipulating DNA molecules through cutting and ligating sequences. The authors stress the importance of ML methods in the design of biochips based on biomolecular computers, as accurate knowledge of unique DNA sequences is a fundamental aspect of these solutions.

The study highlights the potential of biomolecular computers in constructing biochips and emphasizes the significance of deterministic input-driven queue automata as a theoretical model for these systems. The use of specific restriction enzymes, particularly type IIB restriction endonucleases, is emphasized for the design of biomolecular computers with memory capabilities, such as queue automata. The paper introduces the concept of "Queue-PCR" as an innovative way to automate the polymerase chain reaction (PCR) method using biomolecular computers, thereby suggesting new avenues for the automation of molecular genetics techniques.

Paper [9] focuses on the application of ML algorithms to predict the clinical evolution of patients diagnosed with COVID-19. It aims to optimize the diagnostic process by utilizing predictive modeling to classify the clinical course of COVID-19 cases. The research involves a comparative analysis of various classification algorithms, including k-nearest neighbors, naïve Bayes, decision trees (DT), multilayer perceptrons (MLPs), and support vector machines. It analyzes 30,000 cases during the training and testing phases of the prediction models. The authors underscore the significance of accurate predictions for patients' vital prognosis and the efficiency of initial consultations in hospitals.

The conclusion of this study highlights the achievement of predicting the clinical evolution of COVID-19 patients using optimized ML models. The MLP algorithm is identified as the most effective for this purpose, based on comparative benchmarks. The research suggests potential future work, including analyzing clinical data using different algorithms, applying ensemble learning, and exploring additional neural network algorithms. However, the study acknowledges limitations such as data quality concerns in medical applications of ML, which can impact diagnoses and introduce biases.

Paper [10] explores the use of generative adversarial networks (GANs) for regression tasks, focusing on multi-output regression in non-image data. The study introduces the concept of MOR-GANs, which employ Wasserstein GAN (WGAN) as a regression method. The paper compares the performance of MOR-GANs with Gaussian process regression (GPR) on various datasets and introduces a prediction algorithm for GANs to generate responses based on independent variables.

The authors emphasize that WGANs perform well in regression tasks, often surpassing GPR, and showcase their effectiveness across diverse datasets. MOR-GANs show notable performance in handling variable uncertainty, multi-modal distributions, and multi-output regression tasks. Importantly, this performance is achieved without requiring extensive modifications to the GAN architecture. The authors also speculate on potential applications in domains like image reconstruction and high-dimensional modeling, where MOR-GANs could provide invaluable insights and predictions.

In [11], a novel compressed convolutional neural network designed to address the challenges of human detection in computer vision, ReSTiNet, is introduced. Human detection is crucial for applications like public safety and security surveillance. ReSTiNet aims to incorporate a compact size, high detection speed, and accuracy in its design, inspired by recent advances in deep learning techniques. The main aim of ReSTiNet is to create a more capable human detection model suitable for portable devices with limited processing power. This lightweight model enhances the performance of intelligent surveillance systems without increasing hardware costs or processing demands. The paper emphasizes the importance of fire modules, their placement, and the integration of residual connections within the architecture.

The proposed ReSTiNet model is based on Tiny-YOLO architecture, and incorporates fire modules from SqueezeNet. It strategically adjusts the number and placement of these modules to reduce the model's parameter count and overall size. Residual connections are integrated within the fire modules to enhance feature propagation and information flow, resulting in improved detection speed and accuracy. Performance of ReSTiNet surpasses other lightweight models, such as MobileNet and SqueezeNet, in terms of mean average precision. The study concludes that ReSTiNet can be adapted to various deep convolutional neural networks for compression purposes. The model's performance will be further optimized for high-resolution images in future work, particularly for datasets like EuroCity Persons.

Finally, paper [12] introduces the natural language policy translator (NLPT) 2.0, an extended version of the NLPT 1.0 system, aimed at systematically translating data privacy policies from natural language to controlled natural language for data sharing agreement (CNL4DSA). With the surge in online social networks, user-generated content has led to data exploitation for various purposes. Privacy policies, often expressed in natural language, outline data handling, usage, and authorization details, but lack automatic control mechanisms. NLPT 2.0 addresses this by enabling translation for enhanced machine processing.

The proposed methodology combines natural language processing, logic programming, and ontologies. The system offers a user-friendly Graphical User Interface that allows non-expert users to input policies in natural language, which the system then translates into CNL4DSA. The study's key aspects include the translation of social network data privacy policies and the effectiveness of the NLPT 2.0 system. Testing involved the use of privacy policies from popular social network platforms. The system demonstrated promising performance in components like ontology creation, fragment extraction, and context extraction, with results ranging from 70% to 95%. While human intervention is required for certain initial vocabulary and ontology definitions, the system aims to become increasingly automatic.

NLPT 2.0 addresses the complexity of parsing intricate phrases in original policies by introducing the role of a Policy Writer. Although some aspects still require human involvement, NLPT 2.0 is a valuable tool for translating privacy policies and enhancing machine analysis. Future work will focus on fully automating the process and addressing the remaining challenges.

Conflicts of Interest: The author declares no conflict of interest.

References

1. Alhammad, N.; Al-Dossari, H. Dynamic Segmentation for Physical Activity Recognition Using a Single Wearable Sensor. *Appl. Sci.* **2021**, *11*, 2633. [CrossRef]
2. Choi, J.; Kim, Y. A Heterogeneous Learning Framework for Over-the-Top Consumer Analysis Reflecting the Actual Market Environment. *Appl. Sci.* **2021**, *11*, 4783. [CrossRef]
3. Rožanec, J.M.; Kažič, B.; Škrjanc, M.; Fortuna, B.; Mladenić, D. Automotive OEM Demand Forecasting: A Comparative Study of Forecasting Algorithms and Strategies. *Appl. Sci.* **2021**, *11*, 6787. [CrossRef]
4. Villaseñor, C.; Gallegos, A.A.; Lopez-Gonzalez, G.; Gomez-Avila, J.; Hernandez-Barragan, J.; Arana-Daniel, N. Ellipsoidal Path Planning for Unmanned Aerial Vehicles. *Appl. Sci.* **2021**, *11*, 7997. [CrossRef]
5. Webber, J.; Mehbodniya, A.; Teng, R.; Arafa, A.; Alwakeel, A. Finger-Gesture Recognition for Visible Light Communication Systems Using Machine Learning. *Appl. Sci.* **2021**, *11*, 11582. [CrossRef]
6. Bokaba, T.; Doorsamy, W.; Paul, B.S. Comparative Study of Machine Learning Classifiers for Modelling Road Traffic Accidents. *Appl. Sci.* **2022**, *12*, 828. [CrossRef]
7. Zhang, Z.; Luo, M.; Hu, Z.; Niu, H. Textual Emotional Tone and Financial Crisis Identification in Chinese Companies: A Multi-Source Data Analysis Based on Machine Learning. *Appl. Sci.* **2022**, *12*, 6662. [CrossRef]
8. Sakowski, S.; Waldmajer, J.; Majsterek, I.; Poplawski, T. DNA Computing: Concepts for Medical Applications. *Appl. Sci.* **2022**, *12*, 6928. [CrossRef]
9. Andrade, E.C.d.; Pinheiro, P.R.; Barros, A.L.B.d.P.; Nunes, L.C.; Pinheiro, L.I.C.C.; Pinheiro, P.G.C.D.; Holanda Filho, R. Towards Machine Learning Algorithms in Predicting the Clinical Evolution of Patients Diagnosed with COVID-19. *Appl. Sci.* **2022**, *12*, 8939. [CrossRef]
10. Phillips, T.R.F.; Heaney, C.E.; Benmoufok, E.; Li, Q.; Hua, L.; Porter, A.E.; Chung, K.F.; Pain, C.C. Multi-Output Regression with Generative Adversarial Networks (MOR-GANs). *Appl. Sci.* **2022**, *12*, 9209. [CrossRef]
11. Sumit, S.S.; Awang Rambli, D.R.; Mirjalili, S.; Ejaz, M.M.; Miah, M.S.U. ReSTiNet: On Improving the Performance of Tiny-YOLO-Based CNN Architecture for Applications in Human Detection. *Appl. Sci.* **2022**, *12*, 9331. [CrossRef]
12. Tanoli, I.K.; Amin, I.; Junejo, F.; Yusoff, N. Systematic Machine Translation of Social Network Data Privacy Policies. *Appl. Sci.* **2022**, *12*, 10499. [CrossRef]

Disclaimer/Publisher's Note: The statements, opinions and data contained in all publications are solely those of the individual author(s) and contributor(s) and not of MDPI and/or the editor(s). MDPI and/or the editor(s) disclaim responsibility for any injury to people or property resulting from any ideas, methods, instructions or products referred to in the content.

Article

Dynamic Segmentation for Physical Activity Recognition Using a Single Wearable Sensor

Nora Alhammad * and Hmood Al-Dossari

College of Computer and Information Sciences, King Saud University, Riyadh 11584, Saudi Arabia; hzaldossari@ksu.edu.sa
* Correspondence: noralhammad@ksu.edu.sa

Featured Application: This article presents an application of dynamic segmentation for physical activity recognition using machine learning techniques.

Abstract: Data segmentation is an essential process in activity recognition when using machine learning techniques. Previous studies on physical activity recognition have mostly relied on the sliding window approach for segmentation. However, choosing a fixed window size for multiple activities with different durations may affect recognition accuracy, especially when the activities belong to the same category (i.e., dynamic or static). This paper presents and verifies a new method for dynamic segmentation of physical activities performed during the rehabilitation of individuals with spinal cord injuries. To adaptively segment the raw data, signal characteristics are analyzed to determine the suitable type of boundaries. Then, the algorithm identifies the time boundaries to represent the start- and endpoints of each activity. To verify the method and build a predictive model, an experiment was conducted in which data were collected using a single wrist-worn accelerometer sensor. The experimental results were compared with the sliding window approach, indicating that the proposed method outperformed the sliding window approach in terms of overall accuracy, which exceeded 5%, as well as model robustness. The results also demonstrated efficient physical activity segmentation using the proposed method, resulting in high classification performance for all activities considered.

Keywords: activity recognition; machine learning; wearable sensors; spinal cord injury; telerehabilitation

1. Introduction

Individuals with spinal cord injuries (SCI) who rely on wheelchairs typically experience associated symptoms such as obesity and low muscular strength. These symptoms may eventually lead to secondary complications, including diabetes and cardiovascular diseases [1,2]. Rehabilitation processes, such as in-home strength exercises, play an essential role in avoiding such symptoms and redeveloping the motor skills that are needed to perform daily activities and promote quality of life [3,4]. Currently, therapists rely on patient surveys to measure their adherence to these activities. However, studies indicate wide variability between self-reported and actually performed physical activity, which can undermine rehabilitation progress [5]. Nevertheless, with rapid technological innovation, physical activity recognition systems are emerging as a more reliable way to detect these activities [6–9].

Based on the approach used to collect data, activity recognition can be broadly classified into two approaches: the vision-based and sensor-based approaches. Although the vision-based approach is information-rich, it often suffers from ethical and privacy concerns, especially in healthcare applications when dealing with patients. By contrast, the devices used in the sensor-based approach, including wearable sensors, can operate with limited cost and power, and they have no restrictions in terms of the surrounding

environment or the location where activities must be performed. As a result, activity recognition systems commonly adopt the sensor-based approach [10].

Several studies have been undertaken to investigate the impact of different sensor positions on overall recognition accuracy. These studies indicate that sensor position should be determined mainly based on the type of activity under study. Forms of locomotion, including walking and running, as well as static activities, such as standing and sitting, can be recognized with an accuracy of between 83% to 95% using lower-limb segments (hip, thigh, and ankle) as the sensor positions. To improve accuracy when recognizing upper-limb activities, sensors are placed on the wrist and upper arm [11]. Within this context, the study in [12] considered different positions, such as hip, belt, wrist, upper arm, ankle, and thigh, to recognize 20 types of activities, including both upper- and lower-limb activities. The results showed high accuracy when combining different positions. However, the study also demonstrated a slight performance decrease when using only the thighs and wrists. In addition to the impact of sensor placement on accuracy, user preferences should be considered to gain acceptance. To address this problem in the design of wearables, a meta-analysis was undertaken in [13]. The study concluded that people prefer wearing sensors on their wrist, followed by the trunk, belt, ankle, and, finally, armpit.

Activity recognition systems have a wide variety of applications, including rehabilitation and physical therapy. These systems allow monitoring of patients and the identification of exercises being performed [14]. In this regard, Pernek et al. [15] proposed a monitoring system consisting of a network of wearable accelerometers and a smartphone to recognize the intensity of specific physical activities (e.g., strength exercises). The system used two Support Vector Machine (SVM) layers to detect the type of activity being performed and determine its intensity. The study demonstrated that the hierarchical algorithm achieved an accuracy of approximately 85% in recognizing a set of upper-body activities. The study in [16] presented a methodology to recognize three fundamental arm movements using two different classifiers: Linear Discriminant Analysis (LDA) and SVM. The overall average accuracy was 88% using data collected from accelerometers and 83% using gyroscope data. With the same objective, Panwar et al. [10] designed a model to recognize three physical activities of the human forearm, relying on data collected from a single wrist-worn accelerometer. Lin et al. [17] proposed a model for recognizing the physical activities performed to rehabilitate frozen shoulder. Based on wireless sensor networks (WSN), the model could recognize six physical activities with an accuracy ranging from 85 to 95%. The study showed the applicability of using these types of models to recognize the rehabilitation exercises that are ubiquitous in healthcare self-management. In [18], Cai et al. developed an upper-limb robotic device to rehabilitate stroke patients. The system works by initially recognizing the activity performed by the healthy side of the patient and then provides mirror therapy to the affected side. The method used surface electromyography (sEMG) signals to train and test the model, and SVM was applied to classify the activities. To provide stroke survivors with feedback to maintain a correct posture during rehabilitation, Zambrana et al. [7] proposed a hierarchical approach using interrail sensors to monitor arm movements. This approach consisted of two levels: the first level distinguishes between movements and non-movements of the arm, while the second level determines whether the movement was purposeful.

Similar to other pattern recognition problems, continuous raw data should be divided into smaller fragments before proceeding to feature extraction and other following operations. The selection and application of an efficient segmentation method substantially influence the classification process, which directly results in accurate activity recognition [19]. The sliding window is the most widely used approach and, to date, it is still considered the best available approach [19–21]. In this method, continuous data obtained from sensors are segmented into windows of either static or dynamic sizes based on time intervals. For the former, two different algorithms are available: fixed-size non-overlapping sliding window and fixed-size overlapping sliding window. The first algorithm is considered a simple segmentation process, where the number of windows can be calculated exactly since no overlap exists. The second algorithm includes data overlap between two consecutive windows, where the percentage overlap can be referred to as the window shift. Since different activities have different periods of motion, the size of the window depends on the type of activity that is evaluated [22]. However, determining the effective window size is considered a critical issue. A short window size may split an activity's signal into two or more consecutive windows, whereas a long window size may combine signals for more than one activity. Ultimately, these cases may affect the accuracy of activity classification because information is lost or noise is introduced into the signal, respectively [23,24].

In dynamic sliding windows, data are segmented into different window sizes according to specific features. One of the challenges is to optimize different window sizes while considering activities with both short and long duration. Numerous studies have sought to resolve the limitation of the sliding window approach. Feda et al. [22] investigated the impact of using different window sizes on the accuracy of recognizing activities with different durations, reporting that a 1.5-second window size may represent the best trade-off. Other researchers have proposed adaptive window size techniques. In this context, Santos et al. [25] used entropy feedback to adjust the window size and time continuously, thereby increasing classification accuracy. Nevertheless, the algorithm is computationally complex since shorter time shifts increase the rate of classifications per second. In [24], Noor et al. presented a segmentation technique based on adjusting the window size according to the probability of the signal. Initially, the approach specifies a small window size suitable for splitting static and dynamic activities. In turn, this size expands dynamically when a transitional activity is encountered, which stems from its longer duration. Similarly, using cluster analysis for period extraction, [21] proposed a technique to differentiate between basic and transitional activities during segmentation. Sheng et al. [26] designed an adaptive time window by using pitch extraction algorithms to divide the data into periodic and non-periodic activities. The study in [27] designed and implemented a segmentation method based on the sliding window autocorrelation technique and the Gaussian model. Using a dataset consisting of readings from an accelerometer embedded in a smartphone, the method successfully divided the data into distinct subsets of activities. Based on a change detection algorithm, an activity segmentation method was presented in [19]. To identify stationary, dynamic, and transitional activities, starting window positions were dynamically detected.

The objective of this research is to propose a novel signal segmentation method for physical activity recognition that can enhance classification performance. Unlike previous studies, this method is concerned with the segmentation of physical activities that belong to the same category (i.e., dynamic activities). To achieve this objective, an experiment was conducted to verify and compare the proposed method with the sliding window approach. The comparison demonstrates the effectiveness of our method, particularly in terms of enhancing recognition accuracy.

The remainder of this paper is organized as follows: Section 2 presents the set of physical activities applied during the rehabilitation of SCI patients; Section 3 offers an overview of the system; Section 4 describes the proposed segmentation method; Section 5 demonstrates the experimental setup; Sections 6 and 7 present and discuss the results, respectively; and finally, Section 8 concludes the paper.

2. Physical Activity

Unlike stroke and other neurological conditions, SCI affects patients' lower limbs. In rare cases, SCI patients may suffer from complete paralysis based on the degree and location of their injury. The focus of this work is on the former type of SCI, where individuals need rehabilitation to avoid having associated symptoms, such as low muscular strength. Rehabilitation through physical activity is also essential for developing upper-limb motor skills, which enable patients to perform daily activities and promote quality of life [3,4].

Whenever the aim is to strengthen the upper limbs, the body parts of focus are the elbows and shoulders [28–30]. The main activities required to strengthen the shoulder muscles are flexion, abduction, extension, internal rotation (IR), and external rotation (ER). In addition, the main activities applied to strengthen the elbow's major muscles are elbow flexion (EF) and elbow extension (EE) [28]. An illustration of these activities is given in Figure 1.

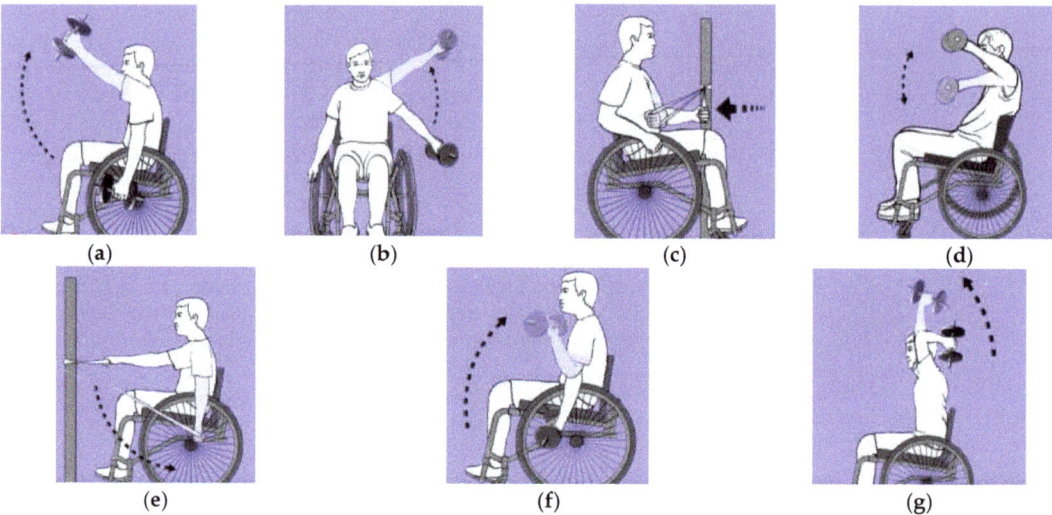

Figure 1. Physical activities used to rehabilitate spinal cord injuries (SCI) patients: (**a**) Shoulder flexion; (**b**) Shoulder abduction; (**c**) Internal rotation; (**d**) External rotation; (**e**) Extension; (**f**) Elbow flexion; (**g**) Elbow extension [28].

3. System Overview

A wireless sensor was used (Shimmer Research, Dublin, Ireland), each consisting of a tri-axial accelerometer, a tri-axial gyroscope, and a tri-axial magnetometer. Due to the efficiency of accelerometers in activity recognition, the dataset used in this research was collected using a single tri-axial accelerometer [31–33]. It is a sensing device used to measure acceleration in three orthogonal directions simultaneously. However, gyroscope and magnetometer were excluded since prior studies indicate that accelerometers provide higher overall accuracy [16]. In addition, the ferromagnetic materials that are commonly available in domestic environments can affect magnetometers. The sensor was configured to collect acceleration data with a sampling frequency of 30 Hz (range $\pm$ 2 g), which has been shown to be sufficient for recognizing similar activities [30,31]. In addition, a previous study demonstrated that the type and intensity of human activities can be recognized using signals with a sampling rate equal to 10 Hz [34].

Sensors are placed on the wrist and upper arm when recognizing upper-limb activities, both of which were examined in this research. However, due to the type of motion being recognized, certain activities, such as EE, EF, and IR, lack upper-arm movements. This meant that the sensor placed on the upper arm could not detect any motion. Accordingly, the wrist was chosen as the sensor position.

In terms of axis orientation, the Y-axis was in parallel with the wrist, pointing toward the fingers and across the X-axis. In addition, the Z-axis pointed away from the backside of the wrist, as shown in Figure 2.

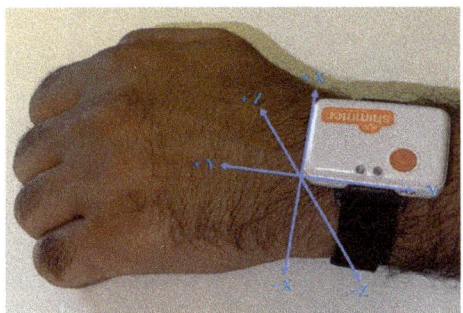

Figure 2. Axis orientation.

4. Proposed Method

Since physical activities are performed sequentially rather than concurrently, a clear activity pattern can be identified by observing the acceleration signal. Figure 3a shows the raw data collected from a tri-axial accelerometer during 10 repetitions of abduction, where each part enclosed within the dotted rectangle represents a single repetition.

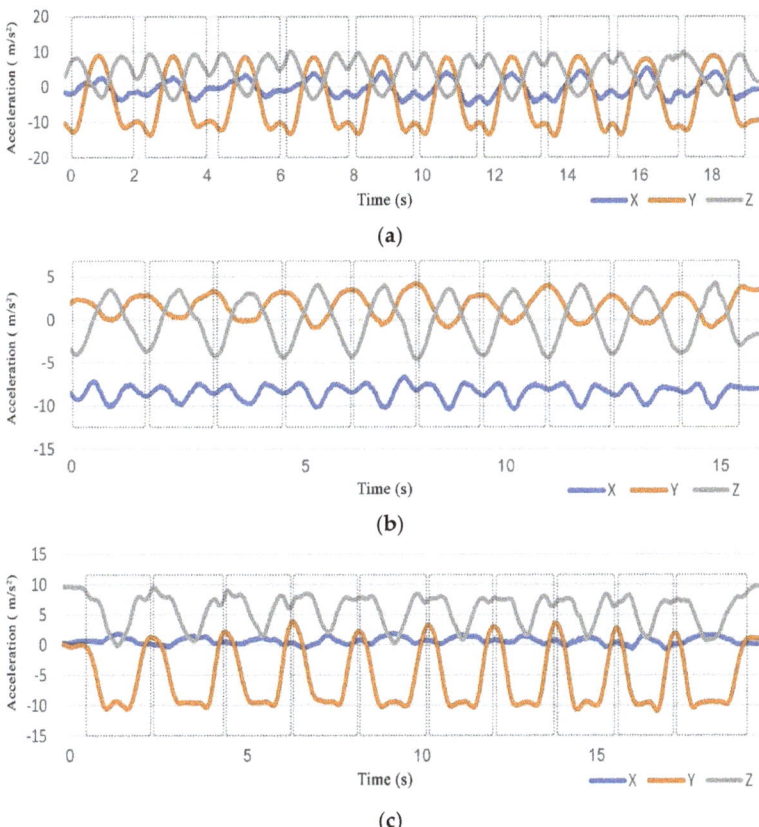

Figure 3. Acceleration signal for 10 repetitions of (**a**) Abduction, (**b**) Internal rotation (IR), and (**c**) Extension.

For all seven activities, each peak along the Y-axis corresponds to a single activity, except for IR and extension, where two consecutive peaks represent the starting and ending points of the activity. Figure 3b,c shows 10 repetitions of IR and extension, respectively, where all data points enclosed within the dotted rectangles belong to a single repetition. The underlying reason for this difference is the movement direction of the activity and the hand position while moving.

The proposed segmentation method consisted of three main steps. The first step involved the selection of peaks in the Y-axis acceleration signal since it best represents the start and end of all types of activities under study when applying the algorithm. Peaks were selected based on a threshold and a distance, which represent the minimum value of a peak and the minimum distance between peaks, respectively. The second step was to select valleys using a second threshold that represented the highest value of a valley. Finally, the signal's characteristics were analyzed for each peak to identify suitable segmentation boundaries. The method is explained in more detail in the rest of this section.

4.1. Selection of Peaks

Peaks, which represent the local maximum values in the Y-axis acceleration signal, were first discerned. To avoid including false-positive peaks, as illustrated in Figure 4a, a threshold value was used. To be detected, a peak must be equal to or greater than Threshold 1. This can be calculated by separately averaging the peaks in the learning dataset of each of the seven physical activities and, in turn, choosing the minimum value among them as follows:

$$\text{Threshold 1} = \min(\text{avg}_{max}(PA_1), \text{avg}_{max}(PA_2), \ldots, \text{avg}_{max}(PA_n)) \quad (1)$$

where avg denotes the average, max is the local maximum in the processed axis (i.e., Y-axis), PA denotes physical activity, and n refers to the number of physical activities to be classified. The identified peaks after applying the threshold are shown in Figure 4b.

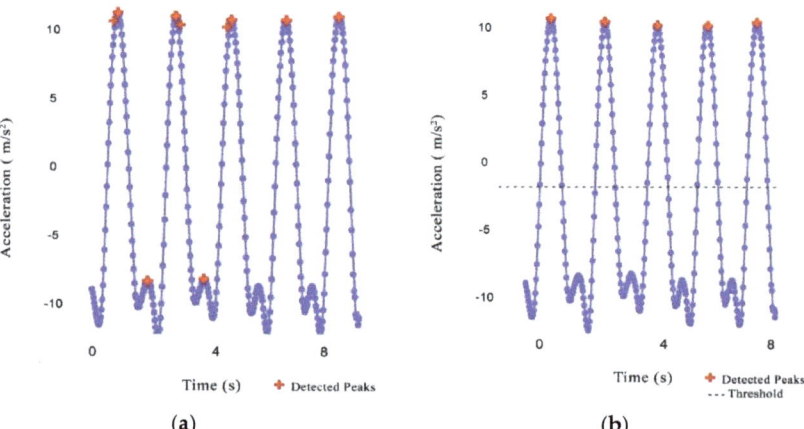

Figure 4. Detected peaks in acceleration signal: (a) Initial selection of peaks; (b) After applying threshold and minimum distance.

Moreover, to avoid detecting more than one peak within the data points that represent a single activity, as shown in Figure 4a, a minimum distance between peaks was assigned. This value can be obtained by calculating the average duration needed to perform the shortest activity as follows:

$$\text{Distance} = \min(\text{avg}_{duration}(PA_1), \text{avg}_{duration}(PA_2), \ldots, \text{avg}_{duration}(PA_n)) \quad (2)$$

4.2. Selection of Valleys

In addition to the peaks obtained from the first step, the method required the identification of valleys (i.e., local minimum values) in the Y-axis acceleration signal. In this process, a second threshold was used to avoid detecting false-positive valleys. A valley was chosen when it was less than or equal to Threshold 2. It can be obtained by averaging the values of true-positive valleys in the learning dataset and, in turn, repeating the process for each type of activity that consists of a single peak (i.e., in this research, abduction, flexion, EE, EF, and ER). The maximum average was assigned as the threshold using the following equation:

$$\text{Threshold 2} = \text{maximum}\ (\text{avg}_{min}\ (PA_1), \text{avg}_{min}\ (PA_2), \ldots, \text{avg}_{min}\ (PA_m)) \qquad (3)$$

where min denotes the local maximum in the processed axis (i.e., Y-axis) and m is the number of physical activities consisting of a single peak in each repetition.

4.3. Determining Segment Boundaries

In dynamic activity segmentation, it was necessary to determine the segment time boundaries to obtain a successful partition among different activities [27]. In the proposed algorithm, there were two types of boundaries for the activities based on the number of peaks in each activity. The first type was the peak boundaries, which was used when a single activity contained two peaks (as in the case of IR and extension). In this type, as the name suggests, these peaks were regarded as the boundaries of the segment. The second type was the valley boundaries, which was applied when an activity consisted of only one peak. In this type, the two valleys that directly preceded and followed each peak were identified to represent the start- and endpoints of the segment, respectively. Therefore, the length of a segment changed dynamically according to the duration of the corresponding activity. To determine the suitable type of boundaries for the segmentation, the algorithm checked the signal characteristics of each identified peak, as illustrated in Figure 5.

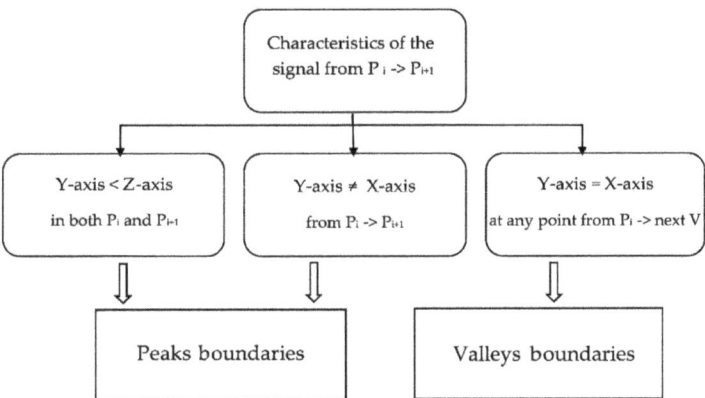

Figure 5. Determining boundary type based on signal characteristics (P: Peak; V: Valley).

Peak boundaries were chosen if the value of Y-axis was smaller than the value of Z-axis at $peak_i$ and $peak_{i+1}$, as shown in Figure 6a. Moreover, the algorithm checked the signal's characteristics between every two consecutive peaks. If there was no intersection between Y-axis and X-axis along these peaks, as illustrated in Figure 6b, peak boundaries were also applied. Otherwise, if an intersection existed at any point between the peak and the valley that directly follows the peak, as shown in Figure 6c–g, valley boundaries were used. The pseudocode that describes how to segment the acceleration signal of physical activities adaptively is shown in Algorithm 1. The input values to Dynamic Segmentation are represented in line 2, and the output value is represented in line 5. The input of the algorithm is a set of tri-axial accelerometer data S, which is divided into multiple segments. The "for" loop in lines 9–28 represents the process of determining the type of boundaries in all peaks except the last one. The "if" and "else if" statements in lines 10–14 and 15–23, respectively, examine the signal's characteristics in each peak and divide the signal using peak or valley boundaries. Lines 28–36 repeat the process for the last peak using only valley boundaries.

Algorithm 1 Dynamic Segmentation

1: **Input:**
2: S: a set of tri-axial accelerometer data
3: **Output:**
4: A set of segments: Seg = {seg_1, seg_2, ..., seg_n}
5: peaks = indices of all peaks in Y-axis using Threshold1 and Distance
6: valleys = indices of all valleys in Y-axis using Threshold2
7: p = total number of peaks
8: v = total number of valleys
9: **for** i = 0 to p-2 **do**
10:    **if** Y-axis value is smaller than Z-axis value at peak(i) and peak(i+1)
11:    OR no intersection between X-axis and Y-axis from peak(i) to peak(i+1) **then**
12:       **for** h = peaks (i) to peaks (i+1) **do**
13:          Add S(h) to Seg_i
14:       **end for**
15:    **else if** intersection exists between X-axis and Y-axis at any point from peak(i) to next valley **then**
16:       **for** k = 1 to v-1 **do**
17:          **if** valleys (k) is the valley that directly follows peaks (i)
18:          AND valleys (k-1) is the valley that directly precedes peaks (i) **then**
19:             For h = valleys (k-1) to valleys (k) **do**
20:                Add S(h) to Seg_i
21:             **end for**
22:          **end if**
23:       **end for**
24:    **else**
25:       i = i+1
26:    **end if**
27: **end for**
28: **for** k = 1 to v-1 **do**
29: **if** valleys (k) is the valley that directly follows peaks (p-1)
30: AND valleys (k-1) is the valley that directly precedes peaks (p-1)
31: AND intersection exists between X-axis and Y-axis from peaks(p-1) to valleys (k) **then**
32:    **for** h = valleys (k-1) to valleys (k) **do**
33:       Add S(h) to Seg_{p-1}
34:    **end for**
35:    **end if**
36: **end for**

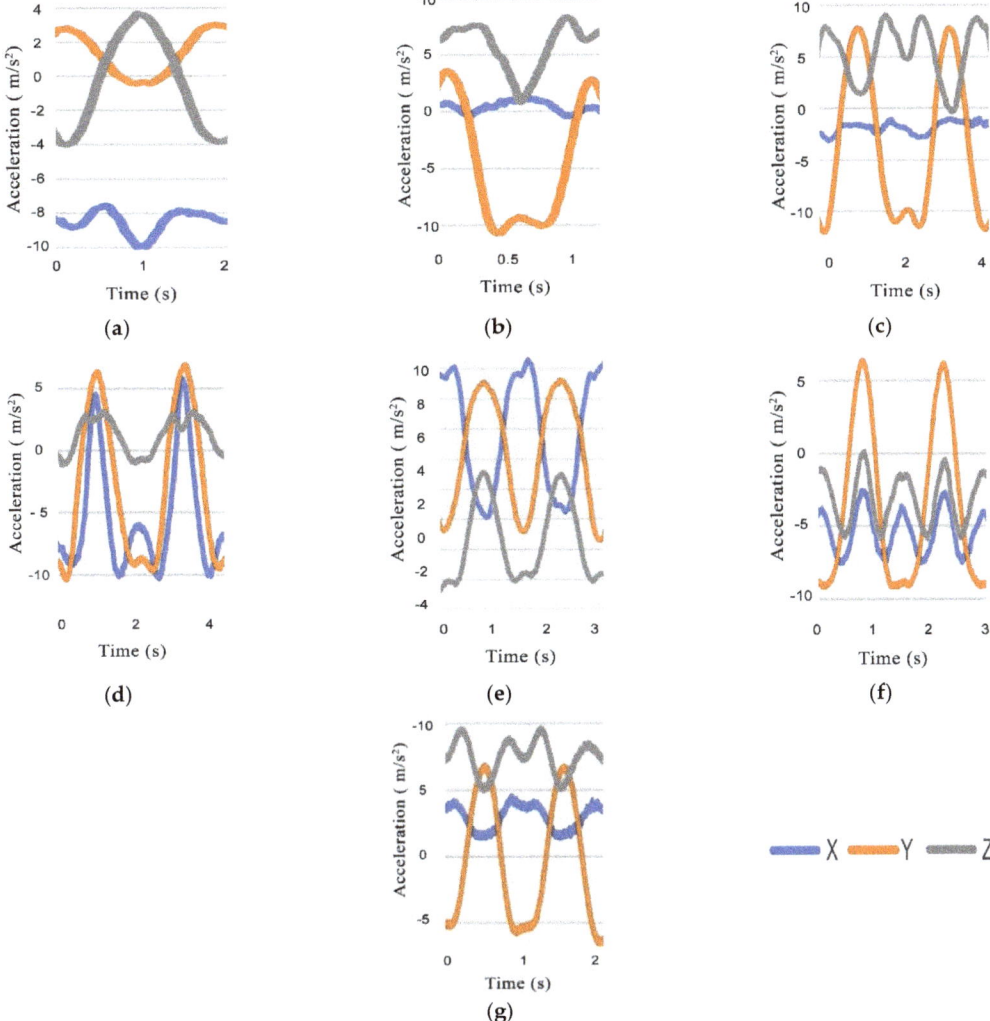

Figure 6. Acceleration signal of two consecutive peaks corresponding to: (**a**) Single extension; (**b**) Single IR; (**c**) Two abductions; (**d**) Two flexions; (**e**) Two elbow extensions (EEs); (**f**) Two elbow flexions (EFs); and (**g**) Two external rotations (ERs).

5. Experimental Setup

An experiment was performed to evaluate and compare the results of the proposed method. This section describes the overall process and experimental details.

5.1. Data Acquisition

This section describes the demographics of the participants. It also offers an overview of the protocol used to collect data and perform the physical activities.

5.1.1. Participants

In the experiment, 10 healthy individuals (3 male, 7 female) aged between 25 and 50 years were recruited to perform the activities. Before the experiment, all participants signed an informed consent form that explained the protocol and procedure.

5.1.2. Activity Session

Before starting the session, participants were given practical advice and instructions for the correct execution of the exercises. Finally, before each activity, a short demonstration video was shown as a reminder for more optimal performance.

Each participant was asked to execute 10 repetitions of all activities, resulting in a total of 700 repetitions. Furthermore, they were asked to separate each group of the same activity with approximately 10 s, thereby marking the start of each new group of repetitions.

5.2. Data Preprocessing

The raw data acquired from wearable sensors, such as accelerometers, are prone to noise and error. Hence, preprocessing is an essential step to obtain the most representative format of physical activities that is suitable for predictive modeling [35,36]. In this research, preprocessing was implemented in two steps:

- Smoothing

A moving average filter (MAF) was applied to smoothen the data and remove high-frequency noise introduced due to physical effects [24]. This process, which is equivalent to lowpass filtering, is important to ensure that small perturbations are insignificant to the model.

An important aspect of the MAF relates to the problem of how to choose the optimal length. This is a key consideration because different values can affect recognition performance. In this research, different values were tested, which led to the discovery that a length of 10 produced smoother data without losing key information.

- Removal of Undesired Data (Cleaning)

Since the participants were asked to separate each group of activity repetitions with approximately 10 s, this meant that part of the collected data corresponded to a time when no activity was undertaken. These parts were removed manually. It is worth noting that this step was done only for the learning dataset, whereas patients in the real-world were not given such directions. In addition, since the proposed method is based on detecting the peaks and valleys, even the existence of such data will not affect the performance of the algorithm.

5.3. Segmentation

To demonstrate the performance improvement of the proposed method on activity recognition, two different segmentation methods were used for comparison purposes. The first method was the commonly used fixed-size sliding window of length 2 s and 50% overlap, which provided the highest recognition accuracy in [15]. This method was chosen because their work involved some activities that were also considered in this research. The second method was the proposed segmentation method. Figure 7 illustrates the result of using both methods for segmenting the acceleration signal of EF.

5.4. Feature Extraction

To generate data that could be suitably fed into a machine learning algorithm, multiple features were calculated from all the segments obtained using both methods. A diverse set of features is available, including time/frequency-domain features as well as heuristic features. For sensor-based human activity recognition, it is common to adopt time-domain features due to their simplicity and effectiveness for activity recognition [15,37]. In this work, only time-domain features were used since frequency-domain features have high computation and memory requirements, which may be not applicable in low-power real-time applications [38]. First, a magnitude (m) value was calculated using the signals (x, y, and z) from the accelerometer ($m = \sqrt{x^2 + y^2 + z^2}$). Furthermore, six time-domain features were considered and extracted from raw data of the three axes (x, y, and z), as well as (m). A list of the features used along with their definitions is presented in Table 1.

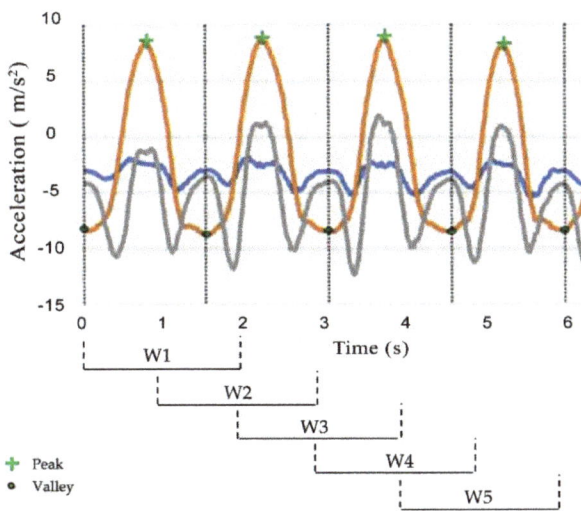

Figure 7. Acceleration signal of four repetitions of EF segmented using sliding window (**lower part**) and the proposed method (**dotted lines**).

Table 1. List of features used (notation: $d \in (x, y, z, m)$; N is the number of data points; i is the index).

Name	Definition
Minimum	$\min(d) =$ lowest $d_i, i = 1, 2, \ldots, N$
Maximum	$\max(d) =$ highest $d_i, i = 1, 2, \ldots, N$
Range	$\text{range}(d) = \max(d) - \min(d)$
Mean	$\text{mean}(d) = \frac{1}{N} \sum_{i=1}^{N} x_i$
Standard Deviation	$SD(d) = \sqrt{\frac{1}{N} \sum_{i=1}^{N} (d_i - \text{mean}(d))^2}$
Root Mean Square	$RMS(d) = \sqrt{\frac{1}{N} (d_1^2 + d_2^2 + \cdots + d_N^2)}$

5.5. Model Training and Validation Strategies

Support vector machine (SVM) was used to train and test the classification model due to its frequent use in previous physical activity studies [16,29,30]. Ten-fold cross-validation was used to train the model, which means that data from nine subjects were randomly divided into training and testing sets using 90 and 10% of the data, respectively. The Waikato Environment for Knowledge Analysis (WEKA) toolkit was used in this work. Using a personal computer with an Intel Core i5-2430M CPU (Toshiba International Corporation, Texas, USA), the total time taken to build the model was 0.43 s.

Ten-fold cross-validation and leave-one-user-out (LOUO) were the evaluation protocols intensively used in the literature. Although 10-fold cross-validation is the most accurate approach for model selection, LOUO performs better in terms of model robustness, and it is recommended for human activity recognition [20]. In the latter protocol, instead of randomly splitting data into evaluation and training sets, it selects data from some subjects for training and data from the remaining for evaluation. As a result, the protocol is considered robust to the overfitting problem since training, and testing data never share samples belonging to the same subject [15]. Algorithm accuracy in this work was evaluated using LOUO, which means that the algorithm was trained using data from nine subjects and then evaluated on the remaining one. This process was repeated until data from each subject were evaluated exactly once, and an average of performance was obtained.

6. Results

Various performance metrics have been used in prior works, including accuracy, which refers to the ratio of correctly predicted observations to the total observations; recall, which refers to the ratio of correctly predicted positive observations to all observations in the actual class; precision, which is the ratio of correctly predicted positive observations to the total predicted positive observations; and F-measure, which is a combination of the precision and recall measures that are used to represent the detection result.

To evaluate the performance improvement of the proposed method, the experiment was conducted in two phases. First, the abovementioned performance metrics were used to determine the recognition performance using both segmentation methods: sliding window and the proposed method. For comparison purposes, only values of similar activities, as in [15], were presented. This study was chosen because it has the greatest number of shared activities with the ones provided in this work (i.e., the shared activities are abduction, flexion, and EF). In addition, it used the fixed-size sliding window protocol for segmentation. In the second phase, for the purpose of determining the effectiveness of the proposed method using the SVM classifier, other common classifiers, including J48, K-Nearest Neighbors (KNN), and Naïve Bayes (NB), were used for comparison.

Table 2 reports the classification performance of the proposed method in comparison to the fixed-size sliding window approach. It indicates that not only a performance improvement in accuracy measures was obtained when using the proposed method but also the values for precision, recall, and F-measure showed statistically significant improvements.

Table 2. Performance comparison using accuracy, recall, and precision measures (mean ± standard deviation) between segmentation using the proposed method and fixed-size sliding window.

	Accuracy	Recall	Precision	F-Measure
Our method	96.67 ± 2.7%	96.67 ± 1.2%	96.97 ± 1.9%	96.82 ± 1.5%
Sliding Window	91.44 ± 5.9%	91.90 ± 3.9%	92.51 ± 4.5 %	92.21 ± 3.8%

Additionally, an evaluation of activity type recognition accuracy and prediction error was undertaken for each of the three physical activities. As shown in Table 3, the algorithm had the greatest difficulties when recognizing abduction and flexion. This was expected because these two activities are similar, especially with regard to the starting and ending points of the movement, as well as the range of motion. However, the algorithm still achieved a recognition accuracy of 96% for these physical activities.

Table 3. Confusion matrix of activity recognition (in %). Rows represent actual exercise, whereas columns show algorithm predictions (cells with value 0 are left blank).

	Abduction	EF	Flexion
Abduction	96	1	3
EF		98	2
Flexion	4		96

EF: Elbow Flexion.

Figure 8 depicts the recall, precision, and F-measure values for each activity obtained by the model using the SVM classifier. Both segmentation methods achieved high classification performance in recognizing EF, and the enhancement achieved by the proposed method was small. However, the enhancement became increasingly large when recognizing more similar activities: abduction and flexion. The increase in recall when using the proposed method was 5% in abduction and approximately 4% in flexion, while precision increased by 5% and 7% in recognizing abduction and flexion, respectively. In addition, our method increased the F-measure of abduction by 7% and flexion by 5%. These results show that the proposed method not only enhanced performance but also increased model robustness.

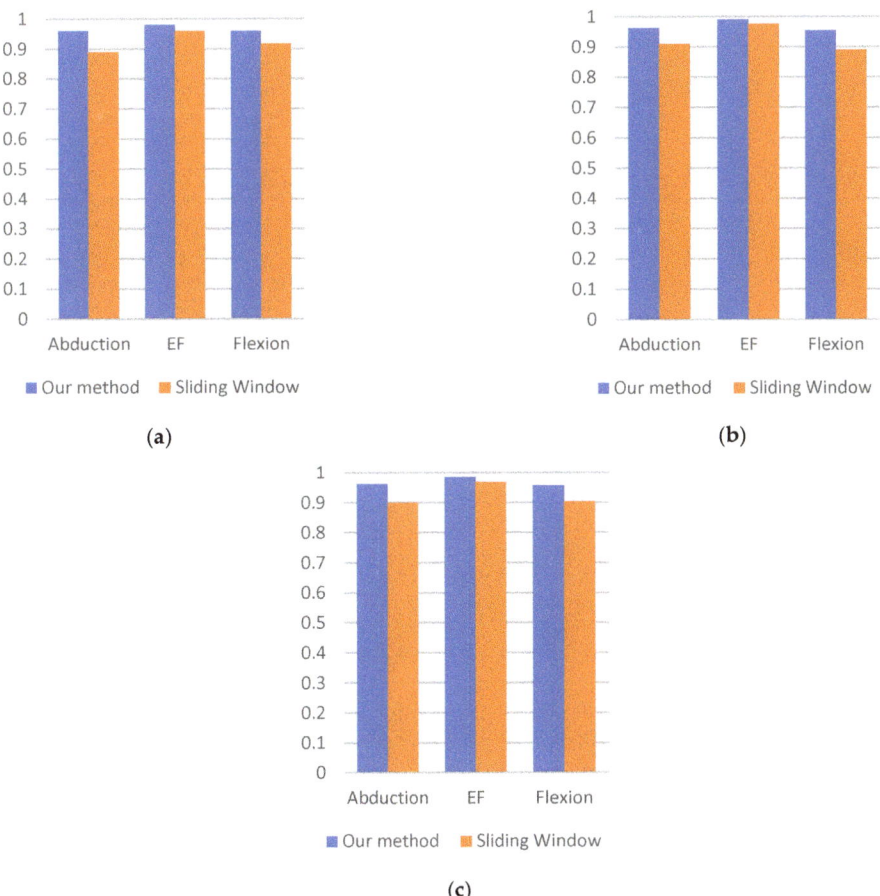

Figure 8. Performance comparison of each activity using: (**a**) Recall; (**b**) Precision; (**c**) F-measure.

To investigate the effectiveness of the proposed method using the SVM classifier, three common machine learning algorithms were further used for the comparison. Table 4 shows the performance of the proposed method and sliding window using NB, J48, and KNN classifiers.

Table 4. Recognition accuracy of both segmentation methods using different classification algorithms.

	SVM	NB	J48	KNN
Our method	96.67 ± 2.7%	91 ± 3.4%	95 ± 5.1%	95.65 ± 1.9%
Sliding Window	91.44 ± 5.9%	84.49 ± 3.9%	89.78 ± 5.4%	90.28 ± 5.4%

7. Discussion

In this study, we proposed and verified a machine learning-based method for physical activity segmentation using wearable sensors. Our method enabled the algorithm to classify specific types of physical activity with an accuracy reaching up to 96%. Overall classification performance improved by approximately 5% compared to a commonly used approach, namely the sliding window. Furthermore, the results in Table 2 clearly indicate that the statistically significant improvement occurred not only in terms of accuracy but also in all performance measures used in this work. This enhancement reflects the effectiveness and applicability of the method on continuous data collected from a single accelerometer.

The algorithm enabled the accurate classification of similar activities, such as abduction and flexion. In contrast, when using sliding window segmentation, the algorithm frequently confused these activities and experienced difficulties in recognizing them. This demonstrates that the impact of the correct segmentation of raw data is not only on performance but also on model robustness.

Table 4 shows that the new segmentation method achieved a recognition rate of more than 91% using four different ML classifiers, and SVM outperformed the others. This is consistent with expectations because SVM is highly regularized and works effectively with small datasets and few classes. Moreover, the results of this table emphasize the effectiveness of the proposed method, which outperformed the sliding window method across all four classifiers with an average of 5.5%.

The results clearly show that wearable sensors are a promising technology for monitoring and performing automated rehabilitation assessments. Despite the performance enhancement obtained using specific sensor types, affordability and usability are also important factors for determining their applicability. The study in [18] used sEMG electrodes to recognize different activities performed by stroke patients. Although the results suggested that sEMG signals provide good accuracy in upper-limb activities, attaching these electrodes is a sensitive process that requires an expert. This type of sensor is impractical for use in certain applications, including monitoring in-home rehabilitation, especially if the set of activities must be repeated daily or multiple times during the day. Contrastingly, the accelerometers used in this research are low-cost and easy-to-use sensors.

This work can be considered as a systematic approach to dynamic signal segmentation, which could be applied to other types of physical activity. However, slight modifications should be taken into account when needed. For the segmentation of a wider range of activities, more signal characteristics might be needed. One possible solution is to exploit statistical and time series analysis to detect the signal variation.

The new method presented in this paper overcomes the limitation of the sliding window approach through the adaptive segmentation of physical activities. However, we acknowledge that certain limitations are evident in our work. First, only an accelerometer was used for physical activity recognition. Although studies have proven the effectiveness and efficiency of accelerometers, additional types of sensors, such as gyroscopes and magnetometers, may improve recognition performance. Second, this work focused on the segmentation of physical activities applied during the rehabilitation of SCI patients. Further research should be undertaken to study the effect of this method on other physical activities. Third, the data were collected in a controlled environment. Future work might consider collecting data from real scenarios in which participants perform activities at home. Finally, the selection of a threshold value depends on the training data. In future work, the threshold could be chosen with the ability to update periodically according to the incoming signal.

In addition to the abovementioned future work, the impact of the method on the rest of the activities will be investigated. In addition, frequency-domain features and additional time-domain features will be identified to facilitate performance enhancement. Finally, the method will be introduced into hospital-based rehabilitation sessions to examine the performance on SCI individuals.

8. Conclusions

In physical activity recognition using machine learning algorithms, data segmentation is an essential step that may influence accuracy. Nevertheless, studies mostly adopt the sliding window technique and rely on the window size used in previous works. Although this approach is considered simple, it might be ineffective, especially for activities with different durations.

This study proposed a novel segmentation method that can be applied to enhance the recognition of physical activities performed in a rehabilitative context. To adaptively segment the raw data, the algorithm identifies the time boundaries to represent the start- and endpoints of each activity. Peak boundaries and valley boundaries are used depending on the signal characteristics.

The proposed algorithm was also verified in this paper. The results, which were generated using data from a single accelerometer located on the wrist, approved the effectiveness and applicability of the method on continuous raw data. Moreover, adopting the proposed method generally improved recognition performance, and the improvement was more substantial for similar activities.

Author Contributions: Conceptualization, N.A.; methodology, N.A.; software, N.A.; validation, N.A.; formal analysis, N.A.; investigation, N.A.; resources, N.A.; data curation, N.A.; writing—original draft preparation, N.A.; writing—review and editing, N.A. and H.A.-D.; visualization, N.A.; supervision, H.A.-D.; project administration, H.A.-D. All authors have read and agreed to the published version of the manuscript.

Funding: The authors would like to thank the Deanship of scientific research in King Saud University for funding and supporting this research through the initiative of the DSR Graduate Students Research Support (GSR).

Conflicts of Interest: The authors declare no conflict of interest.

References

1. Ding, D.; Ayubi, S.; Hiremath, S.; Parmanto, B. Physical activity monitoring and sharing platform for manual wheelchair users. In Proceedings of the 2012 Annual International Conference of the IEEE Engineering in Medicine and Biology Society, San Diego, CA, USA, 28 August 2012–1 September 2012; Volume 2012, pp. 5833–5836. [CrossRef]
2. Harvey, L.A. Physiotherapy rehabilitation for people with spinal cord injuries. *J. Physiother.* **2016**, *62*, 4–11. [CrossRef] [PubMed]
3. O'Sullivan, S.B.; Schmitz, T.J.; Fulk, G. *Physical Rehabilitation*, 7th ed.; F.A. Davis Co.: Philadelphia, PA, USA, 2019.
4. Burns, A.S.; Marino, R.J.; Kalsi-Ryan, S.; Middleton, J.W.; Tetreault, L.A.; Dettori, J.R.; Mihalovich, K.E.; Fehlings, M.G. Type and Timing of Rehabilitation Following Acute and Subacute Spinal Cord Injury: A Systematic Review. *Glob. Spine J.* **2017**, *7*, 175S–194S. [CrossRef] [PubMed]
5. Warms, C.A.; Whitney, J.D.; Belza, B. Measurement and description of physical activity in adult manual wheelchair users. *Disabil. Health J.* **2008**, *1*, 236–244. [CrossRef] [PubMed]
6. Voicu, R.-A.; Dobre, C.; Bajenaru, L.; Ciobanu, R.-I. Human Physical Activity Recognition Using Smartphone Sensors. *Sensors* **2019**, *19*, 458. [CrossRef] [PubMed]
7. Zambrana, C.; Idelsohn-Zielonka, S.; Claramunt-Molet, M.; Almenara-Masbernat, M.; Opisso, E.; Tormos, J.M.; Miralles, F.; Vargiu, E. Monitoring of upper-limb movements through inertial sensors—Preliminary results. *Smart Health.* **2019**, *13*, 100059. [CrossRef]
8. Leving, M.T.; Horemans, H.L.D.; Vegter, R.J.K.; De Groot, S.; Bussmann, J.B.J.; Van Der Woude, L.H.V. Validity of consumer-grade activity monitor to identify manual wheelchair propulsion in standardized activities of daily living. *PLoS ONE* **2018**, *13*, e0194864. [CrossRef]
9. Bisio, I.; Delfino, A.; Lavagetto, F.; Sciarrone, A. Enabling IoT for In-Home Rehabilitation: Accelerometer Signals Classification Methods for Activity and Movement Recognition. *IEEE Internet Things J.* **2016**, *4*, 135–146. [CrossRef]
10. Panwar, M.; Prakash, C.; Piswas, D.; Asharyya, A. CNN based approach for activity recognition using a wrist-worn accelerometer. In Proceedings of the Annual International Conference of the IEEE Engineering in Medicine and Biology Society, EMBS, Jeju Island, Korea, 11–15 July 2017; pp. 2438–2441.
11. Twomey, N.; Diethe, T.; Fafoutis, X.; Elsts, A.; McConville, R.; Flach, P.; Craddock, I. A Comprehensive Study of Activity Recognition Using Accelerometers. *Informatics* **2018**, *5*, 27. [CrossRef]
12. Bao, L.; Intille, S.S. Activity Recognition from User-Annotated Acceleration Data. *Pervasive* **2004**, *3001*, 1–17.
13. Bergmann, J.H.M.; McGregor, A.H. Body-Worn Sensor Design: What Do Patients and Clinicians Want? *Ann. Biomed. Eng.* **2011**, *39*, 2299–2312. [CrossRef]
14. Dostál, O.; Procházka, A.; Vyšata, O.; Ťupa, O.; Cejnar, P.; Vališ, M. Recognition of motion patterns using accelerometers for ataxic gait assessment. *Neural Comput. Appl.* **2020**, *2*, 1–9. [CrossRef]
15. Pernek, I.; Kurillo, G.; Stiglic, G.; Bajcsy, R. Recognizing the intensity of strength training exercises with wearable sensors. *J. Biomed. Inform.* **2015**, *58*, 145–155. [CrossRef]
16. Biswas, D.; Cranny, A.; Gupta, N.; Maharatna, K.; Achner, J.; Klemke, J.; Jobges, M.; Ortmann, S. Recognizing upper limb movements with wrist worn inertial sensors using k-means clustering classification. *Hum. Mov. Sci.* **2015**, *40*, 59–76. [CrossRef]

17. Lin, H.-C.; Chiang, S.-Y.; Lee, K.; Kan, Y.-C. An Activity Recognition Model Using Inertial Sensor Nodes in a Wireless Sensor Network for Frozen Shoulder Rehabilitation Exercises. *Sensors* **2015**, *15*, 2181–2204. [CrossRef]
18. Cai, S.; Chen, Y.; Huang, S.; Wu, Y.; Zheng, H.; Li, X.; Xie, L. SVM-based classification of sEMG signals for upper-limb self-rehabilitation training. *Front. Neurorobot.* **2019**, *13*, 1–10. [CrossRef]
19. Ni, Q.; Patterson, T.; Cleland, I.; Nugent, C. Dynamic detection of window starting positions and its implementation within an activity recognition framework. *J. Biomed. Inform.* **2016**, *62*, 171–180. [CrossRef] [PubMed]
20. Wang, G.; Li, Q.; Wang, L.; Wang, W.; Wu, M.; Liu, T. Impact of Sliding Window Length in Indoor Human Motion Modes and Pose Pattern Recognition Based on Smartphone Sensors. *Sensors* **2018**, *18*, 1965. [CrossRef] [PubMed]
21. Li, J.-H.; Tian, L.; Wang, H.; An, Y.; Wang, K.; Yu, L. Segmentation and Recognition of Basic and Transitional Activities for Continuous Physical Human Activity. *IEEE Access* **2019**, *7*, 42565–42576. [CrossRef]
22. Fida, B.; Bernabucci, I.; Bibbo, D.; Conforto, S.; Schmid, M. Varying behavior of different window sizes on the classification of static and dynamic physical activities from a single accelerometer. *Med. Eng. Phys.* **2015**, *37*, 705–711. [CrossRef]
23. Ni, Q.; Zhang, L.; Li, L. A Heterogeneous Ensemble Approach for Activity Recognition with Integration of Change Point-Based Data Segmentation. *Appl. Sci.* **2018**, *8*, 1695. [CrossRef]
24. Noor, M.H.M.; Salcic, Z.; Wang, K.I.-K. Adaptive sliding window segmentation for physical activity recognition using a single tri-axial accelerometer. *Pervasive Mob. Comput.* **2017**, *38*, 41–59. [CrossRef]
25. Santos, L.; Khoshhal, K.; Dias, J. Trajectory-based human action segmentation. *Pattern Recognit.* **2015**, *48*, 568–579. [CrossRef]
26. Zhang, S.; Chen, H.; Jiang, C.; Zhang, S. An adaptive time window method for human activity recognition. In Proceedings of the 2015 IEEE 28th Canadian Conference on Electrical and Computer Engineering, Halifax, NS, Canada, 3–6 May 2015; pp. 1188–1192. [CrossRef]
27. Ling, Y. Automatic human daily activity segmentation applying smart sensing technology. *Int. J. Smart Sens. Intell. Syst.* **2015**, *8*, 1624–1640. [CrossRef]
28. Physio Therapy Exercises. Available online: https://www.physiotherapyexercises.com (accessed on 3 October 2019).
29. Nas, K.; Yazmalar, L.; Şah, V.; Aydin, A.; Öneş, K. Rehabilitation of spinal cord injuries. *World J. Orthop.* **2015**, *6*, 8–16. [CrossRef] [PubMed]
30. Côté, M.-P.; Murray, M.; Lemay, M.A. Rehabilitation Strategies after Spinal Cord Injury: Inquiry into the Mechanisms of Success and Failure. *J. Neurotrauma* **2017**, *34*, 1841–1857. [CrossRef] [PubMed]
31. Janidarmian, M.; Fekr, A.R.; Radecka, K.; Zilic, Z. A Comprehensive Analysis on Wearable Acceleration Sensors in Human Activity Recognition. *Sensors* **2017**, *17*, 529. [CrossRef] [PubMed]
32. Ignatov, A. Real-time human activity recognition from accelerometer data using Convolutional Neural Networks. *Appl. Soft Comput.* **2018**, *62*, 915–922. [CrossRef]
33. Garciamasso, X.; Serra-Añó, P.; Gonzalez, L.M.; Ye-Lin, Y.; Prats-Boluda, G.; Garcia-Casado, J. Identifying physical activity type in manual wheelchair users with spinal cord injury by means of accelerometers. *Spinal Cord* **2015**, *53*, 772–777. [CrossRef]
34. Siirtola, P.; Laurinen, P.; Roning, J.; Kinnunen, H. Efficient accelerometer-based swimming exercise tracking. In Proceedings of the 2011 IEEE Symposium on Computational Intelligence and Data Mining (CIDM), Paris, France, 11–15 April 2011; IEEE: New York, NY, USA, 2011; pp. 156–161.
35. Han, S.; Meng, Z.; Omisore, O.; Akinyemi, T.; Yan, Y. Random Error Reduction Algorithms for MEMS Inertial Sensor Accuracy Improvement—A Review. *Micromachines* **2020**, *11*, 1021. [CrossRef]
36. Erdaş, B.; Atasoy, I.; Açici, K.; Oğul, H. Integrating Features for Accelerometer-based Activity Recognition. *Procedia Comput. Sci.* **2016**, *58*, 522–527. [CrossRef]
37. Hiremath, S.V.; Intille, S.S.; Kelleher, A.; Cooper, R.A.; Ding, D. Detection of physical activities using a physical activity monitor system for wheelchair users. *Med. Eng. Phys.* **2015**, *37*, 68–76. [CrossRef] [PubMed]
38. Elhoushi, M.; Georgy, J.; Noureldin, A.; Korenberg, M.J. A Survey on Approaches of Motion Mode Recognition Using Sensors. *IEEE Trans. Intell. Transp. Syst.* **2017**, *18*, 1662–1686. [CrossRef]

Article

A Heterogeneous Learning Framework for Over-the-Top Consumer Analysis Reflecting the Actual Market Environment

Jaeun Choi [1] and Yongsung Kim [2,*]

[1] Department of Artificial Intelligence Software, Kyungil University, Gyungbuk 38428, Korea; juchoi@kiu.kr
[2] Department of Software Engineering, Cyber University of Korea, Seoul 03051, Korea
* Correspondence: kys1001@cuk.edu; Tel.: +82-2-6361-1948

Abstract: The over-the-top (OTT) market for media consumption over wired and wireless Internet is growing. It is, therefore, crucial that service providers and carriers participating in the OTT market analyze consumer traffic for pricing, service delivery, infrastructure investments, etc. The OTT market has many consumer groups, but the proportion of users is not consistent in each. Furthermore, as multimedia consumption has increased owing to the COVID-19 epidemic, the OTT market has changed rapidly. If this is not reflected, the analysis will not be accurate. Therefore, we propose a framework that can classify consumers well based on actual OTT market environment conditions. First, by applying our proposed conditional probability-based method to basic machine learning techniques, such as support vector machine, *k*-nearest neighbor, and decision tree, we can improve the classification performance, even for an imbalanced OTT consumer distribution. Then, it is possible to analyze the changing consumer trends by dynamically retraining the incoming OTT consumer data. Conventional methods result in low classification accuracy in low-number classes, but our method shows an improvement of 5.3–19.2% based on recall. Moreover, conventional methods have shown large fluctuations in performance as the OTT market environment has changed, but our framework consistently maintains high performance.

Keywords: consumer analysis; cost-sensitive learning; imbalanced dataset; machine learning; over-the-top; training data update

Citation: Choi, J.; Kim, Y. A Heterogeneous Learning Framework for Over-the-Top Consumer Analysis Reflecting the Actual Market Environment. *Appl. Sci.* **2021**, *11*, 4783. https://doi.org/10.3390/app11114783

Academic Editor: Grzegorz Dudek

Received: 20 April 2021
Accepted: 21 May 2021
Published: 23 May 2021

Publisher's Note: MDPI stays neutral with regard to jurisdictional claims in published maps and institutional affiliations.

Copyright: © 2021 by the authors. Licensee MDPI, Basel, Switzerland. This article is an open access article distributed under the terms and conditions of the Creative Commons Attribution (CC BY) license (https://creativecommons.org/licenses/by/4.0/).

1. Introduction

Digital media consumption worldwide is exploding alongside wired and wireless Internet access speeds and bandwidth since the COVID-19 pandemic started. Consumers now have access to media content they want, anytime and anywhere, at cheap prices. YouTube, Netflix, Hulu, Amazon Prime, and Roku are now threatening the existence of traditional media markets [1]. These new over-the-top (OTT) services are defined as "video contents provided through paths based on the internet or internet protocol (IP)" [2]. OTT services are spreading rapidly because consumers can select personalized content and platforms based on their own schedules. The global OTT market is expected to reach USD 1039.03B by 2027 with an average annual growth rate of 29.4% from 2020 to 2027 [3]. In the US (the largest OTT market), there were 182-million OTT subscribers as of 2019 [4], and YouTube (the most popular digital broadcasting platform), was watched by 84.2% of the US digital video viewers; Netflix was watched by 67.6% [5]. As the OTT market has grown, various global service providers and telecommunication carriers have competed intensely.

As some indoor and outdoor activities were restricted owing to COVID-19, demand for video streaming skyrocketed as movie theaters shut down. Subscription video on demand, the most typical OTT method, is a monthly subscription model that allows users to view all platform content for a gateway fee. Subscriptions have increased by approximately 10% since COVID-19 started [6]. Similar phenomena have led to a significant increase in consumer traffic consumption. As the OTT market grows rapidly, an analysis methodology specialized for the OTT market is required. Focusing on the OTT market, we intend to propose a market analysis methodology that will be required by players participating in the OTT market.

1.1. Motivation and Objective

Due to the growth of the OTT market, the revenue generated by the consumer growth is positive from the standpoint of OTT service providers, but content delivery network (CDN) service costs also have grown [7]. To generate profits, OTT companies must analyze and capitalize network usage. Network operators are also struggling because of the growth in OTT traffic. A problem occurs in terms of profitability if the service fees are not commensurate to the provided services [8]. In particular, because it is important for an OTT company to ensure quality of service (QoS), it is essential to manage the network effectively [9]. In the case of live streaming, which now accounts for a considerable portion of OTT, QoS expectations have placed a large burden on telecommunication carriers [10]. To address these challenges, carriers offer a variety of service contracts. Normally, if allocated bandwidth is exceeded, a service degradation is often applied [11]. This allows telecommunication carriers to better manage large and complex network resources. However, throttling often causes complaints from customers with changing needs. Therefore, both providers and consumers have a learning curve. As such, companies participating in the OTT market need to be able to more accurately classify the OTT service patterns of consumers to maintain contracts and create profits.

Many studies have been conducted to analyze the traffic of traditional networks. In particular, there have been many studies recently that have applied artificial intelligence and machine learning (ML) based methods for analyzing common Internet traffic. However, these methods generally target general-purpose traffic, and very few studies have analyzed OTT service traffic [12,13]. While these studies are significant in that they dealt with ML methods specialized for OTT traffic classification, they neglected real-world problems that were common to the OTT market. OTT consumers range from heavy users who watch tremendous amounts of OTT content, to light users who rarely watch, and the proportions are not the same [12,14]. If ML is applied without considering these imbalances, the classification accuracy drops for the smaller user group [15]. OTT usage patterns change rapidly over time, such as during the COVID-19 pandemic. Because new OTT services are continually offered, and telecommunication carriers offer various subscription-fee schemes, consumer usage patterns also change. Conventional studies on OTT traffic have not considered the dataset changes caused by these phenomena. They generally perform ML and classification for the data once, which does not reflect continuous changes. Hence, classification accuracy declines over time. Our research objective is to propose a method to analyze OTT consumers well, based on actual market environment conditions.

1.2. Contribution

In this study, we propose an OTT user classification method that responds to real-world problems. OTT users can be divided into several groups according to their data usage, and the number of members for each group is not consistent. While existing studies show good performance in classifying groups composed of similar numbers, their classification accuracy for classes with small numbers reduces with the imbalanced data environments encountered in real-world situations. We thus propose a framework to solve this problem as this is an issue that is readily discoverable in the OTT market but has not yet been considered as a research topic. First, when classifying a class with small numbers using ML, we tried to increase the classification accuracy by setting the weight for the error occurring in the class higher than the error occurring in a class with a large number of members. As the weights were set high, and the ML classifier was set to avoid errors with high weights, we were able to improve the classification accuracy of classes with a small number. To set the weight of the error, the probability of indicating the class to which a sample belongs was calculated based on the costs of misclassification errors, and, by setting the cost high, the weight for a specific error could be set high. In addition, in order to respond to changes in consumer trends, we constructed a module that can periodically update the training data. Unlike existing studies that do not take changes in trends into account, our framework periodically updates training data, which allows us to respond to frequent trend changes with regard to OTT users. According to experimental results, it can be seen that, even though consumer trends change, our framework shows a constant performance; however, the performance of existing methods degrades severely. As such, our study suggests ways to solve the practical problems encountered in the OTT market. In other words, it has great significance as the OTT user analysis framework reported here can be utilized to realistically analyze OTT users.

The remainder of this paper is organized as follows. Section 2 discusses the importance of analyzing OTT-related trends and usage patterns. Furthermore, we examine the limitations of conventional studies. Section 3 introduces the OTT user analysis framework proposed in this study, and Section 4 examines the experimental results. Finally, Section 5 presents conclusions and a brief description of future studies.

2. Literature Review
2.1. OTT Services

Recent statistics show that OTT consumers are moving away from traditional television (TV)-based content viewing. In the US market, the proportion of those who have subscribed to a streaming video service at least once (68%) has already surpassed the ratio of paid TV subscribers (65%). Furthermore, the average number of streaming subscriptions has increased by 33% since the beginning of the COVID-19 outbreak [16]. As of December 2020, US consumers spent an average of USD 47 per month, a significant increase from the USD 38 reported in April of the same year [17].

An increasing number of companies are entering the OTT market, intensifying competition. In the second quarter of 2020, Netflix had the highest streaming proportion in the US market, accounting for 34%. This was followed by the traditional OTT powerhouses of YouTube, Hulu, and Amazon Prime, with 20, 11, and 8%, respectively. Disney Plus then launched, quickly garnering 4% [18] after acquiring the 21st Century Fox library [19]. Because existing OTT companies already dominate the market to some extent, TV broadcasting companies, telecommunication carriers, and cable operators are now releasing their own apps or investing in other platforms. After acquiring Warner Media, AT&T launched an OTT service leveraging their new HBO content [20].

The rapidly changing market is looming as both a threat and an opportunity for OTT operators. Notably, it is expected that many subscriptions will not be renewed after COVID-19 restrictions are lifted. Thus, OTT operators must find ways to retain customers. For this, the Boston Consulting Group has advised OTT operators to analyze user patterns and to classify them into groups for customized strategies [6]. Pricing plans comprise an important customer lure. The biggest reason that customers cancel subscriptions is the expense, and this accounts for 36% of all cancellations [16].

Telecommunication carriers, cable operators, and Internet-protocol TV (IPTV) operators are struggling under the competitive OTT environment [21,22]. For example, the IPTV market overlaps and encroaches many OTT services. Bundled service strategies are sometimes required to prevent IPTV subscriptions from being canceled for OTT viewing [23]. In South Korea, KT, the operator with the highest IPTV market share, is partnering with Netflix to create synergies. Netflix is using this opportunity to enter the South Korean market. Additionally, KT will receive network fees by providing Internet bandwidth to Netflix. Furthermore, an increase in the number of KT customers is expected when Netflix is provided as a bundled service [24]. Mobile network providers are also required to make infrastructure investments to maintain the quality of live streaming. With the spread of 5G, an increasing number of users are enjoying OTT services wirelessly. However, failure to provide a stable QoS will result in customer churn. In fact, about 30% of consumers are willing to for pay premium prices if the mobile networks, especially 5G, can deliver better video quality and reduce buffering [25]. As more consumers use real-time services, network operators face difficulties because of infrastructure investments [10,26]. Network operators must build a sound service-quality degradation strategy that minimizes network resource consumption, while also satisfying consumer demand and QoS. As such, it is crucial for all providers to establish appropriate pricing schemes for the OTT environment.

Various studies have been conducted on pricing systems related to content providers, network operators, and service users based on net neutrality. These include a study based on QoS [9], a study based on the quality of experience [27], a study using shadow prices [28], and a study based on CDNs [29] or software defined networks [30] (see Section 2.1 of our previous study [13] for a brief description of these constructs). Although there are differences in these detailed methods, most studies have proposed pricing schemes based on network use per user per month. Hence, it is a top priority for OTT and network providers to identify the traffic usage patterns of OTT users to determine the most efficient pricing scheme. It is thus important to effectively classify and group OTT users. Then, they can implement suitable pricing strategies. Clearly classifying OTT users is the first step. In this study, we propose a ML-based framework specialized for OTT user traffic analyses in a real-world environment.

2.2. Review of Classification Using ML

Machine and deep learning methods are widely used for user traffic analyses, owing to advancements in artificial intelligence technology. Many relevant techniques have been studied, including decision tree, a traditional ML method [31,32], support vector machine (SVM) [33–35], k-nearest neighbor (KNN) [36,37], hidden Markov model [38,39], and k-means [40,41]. There have been recent studies on traffic analyses using deep learning, which has strengths in terms of accuracy [42–44]. Although there are some differences in the techniques and forms of the applications, they all tend to capture and analyze traffic based on features. Analysis targets range from captured packets to open datasets, but little consideration has been given to OTT data.

Rojas et al. proposed a method of classifying users based on OTT usage data [11,12,45]. They used various ML methods to analyze OTT traffic and classified consumers into three consumption categories: high, medium, and low. Their study is highly significant in that it was the first to attempt to classify OTT users. Their dataset contained real-world data that were equally weighted based on the three consumption classes. However, their validation was performed in an environment different from a real one, and equal weighting was problematic, as we discuss herein. Our previous study was significant in that a deep learning method was applied alongside traditional ML methods [13]. In particular, we proposed a framework to overcome the temporal disadvantages of applying a deep learning method alone. Nevertheless, our study had a limitation in that a dataset detached from the real-world environment was used. In this study, we propose a method that overcomes these limitations.

2.3. Problem Statement

2.3.1. Class-Imbalance Problem

There are diverse demographics of consumers that consume OTT services. Gen-Z's (born between 1997 and 2006) and Millennials' (born between 1983 and 1996) lives have included breakthrough technologies and cultural changes that now include OTT services. Statistics show that the Millennials and Gen-Zs use 17 and 14 subscription services each, respectively, whereas Baby-Boomers subscribe to eight on average [16]. A similar phenomenon was observed in network usage statistics. Seventy percent of Gen-Zs subscribe to Netflix; however, as age increases, the subscription rate decreases, with only 39% of Baby-Boomers subscribing to it [46]. When consumers are grouped by country, the characteristics differ among groups again. Consumers in populous India spend more than 45B h using video streaming services, more than double that of US consumers. The country having the highest video content per capita is South Korea, where almost 2000 h are spent per person [47].

As such, OTT market consumers can be divided into various groups, and the number of group members varies widely. According to Walelgne et al. [14], who analyzed the data traffic of mobile users (including OTT), heavy users who comprise only 2–4% of the total consume the most data. They collected mobile traffic from Finland, Germany, the UK, Japan, and Brazil and classified users using a clustering method. In Finland, which had the largest number of research samples, the proportions of heavy, regular, and light users were 3.5, 41.9, and 54.6%, respectively, and the data used for uploads and downloads by each group comprised 328.7, 64.3, and 9.4 MB, respectively. Heavy users, comprising only about 3% of the total, used more data than approximately 97% of the other users. A similar phenomenon was found in other countries, although the proportions were different [14]. Furthermore, similar trends were found in a study that grouped users by analyzing actual OTT traffic. According to Rojas et al., the high, medium, and low consumption groups consisted of 84, 50, and 582 persons, respectively [12].

Similar to the case of OTT user groups, very small or very large numbers of samples for particular classes are often observed in real-world environments [48]. Hence, analysis results will likely be biased toward the most populous classes [49]. With ML, this problem is called the "class-imbalance problem" and is viewed as one of ten major problems to overcome [50]. As reviewed above, very few studies have analyzed OTT traffic, and some did not consider the class-imbalance problem at all, which is easily seen in the OTT demographics. If this problem is not considered, performance deterioration problems will occur with real-world grouping and pricing strategy computations. Therefore, we propose a method to overcome such problems for ML methods, as applied to an actual OTT environment.

In areas other than OTT, the class-imbalance problem is often encountered when classification is performed. For example, many studies on the detection of Twitter spam have overlooked this problem. However, other studies applied methods of artificially re-sampling the data to solve this problem [51,52]. Nevertheless, if re-sampling is performed based on a small amount of data, there will be the problem that the minor classes have the characteristics of only a small amount of collected data. To overcome this, cost-based methods have been applied in the binary classification field [15,53]. These adjust the cost of misclassifications to reduce them for the smaller classes. While employing a cost-based approach in this study, we leverage a method that can be applied to a dataset comprising many classes in accordance with the characteristics of OTT users.

2.3.2. Rapid Changes in the OTT Market

The OTT market has been active for less than a decade, and many companies are competing to lead the market. As mentioned, the landscape of the OTT market is expected to change continuously in the future as media providers, telecommunication operators, and OTT companies compete for market share. According to a survey, many consumers intend to cancel one out of five newly acquired subscription services, and one out of ten previously acquired services after post-pandemic normalization [6]. This is because the time spent on entertainment will likely be reduced when consumers return to their normal routines [16].

Most ML-based classification methods perform learning based on previously collected data. Therefore, it is known that the classification accuracy increases with more learned data. When analyzing OTT consumers, this can be problematic if the training is performed using only previously collected data. Because the OTT market is rapidly changing, it will not be possible to respond to new changes, and the accuracy of the analysis will decrease. Most existing studies performed training based on initially collected data with no plans to continuously update the training datasets. This study, however, proposes a framework for ML and analysis that reflects the evolving patterns of consumers.

3. Research Design

3.1. Model Design: An Overview

We propose a ML-based framework that facilitates the effective classification of OTT users in a real market environment. First, OTT consumer classification is performed to increase the classification accuracy related to the class-imbalance situation. Then, we propose a module that updates the training data at predetermined intervals to reflect the continuously changing trends. Figure 1 illustrates the modules of the proposed framework. The details of each are discussed in the following sections.

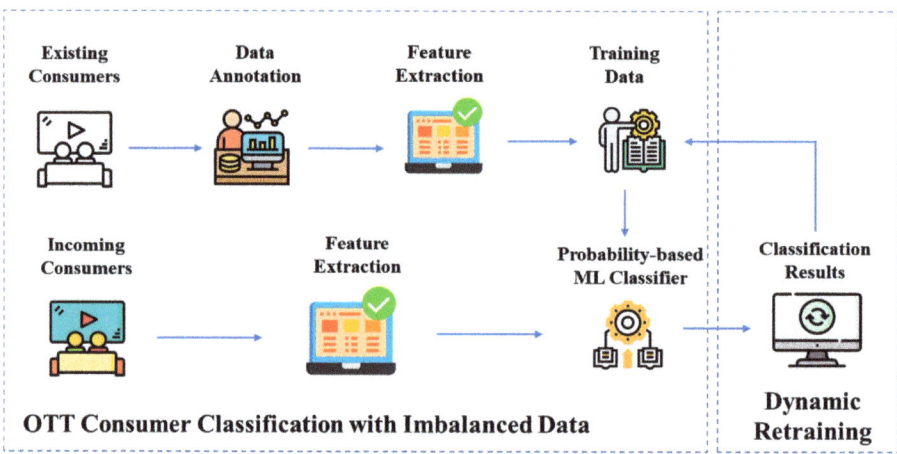

Figure 1. Modules of the proposed framework.

3.2. OTT Consumer Classification with Imbalanced Data

The first step in our proposed framework is to analyze the traffic of OTT users by using ML to classify them into groups. For consumer classification, data annotation with the help of experts is first needed after collecting the data usage patterns of existing OTT users. In this method, OTT consumer traffic is classified into three types. Consumers with high OTT usage are classified as "high consumption", those with a low usage are classified as "low consumption", and those with average usage are classified as "medium consumption". As discussed, data consumption differs significantly among the three types. According to Rojas et al., low consumption users account for 81.3% of the total, while high and medium consumption users account for only a small portion of the total [12].

After collecting OTT user traffic and performing annotation, feature extraction is performed. Features refer to individual and measurable properties of data for ML. The more significant features that are extracted, the higher is the accuracy of the classification. In this study, the public dataset released by Rojas et al. was used; thus, our feature sets are also based on their study [12]. As our study's objective is to classify consumers by analyzing patterns of OTT users, it is important to know how much data users have consumed for each OTT application. Therefore, by utilizing the amount of time and data used by consumers for each OTT application as the main features, consumers can be classified based on their usage patterns. A detailed description of the datasets and features used in this study is provided in Section 4.1.

After extracting features based on collected consumer data, they are used as training data. Afterward, when incoming consumers' information that needs to be analyzed comes in, features are first extracted. Subsequently, through ML that uses the training data built earlier, the group to which the incoming consumer belongs to is determined. In this process we face the problem of deteriorating classification accuracy due to the class imbalance, as discussed above. In order to improve performance, even in such a situation, we propose a method to calculate the probability of which class each data sample belongs to based on the cost. To better classify the classes, we use different costs for misclassification errors so that mistakes are eventually minimized [15,54]. In particular, the OTT consumer dataset consists of three classes and we propose the appropriate formulation and cost matrix. Table 1 shows the asymmetric cost matrix for OTT consumer classes.

Table 1. Asymmetric misclassification cost matrix.

	Actual High	Actual Medium	Actual Low
Predicted High	$C(h, h)$	$C(m, h)$	$C(l, h)$
Predicted Medium	$C(h, m)$	$C(m, m)$	$C(l, m)$
Predicted Low	$C(h, l)$	$C(m, l)$	$C(l, l)$

Misclassification refers to the incorrect classification of users. If a user who belongs to the actual high class is classified as medium or low, the costs that occur in this case are $C(h, m)$ and $C(h, l)$, respectively. In the case of OTT consumers, because the number of users belonging to the actual high or medium classes is extremely small compared with those in the actual low class, the classification accuracy for the two classes is inevitably low. Because our goal is to improve classification accuracy for classes having small sample sizes, we need to reduce the number of misclassifications of users who actually belong to the high or medium class. We do this with $C(h, m)$ and $C(h, l)$, which are applied to misclassifications of high consumption users, and $C(m, h)$ and $C(m, l)$, which are applied to misclassifications of medium consumption users. They should be set higher than $C(l, h)$ and $C(l, m)$, the costs occurring due to misclassifying low consumption users. If the costs are set high, misclassifications will be reduced. On the other hand, if the classification is properly performed, the costs are $C(h, h)$, $C(m, m)$, and $C(l, l)$ for each respective class. Because there is no risk to the classification system in the case of proper classification, the three above costs should all be set to zero.

Upon completion of cost-setting, classification is performed to determine the class to which samples belong. When a sample is given, the probability of indicating the class to which it belongs is calculated. Supposing that E is the entire dataset. Then, E_i is a resample of E with n examples. The probability that an example, x, belongs to a class, j, is as follows [54]:

$$P(j|x) = \frac{1}{\sum_i 1} \sum_i P(j|x, M_i), \quad (1)$$

where i ranges from 1 to m, and m is the number of newly produced resamples. Then, M_i is a model created by applying a classification learning algorithm to E_i. Here, the risk occurring when x is classified as a class s can be defined as follows [15]:

$$R(s|x) = \sum_j P(j|x)C(s, j). \quad (2)$$

We must minimize the risk of sample assignment. Therefore, class s, which satisfies Equation (3), becomes the class to which x is assigned:

$$\text{argmin}_s R(s|x). \quad (3)$$

For OTT user classification, because there are three classes, the variables, s and j, indicate the degrees of freedom for high, medium, and low classes.

Various ML algorithms can be used to generate a model, M_i, which is used for probability calculation when performing consumer classifications. In this study, we use common ML methods, including decision tree, SVM, and KNN, because we need to determine whether the performance can increase in an imbalanced data environment when our framework is applied. This allows us to check whether data encountered in real-world situations can be accurately classified, regardless of which ML algorithm is used. The ML algorithms used in this study are presented in Section 4.2.

3.3. Dynamic Retraining Module

Another problem encountered when analyzing OTT users in real-world situations is the that where the data characteristics change continuously. Studies on conventional ML-based classifications tend to continuously utilize data that were initially collected after annotation. The critical disadvantage of this method is that newly changed characteristics are not reflected. To overcome this, Chen et al. proposed a method for updating training data at fixed intervals [55]. Based on their studies, we propose a method suitable for OTT user analysis.

To classify OTT users, data are collected first, then they are labeled by an expert. If the collected dataset is T_{init}, the classification algorithm, L, is used to perform training using T_{init}. The classifier, C_{init}, is composed as follows:

$$C_{init} = L(T_{init}). \tag{4}$$

Our proposed framework also uses C_{init}, which is based on labeled data that have already been collected. However, although most studies continue to use only C_{init}, we update the training data continuously. If the pre-set time interval, τ, elapses, the classification result of the data that were already collected is obtained. If an additionally collected dataset of high consumption users is H_t, that of medium consumption users is M_t, and that of low consumption users is L_t. Here, t is a time unit that increases by one whenever the pre-set time interval, τ, elapses. The newly added dataset, T_{new}, can be summarized as Equation (5), and the classifier C_{new} that reflects it is Equation (6):

$$T_{new} = \sum_t (H_t \cup M_t \cup L_t), \tag{5}$$

$$C_{new} = L(T_{init} \cup T_{new}). \tag{6}$$

Periodically, at a given time interval, the training dataset will incorporate the newly changed characteristics of each user group. C_{new}, is updated based on retraining to facilitate accurate classification while accounting for changes. This enables flexible responses and updated learning.

4. Results and Discussion

Section 4.1 describes the dataset and evaluation metrics used in this study. Section 4.2 verifies the performance improvement in an environment with a given imbalanced dataset when our framework is applied. Section 4.3 verifies how well it can respond to the trend changes if the training dataset is updated periodically.

4.1. Dataset Description and Evaluation Metrics

To validate the method proposed in this study, we used a dataset released by Rojas et al., who captured data directly for 10 days from the Universidaa del Caucau Unicauca network in 2019. The dataset comprises a total of 113 features and samples from 1249 users classified into three classes: high, medium, and low consumption.

OTT data are well-represented, and analyses were performed for a total of 56 applications, including typical OTT services (e.g., Netflix, YouTube, Twitch, and Spotify). The traffic flow was analyzed for each, and features were extracted, as shown in Table 2 [12].

Table 2. Feature description.

Feature Name	Feature Description
src_ip_numeric	Decimal representation of the IP address of the user
ApplicationName_time_occupation	Time spent by the user for each OTT service
Application-Name.Flow.Bytes.Per.Sec	Byte size used per second by the user for each OTT service

The number of samples in each dataset class differed from those in real situations. There were 406 high-consumption samples, 333 medium-consumption samples, and 510 low-consumption samples, which were readjusted to balance the classes. We used an analytical approach that shows good performance, even if training is performed to reflect real-world data. We used the SMOTE method to adjust the above-described open dataset according to the proportions of an actual situation [56]. We set the number of samples for each class to 5610 for low, 566 for medium, and 812 for high.

Recall, precision, and F-measure were considered as evaluation metrics and were calculated based on true positive (TP), false positive (FP), and false negative (FN) results. In this study, data composed of three classes were classified, and we will first look at the concepts of TP, FP, and FN using examples of a high-consumption group. TP refers to the rate at which the sample belonging to the actual high class is predicted to be high. FP and FN are values indicating an error, FP indicates that a sample that actually belongs to low or medium class is incorrectly classified as high class, and FN indicates that a sample that belongs to high is incorrectly classified as low or medium class. TP, FP, and FN of medium and low classes can also be obtained in the same manner. Recall is equivalent to TP, a numerical value that indicates correct classifications. Precision is the probability of the data belonging to that class. F-measure shows the accuracy by finding the harmonic mean of the precision and recall; see Equation (7):

$$Recall = \frac{TP}{TP + FN}, \quad Precision = \frac{TP}{TP + FP}, \quad F - Measure = \frac{2 \cdot Recall \cdot Precision}{Recall + Precision}. \quad (7)$$

4.2. Performance Comparison with Imbalanced Dataset

To compare the performance between the proposed framework and existing studies, J48-decision tree, KNN, rule-based PART, and SVM algorithms were used for comparison. As previously discussed, there are few existing studies classifying OTT consumers, and these studies derive insights by applying popular ML or deep learning algorithms targeting OTT consumers [11–13,45]. Therefore, in this study, we compared the performance of our proposed framework with the widely used ML techniques for performance comparison with the existing research methodologies. See Section 3.1.1 of our previous study [13] for a brief description of comparison algorithms. These were implemented using scikit-learn [57] and Weka [58]. In the case of J48, the seed was fixed to 1, and the confidence factor was set to 0.25. In the case of KNN, k was set to five; and a polynomial kernel was used for the SVM. In the case of PART, the number of folds used for pruning was set to five.

To check how much the performance declines when using an imbalanced dataset, we first compared the performance using the original and the refined dataset with a similar number of samples. Table 3 shows the performance differences. Apart from these, the accuracy increases significantly for the low consumption user group, because its proportion is large, which results in biased training toward that group. In contrast, the medium and high consumption groups showed performance drops in the unbalanced dataset compared with the refined one. In particular, the recall, which indicates whether the data belong to the pertinent group, decreases significantly in the unbalanced dataset. A drop of approximately 3–4% was observed even when the J48 algorithm was used, which resulted in the lowest drop, and a 6–10% drop was observed when the KNN and PART algorithms were used. In the case of SVM, a drop of almost 30% was observed in the high consumption group. As such, if the imbalanced dataset that reflects a real-world situation is classified using a conventional method, the classification accuracy declines for classes having small proportions. This can be a big problem for companies that need to analyze consumers and develop customized strategies.

Table 3. Performance comparison between refined data and imbalanced data by ML algorithms.

ML Algorithms	Class	Refined Dataset			Imbalanced Dataset		
		Recall	Precision	F-Measure	Recall	Precision	F-Measure
J48	Low	0.941	0.950	0.946	0.992	0.984	0.988
	Medium	0.955	0.933	0.944	0.917	0.917	0.917
	High	0.948	0.955	0.952	0.915	0.966	0.940
KNN	Low	0.951	0.933	0.942	0.999	0.967	0.983
	Medium	0.958	0.967	0.962	0.852	0.992	0.916
	High	0.946	0.962	0.954	0.863	0.997	0.925
PART	Low	0.925	0.872	0.898	0.991	0.961	0.976
	Medium	0.886	0.905	0.895	0.825	0.945	0.881
	High	0.901	0.958	0.929	0.839	0.958	0.894
SVM	Low	0.961	0.965	0.963	0.999	0.940	0.968
	Medium	0.973	0.961	0.967	0.843	0.988	0.909
	High	0.975	0.980	0.978	0.664	0.994	0.796

We proposed a framework to improve the classification accuracy for imbalanced datasets encountered in real-world environments. In this section, we verify the accuracy improvement when our framework is applied. In the next section, we validate the performance improvement when retraining is implemented. We used J48, KNN, PART, and SVM algorithms, which were selected for comparison, to generate the M_i of Equation (1). Their environment settings are the same as those used previously. Our framework requires an additional cost-setting, and the cost was set as follows. The cost of misclassifying the low-consumption group was set to one in all algorithms. The cost of misclassifying the medium consumption group was set to 10 for J48 and SVM algorithms, 20 for the KNN, and 15 for the PART. The cost of misclassifying the high consumption group was set to 10 for J48 and PART, and 20 for the KNN and SVM. Table 4 shows the performance of the proposed framework. All four algorithms showed a slight performance drop in the low consumption group but maintain a 96–99% level in terms of recall, because there were many samples. On the other hand, in the case of the medium and high consumption groups, the performance was low when the imbalanced dataset was used as is. However, it increased significantly when our framework was used. Most algorithms showed a recall of the mid-to-high 90% range, and in particular, the high consumption group of the SVM algorithm showed that the recall, which dropped to 66.4%, increased up to 85.6%. In Figure 2, which compares the recall between the cases of using the refined and imbalanced datasets and the case of using our framework, it is confirmed that our framework shows good performance, even in real-world situations. This means that, although the existing algorithms alone cannot properly classify the propensity of OTT consumers encountered in the real world, our proposed algorithm facilitates proper classification of data reflecting real-world situations.

Table 4. Performance comparison between conventional methods and our framework in an imbalanced data environment.

ML Algorithms	Class	Imbalanced Dataset			Our Framework		
		Recall	Precision	F-Measure	Recall	Precision	F-Measure
J48	Low	0.992	0.984	0.988	0.967	0.995	0.981
	Medium	0.917	0.917	0.917	0.972	0.820	0.889
	High	0.915	0.966	0.940	0.968	0.910	0.938
KNN	Low	0.999	0.967	0.983	0.997	0.989	0.993
	Medium	0.852	0.992	0.916	0.959	0.977	0.968
	High	0.863	0.997	0.925	0.954	0.997	0.975
PART	Low	0.991	0.961	0.976	0.975	0.977	0.976
	Medium	0.825	0.945	0.881	0.889	0.857	0.873
	High	0.839	0.958	0.894	0.903	0.911	0.907
SVM	Low	0.999	0.940	0.968	0.996	0.981	0.988
	Medium	0.843	0.988	0.909	0.898	0.906	0.902
	High	0.664	0.994	0.796	0.856	0.946	0.899

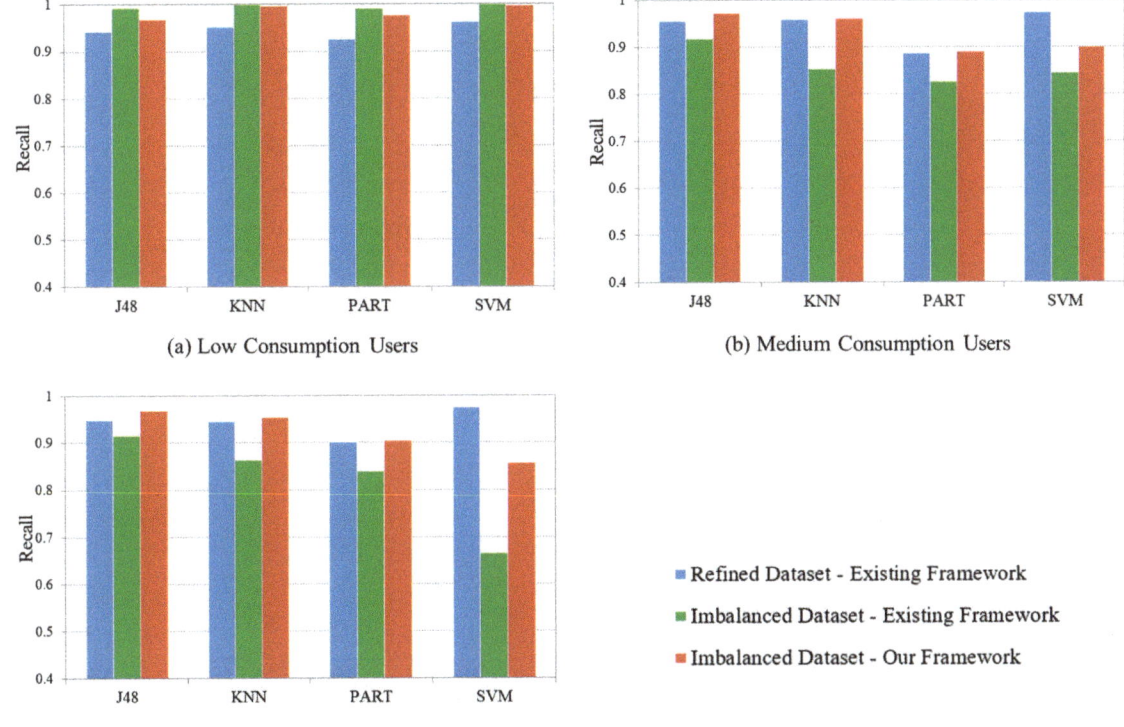

Figure 2. Comparison of recall between different user groups: (**a**) low consumption users; (**b**) medium consumption users; (**c**) high consumption users.

4.3. Performance Comparison with the Dynamic Retraining Module

In the previous section, learning and classification were conducted under the assumption that all data were collected in advance. This assumption is easily observed in most ML-based classification studies. However, this is far from reality. Therefore, we provide a module that accommodates new retention by including the results of the previous cycle in the training data at every fixed cycle. In this section, we verify the performance of the proposed module. We divided the imbalanced dataset used in the previous section into 10 sub-datasets to reflect the changes in the OTT market environment. If each sub-dataset is assumed to contain data collected for a single day, the dataset is divided into 10 sub-datasets from days 1 to 10. Because the dataset is based on data collected over 10 days, this is a reasonable assumption. First, to check whether the conventional methods properly respond to the changes in the OTT market environment, we used the data collected on day 1 as the training data and those collected on days 2–10 as the test data to measure performance. To evaluate the performance, we measured after retraining using the data classification results of up to the previous day daily. Figure 3 shows the change in recall on each day for each group, and Figure 4 shows the change in F-measure for each day for each group.

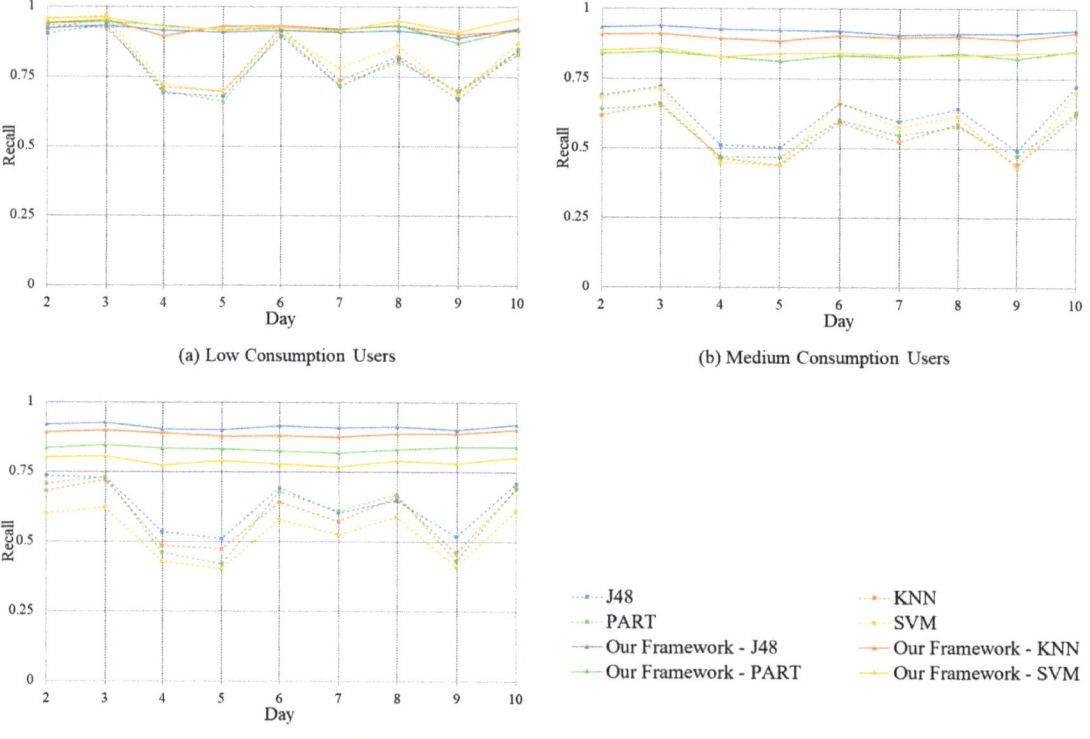

Figure 3. Change of recall on each for each user group: (**a**) low consumption users; (**b**) medium consumption users; (**c**) high consumption users.

First, recall was compared for each group, as shown in Figure 3. In the case of our proposed method, stable recall values were maintained without significant changes, even when time elapsed. However, in the case of conventional methods, the deviation was very large between different days. Even in the low consumption group with many samples, the performance was significantly different between our proposed method and that of conventional methods, and in the case of medium and high consumption groups, the recall dropped below 50% on severe days when only the conventional methods were used. This means that more than half of the consumers belonging to those groups were not correctly classified, which may have a critically adverse effect on the reliability of the analysis results. Similar trends were observed from the comparison of the F-measure for each group, as shown in Figure 4. Although our method shows a stable overall performance, the conventional methods show large deviations between different days. This means that if the conventional methods are used alone, changes in OTT trends cannot be reflected, resulting in a decreased classification accuracy. In contrast, our framework facilitates a proper response to trend changes over time.

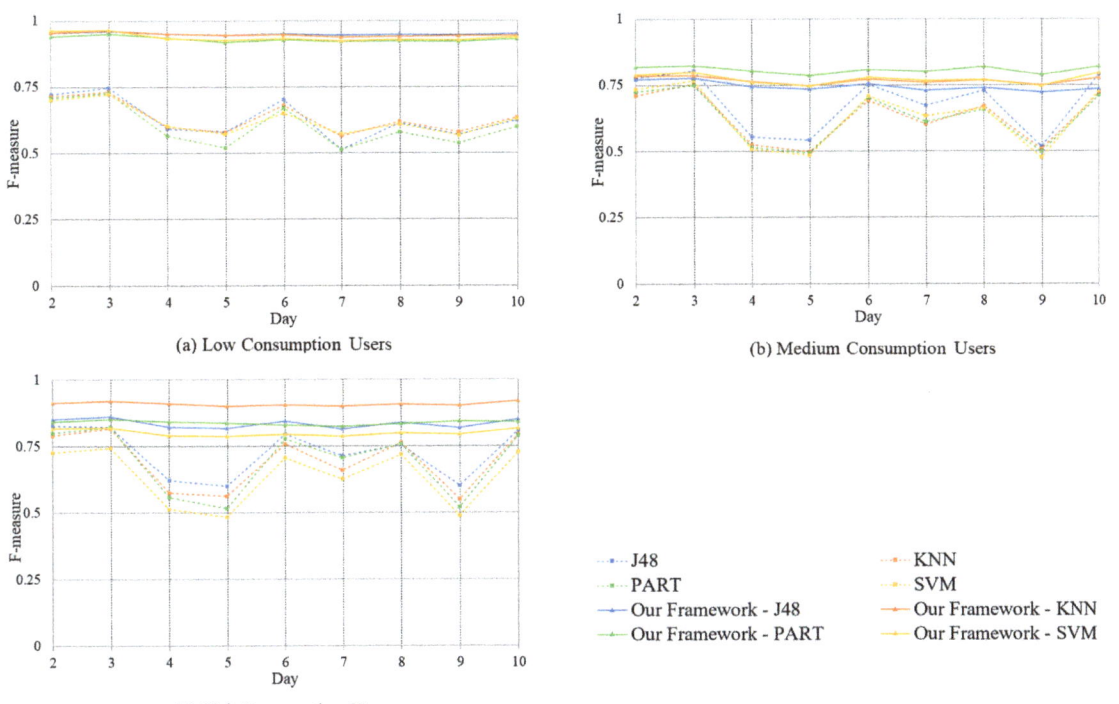

Figure 4. Change of F-measure on each day for each user group: (**a**) low consumption users; (**b**) medium consumption users; (**c**) high consumption users.

5. Conclusions

In this study, we proposed an ML-based framework for OTT user analysis, which is an important factor for various companies in the OTT market. Specifically, we used a probability based on cost while utilizing an ML-based consumer classification method to obtain good performance even with an imbalance between user groups, which is seen in the actual OTT market environment as well. Our method showed a higher performance compared with conventional ones, even for an imbalanced dataset. Furthermore, our framework continually updated the training dataset in response to the ever-changing OTT market environment. For conventional methods, it is difficult to respond to trend changes, because the classification is performed based on pre-learned data. However, ours performs better despite the trend changes.

This study is significant in that it provides a direction to solve the problem that is easily encountered by various companies participating in the OTT market. Conventional ML-based classification studies are often conducted based on refined datasets, not datasets that can be encountered in the real world. In such cases, the accuracy may be high, but when they are used in real-world environments, the accuracy may drop, making them difficult to use for practical applications. Furthermore, extant studies often performed ML and analysis based on previously collected data without considering the constantly changing propensity of consumer behavior. However, our study can help companies analyze consumers in this environment, because our method provides stable performance in actual changing situations.

In the future, a specific methodology will be required for cost-setting when cost-based classification is performed. In this study, we conducted experiments by setting the costs higher when a larger number of errors occurred. In the future, we must consider how to systemize this and automatically select the appropriate costs. Furthermore, additional analyses are required based on a variety of OTT user data. To the best of our knowledge, the dataset used in this study is the latest open dataset specific to OTT service users. In the future, if additional open datasets are available, validation and improvements should be studied based on those sets.

Author Contributions: Conceptualization, J.C. and Y.K.; methodology, J.C. and Y.K.; software, J.C.; validation, J.C. and Y.K.; formal analysis, J.C.; investigation, J.C. and Y.K.; resources, J.C.; data curation, J.C.; writing—original draft preparation, J.C.; writing—review and editing, Y.K.; visualization, J.C.; supervision, J.C. and Y.K.; project administration, J.C.; funding acquisition, Y.K. Both authors have read and agreed to the published version of the manuscript.

Funding: This work was supported by the National Research Foundation of Korea (NRF) grant funded by the Korea government (MSIT) (No. 2020R1G1A1099559).

Institutional Review Board Statement: Not applicable.

Informed Consent Statement: Not applicable.

Data Availability Statement: Not applicable.

Conflicts of Interest: The authors declare no conflict of interest.

References

1. Joshi, H. *Digital Media: Rise of on-Demand Content*; Gurgaon, Deloitte Publishing: Gurgaon, India, 2015.
2. Federal Communications Commission. Annual Assessment of the Status of Competition in the Market for the Delivery of Video Programming. MB Docket No. 14-16. FCC 15-41. 2015. Available online: https://www.federalregister.gov/documents/2015/07/24/2015-18215/annual-assessment-of-the-status-of-competition-in-the-market-for-the-delivery-of-video-programming (accessed on 23 May 2021).
3. Rake, R.; Gaikwad, V.; Over-the-top (OTT) Market Outlook—2027. Allied Market Research. 2020. Available online: https://www.alliedmarketresearch.com/over-the-top-services-market (accessed on 19 April 2021).
4. von Abrams, K. The Global Media Intelligence Report. *eMarketer*. 2018. Available online: https://www.emarketer.com/content/global-media-intelligence-2018, (accessed on 19 April 2021).
5. Benes, R. US Digital Video. *eMarketer*. 2019. Available online: https://www.emarketer.com/content/us-digital-video-2019, (accessed on 19 April 2021).
6. Rose, J.; Zuckerman, N.; Sheerin, A.; Mank, T.; Schmitz, L.-K.L.; Cadicamo, A. Can Subscription Video Providers Hold on to Their New Customers? *Boston Consulting Group*. 2020. Available online: https://www.bcg.com/publications/2020/can-subscription-video-providers-hold-on-to-their-new-customers (accessed on 19 April 2021).
7. Research and Markets. United States Over the Top (OTT) Market —Growth, Trends, Forecasts (2020–2025). 2020. Available online: https://www.researchandmarkets.com/r/e46wk0 (accessed on 19 April 2021).
8. Sujata, J.; Sohag, S.; Tanu, D.; Chintan, D.; Shubham, P.; Sumit, G. Impact of Over the Top (OTT) Services on Telecom Service Providers. *Indian J. Sci. Techn.* **2015**, *8*, 145–160. [CrossRef]
9. Dai, W.; Baek, J.W.; Jordan, S. Neutrality between a vertically integrated cable provider and an over-the-top video provider. *J. Commun. Netw.* **2016**, *18*, 962–974. [CrossRef]
10. Hu, M.; Zhang, M.; Wang, Y. Why do audiences choose to keep watching on live video streaming platforms? An explanation of dual identification framework. *Comput. Human Behav.* **2017**, *75*, 594–606. [CrossRef]
11. Rojas, J.S.; Rendon, A.; Corrales, J.C. Consumption Behavior Analysis of Over the Top Services: Incremental Learning or Traditional Methods? *IEEE Access* **2019**, *7*, 136581–136591. [CrossRef]
12. Rojas, J.S.; Pekar, A.; Rendon, A.; Corrales, J.C. Smart User Consumption Profiling: Incremental Learning-Based OTT Service Degradation. *IEEE Access* **2020**, *8*, 207426–207442. [CrossRef]
13. Choi, J.; Kim, Y. Time-Aware Learning Framework for Over-The-Top Consumer Classification Based on Machine- and Deep-Learning Capabilities. *Appl. Sci.* **2020**, *10*, 8476. [CrossRef]
14. Walelgne, E.A.; Asrese, A.S.; Manner, J.; Bajpai, V.; Ott, J. Clustering and predicting the data usage patterns of geographically diverse mobile users. *Comput. Netw.* **2021**, *187*. [CrossRef]

15. Zhao, C.; Xin, Y.; Li, X.; Yang, Y.; Chen, Y. A Heterogeneous Ensemble Learning Framework for Spam Detection in Social Networks with Imbalanced Data. *Appl. Sci.* **2020**, *10*, 936. [CrossRef]
16. Westcott, K.; Loucks, J.; Downs, K.; Arkenberg, C.; Jarvis, D. Digital Media Trends Survey, 14th Edition. *Deloitte*. 2020. Available online: https://www2.deloitte.com/us/en/insights/industry/technology/digital-media-trends-consumption-habits-survey/summary.html/#endnote-1 (accessed on 19 April 2021).
17. J.D. Power. New Streaming Services Cut into Netflix's Market Share, While "The Mandalorian" Drives Disney+ Viewership. 2021. Available online: https://discover.jdpa.com/hubfs/Files/Industry%20Campaigns/TMT/New%20Streaming%20Services%20Cut%20into%20Netflixs%20Market%20Share%20While%20The%20Mandalor._.pdf (accessed on 19 April 2021).
18. Nielsen. The Nielsen Total Audience Report: August 2020. Available online: https://www.nielsen.com/us/en/insights/report/2020/the-nielsen-total-audience-report-august-2020/ (accessed on 19 April 2021).
19. Webb, K. Disney Plus can't Compete with Netflix when it Comes to Original Content, but its Affordable Price and Iconic Franchises Make it a Great Value for Families. *Business Insider*. 2020. Available online: https://www.businessinsider.com/disney-plus-review (accessed on 19 April 2021).
20. Spangler, T.; Littleton, C. HBO Max and HBO Have 36.3 Million Subscribers, Up 5% From End of 2019, AT&T Says. *VARIETY*. 2020. Available online: https://variety.com/2020/digital/news/hbo-max-subscribers-subscribers-q2-att-1234714316/ (accessed on 19 April 2021).
21. Kim, J.; Kim, S.; Nam, C. Competitive dynamics in the Korean video platform market: Traditional pay TV platforms vs. OTT platforms. *Telemat. Informat.* **2016**, *33*, 711–721. [CrossRef]
22. Park, E.-A. Business strategies of Korean TV players in the age of over-the-top(OTT) video service. *Int. J. Commun.* **2018**, *12*, 4646–4667.
23. Kim, J.; Nam, C.; Ryu, M.H. IPTV vs. emerging video services: Dilemma of telcos to upgrade the broadband. *Telecom. Pol.* **2019**, *44*. [CrossRef]
24. Kim, Y.C. Netflix May Pay for KT's Network. *The Korea Times*. 2020. Available online: http://www.koreatimes.co.kr/www/tech/2020/07/133_293720.html (accessed on 19 April 2021).
25. PWC. The Promise of 5G. 2018. Available online: https://www.pwc.com/us/en/advisory-services/publications/consumer-intelligence-series/promise-5g.pdf (accessed on 19 April 2021).
26. Johnson, M.R.; Woodcock, J. "And Today's Top Donator is": How Live Streamers on Twitch.tv Monetize and Gamify Their Broadcasts. *Soc. Med. Soc.* **2019**, *5*. [CrossRef]
27. Floris, A.; Ahmad, A.; Atzori, L. QoE-aware OTT-ISP Collaboration in Service Management: Architecture and Approaches. *ACM Trans. Multimedia Comput. Commun. Appl.* **2018**, *1*, 1–23. [CrossRef]
28. Nevo, A.; Turner, J.L.; Williams, J.W. *User-Based Pricing and Demand for Residential Broadband*; NBER Working Paper 21321; National Bureau of Economic Research: Cambridge, MA, USA, 2015. [CrossRef]
29. Oliveira, T.; Fiorese, A.; Sargento, S. Forecasting Over-the-Top Bandwidth Consumption Applied to Network Operators. In Proceedings of the 2018 IEEE Symposium on Computers and Communications (ISCC), Natal, Brazil, 25–28 June 2018; IEEE: Piscataway, NJ, USA, 2018; pp. 859–864. [CrossRef]
30. Naudts, B.; Flores, M.; Mijumbi, R.; Verbrugge, S.; Serrat, J.; Colle, D. A dynamic pricing algorithm for a network of virtual resources. *Int. J. Netw. Mgmt.* **2017**, *27*, e1960. [CrossRef]
31. Branch, P.; But, J. Rapid and generalized identification of packetized voice traffic flows. In Proceedings of the 37th Annual IEEE Conference on Local Computer Networks, Clearwater Beach, FL, USA, 22–25 October 2012; IEEE: Piscataway, NJ, USA, 2012; pp. 85–92. [CrossRef]
32. Bujlow, T.; Riaz, T.; Pedersen, J.M. A method for classification of network traffic based on C5.0 Machine Learning Algorithm. In Proceedings of the 2012 International Conference on Computing, Networking and Communications (ICNC), Maui, HI, USA, 30 January–2 February 2012; IEEE: Piscataway, NJ, USA, 2012; pp. 237–241. [CrossRef]
33. Yuan, R.; Li, Z.; Guan, X.; Xu, L. An SVM-based machine learning method for accurate internet traffic classification. *Inf. Sys. Front.* **2010**, *12*, 149–156. [CrossRef]
34. Shi, H.; Li, H.; Zhang, D.; Cheng, C.; Wu, W. Efficient and robust feature extraction and selection for traffic classification. *Comput. Netw.* **2017**, *119*, 1–16. [CrossRef]
35. Wang, P.; Lin, S.C.; Luo, M. A framework for QoS-aware traffic classification using semi-supervised machine learning in SDNs. In Proceedings of the 2016 IEEE International Conference on Services Computing (SCC), San Francisco, CA, USA, 27 June–2 July 2016; IEEE: Piscataway, NJ, USA, 2016; pp. 760–765. [CrossRef]
36. Dong, Y.-n.; Zhao, J.-j.; Jin, J. Novel feature selection and classification of Internet video traffic based on a hierarchical scheme. *Comput. Netw.* **2017**, *119*, 102–111. [CrossRef]
37. Bar-Yanai, R.; Langberg, M.; Peleg, D.; Roditty, L. Realtime classification for encrypted traffic. In Proceedings of the International Symposium on Experimental Algorithms, Ischia Island, Italy, 20–22 May 2010; Festa, P., Ed.; Springer: Berlin, Germany; pp. 373–385. [CrossRef]
38. Ertam, F.; Avcı, E. A new approach for internet traffic classification: GA-WK-ELM. *Measurement* **2017**, *95*, 135–142. [CrossRef]
39. Davis, J.J.; Foo, E. Automated feature engineering for HTTP tunnel detection. *Comput. Secur.* **2016**, *59*, 166–185. [CrossRef]
40. Zhang, J.; Xiang, Y.; Zhou, W.; Wang, Y. Unsupervised traffic classification using flow statistical properties and IP packet payload. *J. Comput. Sys. Sci.* **2013**, *79*, 573–585. [CrossRef]

41. Du, Y.; Zhang, R. Design of a method for encrypted P2P traffic identification using K-means algorithm. *Telecom. Sys.* **2013**, *53*, 163–168. [CrossRef]
42. Lotfollahi, M.; Siavoshani, M.J.; Zade, R.S.H.; Saberian, M. Deep packet: A novel approach for encrypted traffic classification using deep learning. *Soft Comput.* **2020**, *24*, 1999–2012. [CrossRef]
43. Aceto, G.; Ciuonzo, D.; Montieri, A.; Pescapé, A. Mobile encrypted traffic classification using deep learning. In Proceedings of the 2018 Network Traffic Measurement and Analysis Conference (TMA), Vienna, Austria, 26–29 June 2018; IEEE: Piscataway, NJ, USA, 2018; pp. 1–8. [CrossRef]
44. Aceto, G.; Ciuonzo, D.; Montieri, A.; Pescapè, A. MIMETIC: Mobile encrypted traffic classification using multimodal deep learning. *Comput. Netw.* **2019**, *165*, 106944. [CrossRef]
45. Rojas, J.S.; Gallón, Á.R.; Corrales, J.C. Personalized Service Degradation Policies on OTT Applications Based on the Consumption Behavior of Users. In Proceedings of the Computational Science and Its Applications, Melbourne, Australia, 2–5 July 2018; Springer: Cham, Switzerland, 2018; pp. 543–557. [CrossRef]
46. Stoll, J. Netflix Subscriptions in the U.S. 2020, by Generation. *Statista*. 2021. Available online: https://www.statista.com/statistics/720723/netflix-members-usa-by-age-group/#statisticContainer (accessed on 19 April 2021).
47. AppAnnie. The State of Mobile 2020 Report. 2019. Available online: https://www.appannie.com/en/go/state-of-mobile-2020/ (accessed on 19 April 2021).
48. Li, C.; Liu, S. A comparative study of the class imbalance problem in Twitter spam detection. *Concurr. Comput.* **2018**, *30*, e4281. [CrossRef]
49. Liu, S.; Wang, Y.; Zhang, J.; Chen, C.; Xiang, Y. Addressing the class imbalance problem in twitter spam detection using ensemble learning. *Comput. Sec.* **2017**, *69*, 35–49. [CrossRef]
50. Yang, Q.; Wu, X. 10 challenging problems in data mining research. *Int. J. Inf. Technol. Decis. Mak.* **2006**, *5*, 597–604. [CrossRef]
51. Inuwa-Dutse, I.; Liptrott, M.; Korkontzelos, I. Detection of spam-posting accounts on Twitter. *Neurocomputing* **2018**, *315*, 496–511. [CrossRef]
52. Kudugunta, S.; Ferrara, E. Deep neural networks for bot detection. *Inform. Sci.* **2018**, *467*, 312–322. [CrossRef]
53. Sze-To, A.; Wong, A.K. A weight-selection strategy on training deep neural networks for imbalanced classification. In Proceedings of the International Conference Image Analysis and Recognition, Montreal, QC, Canada, 5–7 July 2017; Karray, F., Campilho, A., Cheriet, F., Eds.; Springer: Cham, Switzerland, 2017; pp. 3–10. [CrossRef]
54. Domingos, P. Metacost: A general method for making classifiers cost-sensitive. In Proceedings of the 5th ACM SIGKDD International Conference on Knowledge Discovery and Data Mining, San Diego, CA, USA, 15–18 August 1999; pp. 155–164.
55. Chen, C.; Zhang, J.; Xiang, Y.; Zhou, W. Asymmetric self-learning for tackling twitter spam drift. In Proceedings of the 2015 IEEE Conference on Computer Communications Workshops (INFOCOM WKSHPS), Hong Kong, China, 26 April–1 May 2015; IEEE: Piscataway, NJ, USA, 2015; pp. 208–213. [CrossRef]
56. Chawla, N.V.; Bowyer, K.W.; Hall, L.O.; Kegelmeyer, W.P. SMOTE: Synthetic minority over-sampling technique. *J. AI Res.* **2002**, *16*, 321–357. [CrossRef]
57. Pedregosa, F.; Varoquaux, G.; Gramfort, A.; Michel, V.; Thirion, B.; Grisel, O.; Blondel, M.; Prettenhofer, P.; Weiss, R.; Dubourg, V.; et al. Scikit-learn: Machine learning in Python. *J. Mach. Learn. Res.* **2011**, *12*, 2825–2830.
58. Eibe, F.; Hall, M.A.; Witten, I.H.; Kaufmann, M. The WEKA workbench. Online appendix. In *Data Mining: Practical Machine Learning Tools and Techniques*, 4th ed.; Morgan Kaufmann: Burlington, VT, USA, 2016.

Article

Automotive OEM Demand Forecasting: A Comparative Study of Forecasting Algorithms and Strategies

Jože M. Rožanec [1,2,3,*], Blaž Kažič [1,2,3], Maja Škrjanc [1,2,3], Blaž Fortuna [1,2] and Dunja Mladenić [1]

1. Jožef Stefan Institute, Jamova 39, 1000 Ljubljana, Slovenia; blaz.kazic@qlector.com (B.K.); maja.skrjanc@qlector.com (M.Š.); blaz.fortuna@qlector.com (B.F.); dunja.mladenic@ijs.si (D.M.)
2. Qlector d.o.o., Rovšnikova 7, 1000 Ljubljana, Slovenia
3. Jožef Stefan International Postgraduate School, Jamova 39, 1000 Ljubljana, Slovenia
* Correspondence: joze.rozanec@ijs.si

Featured Application: The outcomes of this work can be applied to B2B discrete demand forecasting in the automotive industry and probably generalized to other demand forecasting domains.

Abstract: Demand forecasting is a crucial component of demand management, directly impacting manufacturing companies' planning, revenues, and actors through the supply chain. We evaluate 21 baseline, statistical, and machine learning algorithms to forecast smooth and erratic demand on a real-world use case scenario. The products' data were obtained from a European original equipment manufacturer targeting the global automotive industry market. Our research shows that global machine learning models achieve superior performance than local models. We show that forecast errors from global models can be constrained by pooling product data based on the past demand magnitude. We also propose a set of metrics and criteria for a comprehensive understanding of demand forecasting models' performance.

Keywords: demand forecasting; smart manufacturing; artificial intelligence; supply chain agility; digital twin

Citation: Rožanec, J.M.; Kažič, B.; Škrjanc, M.; Fortuna, B.; Mladenić, D. Automotive OEM Demand Forecasting: A Comparative Study of Forecasting Algorithms and Strategies. *Appl. Sci.* 2021, *11*, 6787. https://doi.org/10.3390/app11156787

Academic Editor: Grzegorz Dudek

Received: 30 June 2021
Accepted: 21 July 2021
Published: 23 July 2021

Publisher's Note: MDPI stays neutral with regard to jurisdictional claims in published maps and institutional affiliations.

Copyright: © 2021 by the authors. Licensee MDPI, Basel, Switzerland. This article is an open access article distributed under the terms and conditions of the Creative Commons Attribution (CC BY) license (https://creativecommons.org/licenses/by/4.0/).

1. Introduction

Supply (the *"amount of something ready to be used"* [1]) and demand (*"the fact of customers buying goods... and the amount that they buy"* [1] at a given point in time) are two key elements continually interacting in the market. The ability to accurately forecast future demand enables manufacturers to make operational and strategic decisions on resources (allocation and scheduling of raw material and tooling), workers (scheduling, training, promotions, or hiring), manufactured products (market share increase and production diversification), and logistics for deliveries [2]. Accurate demand forecasts reduce inefficiencies, such as high stocks or stock shortages, which have a direct impact on the supply chain (e.g., reducing the bullwhip effect [3,4]), and prevent a loss of reputation [5].

There is consensus that greater transparency between related parties helps to mitigate the issues mentioned above [6,7]. Such transparency can be achieved through automation and digitalization (e.g., implementing Electronic Data Interchange software), by sharing manufacturing processes' data, and making it timely available to internal stakeholders and relevant external parties where appropriate [8]. In addition, the ability to apply intelligence to multiple stages across the supply chain can improve its performance [9]. Such ability and the capability to get up-to-date information regarding any aspect of the manufacturing plant enable the creation of up-to-date forecasts and provide valuable insights for decision-making.

Multiple authors found that machine learning outperforms statistical methods for demand forecasting [10,11]. Machine learning methods can be used to train a single model per target demand or a global model to address them all. When designing the models, it is crucial to consider which data is potentially relevant to such forecasts. Multiple factors may affect the product's demand. First, it is necessary to understand if the products can be considered inelastic (their demand is not sensitive to price fluctuations), complementary, or be substituted for alternative products. Second, intrinsic product qualities, such as being a perishable or luxury item, or their expected lifetime, may be relevant to demand. Finally, the manufacturer must also consider the kind of market it operates on and the customer expectations. When dealing with demand forecasting in the automotive industry, most authors do not use only demand data but also incorporate data regarding exogenous factors that influence demand.

Demand forecasting has direct consequences on decision-making. As such, forecasts are expected to be accurate so that they can be relied upon. When training machine learning models, more significant amounts of good quality data can help the model better learn patterns and provide more accurate forecasts. This intuition is considered when building global models. On the other side, while for local models, the forecast error is constrained to past data of a single time series, in global models, the forecasting error is influenced by patterns and values observed in other time series, which can lead to greater errors as well. In this work, we explore a strategy to constrain such forecasting errors in global models. Furthermore, providing a greater amount of data should be considered regarding products' demand and its context. To that end, we enrich the demand data with data from complementary data sources, such as world Gross Domestic Product (GDP), unemployment rates, and fuel prices.

This work compares 21 statistical and machine learning algorithms, building local and global forecasting models. We propose two data pooling strategies to develop global time series models. One of them successfully constrains the global time series models' forecasting errors. We also propose a set of metrics and criteria for the evaluation of demand forecasts for smooth and erratic demands [12]. The error bounding data pooling strategy enables us to gain the benefits of training machine learning models on larger amounts of data (increased forecast accuracy) while avoiding anomalous forecasts by constraining the magnitude of maximum forecasting errors. The metrics and evaluation criteria aim to characterize the given forecasts and provide better insight when deciding on the best-performing model. We expect the outcomes of this work to provide valuable insights for the development and assessment of demand forecasting models related to the automotive industry, introducing forecasting models and evaluation strategies previously not found in the scientific literature.

To evaluate the performance of our models, we consider the mean absolute scaled error (MASE) [13] and the R^2-adjusted (R^2adj) metrics. We compute the uncertainty ranges for each forecast and compare if differences between forecasts are statistically significant by performing a Wilcoxon paired rank test [14]. Finally, we analyze the proportion of products with forecasting errors below certain thresholds and the proportion of forecasts that result in under-estimates.

The rest of this paper is structured as follows. Section 2 presents related work. Section 3 describes the methodology we followed to gather and prepare data, create features, and build and evaluate the demand forecasting models. Section 4 details the experiments performed and the results obtained. Finally, Section 5 presents the conclusions and an outline of future work.

2. Related Work

Products' demand forecasting is a broad topic addressed by many authors in the scientific literature. Different demand patterns require specific approaches to address their characteristics. Multiple authors proposed demand classification schemas to understand which techniques are appropriate for a particular demand type. For example, the work in [15] focused on demand variance during lead times, while the work in [16] introduced the concept of average demand interval (ADI), which was later widely adopted.

$$ADI = \frac{Total\ Periods}{Total\ Demand\ Buckets} \quad (1)$$

The work in [12] complemented this view of demand introducing the coefficient of variation (CV). Both concepts allow us to divide demand types into quadrants, classifying them as intermittent, lumpy, smooth, and erratic demands (see Figure 1). Smooth and intermittent demand have little variability in demand quantities. Smooth demand has little variability regarding demand intervals over time, while intermittent demand displays a higher demand interval variability. Erratic and lumpy demands have higher variability in demand quantities, which comprehends an additional forecasting model challenge. Erratic demand has little variability regarding demand intervals over time. In lumpy ones, this is an essential factor to be considered. Following demand types proposed in [12], in this work, we focus on smooth and erratic demands.

$$CV = \frac{Demand\ Standard\ Deviation}{Demand\ Mean} \quad (2)$$

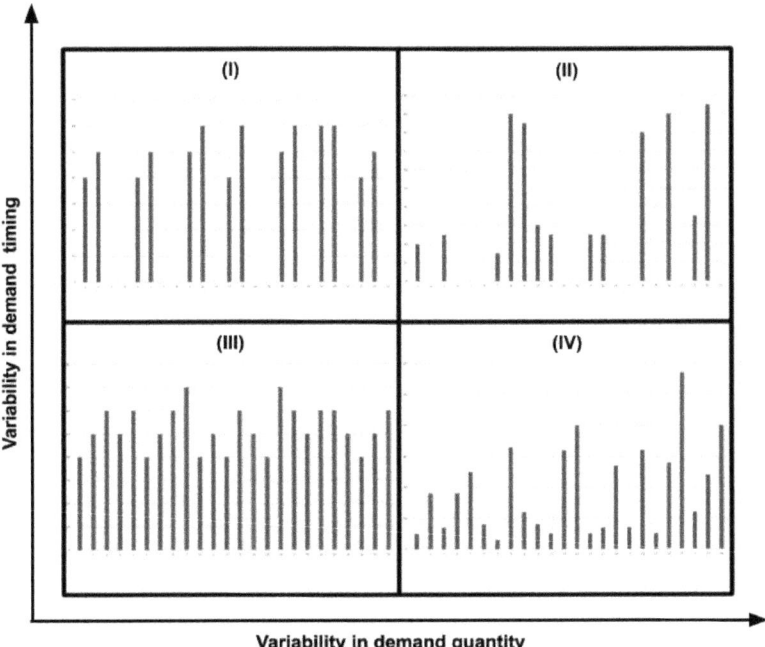

Figure 1. Demand types classification by Syntetos et al. [12]. Quadrants correspond to (**I**) intermittent, (**II**) lumpy, (**III**) smooth, and (**IV**) erratic demand types.

Planners, who regularly create demand forecasts, must understand the products they sell, the market they target, the economic context, and customer expectations. Over time they learn how buyers behave, the vast array of factors that can influence product demand, and create their estimates. Each planner can weigh different factors and have distinct ways to ponder them. Most of this information can be collected and fed to machine learning (ML) models, which learn how demand behaves over time to provide a forecast. In the scientific literature addressing demand forecasting in the automotive industry, most authors do not use only demand data, but also incorporate data regarding exogenous factors that influence demand, such as the effect of personal income on car ownership [17,18], or the effect of the GDP [5,17,19,20], inflation rate [18,19], unemployment rate [5], population density[20], and fuel prices [5,18,20–22] on vehicles demand.

Demand distributions can also be considered as another source of information for demand forecasting: research performed by many authors confirmed a relationship exists between demand types and demand distributions [23–26].

A wide range of models was explored in the literature addressing car, and car components demand forecasting. Ref. [5] developed a custom additive forecasting model with seasonal, trend, and calendar components. The authors used a phase average to compute the seasonal component, experimented with Multiple Linear Regression (MLR) and Support Vector Machine (SVM) for trend estimation, and used a Linear Regression to estimate the number of working days within a single forecasting period (calendar component). The models were built with car sales data from Germany, obtaining the best results when estimating trends with an SVM model and providing forecasts quarterly. Models' performance was measured using Mean Absolute Error (MAE) and Mean Absolute Percentage Error (MAPE) metrics. Ref. [18] compared three models: an adaptive network-based fuzzy inference system (ANFIS), an autoregressive integrated moving average model (ARIMA), and an artificial neural network (ANN). The forecasting models were built considering new automobile monthly sales in Taiwan, obtaining the best results with the ANFIS model. Ref. [21] developed an ANN model considering the inflation rate, pricing changes in crude oil, and past sales. They trained and evaluated the model on data from the Maruti Suzuki Ltd. company from India, measuring the models' performance with the Mean Squared Error (MSE) metric. Ref. [27] compared three models: ANFIS, ANN, and a Linear Regression. They are trained on car sales data from the Maruti car Industry in India and compared with the root mean squared error (RMSE) metric. The authors report that the best performance was obtained with the ANFIS model. Ref. [28] compared the ARIMA and the Holt–Winters models using demand data regarding remanufactured alternators and starters manufactured by an independent auto parts remanufacturer. They measured performance using the MAPE and average cumulative absolute percentage errors (CAPE) metrics, obtaining the best results for the Holt–Winters models. Ref. [29] developed three models (ANN, Linear Regression, and Exponential Regression) based on data from the Kia and Hyundai corporations in the US and Canada. Results were measured with the MSE metric, obtaining the best one with the ANN model. Ref. [19] analyzed the usage of genetic algorithms to tune the parameters from ANFIS models built with data from the Saipa group, a leading automobile manufacturer from Iran. Measuring RMSE and R^2, they achieved the best results with ANFIS models tuned with genetic algorithms compared to ANFIS and ANN models without any tuning. Ref. [30] compared custom deep learning models trained on real-world products' data provided by a worldwide automotive original equipment manufacturer (OEM). Ref. [31] developed an long short-term memory (LSTM) model based on car parts sales data in Norway and compared it against Simple Exponential Smoothing, Croston, Syntetos-Boylan Approximation (SBA), Teunter-Syntetos-Babai, and Modified SBA. Best results were obtained with the LSTM model when comparing models' mean error (ME) and MSE. Ref. [22] developed tree models (autoregressive moving average (ARMA), Vector Autoregression (VAR) model, and the Vector Error Correction Model (VECM)) to forecast automobile sales in China. The models were compared based on their performance measured with RMSE and MAPE metrics, finding the best results with the VECM model. The VECM model was also applied by [20], when forecasting cars demand for the state of Sarawak in Malaysia. Finally, Ref. [32] compared forecasts obtained from different moving average (MA) algorithms (simple MA, weighted MA, and exponential MA) when applied to production and sales data from the Gabungan Industri Kendaraan Bermotor Indonesia. Considering the Mean Absolute Deviation, the best forecasts were obtained with the Exponential Moving Average.

Additional insights regarding demand forecasting can be found in research related to time series forecasting in other domains. Refs. [33,34] described the importance of time series preprocessing regarding trend and seasonality, though [35,36] found the ANN models could learn seasonality. The use of local and global forecasting models for time series forecasting was researched in detail by [35]. Local forecasting models model each time series individually as separate regression problems. In contrast, global forecasting models assume there is enough similarity across the time series to build a single model to forecast them all. Researchers explored the use of global models either clustering time series [36,37], or creating a single model for time series that cannot be considered related to each other [38]. They achieved good performance in both cases.

3. Methodology

To address the demand forecasting problem, we followed a hybrid of the agile and cross-industry standard process for data mining (CRISP-DM) methodologies [39]. From the CRISP-DM methodology, we took the proposed steps: focus first on understanding the business and the available data, later tackle the data preparation and modeling, and, finally, evaluate the results. We did not follow these steps sequentially, but rather moved several times through them forward and backward, based on our understanding and feedback from end users, as is done in agile methodologies. We describe the work performed in each phase in the following subsections.

3.1. Business Understanding

The automotive industry accounts for one of the largest economies in the world, by revenue [40]. It is also considered a strong employment multiplier, a characteristic that is expected to grow stronger with the incorporation of complex digital technologies and the fusion with the digital industry [41]. Environmental concerns have prompted multiple policies and agreements, which foster the development of more environment friendly vehicles and rethinking of current mobility paradigms [42–44]. Nevertheless, global vehicle sales and automotive revenue are expected to continue to grow in the future [45,46].

Demand forecasting is a critical component to supply chain management as its outcomes directly affect the supply chain and manufacturing plant organization. In our specific case, demand forecasts for the automotive industry engine components worldwide were required on a monthly level, six weeks in advance. In Section 2, we highlighted related work, data, and techniques used by authors in the automotive industry. On top of data sources suggested in the literature for deriving machine learning features (past demand data, GDP, unemployment rates, and oil price), we incorporated three additional data sources based on experts' experience: Purchasing Managers' Index (PMI), copper prices, and sales plans.

PMI is a diffusion index obtained from monthly surveys sent to purchasing managers from multiple manufacturing companies. It summarizes expectations regarding whether the market will expand, contract, or stay the same and how strong the growth or contraction will be.

Prices of the products we forecast are tied to copper price variations used to manufacture them. Therefore, we consider the price of this metal and create derivative features to capture how it influences the products' price and how it may influence it in the future.

The strategic sales department creates sales plans on a yearly and quarterly basis. Experts consider projected sales to be a good proxy of future demand as they inform buyers' purchase intentions. We found research that backs their claim (see, e.g., in [47]), showing that purchase intentions contribute to the forecast's accuracy. The research done in [48] shows that purchase intentions are good predictors of future demand for durable products and that this accuracy is higher for short time horizons. Research also shows that the purchase intention bias can be adjusted with past sales data.

Much research was performed on the effect of aggregation on time series [34,49–51], showing that a higher aggregation improves forecast results. Though research shows optimal demand aggregation levels exist [52], we considered forecasts at a monthly level to reflect business requirements specific to our use case.

To understand demand forecasting models' desired behavior and performance, we consulted industry experts. They agreed that one-third of demand forecasts produced by planners have up to 30% error, and up to 20% forecasts may have more than 90% error.

They also pointed out that 40% of all forecasts result in under-estimates. When issuing a forecast, it is more desirable to have over-estimates than under-estimates. We consider these facts to assess the forecast results.

We address demand analysis in detail in Section 3.2.

3.2. Data Understanding

We make use of several data sources when forming features for machine learning, described in Table 1. We distinguish between internal data sources (non publicly available data regarding a manufacturing company provided by that same company) and external data sources used for the data enrichment process.

Table 1. Data sources. In the first and second columns, we indicate the kind of data we retrieve and its source. The third column provides information on how frequently new data is available. In contrast, the last column describes the aggregation level at which the data is published. Periodicity and aggregation levels can be at a yearly, quarterly, monthly, or daily level and are denoted by "Y", "Q", "M", or "D", respectively. The London Metal Exchange published copper prices for weekdays.

Data	Source	Periodicity	Aggregation Level
History of deliveries	Internal	D	D
Sales Plan	Internal	Y,Q	M
Gross Domestic Product (GDP)	World Bank	Y	Y
Unemployment rate	World Bank	Y	Y
Crude Oil price	World Bank	M	M
Purchasing Managers' Index (PMI)	Institute of Supply Chain Management	M	M
Copper price	London Metal Exchange	D	D
Car sales	International Organization of Motor Vehicle Manufacturers	Y	Y

When performing preliminary data analysis over the seven years of data, we found that GDP, crude oil prices, PMI values, and demand (see Figure 2) show a different pattern before and after the *year 4* of our dataset. When searching for possible root causes, we observed that in *year 4* some significant economic and political events took place affecting the economy worldwide. Among them, we found a stock market crash of a relevant country, a decrease in crude oil production, and several political events that affected the market prospects.

We consider demand quantity as the executed orders of a given product leaving the manufacturing plant on a specific date. Even though demand data is available daily, we aggregate them monthly, satisfying business requirements and providing smoother curves and ease of forecasting. We also consider that months have different working days (due to weekdays and holidays). Thus, we computed the average demand per working day for each month. Future demand can be estimated using the average demand per working day, multiplying by the number of working days in the target month.

Based on the demand classification in [12], we analyzed how many products correspond to erratic and smooth demands. We create features to capture this behavior. We present the products demand segmentation in Table 2. From the works in [23,24,26,53], we understand that demands of a given type follow a certain distribution. Thus, most manufacturing companies' products may have a slightly different demand behavior but share enough characteristics that would reflect common patterns. We observed that demand values for each product follow a geometric distribution.

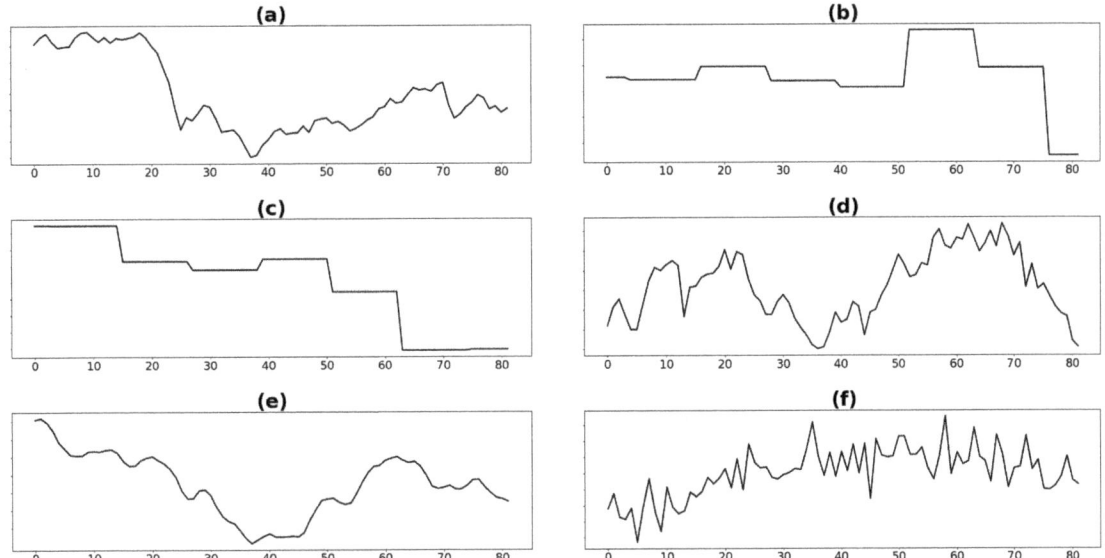

Figure 2. Median values for (**a**) crude oil price, (**b**) GDP, (**c**) unemployment rate worldwide, (**d**) PMI, (**e**) copper price (last three months average), and (**f**) demand.

Table 2. Demand segmentations, by demand type as per [12], and by demand magnitude, considering demanded quantities per month.

Years	By Demand Type		By Demand Magnitude				
	Smooth	Erratic	10	100	1 K	10 K	100 K
All years	13	43	13	2	5	26	10
Last 3 years	19	37	10	1	4	28	13

To discover potential patterns, we made use of different visualizations.

Demand seasonality was assessed with correlograms (see Figure 3), which show what lags in time most frequently display a statistically significant correlation (with a p-value = 0.05). Considering all data available, we found the strongest correlations for products at three, four, five, eight, and eleven months before the target month. However, we observed a different pattern in the last three years of data: the strongest correlations occurred at eight, ten, and eleven months before the target. Therefore, we choose only those statistically significant when analyzing correlation values, considering a confidence interval of 95%.

Plotting products' monthly demand for every year, as shown in Figure 4, we found that most products were likely to behave similarly over the years for a given month.

When assessing demand data sparsity, we analyzed how many non-zero demand data points we have for each product and the demand magnitudes we observe in each case. We present the data in Table 2. Higher aggregation levels regarding the time dimension allow reducing variability in time. However, aggregate data at a higher than monthly level are not applicable in our case.

3.3. Data Preparation

The first step we followed for data preparation was to remove records that would fall into the black period for any given point in time and thus avoid provide our models any indication about the future (except for the target we aim to predict). In our case, we consider a forecasting horizon of six weeks until the beginning of the target month, as depicted in Figure 5.

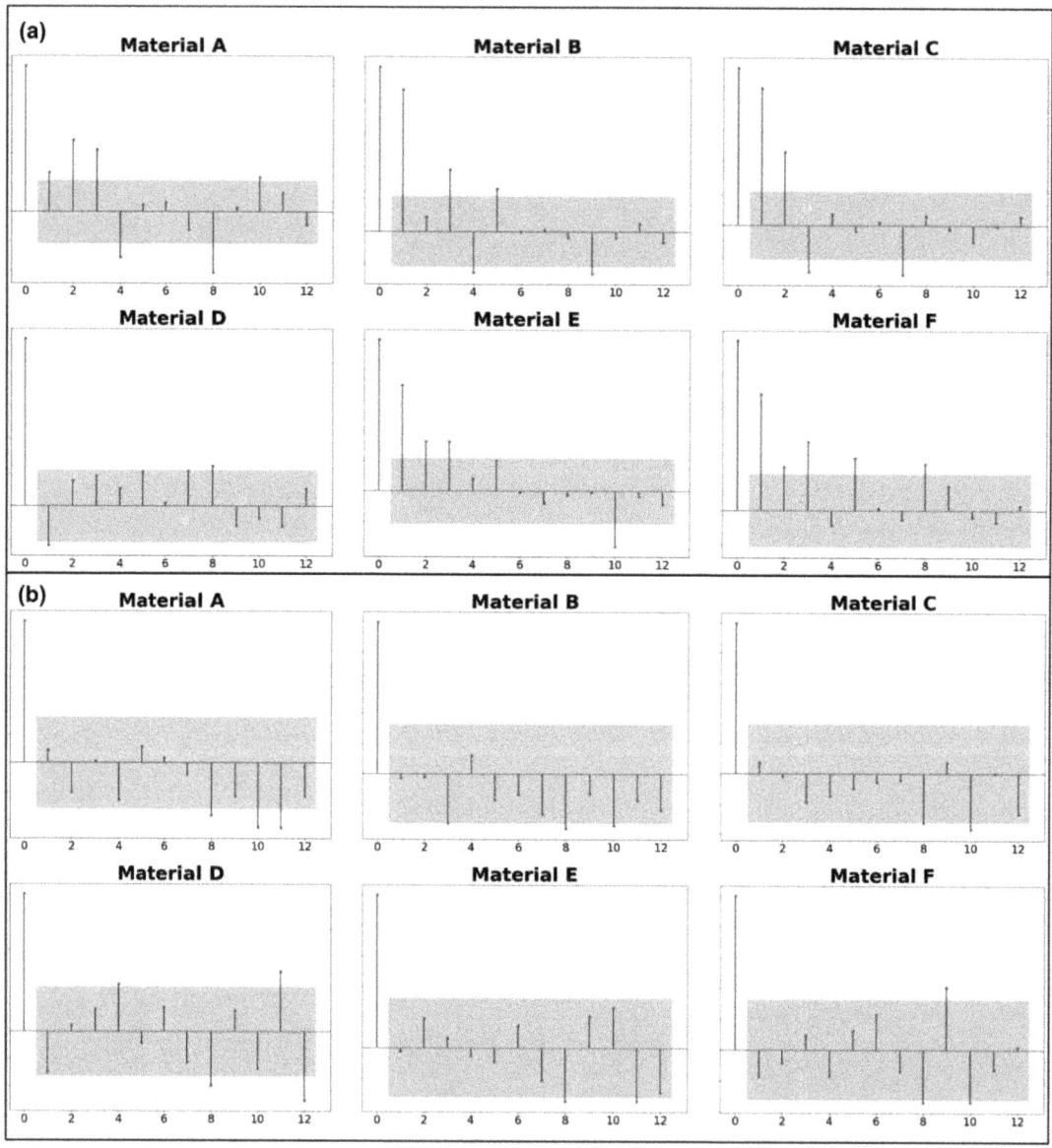

Figure 3. Sample demand correlograms, indicating seasonality patterns. The correlogram in panel (**a**) is computed over the seven years of data, while correlogram in (**b**) is computed over last three years.

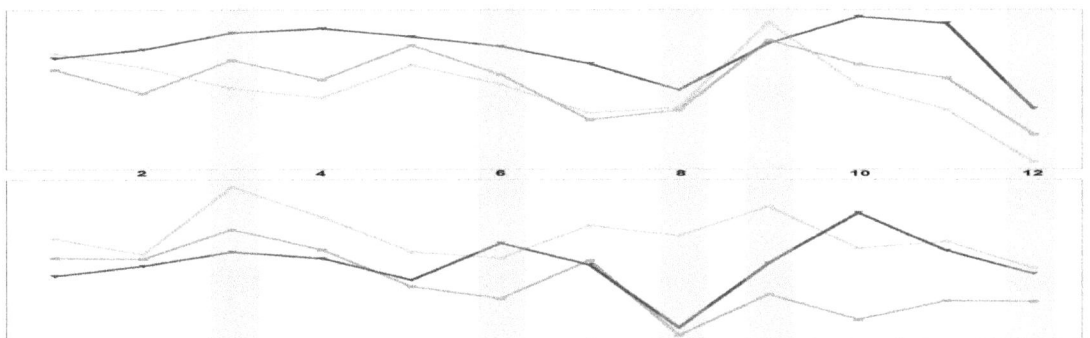

Figure 4. Monthly demand over the years of selected products. We compare the last three years of data.

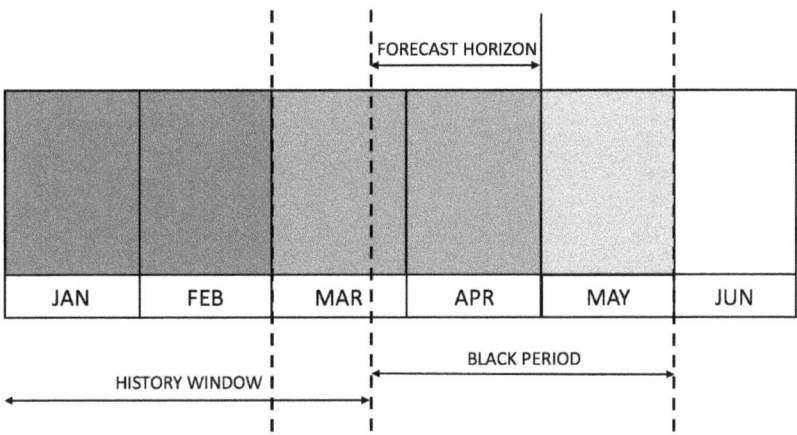

Figure 5. Relevant points in time we considered for forecasting purposes. There is a six-week slot between the moment we issue the forecast and the month we predict. The day of the month considered issuing the prediction is fixed.

For sales plans, we performed data fusion, merging annual and quarterly plans into a single one. In each case, we considered black periods, dates on which each plan becomes available, and the granularity level at which those estimates are provided.

PMI values are informed by the Institute of Supply Chain Management at the beginning of each month, based on the previous month's survey results. For crude oil prices, we considered the ones provided by the World Bank on a monthly level. We considered the same source for worldwide unemployment rates and GDP values, published yearly and available from March onwards. Every year in early March, the International Organization of Motor Vehicle Manufacturers publishes statistics regarding yearly worldwide car sales, which we used as well. Statistics regarding vehicle production worldwide are incomplete, and thus we did not consider them in this research. For copper prices, we took the London Metal Exchange value for each weekday of the year. We then computed the average price over the last three months. Finally, we computed features based on price adjustments applied to final products based on copper price fluctuations.

All sources of data are merged into a single dataset and aggregated at a product and monthly level.

3.3.1. Feature Creation

We can characterize demand data as a time series per product, each of which may present some level, trend, and seasonality. Therefore, we require a proper assessment of these aspects to create good statistical and ML models. While statistical models use only data regarding past demand to predict the future, ML models can leverage a more extensive set of features. These features provide insights into different factors affecting product demand and are taken into account to make predictions. We created a total of 708 features, some of which we describe below.

We computed rolling summary statistics such as average, maximum, and minimum demand over the last three months to address the time series level. In addition, we computed the same features for a weighted average and minimum and maximum values regarding the target month's past demand.

Trends help us understand demand growth or contraction and must be considered in forecasting models. However, different approaches may be helpful for statistical and ML models. The statistical models assume that the forecasted time series is stationary. To fulfill this assumption, we applied first-level differencing, which is suitable to address stochastic trends. For ML models, we created features to describe trends and capture monthly or interannual growth or contraction of GDP, unemployment rates, car sales, crude oil, copper prices, and demand. We also created features such as relations between observed demand and sales plans to capture common distortions that may take place on sales plans. Finally, we created derivative features that indicate growth or contraction for given months and more extended periods and detect and tag time series peaks from trend data.

We assessed seasonality using correlograms (see Figure 3). In addition, we incorporated demand at the lag values described before as proxies of potential demand.

We created naïve features to capture time characteristics to represent the month, a quarter, and workdays for given months. We used information regarding weekdays, national and collective holidays to compute the average demand per workday.

Values such as lagged demands, average, maximum, or minimum value of the last n observed months, and values from sales plans for target month, the weighted average of past demands for target month, and given product could act as reasonable approximations of demand values. Average demand per workday can be used to project expected demand on the target month, multiplying it by the number of workdays in the manufacturing plants. These demand approximations can be further adjusted using trend information.

We created two features to signal demand event occurrence: one based on product data sales plan, and the second one considering values from a probability density function on lagged demand values.

When building a single model for multiple products, it can be helpful to have some features convey information regarding demand similarity. Among others, we provide one-hot encoded features indicating demand-type as described in [12], considering demand behavior ever since we have data about the product and the last twelve and six months of the point in time we consider. To identify a similar context in which demand occurs, we binned GDP, unemployment rate, crude oil prices, car sales, and demand data into four bins of equal length for each case. Such features may also help identify specific cases, such as *year 4*, when context differs from most observed history.

3.3.2. Feature Selection

Feature selection reduces the number of features used to build a model, producing a succinct one that is quick to train, analyze, and understand.

We performed feature selection by combining the manual addition of common sense features with those suggested by a Gradient Boosted Regression Trees (GBRT) model, which is not sensitive to data distribution and allows us to rank features based on how much they reduce variance concerning target values. We only use the data that is later used to train the models and ensure that the test data remains unseen. We performed feature selection to extract the most relevant features in all experiments, considering all products rather than for each product separately. In every case, we selected K features, obtaining K from $\sqrt{N}$, where N is the number of instances in the training subset, as suggested in [54], and empirically verified these features within our setting. Some of the best features are presented in Table 3.

Table 3. Top 15 features selected by the GBRT model considering the last three years of data. We did not remove correlated features in this case.

Feature	Brief Description
wdp_{3m}	Estimate of target demand based on average demand per working day on third month before predicted month, and amount of working days on target month.
$sp \cdot \frac{demand_{pastwavg}}{sp_{pastwavg}}$	Planned sales for target month adjusted with ratio of weighted averages of past demand and past planned sales for given month.
$demand_{lag4m} \cdot \frac{UE_{3m}}{UE_{15m}}$	Lagged demand (4 months before target month), adjusted by the ratio of unemployment rates three, and fifteen months before the month we aim to predict.
sp_{lag12m}	Planned sales for last year, same month we aim to predict.
$sp \cdot \frac{UE_{3m}}{UE_{15m}}$	Planned sales, adjusted by the ratio of unemployment rates three and fifteen months before the month we aim to predict.
sp	Planned sales for target month
$demand_{lag3m} \cdot \frac{GDP_{3m}}{GDP_{15m}}$	Lagged demand (3 months before target month), adjusted by the ratio of GDP three and fifteen months before the month we aim to predict.
$sp \cdot \frac{GDP_{3m}}{GDP_{15m}}$	Planned sales for target month, adjusted by the ratio of GDP three and fifteen months before the month we aim to predict.
$demand_{lag3m}$	Lagged demand (3 months before target month)
$wdp_{12} \cdot \frac{sp}{sp_{pastwavg}}$	Estimate of target demand based on average demand per working day a year before the predicted month and amount of working days on target month. Adjusted by the the ratio between planned sales for target month and the weighted average of planned sales for the same month over past years.
wdp_{8m}	Estimate of target demand based on average demand per working day on eighth month before predicted month and amount of working days on target month.
$wdp_{5m} \cdot \frac{UE_{3m}}{UE_{15m}}$	An estimate of target demand based on average demand per working day on the fifth month before predicted month and amount of working days on target month. Adjusted by the ratio of unemployment rates three and fifteen months before the month we aim to predict.
$wdp_{12m} \cdot \frac{PMI_{13m}}{PMI_{14m}}$	An estimate of target demand based on average demand per working day a year before predicted month and the amount of working days on target month. Adjusted by the ratio between PMI values 13, and 14 months beforethe target month.
$demand_{lag3m_{scaled}}$	Lagged demand (3 months before target month) - scaled between 0–1, considering products past demand values.
$wdp_{3m} \cdot \frac{GDP_{3m}}{GDP_{15m}}$	Estimate of target demand based on average demand per working day on third month before predicted month, and amount of working days on target month. Adjusted by the ratio of GDP three and fifteen months before the month we aim to predict.

3.4. Modeling

3.4.1. Feature Analysis and Prediction Techniques

ML algorithms may have different requirements regarding data preprocessing in order to ensure the best learning conditions. We thus analyzed data distributions and identified which steps were required in each case to satisfy those requirements.

For ML algorithms, we standardized (3) the features so that they would have zero mean and unit variance Equation (3), except for the case of the Multiple Linear Perceptron Regressor (MLPR), where we scaled the values of the features between zero and one Equation (4). Standardization enhances the model's numerical stability, makes some algorithms consider all features equally important, and shortens ML models' training times [55].

$$x_{scaled} = \frac{X - \overline{X}}{\sigma} \qquad (3)$$

$$x_{scaled} = \frac{X - min(X)}{max(X) - min(X)} \qquad (4)$$

We took into account 21 forecasting techniques. We considered the naïve forecast (last observed value as prediction) as the baseline method. We train twelve different batch ML models: on top of MLR, support vector regressor (SVR) [56], and multilayer perceptron regressor (MLPR) [57], which we found were used in automotive demand forecasting literature, we also evaluate Ridge [58]; Lasso [59]; Elastic Net [60]; K-nearest-neighbor regressor (KNNR) [61]; tree-based regressors (decision tree regressor (DTR), random forest regressor (RFR), and GBRT); a voting ensemble created using the most promising and diverse algorithms (KNNR, SVR, and RFR); as well as a stacked regression [62] considering KNNR, SVR, and RidgeCV as underlying estimators; and a GBRT model as final regressor. We also take into account four streaming ML algorithms: Adaptive Random Forest Regressor (ARFR) [63], Hoeffding Tree Regressor (HTR) [64], and Hoeffding Adaptive Tree Regressor (HATR) [65]. Additionally, we also consider forecasts obtained as the average demand for the last three months (MA(3)) and the ones obtained from statistical forecasting methods (exponential smoothing, random walk, ARIMA(1,1,0), and ARIMA(2,1,0)). We did not create deep learning models since we consider that not enough data was available to train them.

When training the models, we used MSE as the loss function where possible. We choose MSE because it has the desired property of penalizing higher errors more, thus reducing substantial discrepancies in predicted values.

3.5. Evaluation

From the literature review in Section 2 we observed that authors mostly used ME, MSE, RMSE, CAPE, MAPE, and R^2 metrics to measure the performance of the demand forecasting models related to the automotive industry. While ME, MSE, and RMSE are widely adopted, they all depend on the magnitude of the predicted and observed demands and thus cannot be used to compare groups of products with a different demand magnitude. This issue can be overcome with MAPE or CAPE metrics, though MAPE puts a heavier penalty on negative errors, preferring low forecasts—an undesired property in demand forecasting. Though R^2 is magnitude agnostic, it has been noticed that its value can increase when new features are added to the model [66].

To evaluate the performance of our models, we consider two metrics: MASE and R^2adj. MASE informs the ratio between the MAE of the forecast values against the MAE of the naïve forecast, is magnitude agnostic, and not prone to distortions. R^2adj, informs how well predictions adjust to target values. In addition, it weights the number of features used to make the prediction, preferring succinct models that use fewer features for the same forecasting performance.

We compute an uncertainty range for each forecast, which illustrates possible bounds in which future demand values may be found. We also perform the Wilcoxon paired rank test [14] to assess if forecasts of a given model are significantly better than others.

Summary metrics may not be enough to understand the goodness of fit of a particular model [67,68]. Therefore, based on experts' opinions described in Section 3, and available demand characterizations, we analyzed the proportion of products with forecasting errors below certain thresholds (5%, 10%, 20%, and 30%), and the proportion of forecasts that resulted in under-estimates.

Though some research highlighted the importance of measuring forecast utility related to inventory performance (see, e.g., in [69,70]), this remains out of the scope of this work.

4. Experiments and Results

In this section, we describe the experiments we conducted (summarized in Table 4) and assess their results with metrics and criteria we described in Section 3.5. We summarize the outcomes in Table 5, to understand if a particular model performs significantly better than others. To evaluate the models, we used nested cross-validation [71], which is frequently used to evaluate time series models. To ensure conditions on ML streaming models were comparable to ML batch models, we implemented the nested cross-validation evaluation strategy. By doing so, we ensured the streaming model did not see new events until the required month was predicted. In order to test the models, we set apart the last six months of data. We published the nested cross-validation implementation for streaming models it in the following repository: https://github.com/JozefStefanInstitute/scikit-multiflow (accessed date 21 July 2021).

Table 4. Description of experiments performed. Regarding the feature selection procedure, we consider two cases: (I) top features ranked by a GBRT model and curated by a researcher, and (II) top features ranked by a GBRT model, removing those with strong collinearity, curated by a researcher as well. N in the *"Number of features"* column refers to the number of instances in a given dataset.

Years of Data	Experiment	Feature Selection	Number of Features
All years available	Experiment 1	I	6
	Experiment 2	II	6
Last three years	Experiment 3	I	6
	Experiment 4	II	6
	Experiment 5	II	6
	Experiment 6	II	6
	Experiment 7	II	$\sqrt{N}$
	Experiment 8	II	$\sqrt{N}$
	Experiment 9	II	$\sqrt{N}$
	Experiment 10	II	$\sqrt{N}$
	Experiment 11	Only past demand	1

Table 5. Median of results obtained for each ML experiment. We abbreviate *under-estimates* as *UE*. In Experiments 9–10, streaming models based on Hoeffding bound show poor performance, resulting in negative R^2adj values. We highlight the best results in bold.

Experiment	R^2adj	MASE	5% Error	10% Error	20% error	30% Error	UE	90%+ Error
Experiment 1	0.8584	1.1450	**0.0670**	0.1086	0.2039	0.3051	**0.3854**	0.4077
Experiment 2	0.8447	1.1450	0.0655	0.1101	0.1920	0.2887	0.4182	0.3928
Experiment 3	**0.9067**	0.9150	0.0655	**0.1280**	**0.2351**	0.3095	0.4256	0.3928
Experiment 4	0.8998	0.9750	0.0655	0.1176	0.2143	0.3051	0.4152	0.4018
Experiment 5	0.8757	0.3900	0.0536	0.1116	0.2173	0.3140	0.4762	0.3497
Experiment 6	0.8679	0.3350	0.0565	0.1012	0.1875	0.2768	0.4851	0.3601
Experiment 7	0.8903	0.3550	0.0521	0.1131	0.2247	**0.3155**	0.4851	**0.3408**
Experiment 8	0.8786	**0.3100**	0.0506	0.0938	0.1890	0.2813	0.4658	0.3497
Experiment 9	−0.1611	0.8100	0.0357	0.0714	0.1428	0.2143	0.7321	0.3601
Experiment 10	−1.5344	0.5300	0.0178	0.0536	0.1250	0.2143	0.7143	0.4613

In Experiments 1–4, we assessed how events in year 4 affected model learning and if they significantly degraded forecasts. We also compared two different sets of features, resulting from two different procedures to obtain them. We obtained the best performance with local models trained over the last three years of data. Removing features with high collinearity did not enhance the median of R^2adj and MASE. Therefore, we consider Experiment 3 performed best, having the best MASE and R^2adj values. In contrast, the rest of the evaluation criteria values were acceptable.

Next, we analyzed if grouping products by specific criteria would enhance the quality of the predictions. We trained these global models over the last three years of data, considering insights obtained from Experiments 1–4. Following the *ceteris paribus* principle, we considered the same features as for Experiment 3. We experimented with grouping products based on the median magnitude of past demand (Experiment 5) and demand-type (Experiment 6). We observed that even though the median of R^2adj was lower, and the under-estimates ratio higher, compared to results in previous experiments, the median MASE values decreased by more than 40%. Models based on the median of past demand had the best results in most aspects, including the proportion of forecasts with more than 90% error. Encouraged by these results, we conducted Experiments 7–8, preserving the grouping criteria but adapting the number of features considered according to the amount of data available in each sub-group. In Experiment 7, we grouped them based on the magnitude of the median of past demand. In contrast, in Experiment 8, we grouped products based on demand type. In both cases, we observed that R^2adj values and under-estimates ratios improved, and MASE values remained low. We consider the best results were obtained in Experiment 7, which achieved the best values in all evaluation criteria, except for MASE. We ranked models of these two experiments by R^2adj, and took the top three. We obtained SVR, voting, and stacking models for Experiment 7 and SVR, voting, and RFR models for Experiment 8. The models from Experiment 8 exhibited lower MASE in all cases, a better ratio of under-estimates, and a better proportion of forecasts with an error ratio higher than 90%. Top 3 models from Experiment 8 remained competitive regarding R^2adj and proportion of forecasts with error ratio bounded to 30% or less error.

We assessed the statistical significance of both groups' models in all the performance aspects mentioned above, at a *p*-value = 0.05. The models had no significant difference in the same group regarding R^2adj and MASE. However, the difference was significant between voting models in both groups for these two metrics. The difference was also significant between the voting model from Experiment 7 and the RFR model from Experiment 8 for the MASE metric. Considering the proportion of forecasts with errors lower than 30%, we observed no differences between both groups' models. However, differences between SVR and voting models in Experiment 8 were significant. Finally, differences regarding the number of under-estimates were statistically significant between all top three models from Experiment 7 against SVR and RFR models of Experiment 8. For this particular performance aspect, the stacking model from Experiment 7 only achieves significance against the voting model from Experiment 8.

Having explored a wide range of batch ML models, we conducted Experiments 9–10 with streaming ML models, following the same conditions as Experiment 7–8, but creating a global streaming model for each magnitude of the median of past demand demand-type. This experiment aimed to understand the performance of streaming ML models against the widely used ML batch models and confirm if they behaved the same regarding error bounds as models in Experiments 7–8. We found that streaming models based on Hoeffding inequality did not learn well. On the other side, the Adaptive Random Forest Regressor displayed a better performance. While its R^2adj was lower than the top 3 models from Experiment 8, it achieved the best MASE in Experiment 10. It also was among best proportion predictions with less than 5%, 10%, 20%, and 30% error or more than 90% error. However, the proportion of under-estimates, a parameter of crucial importance in our use case, hindered these performance results. ML streaming models had among the highest proportions of under-estimates of all created forecasting models. The highest proportion of under-estimates was obtained in ML streaming models based on the Hoeffding inequality, reaching a median of underestimates above 70%.

In Experiments 5–10, we consistently observed global models created considering the magnitude of the median of past demand outperformed those created based on demand-type when considering the proportion of forecasts with an error higher to 90%. On the other side, global models based on demand-type scored better on MASE. However, these differences did not prove statistically significant in most cases when comparing top-ranking models of both groups.

Having explored different ML models, we then trained statistical models for each product considering demand data available for the last three years (Experiment 11) and contrasted results obtained with the top three models from Experiment 8 (see Table 6). When preparing demand data for the statistical models, we applied differencing to remove stochastic trends. We observed that the ML models outperformed the statistical ones in almost every aspect. R^2adj was consistently low for statistical models, and though their MASE was better compared to the baseline models, ML models performed better. When assessing the ratio of forecasts with less than 30% error, ML models displayed a better performance. We observed the same when analyzing the under-estimates ratio. Even though the random walk had a low under-estimates ratio, the rest of the metrics indicate the random walk model provides poor forecasts. We consider the best overall performers are the SVR, RFR, and GBRT models, which achieved near-human performance in almost every aspect considered in this research. Even though differences regarding R^2adj, MASE, and the ratio of forecasts with less than 30% error are not statistically significant between them in most cases, they display statistically significant differences when analyzing under-estimates.

Table 6. Results we obtained for the top 3 performing models from Experiment 8 (ML batch models), best result for experiments 9–10 (ML streaming models), and baseline and statistical models. We abbreviate *under-estimates* as *UE*.

Algorithm Type	Algorithm	R^2adj	MASE	5% Error	10% Error	20% Error	30% Error	UE	90+% Error
ML batch	SVR	**0.9212**	0.2600	0.0774	0.1101	0.2321	0.3333	0.4077	0.3304
	Voting	0.9059	0.2800	0.0625	0.0923	0.1786	0.2798	0.4792	0.3393
	RFR	0.8953	0.2900	0.0417	0.1012	0.2173	0.3244	**0.3423**	0.3482
ML streaming	ARFR (Experiment 9)	0.8728	0.3300	0.0744	0.1339	0.2500	0.3274	0.5387	0.3452
	ARFR (Experiment 10)	0.8205	**0.2200**	0.0744	0.1280	0.2232	0.3274	0.5268	0.3423
Baseline	MA(3)	0.8938	0.8800	0.1190	0.1667	0.2530	0.3482	0.3571	0.3065
	Naïve	0.8519	1.0000	**0.2024**	**0.2411**	**0.3423**	**0.4137**	0.4137	0.3214
Statistical	ARIMA(2.1.0)	0.3846	0.4500	0.0476	0.0774	0.1429	0.1875	0.5536	0.5208
	Exponential smoothing	0.3258	0.3600	0.0506	0.1161	0.1905	0.2738	0.5923	0.4434
	ARIMA(1.1.0)	0.2840	0.5200	0.0387	0.0744	0.1012	0.1726	0.5119	0.6071
	Random walk	−0.6705	0.9000	0.0327	0.0387	0.0655	0.0923	0.3780	0.7678

5. Conclusions

This research compares 21 forecasting techniques (baseline, statistical, and ML algorithms) to provide future demand estimates for an automotive OEM company located in Europe. We use various internal and external data sources that describe the economic context and provide insights on future demand. We considered multiple metrics and criteria to assess forecasting models' performance (R^2adj, MASE, the ratio of forecasts with less than 30% error, and the ratio of forecasts with under-estimates)—all of them magnitude-agnostic. These metrics and criteria allow us to characterize results to be comparable regardless of the underlying data. We also assess the statistical significance of results, something we missed in most related literature.

The obtained results show that grouping products according to their demand patterns or past demand magnitude enhances the performance of ML models. We observed that the best MASE performance was obtained on models created for a group of products with the same demand type. Furthermore, when training global models based on the median of past demand, models usually achieved a better R^2adj and a better bound on high forecast errors. However, these values were not always statistically significant.

Our experimental evaluation indicates that the best performing models are SVR, voting ensemble, and RFR trained over product data of the same demand type. The SVR and RFR models achieved near-human performance for the ratio of forecasts under 30% error, and the RFR model scored close to human performance regarding under-estimates. However, none of the models achieved close to human performance on the proportion of forecasts with a high error (more than 90%). How to efficiently detect and bound such cases remains a subject of future research.

When comparing batch and streaming ML models' performance, we observed that ML batch models displayed a more robust performance. From the streaming algorithms, the ARFR achieved competitive results, except for a high ratio of under-estimates. This critical aspect must not be overlooked. Models based on the Hoeffding inequality did not learn well and had poor performance, and further research is required to understand the reasons hindering these models' learning process.

Building a single demand forecasting model for multiple products not only drives better performance, but has engineering implications: fewer models need to be trained and deployed into production. The need for regular deployments can be further reduced by using ML streaming models. This advantage gains importance when considering ever shorter forecasting horizons as it avoids the overhead regular model re-trainings and model deployments. We consider timely access to real data and the ability to regularly update machine learning models as factors that enable digital twins' creation. Such digital twins not only provide accurate forecasts but allow estimating different what-if scenarios of interest.

We envision at least two directions for future work. First, further research is required to develop effective error bounding strategies for demand forecasts. We want to explore the usage of ML anomaly detection methods to identify anomalous forecasts issued by global models and develop strategies to address such anomalies. Second, research is required to provide explanations that inform the context considered by the ML model and models' forecasted values and uncertainty. We understand that accurate forecasts are a precondition to building users' trust in a demand forecasting software. Nevertheless, accurate forecasts alone are not enough. ML models explainability is required to help the user understand the reasons behind a forecast, decide if it can be trusted, and gain more profound domain knowledge.

Author Contributions: Conceptualization, J.M.R., B.K., M.Š., B.F. and D.M.; methodology, J.M.R., B.K., M.Š., B.F. and D.M.; software, J.M.R. and B.K.; validation, J.R., B.K., M.Š. and B.F.; formal analysis, J.M.R., B.K., M.Š. and B.F.; investigation, J.M.R., M.Š. and B.F.; resources, J.M.R., B.K., M.Š. and B.F.; data curation, J.M.R., B.K., M.Š. and B.F.; writing—original draft preparation, J.M.R.; writing—review and editing, J.M.R., M.Š., B.F. and D.M.; visualization, J.M.R.; supervision, B.F. and D.M.; project administration, M.Š., B.F. and D.M.; funding acquisition, B.F. and D.M. All authors have read and agreed to the published version of the manuscript.

Funding: This work was supported by the Slovenian Research Agency and European Union's Horizon 2020 program project FACTLOG under grant agreement number H2020-869951.

Institutional Review Board Statement: Not applicable.

Informed Consent Statement: Not applicable.

Data Availability Statement: Not applicable.

Conflicts of Interest: The authors declare no conflicts of interest.

Abbreviations

The following abbreviations are used in this manuscript:

ADI	Average Demand Interval
ANFIS	Adaptive Network-based Fuzzy Inference System
ANN	Artificial Neural Network

ARFR	Adaptive Random Forest Regressor
ARIMA	autoregressive integrated moving average model
ARMA	Autoregressive Moving Average
CAPE	Cumulative Absolute Percentage Errors
CRISP-DM	CRoss-Industry Standard Process for Data Mining
CV	Coefficient of Variation
DTR	Decision Tree Regressor
GBTR	Gradient Boosted Regression Trees
GDP	Gross Domestic Product
HATR	Hoeffding Adaptive Tree Regressor
HTR	Hoeffding Tree Regressor
KNNR	K-Nearest-Neighbor Regressor
MA	Moving Average
MAE	Mean Absolute Error
MAPE	Mean Absolute Percentage Error
MASE	Mean Absolute Scaled Error
ME	Mean Error
ML	Machine Learning
MLPR	Multiple Linear Perceptron Regressor
MLR	Multiple Linear Regression
MSE	Mean Squared Error
OEM	Original Equipment Manufacturer
PMI	Purchasing Managers' Index
R^2	Coefficient of determination
R^2adj	Coefficient of determination - adjusted
RFR	Random Forest Regressor
RMSE	Root Mean Squared Error
SBA	Syntetos–Boylan Approximation
SVM	Support Vector Machine
SVR	Support Vector Regressor
UE	Under-estimates
VAR	Vector Autoregression
VECM	Vector Error Correction Model

References

1. Cambridge University Press. *Cambridge Learner's Dictionary with CD-ROM*; Cambridge University Press: Cambridge, UK, 2007.
2. Wei, W.; Guimarães, L.; Amorim, P.; Almada-Lobo, B. Tactical production and distribution planning with dependency issues on the production process. *Omega* **2017**, *67*, 99–114. [CrossRef]
3. Lee, H.L.; Padmanabhan, V.; Whang, S. The bullwhip effect in supply chains. *Sloan Manag. Rev.* **1997**, *38*, 93–102. [CrossRef]
4. Bhattacharya, R.; Bandyopadhyay, S. A review of the causes of bullwhip effect in a supply chain. *Int. J. Adv. Manuf. Technol.* **2011**, *54*, 1245–1261. [CrossRef]
5. Brühl, B.; Hülsmann, M.; Borscheid, D.; Friedrich, C.M.; Reith, D. A sales forecast model for the german automobile market based on time series analysis and data mining methods. In *Industrial Conference on Data Mining*; Springer: Berlin/Heidelberg, Germany, 2009; pp. 146–160
6. de Almeida, M.M.K.; Marins, F.A.S.; Salgado, A.M.P.; Santos, F.C.A.; da Silva, S.L. Mitigation of the bullwhip effect considering trust and collaboration in supply chain management: a literature review. *Int. J. Adv. Manuf. Technol.* **2015**, *77*, 495–513. [CrossRef]
7. Dwaikat, N.Y.; Money, A.H.; Behashti, H.M.; Salehi-Sangari, E. How does information sharing affect first-tier suppliers' flexibility? Evidence from the automotive industry in Sweden. *Prod. Plan. Control.* **2018**, *29*, 289–300. [CrossRef]
8. Martinsson, T.; Sjöqvist, E. Causes and Effects of Poor Demand Forecast Accuracy A Case Study in the Swedish Automotive Industry. Master's Thesis, Chalmers University of Technology/Department of Technology Management and Economics, Gothenburg, Sweden, 2019
9. Ramanathan, U.; Ramanathan, R. *Sustainable Supply Chains: Strategies, Issues, and Models*; Springer: New York, NY, USA, 2020
10. Gutierrez, R.S.; Solis, A.O.; Mukhopadhyay, S. Lumpy demand forecasting using neural networks. *Int. J. Prod. Econ.* **2008**, *111*, 409–420. [CrossRef]
11. Lolli, F.; Gamberini, R.; Regattieri, A.; Balugani, E.; Gatos, T.; Gucci, S. Single-hidden layer neural networks for forecasting intermittent demand. *Int. J. Prod. Econ.* **2017**, *183*, 116–128. [CrossRef]
12. Syntetos, A.A.; Boylan, J.E.; Croston, J. On the categorization of demand patterns. *J. Oper. Res. Soc.* **2005**, *56*, 495–503. [CrossRef]
13. Hyndman, R.J.; others. Another look at forecast-accuracy metrics for intermittent demand. *Foresight Int. J. Appl. Forecast.* **2006**, *4*, 43–46.

14. Wilcoxon, F. Individual comparisons by ranking methods. In *Breakthroughs in Statistics*; Springer: New York, NY, USA, 1992; pp. 196–202.
15. Williams, T. Stock control with sporadic and slow-moving demand. *J. Oper. Res. Soc.* **1984**, *35*, 939–948. [CrossRef]
16. Johnston, F.; Boylan, J.E. Forecasting for items with intermittent demand. *J. Oper. Res. Soc.* **1996**, *47*, 113–121. [CrossRef]
17. Dargay, J.; Gately, D. Income's effect on car and vehicle ownership, worldwide: 1960–2015. *Transp. Res. Part Policy Pract.* **1999**, *33*, 101–138. [CrossRef]
18. Wang, F.K.; Chang, K.K.; Tzeng, C.W. Using adaptive network-based fuzzy inference system to forecast automobile sales. *Expert Syst. Appl.* **2011**, *38*, 10587–10593. [CrossRef]
19. Vahabi, A.; Hosseininia, S.S.; Alborzi, M. A Sales Forecasting Model in Automotive Industry using Adaptive Neuro-Fuzzy Inference System (Anfis) and Genetic Algorithm (GA). *Management* **2016**, *1*, 2. [CrossRef]
20. Ubaidillah, N.Z. A study of car demand and its interdependency in sarawak. *Int. J. Bus. Soc.* **2020**, *21*, 997–1011. [CrossRef]
21. Sharma, R.; Sinha, A.K. Sales forecast of an automobile industry. *Int. J. Comput. Appl.* **2012**, *53*, 25–28. [CrossRef]
22. Gao, J.; Xie, Y.; Cui, X.; Yu, H.; Gu, F. Chinese automobile sales forecasting using economic indicators and typical domestic brand automobile sales data: A method based on econometric model. *Adv. Mech. Eng.* **2018**, *10*, 1687814017749325. [CrossRef]
23. Kwan, H.W. On the Demand Distributions of Slow-Moving Items. Ph.D. Thesis, University of Lancaster, Lancaster, UK, 1991
24. Eaves, A.H.C. Forecasting for the Ordering and Stock-Holding of Consumable Spare Parts. Ph.D. Thesis, Lancaster University, Lancaster, UK, 2002
25. Syntetos, A.A.; Babai, M.Z.; Altay, N. On the demand distributions of spare parts. *Int. J. Prod. Res.* **2012**, *50*, 2101–2117. [CrossRef]
26. Lengu, D.; Syntetos, A.A.; Babai, M.Z. Spare parts management: Linking distributional assumptions to demand classification. *Eur. J. Oper. Res.* **2014**, *235*, 624–635. [CrossRef]
27. Dwivedi, A.; Niranjan, M.; Sahu, K. A business intelligence technique for forecasting the automobile sales using Adaptive Intelligent Systems (ANFIS and ANN). *Int. J. Comput. Appl.* **2013**, *74*, 975–8887. [CrossRef]
28. Matsumoto, M.; Komatsu, S. Demand forecasting for production planning in remanufacturing. *Int. J. Adv. Manuf. Technol.* **2015**, *79*, 161–175. [CrossRef]
29. Farahani, D.S.; Momeni, M.; Amiri, N.S. Car sales forecasting using artificial neural networks and analytical hierarchy process. In Proceedings of the Fifth International Conference on Data Analytics: DATA ANALYTICS 2016, Venice, Italy, 9–13 October 2016; p. 69
30. Henkelmann, R. A Deep Learning based Approach for Automotive Spare Part Demand Forecasting. Master Thesis, Otto von Guericke Universitat Magdeburg, Magdeburg, Germany, 2018
31. Chandriah, K.K.; Naraganahalli, R.V. RNN/LSTM with modified Adam optimizer in deep learning approach for automobile spare parts demand forecasting. *Multimed. Tools Appl.* **2021**, 1–15. [CrossRef]
32. Hanggara, F.D. Forecasting Car Demand in Indonesia with Moving Average Method. *J. Eng. Sci. Technol. Manag.* **2021**, *1*, 1–6.
33. Zhang, G.P.; Qi, M. Neural network forecasting for seasonal and trend time series. *Eur. J. Oper. Res.* **2005**, *160*, 501–514. [CrossRef]
34. Athanasopoulos, G.; Hyndman, R.J.; Song, H.; Wu, D.C. The tourism forecasting competition. *Int. J. Forecast.* **2011**, *27*, 822–844. [CrossRef]
35. Montero-Manso, P.; Hyndman, R.J. Principles and algorithms for forecasting groups of time series: Locality and globality. *arXiv* **2020**, arXiv:2008.00444.
36. Salinas, D.; Flunkert, V.; Gasthaus, J.; Januschowski, T. DeepAR: Probabilistic forecasting with autoregressive recurrent networks. *Int. J. Forecast.* **2020**, *36*, 1181–1191. [CrossRef]
37. Bandara, K.; Bergmeir, C.; Smyl, S. Forecasting across time series databases using recurrent neural networks on groups of similar series: A clustering approach. *Expert Syst. Appl.* **2020**, *140*, 112896. [CrossRef]
38. Laptev, N.; Yosinski, J.; Li, L.E.; Smyl, S. Time-series extreme event forecasting with neural networks at uber. In Proceedings of the International Conference on Machine Learning, Sydney, Australia, 6–11 August 2017; Volume 34, pp. 1–5
39. Wirth, R.; Hipp, J. CRISP-DM: Towards a standard process model for data mining. In *Proceedings of the 4th International Conference on the Practical Applications of Knowledge Discovery and Data Mining*; Springer: London, UK, 2000; pp. 29–39.
40. Wang, C.N.; Tibo, H.; Nguyen, H.A. Malmquist productivity analysis of top global automobile manufacturers. *Mathematics* **2020**, *8*, 580. [CrossRef]
41. Tubaro, P.; Casilli, A.A. Micro-work, artificial intelligence and the automotive industry. *J. Ind. Bus. Econ.* **2019**, *46*, 333–345. [CrossRef]
42. Ryu, H.; Basu, M.; Saito, O. What and how are we sharing? A systematic review of the sharing paradigm and practices. *Sustain. Sci.* **2019**, *14*, 515–527. [CrossRef]
43. Li, M.; Zeng, Z.; Wang, Y. An innovative car sharing technological paradigm towards sustainable mobility. *J. Clean. Prod.* **2021**, *288*, 125626. [CrossRef]
44. Svennevik, E.M.; Julsrud, T.E.; Farstad, E. From novelty to normality: reproducing car-sharing practices in transitions to sustainable mobility. *Sustain. Sci. Pract. Policy* **2020**, *16*, 169–183. [CrossRef]
45. Heineke, K.; Möller, T.; Padhi, A.; Tschiesner, A. *The Automotive Revolution is Speeding Up*; McKinsey and Co.: New York, NY, USA, 2017.

46. Verevka, T.V.; Gutman, S.S.; Shmatko, A. Prospects for Innovative Development of World Automotive Market in Digital Economy. In Proceedings of the 2019 International SPBPU Scientific Conference on Innovations in Digital Economy, Saint Petersburg, Russian, 14–15 October 2019; pp. 1–6
47. Armstrong, J.S.; Morwitz, V.G.; Kumar, V. Sales forecasts for existing consumer products and services: Do purchase intentions contribute to accuracy? *Int. J. Forecast.* **2000**, *16*, 383–397. [CrossRef]
48. Morwitz, V.G.; Steckel, J.H.; Gupta, A. When do purchase intentions predict sales? *Int. J. Forecast.* **2007**, *23*, 347–364. [CrossRef]
49. Hotta, L.; Neto, J.C. The effect of aggregation on prediction in autoregressive integrated moving-average models. *J. Time Ser. Anal.* **1993**, *14*, 261–269. [CrossRef]
50. Souza, L.R.; Smith, J. Effects of temporal aggregation on estimates and forecasts of fractionally integrated processes: A Monte-Carlo study. *Int. J. Forecast.* **2004**, *20*, 487–502. [CrossRef]
51. Rostami-Tabar, B.; Babai, M.Z.; Syntetos, A.; Ducq, Y. Demand forecasting by temporal aggregation. *Nav. Res. Logist. (NRL)* **2013**, *60*, 479–498. [CrossRef]
52. Nikolopoulos, K.; Syntetos, A.A.; Boylan, J.E.; Petropoulos, F.; Assimakopoulos, V. An aggregate–disaggregate intermittent demand approach (ADIDA) to forecasting: empirical proposition and analysis. *J. Oper. Res. Soc* **2011**, *62*, 544–554. [CrossRef]
53. Syntetos, A.; Babai, M.; Altay, N. Modelling spare parts' demand: An empirical investigation. In Proceedings of the 8th International Conference of Modeling and Simulation MOSIM, Hammamet, Tunisia, 10–12 May 2010; Citeseer: Forest Grove, OR, USA, 2010; Volume 10
54. Hua, J.; Xiong, Z.; Lowey, J.; Suh, E.; Dougherty, E.R. Optimal number of features as a function of sample size for various classification rules. *Bioinformatics* **2005**, *21*, 1509–1515. [CrossRef]
55. Varma, S.; Simon, R. Bias in error estimation when using cross-validation for model selection. *BMC Bioinform.* **2006**, *7*, 91. [CrossRef]
56. Drucker, H.; Burges, C.J.; Kaufman, L.; Smola, A.J.; Vapnik, V. Support vector regression machines. In Proceedings of the Advances in Neural Information Processing Systems, Denver, CO, USA, 2–5 December 1997; pp. 155–161
57. Rosenblatt, F. The perceptron: A probabilistic model for information storage and organization in the brain. *Psychol. Rev.* **1958**, *65*, 386. [CrossRef]
58. Hoerl, A.E.; Kennard, R.W. Ridge regression: Biased estimation for nonorthogonal problems. *Technometrics* **1970**, *12*, 55–67. [CrossRef]
59. Tibshirani, R. Regression shrinkage and selection via the lasso. *J. R. Stat. Soc. Ser. B* **1996**, *58*, 267–288. [CrossRef]
60. Zou, H.; Hastie, T. Regularization and variable selection via the elastic net. *J. R. Stat. Soc. Ser. B* **2005**, *67*, 301–320. [CrossRef]
61. Altman, N.S. An introduction to kernel and nearest-neighbor nonparametric regression. *Am. Stat.* **1992**, *46*, 175–185.
62. Wolpert, D.H. Stacked generalization. *Neural Netw.* **1992**, *5*, 241–259. [CrossRef]
63. Gomes, H.M.; Barddal, J.P.; Ferreira, L.E.B.; Bifet, A. Adaptive random forests for data stream regression. In Proceedings of the European Symposium on Artificial Neural Networks, Computational Intelligence and Machine Learning (ESANN), Bruges, Belgium, 2–4 October 2018
64. Domingos, P.; Hulten, G. Mining high-speed data streams. In Proceedings of the Sixth ACM SIGKDD International Conference on Knowledge Discovery and Data Mining, Boston, MA, USA, 20–23 August 2000; pp. 71–80
65. Bifet, A.; Gavaldà, R. Adaptive learning from evolving data streams. In *International Symposium on Intelligent Data Analysis*; Springer: New York, NY, USA, 2009; pp. 249–260
66. Ferligoj, A.; Kramberger, A. Some Properties of R 2 in Ordinary Least Squares Regression. 1995
67. Armstrong, J.S. Illusions in regression analysis. *Int. J. Forecast.* **2011**, *28*, 689–694. [CrossRef]
68. Tufte, E.R. *The Visual Display of Quantitative Information*; Graphics Press: Cheshire, CT, USA, 2001; Volume 2.
69. Ali, M.M.; Boylan, J.E.; Syntetos, A.A. Forecast errors and inventory performance under forecast information sharing. *Int. J. Forecast.* **2012**, *28*, 830–841. [CrossRef]
70. Bruzda, J. Demand forecasting under fill rate constraints—The case of re-order points. *Int. J. Forecast.* **2020**, *36*, 1342–1361. [CrossRef]
71. Stone, M. Cross-validatory choice and assessment of statistical predictions. *J. R. Stat. Soc. Ser. B* **1974**, *36*, 111–133. [CrossRef]

Article

Ellipsoidal Path Planning for Unmanned Aerial Vehicles

Carlos Villaseñor [1], Alberto A. Gallegos [2], Gehova Lopez-Gonzalez [2], Javier Gomez-Avila [1], Jesus Hernandez-Barragan [1] and Nancy Arana-Daniel [1,*]

[1] Department of Computer Science, University of Guadalajara, 1421 Marcelino García Barragán, Guadalajara 44430, Mexico; carlos.villasenor@academicos.udg.mx or cvillasenor@neural10.com (C.V.); jenrique.gomez@academicos.udg.mx (J.G.-A.); josed.hernandezb@academicos.udg.mx (J.H.-B.)
[2] Department of Artificial Intelligence, Neural10 S de RL de CV, Av. Aviación 5051, Zapopan 45019, Mexico; agallegos@neural10.com (A.A.G.); jlopez@neural10.com (G.L.-G.)
* Correspondence: nancy.arana@academicos.udg.mx

Abstract: The research in path planning for unmanned aerial vehicles (UAV) is an active topic nowadays. The path planning strategy highly depends on the map abstraction available. In a previous work, we presented an ellipsoidal mapping algorithm (EMA) that was designed using covariance ellipsoids and clustering algorithms. The EMA computes compact in-memory maps, but still with enough information to accurately represent the environment and to be useful for robot navigation algorithms. In this work, we develop a novel path planning algorithm based on a bio-inspired algorithm for navigation in the ellipsoidal map. Our approach overcomes the problem that there is no closed formula to calculate the distance between two ellipsoidal surfaces, so it was approximated using a trained neural network. The presented path planning algorithm takes advantage of ellipsoid entities to represent obstacles and compute paths for small UAVs regardless of the concavity of these obstacles, in a very geometrically explicit way. Furthermore, our method can also be used to plan routes in dynamical environments without adding any computational cost.

Keywords: path planning; unmanned aerial vehicles; neural networks; evolutionary algorithms

1. Introduction

Autonomous Unmanned Aerial Vehicles (UAVs) play an important role in both military and civilian applications. In contrast with manned aircrafts, UAVs are able to perform complex and dangerous tasks with high maneuverability and low cost [1,2]. An important problem to solve in order to achieve a certain level of autonomy is path planning. In the past, the best path was selected as the shortest distance to a goal; now, the best path is associated with the traveled distance and energy consumption [3]. If more parameters, besides distance, are considered, the path planning problem can been stated as an optimization problem, and population based algorithms have been used in many cases to solve it successfully [4–8].

In [9], we described a novel algorithm for path planning, which uses conformal geometric algebra to generate maps using spheres. By using spheres, we gain in terms of the number of parameters needed for representing the maps and these maps are rich in information. For example, we need the same number of parameters for representing a sphere as for a plane, but the plane also needs an extra number of parameters for bounding the plain. Moreover, the spheres are easy to operate in conformal geometric algebra.

The algorithm employs the characteristics of the spheres described in this algebra to navigate through the maps by combining them with Teaching-Learning Based Optimization (TLBO). In this paper, we compared different evolutionary optimization algorithms where TLBO had the best result.

On the other hand, we also explored approaching the robotic mapping problem by using ellipsoidal representations [10]. These ellipsoidal geometric entities are coded in the geometric algebra $G_{6,3}$. The resulting map is compact and rich in information as we showed in [10].

The problem of robotic mapping consists of constructing a spatial representation of the environment, which is helpful for the robot [11]. There are classic mapping abstractions, such as grid occupancy [12], where cubes represent the objects. This abstraction is memory efficient but discretizes the environment; furthermore, it is useful for office-like environments but is not adequately suited for outdoor environments.

We can also find variable size grid occupancy [13], where we can change the resolution of the grid. With particular modification, we can model dynamic maps with this abstraction [14].

There are other map abstractions such as multiplanar maps [15], landmarks, and points of obstacles [16]. A mapping algorithm called OctoMap was proposed in [17,18]. OctoMap has variable resolution grid occupancy representation with a probabilistic construction. We include in Table 1 a qualitative comparison between ellipsoidal maps and Octomap.

Table 1. EMA and OctoMap properties.

Property	EMA	OctoMap
Basic geometric entity	Ellipsoids	Cubes
Variate granularity	Yes	Yes
Construction scheme	Any clustering algorithm	Hierarchical
Robust to outliers	Yes	Yes

In Figure 1, we present an example of a cloud point (left) [19] and its ellipsoidal map (right).

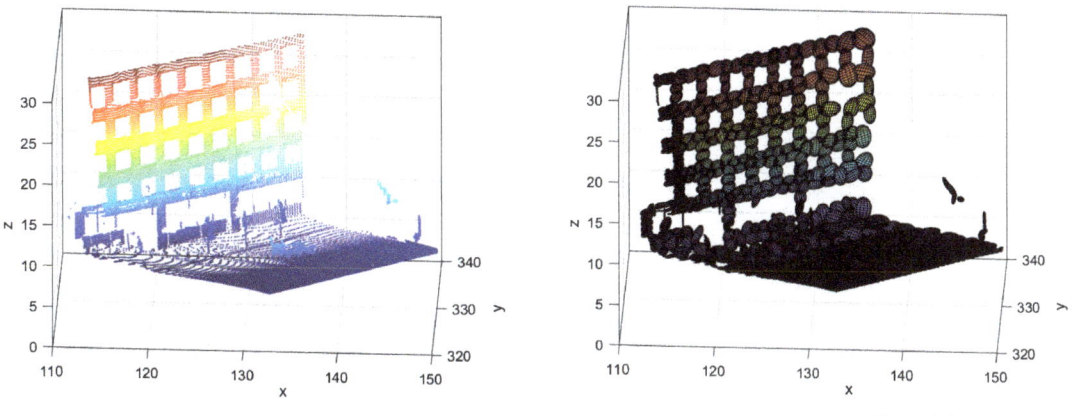

(a) Cloud point (83,459 points).   (b) Ellipsoidal Map (700 ellipsoids).

Figure 1. Example of an ellipsoidal map generated with the ellipsoidal mapping algorithm presented in [10].

In this work, we present a novel algorithm for path planning in 3D environments for small UAVs. This algorithm works on ellipsoidal mapping provided by the algorithm in [10]. There is no closed form for calculating the distance between two ellipsoidal surfaces and using an iterative algorithm will be computational expensive.

We propose to solve this problem by training a dense neural network for approximating the distance between two ellipsoids. We propose a new fitness function to find the path with the TLBO algorithm.

The TLBO algorithm was chosen because it obtained the best performance in a similar problem presented in [9]. We refer the reader to [9] for a performance comparison on metaheuristics for similar path-planning.

The paper is organized as follows: in Section 2, we introduce our solution to efficiently calculate the distance between ellipsoids and we show the training and generalization results. In Section 3, we offer a brief review of the TLBO algorithm and we develop the fitness function for path planning in ellipsoidal maps. Then, the simulation and results of the proposed algorithm are presented in Section 4. Finally, in Section 5, we offer a conclusion and future directions based on this work.

2. Approximating the Distance Function with Neural Networks

Our goal was to develop a path planning algorithm to work with the ellipsoidal maps to take advantage of these maps being compact-in-memory yet rich-in-information. The hypothesis to achieve the above goal was to design an algorithm that could compute a path using the distance between the envelope ellipsoids of the obstacles, and the ellipsoid that models the UAV. The computed path maintains the vehicle safe free space between itself and the occupied places.

To know how much free space exists between ellipsoids, we needed to solve the non-trivial key problem of finding a method to compute the distance between them due to the fact that there is not a closed way to do it. We propose a machine learning method to solve the above computation using neural networks to overcome the problem that represents the great computational costs of using iterative algorithms to calculate distances in maps, where the number of ellipsoids is large.

To solve this problem efficiently, we use a dense neural network to estimate the distance between two ellipsoids. One ellipsoid will represent a small UAV and the other will represent an obstacle.

We can train a neural network for the regression problem. To generate a dataset for training, we randomly generate a pose for the UAV (yaw, pitch and roll). We fix the semi-axes of the ellipsoid representing the UAV with $(0.5, 0.5, 0.3)$ in meters. Furthermore, we generate a random ellipsoid around the UAV. We calculate a cloud mesh for every ellipsoid and estimate the distance between the UAV by using a brute force approach. In Figure 2, we present an example of generated samples and their estimated distance.

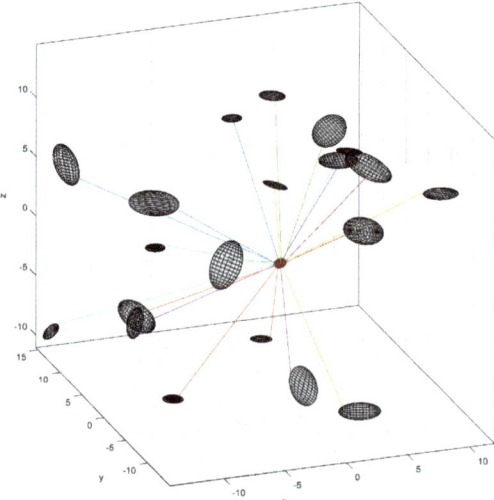

Figure 2. Examples of random generated samples for training.

One problem with this approach is to find a correct normalization of the data. If the input data of a neural network is not well normalized it could lead to slow or biased learning. In the following, we describe a novel normalization method that achieves good results on the neural network performance.

Firstly, the small UAV is represented by an ellipsoid with fixed semi-axes. These semi-axes are not considered in the learning problem, because the neural network can learn them as well. We will fix the UAV position at the center of the 3D space. Then, the position and the semi-axes are not input data for the neural network. The UAV is represented only with the angles $(yaw, pitch, roll) \in [0, 2\pi]^3$.

In the second instance, the 3D points on the map representing the obstacles are mapped using ellipsoids. As we presented in [10], we applied a clustering technique to the cloud point. Each cluster is a set of 3D points $\left\{[x_i, y_i, z_i]^T\right\}_{i=1}^n$, with center of mass $[\mu_x, \mu_y, \mu_z]^T$.

We can also calculate the pair-wise covariance between two variables; for example, for x and y coordinates, the covariance is calculated with (1):

$$\sigma_{xy} = \sigma_{yx} = \sum_{i=1}^n \frac{(x_i - \mu_x)(y_i - \mu_y)}{n}. \tag{1}$$

With the pair-wise covariances, we construct the covariance matrix is defined with (2). The parameters $(c_1, \ldots, c_9)$ carry the information of an ellipsoid that covers all non-outlier data points.

$$\Sigma = \begin{bmatrix} \sigma_{xx} & \sigma_{xy} & \sigma_{xz} \\ \sigma_{xy} & \sigma_{yy} & \sigma_{yz} \\ \sigma_{xz} & \sigma_{yz} & \sigma_{zz} \end{bmatrix} = \begin{bmatrix} c_1 & c_2 & c_3 \\ c_4 & c_5 & c_6 \\ c_7 & c_8 & c_9 \end{bmatrix} \tag{2}$$

The obstacle ellipsoids will be represented with the normalized covariance matrix. This parametrization is chosen because it is the output of the multi-ellipsoidal mapping algorithm presented in [10]. Other parametrizations lead to a high computational cost; for instance, one could use the angles of rotation and the semi-axes, but this will require the spectral decomposition of the covariance matrix.

In Figure 3, we present a 2D scheme of the maximum and minimum distances between two ellipses. The desired distance will be between the minimum and the maximum distances and it will depend on the orientation of the ellipses.

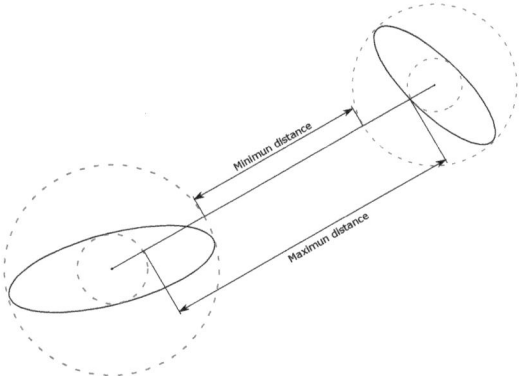

Figure 3. Minimum and maximum distance between ellipses.

The positions of the UAV and obstacles are difficult to normalize. If we normalize using common techniques like max-min or the standard normalization the neural network could output strange values for ellipsoid outside this normalization. To avoid this situation, we will code the relative position with a normalized vector from the UAV center to the obstacle center (u_x, u_y, u_z).

Instead of doing regression with the real distance between the ellipsoids, we just estimate a correction variable δ if we subtract this value from the centers distance of the ellipsoids, we can calculate the distance between ellipsoids, as we show in (3):

$$dist(E_1, E_2) = ||\text{Center}_1 - \text{Center}_2||_2 - \delta. \tag{3}$$

The δ correction factor depends only on the relative position of the obstacle ellipsoid and the UAV ellipsoid and their orientations. We can approximate this correction factor with a neural network. In Figure 4, we present the normalized input vector and the neural network architecture.

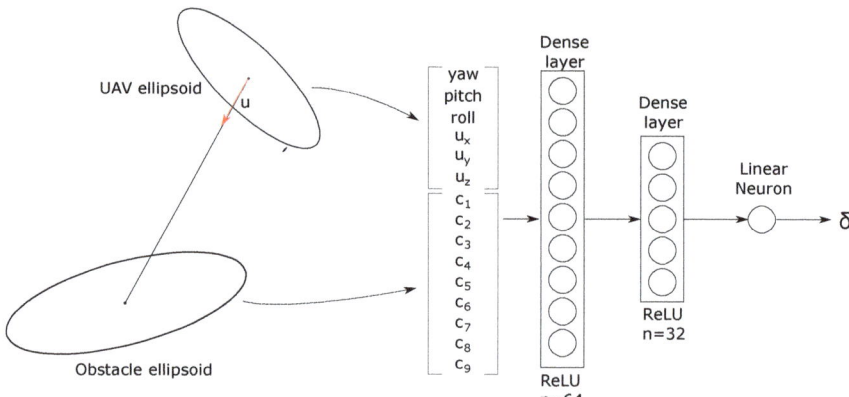

Figure 4. Neural network architecture.

We generate 185,000 random examples that took one day to calculate. We distribute these samples the following way: 149,850 samples for training, 16,650 for validating and hyper-parameter tuning, and 18,500 for testing. We trained this neural network for 50 epochs. In Figure 5, we show the training and validation evolution on the mean squared error (MSE). We got 0.0016 final MSE for training and 0.0017 final MSE for validation.

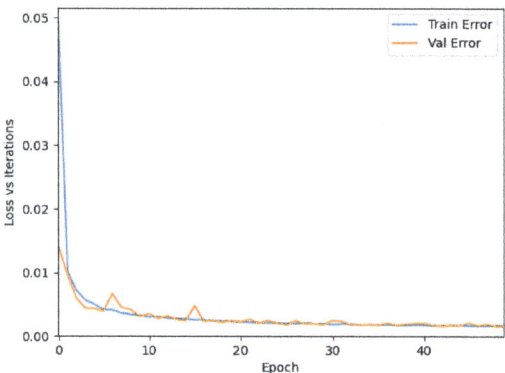

Figure 5. Neural Network Training Results.

In Table 2, we present the training results. In particular, we present the R^2-score where the best possible value is one, we also show the mean absolute error (MAE) and the median absolute error (MedianAE), in order to give a good sense of the capabilities of the neural network.

Table 2. Neural Network training results.

	R^2-Score	MAE (Meters)	MedianAE (Meters)
Train set	0.9928	0.0302	0.0238
Test set	0.9922	0.0308	0.0241

The neural network achieves a high performance in predicting the correction factor and by using (3), we can accurately calculate the distance between the UAV and the obstacle ellipsoids. The Network was programmed on Keras/Tensorflow, then the network natively can run on a graphical process unit (GPU) for high performance. After testing, we can calculate the distance between a UAV ellipsoid and 200 obstacles in a mean time of 0.1208 s (We use a RTX 2060 GPU). With this result, we can assure that the application of path planning over ellipsoidal maps is computationally affordable.

Finally, we run an experiment on a virtual environment by placing the UAV in a grid position and calculating the minimum distance to the closest object. In Figure 6, we show the result of the experiment. The warmer colors represent greater distances. Notice that the neural network can calculate an accurate map that is compact in memory and rich in information.

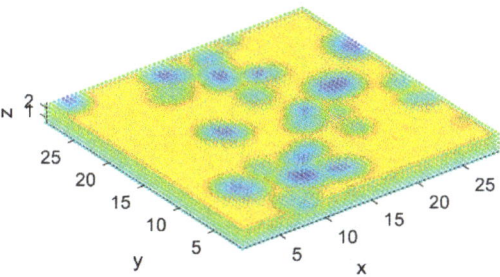

Figure 6. Distance map. The warmer colors represent greater distances (20 random ellipsoids).

In the next section, we develop the path planning algorithm based on this neural network by using a bio-inspired algorithm with a greedy approach.

3. Teaching-Learning Based Optimization

TLBO is an optimization algorithm based on the teaching of knowledge from a teacher to his or her students on a classroom [20]. This population based algorithm has two main phases, in which it generates new knowledge: the teacher and the learner phase.

The teacher phase is inspired by the transmission of knowledge from a teacher to the students, and centers efforts to increase the average score of the class. The learner phase is inspired by the knowledge shared among students; the students with more information will be beneficial as the other learners learn new information from them. The teacher is the best solution so far in the current iteration.

3.1. Teacher Phase

A good teacher will try to increase the knowledge of the students/learners based on his or her own knowledge over time/iterations. But no matter how good a teacher is, because of many factors this can only be done to some extent in a classroom composed of n students. It can be said that the mean of the new knowledge of the class will be moved in some extent towards the teacher's knowledge, but it will also depend on the capabilities of the class [21].

The following equation shows the intent of the teacher X_T to influence, to some degree, each individual X_i (composed of the drones $(x, y, z, yaw, pitch, roll)$ values) with the help of the mean of knowledge of the whole class $\bar{x}$:

$$X'_i = X_i + r(X_T - T_f \bar{x}), \tag{4}$$

where $T_f \in \{1, 2\}$ is a random value of only two possible values, named the teaching factor; and $r \in [0, 1]$ is a random number. If $f(X'_i)$ provides a better solution than $f(X_i)$ (where f is a fitness function), X'_i replaces X_i as a solution.

3.2. Learner Phase

The learner phase depends on the interchange of knowledge between students. A learner with new information will have an influence on the overall knowledge of the class [22].

This phase consists of adjusting each learner X_i based on another learner X_k, where i and $k \in [1, n] : i \neq k$ [9].

There are two alternatives that could happen for learners X; when the $f(X_i)$ is better than $f(X_k)$ which generates the following learner:

$$X'_i = X_i + r(X_i - X_k) \tag{5}$$

or vice versa, when $f(X_k)$ is better than $f(X_i)$,

$$X'_i = X_i + r(X_k - X_i), \tag{6}$$

X'_i replaces X_i as a solution if it represents a better solution. As can be seen, this phase also includes the teacher solution from the previous phase, but in a less important role.

3.3. Fitness Function

We designed a fitness function that is composed of four terms:

$$f(X_i) = d_t + c + h * (d_t + 1) + s * (d_t + 1), \tag{7}$$

where d_t is the Euclidean distance between a learner X_i and the target point θ (composed of only by x, y and z values); by itself this term helps to attract the population towards the target. c is the obstacle collision indicator:

$$c = \begin{cases} \infty & \text{if any } o_j \leq 0, \\ 0 & \text{otherwise} \end{cases} \tag{8}$$

where o_j is the distance between the leaner X_i and the obstacle j, which is obtained using the neural network described in Section 2. The collision indicator's function is to heavily penalize collisions, since it is of utmost importance to guarantee the UAV's safety.

h represents a heat factor that indicates the proximity of X_i to a set of obstacles $o_d \in o_j : 0 < o_d \leq r_1$, where r_1 is a user defined range of proximity:

$$h = \sum(-log_2(0.001 * o_d) + log_2(r_1)). \tag{9}$$

To give the drone the capability to avoid large convex obstacles inside a room (usually obstacles that go from floor to ceiling), a stuck factor s is added. To obtain s it is necessary to create a set of stuck zones s_z; when the euclidean distance of the (x, y, z) values of teachers τ_{t-1} and τ_t (where τ is the last teacher obtained from a TLBO run and t is the current run) is less than a user defined threshold α, a zone is added to s_z. If the condition is met the (x, y, z) values from τ_t are queued to s_z. The stuck factor is obtained as follows:

$$s = \sum(-log_2(0.001 * s_k) + log_2(r_2)), \tag{10}$$

where s_k is the set of Euclidean distances from a learner X_i to any point in s_z, where $0 < s_k \leq r_2$, and r_2 represents a user defined range of proximity. The pseudocode for path planning is presented in Algorithm 1.

Algorithm 1 Path Planning Algorithm.

1: **procedure** OPTIMIZE
2:     $actual\_pos \leftarrow$ starting position
3:     $X_i \leftarrow$ create learner population
4:     $X'_i \leftarrow$ initialize to zero
5:     $X_T \leftarrow$ obtain teacher from population as a separate value
6:     $ngens \leftarrow$ number of generations
7:     $stop \leftarrow$ stopping value
8:     $tqueue \leftarrow$ teachers queue
9:     $S_z \leftarrow$ set stuck zones list to empty
10:    $X_{Tfitness} \leftarrow fitness(X_i, S_z)$
11:    $\alpha \leftarrow 0.1$ ▷ User defined threshold
12:    **while** $X_{Tfitness} > stop$ **do**
13:       **for** $gen \leftarrow 1$ to $ngens$ **do**
14:          **for** every X_i **do**
15:             $X'_i \leftarrow teacher\_phase(X_i)$ ▷ This step corresponds to (4)
16:             $X'_i \leftarrow bound\_increments(X_i, actual\_pos)$
17:             $X'_{ifitness} \leftarrow fitness(X'_i, S_z)$ ▷ Evaluates (7)
18:             $X_i \leftarrow select\_best(X_i, X'_i)$ ▷ Selects the best candidate between X_i and X'_i
19:          **for** every X_i **do**
20:             $X'_i \leftarrow learner\_phase(X_i)$ ▷ This step corresponds to (5) and (6)
21:             $X'_i \leftarrow bound\_increments(X_i, actual\_pos)$ ▷ Described in Section 4
22:             $X'_{ifitness} \leftarrow fitness(X'_i, S_z)$
23:             $(X_i, X_{ifitness}) \leftarrow select\_best\_learners((X_i, X_{ifitness}), (X'_i, X'_{ifitness}))$
24:       $(X_T, X_{Tfitness}) \leftarrow update\_teacher(X_i, X_{ifitness})$
25:    $tqueue \leftarrow append(X_T, tqueue)$ ▷ Add X_T to queue
26:    $dist = norm(X_T[0:3] - actual\_pos[0:3])$ ▷ Euclidean norm
27:    $actual\_pos \leftarrow X_T$
28:    $X_i \leftarrow initialize()$ ▷ Initialize and obtain fitness values
29:    $X'_i \leftarrow set\_to\_zero()$
30:    $mi \leftarrow max\_index(X_{ifitness})$
31:    **if** $dist < \alpha$ **then**
32:       $S_z \leftarrow append(X_T)$
33:    **else**
34:       $X_{mi} \leftarrow X_T$
     return $tqueue$

4. Simulation and Results

To define the whole path, TLBO was run several times, and each time (except the first one) the learners were initialized randomly within the proximity of τ_{t-1}; for the first iteration the $(x, y, z, yaw, pitch, roll)$ base values where defined arbitrarily. Each TLBO run consisted of 20 iterations and a population of five individuals; r_1 and r_2 were assigned values of 0.35 and 1.5, respectably. As a stopping condition, the Euclidean distance from τ_t and the target θ was used (a distance value less than 0.1). At the end of a run, τ_t is added to the path. As Figure 7 shows.

The values that could be achieved by a learner were bounded, so that the drone could not make abrupt changes that could make it behave unstably from one state to another or fly at very pronounced angles. In each iteration, the values of the learners were bounded by $\tau_{t-1} \pm (0.5, 0.5, 0.5, 0.15, 0.15, 0.25)$. The drone's $(yaw, pitch, roll)$ values were also bounded globally to $\pm[\pi, 0.7, 0.7]$ radians, respectively. The bounds and other values were empirically selected. We included the pitch and roll angles in the search space because some control schemes for UAV such as Backstepping or Inverse Optimal Control need these references [23–25]. However, our proposal can work even when ignoring pitch and roll angles.

Compared to [9], our approach involving the path planning algorithm offers several advantages. Firstly, our approach was designed to work indoors and outdoors alike. Ref. [9] shows several limitations avoiding large convex obstacles inside a room since it does not take them into consideration and this prevents the algorithm to be trapped in certain local minimums. Tthe influence of the obstacles in our approach also only takes into account the nearest obstacles in the range and adds smaller penalty values that do not heavily obfuscate the influence of the distance to a target in the fitness function.

Figures 8–12 show several maps where paths were generated for a drone to follow. All the maps were contained in a room composed of ellipsoids. The room was not plotted for display purposes.

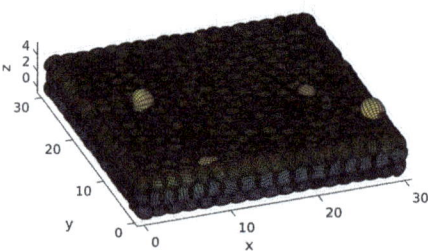

Figure 7. Room composed of ellipsoids looking from the outside (700 ellipsoids represent the walls, floor and roof, and 25 random ellipsoids represent the obstacles).

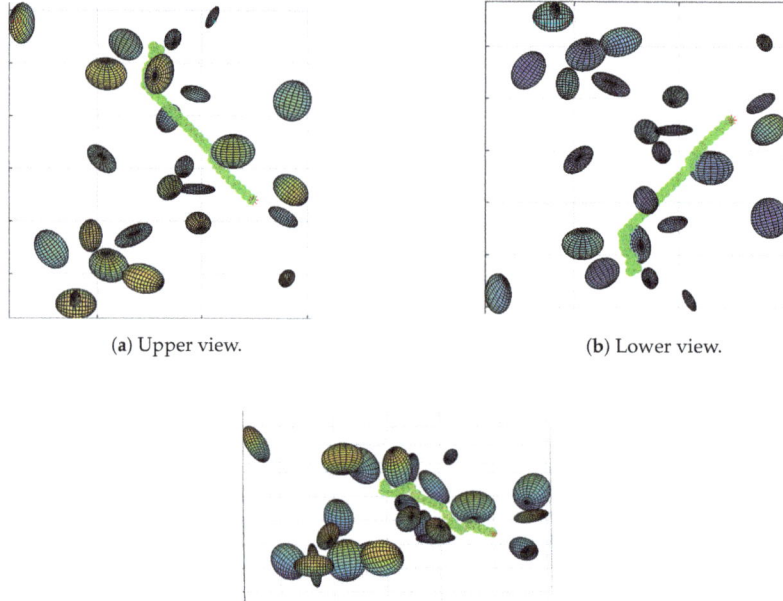

Figure 8. Path of map 1 generated with TLBO. The green ellipsoids represent the path obtained, the asterisk represent the target and the multicolor ellipsoids represent the obstacles. It can be seen that the path is sufficiently smooth for a drone to follow it.

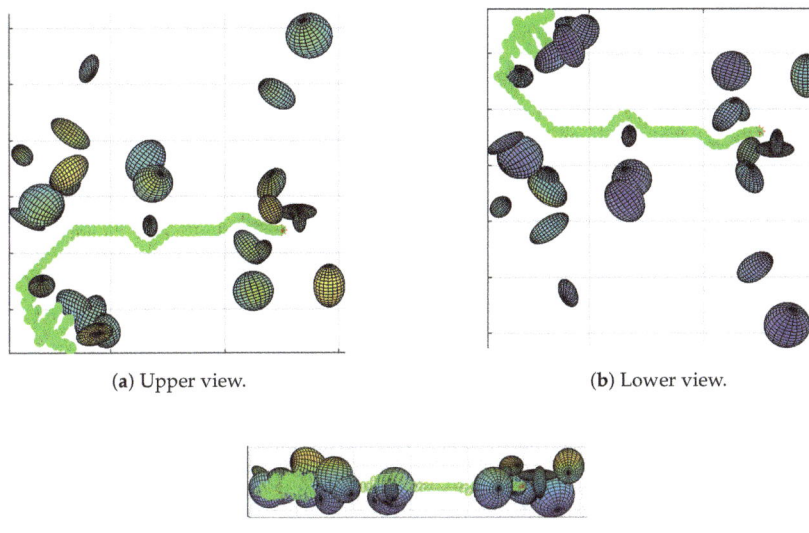

Figure 9. Path of map 2 generated with TLBO. The green ellipsoids represent the drone path and the multicolor ellipsoids represent the obstacles. Although it shows difficulties to find a path, it is safely pushed away the obstacles at the start.

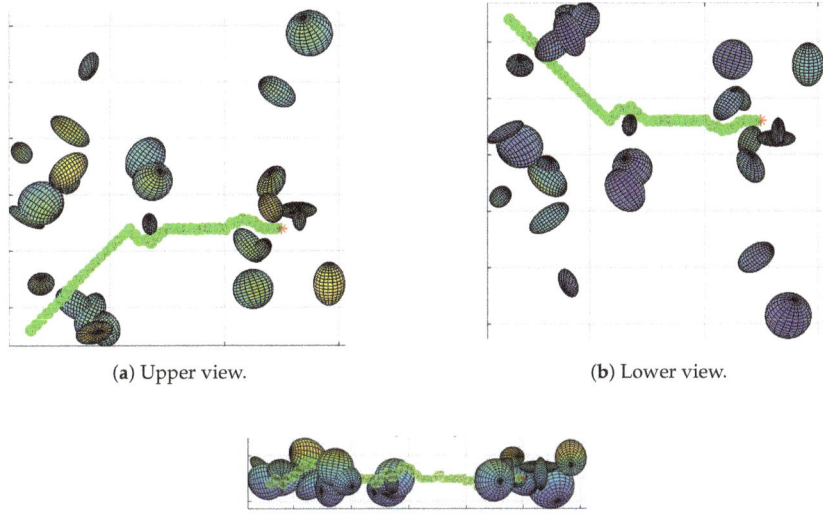

Figure 10. Path of map 2 without the room of ellipsoids. In this case, the ellipsoids, where the map is contained, have been removed. As can be seen, now the UAV can easily find a path above and beside the obstacles.

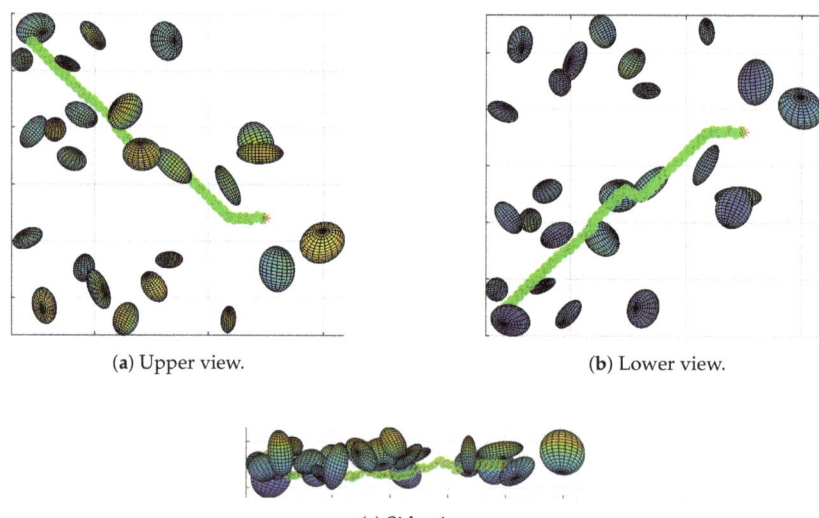

Figure 11. Path of map 3 generated with TLBO. The path represented by the green ellipsoids, are sufficiently smooth for the UAV.

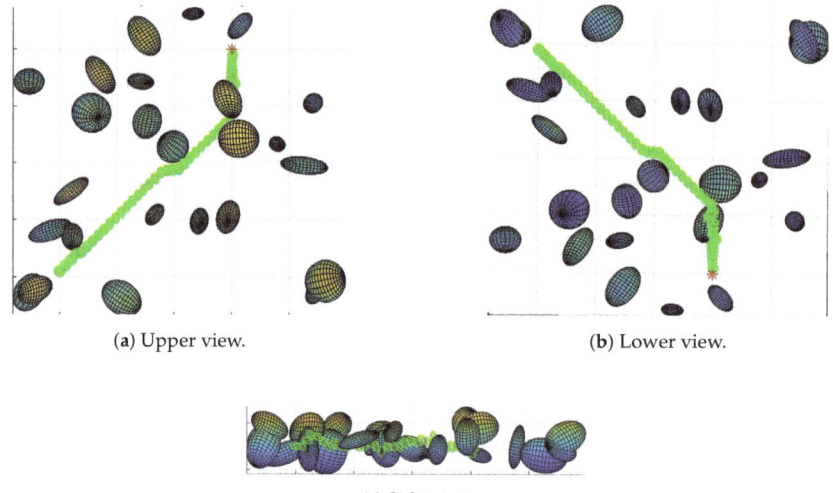

Figure 12. Path of map 4 generated with TLBO. The algorithm founds a smooth path in presence of convex obstacles.

The figures display the path followed by the drone (green ellipsoids) to its target (red asterisk), avoiding on the way several obstacles (multicolor ellipsoids). As can be seen, the drone can easily follow the paths obtained by the algorithm. Maps, like those shown in Figures 8 and 9, show little difficulty finding a path; even in the presence of convex obstacles at the start, the drone is safely pushed away until it finds a way to circumnavigate the obstacles. Comparing Figures 9 and 10 it can be seen that, without the room, the path simply passes above and beside the obstacles.

Comparison with State of the Art Algorithms

In order to validate the proposed method, we compared it with other evolutionary techniques and a well-known path planning algorithm. Firstly, we describe the Rapidly-exploring Random Tree Star (RRT*) [26].

The RRT* algorithm, presented in Algorithm 2, finds a free path from the initial point z_{init} to the final point z_{goal}. We created a tree T with an initial node z_{init}. Next, we grew the tree up for N attempts.

Algorithm 2 Rapidly-exploring Random Tree Star (RRT*).

1: $T \leftarrow$ InitializeTree()
2: $T \leftarrow$ InsertNode($\emptyset$, z_{init}, T)
3: **for** $i = 1$ to N **do**
4:     $z_{rand} \leftarrow$ SampleSpace()
5:     $z_{nearest} \leftarrow$ Nearest(T, z_{rand})
6:     $(z_{new}, U_{new}) \leftarrow$ Steer($z_{nearest}$, z_{rand})
7:     **if** ObstacleFree(z_{new}) **then**
8:         $z_{near} \leftarrow$ Near(T, z_{new})
9:         $z_{min} \leftarrow$ ChooseParent(z_{near}, $z_{nearest}$, z_{new})
10:        $T \leftarrow$ InsertNode(z_{min}, z_{new}, T)
11:        $T \leftarrow$ Rewire(T, z_{near}, z_{min}, z_{new})
     return T

To find the next node in the tree, we randomly sampled a point on the map z_{rand} that is not with an obstacle. We found the nearest node of the tree and renamed it $z_{nearest}$. After steering from $z_{nearest}$ to z_{rand}, this function has heuristics about the robot's kinematics. Then we renamed z_{rand} as z_{new} and found a path U_{new}.

The ObstacleFree function search for collision with obstacles on the line from $z_{nearest}$ to z_{new}; if there were no collisions, we proceeded to add the z_{new} point. We collected the points close to z_{new} within a certain radius. Then we chose the parent node that carried the least cost and renamed z_{min}. Finally, we added the link between z_{min} and z_{new} and rewired the tree to find the minimum cost.

To apply the RRT* algorithm on an ellipsoidal map we developed a collision detection function. We used the Cholesky factorization of the covariance matrices that represent the obstacles. We show this in (11). In the case of the evolutionary algorithms, we can expect longer run-times because of the neural network prediction.

$$\Sigma = LL^T. \tag{11}$$

Using the triangular matrix L, we can calculate if a point x is inside an ellipsoid on the map by using the inequality (12), where μ is the center of the ellipsoid.

$$||L^T(x - \mu)||_2 \leq 1. \tag{12}$$

In Figure 13, we show the resulting path of the RRT* algorithm in the same four maps. Notice that the found paths avoid the obstacles but do not consider the ellipsoid that represents the UAV. We used a maximum of 5000 iterations, but for the mean convergence on the four maps it was 1348 iterations.

Furthermore, we also present experiments with other state-of-the-art evolutionary optimization algorithms. We ran the same tests for the the Differential Evolution (DE) [27] algorithm, the Particle Swarm Optimization (PSO) [28] algorithm, and the Firefly (FF) [29] algorithm.

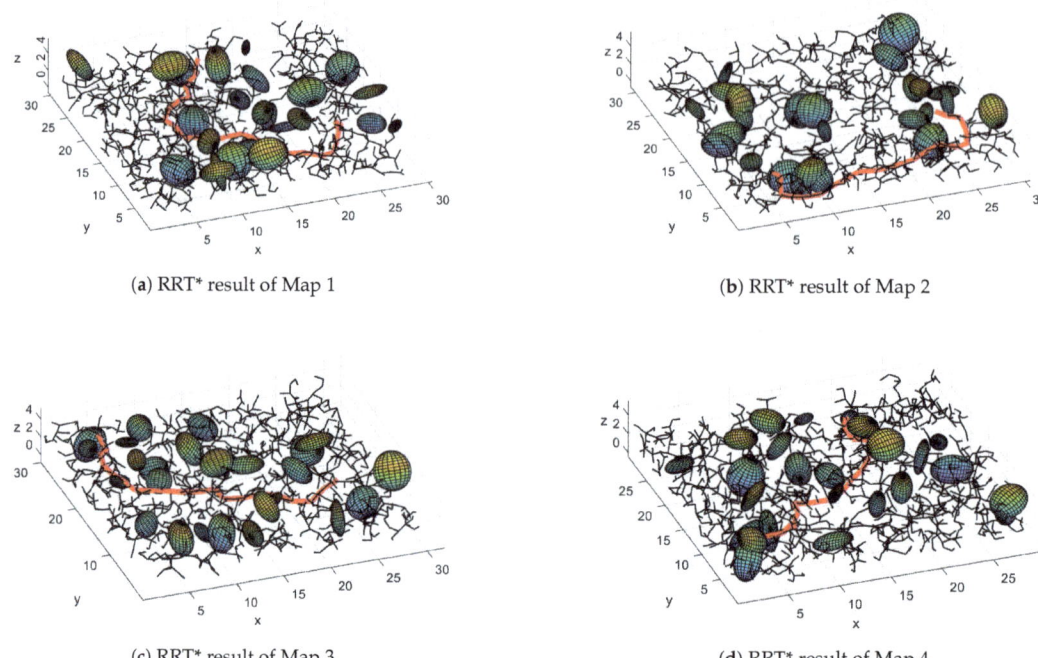

(a) RRT* result of Map 1

(b) RRT* result of Map 2

(c) RRT* result of Map 3

(d) RRT* result of Map 4

Figure 13. RRT* results of the maps 1 to 4. We show the constructed tree in black and the best found path in red.

All the evolutionary algorithms used the same fitness function presented in (7). All the proposed methods are non-deterministic. To ensure the validity of the results, we ran each algorithm experiment 30 times on the same computer. The start and endpoints were the same for all the experiments. In Table 3, we present the comparison of the different methods. Notice that the evolutionary schemes have the best mean performance for maps 1, 3, and 4. In Figure 14, we show the box-and-whisker plots for each map and each method.

Table 3. Experimental results, mean and standard deviation of the distance of the found path for each algorithm.

Algorithm		Map 1	Map 2	Map 3	Map 4
TLBO	mean	25.2912	61.5385	32.9653	34.9789
	STD	2.2956	34.9912	2.5192	9.3455
DE	mean	29.7900	51.7444	35.8763	39.0414
	STD	4.9021	22.3003	3.5688	8.2239
PSO	mean	27.8994	46.1655	32.5432	33.5899
	STD	4.5297	29.2296	1.8954	7.6463
FF	mean	25.6914	46.5815	31.9210	32.5309
	STD	3.1752	19.2983	2.1017	5.0559
RRT*	mean	37.7490	37.0365	39.6117	40.9821
	STD	8.5628	5.1285	3.4001	4.3958

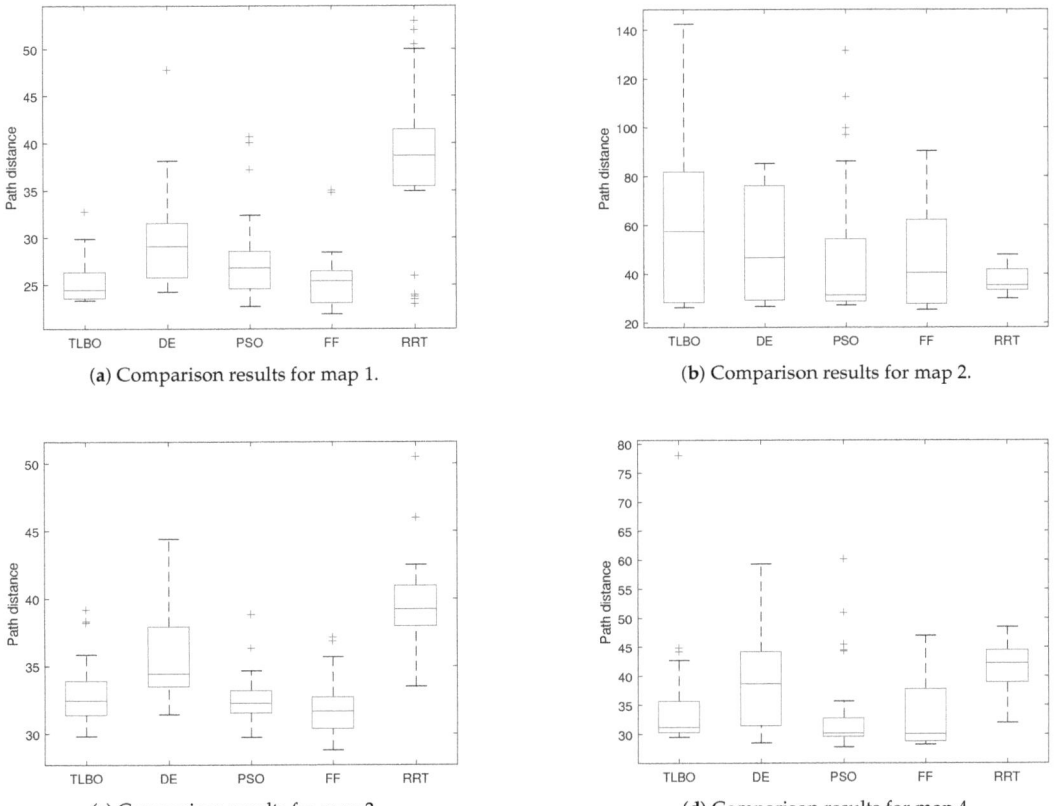

(a) Comparison results for map 1.
(b) Comparison results for map 2.
(c) Comparison results for map 3.
(d) Comparison results for map 4.

Figure 14. Comparison results for four experimental maps and for the five proposed methods.

In Table 4, we include the number of steps in each evolutionary algorithm and the number of nodes in the RRT* algorithm.

Table 4. Experimental results, mean steps to goal point.

Algortihm	Map 1	Map 2	Map 3	Map 4
TLBO	40.70	47.60	52.80	50.80
DE	52.84	47.10	61.30	59.30
PSO	46.33	45.30	49.40	47.93
FF	42.57	56.23	51.83	51.43
RRT*	1412.34	1115.10	1342.47	1516.24

We proved the novel algorithm in a real environment. We used the map from [19], and we created the ellipsoidal map. In Figure 15, we offer the resulting path planning. Notice that this path planning has a good performance even in non-structural environments. In Table 5, we show how the Cholesky factorization allows lower complexity in the RRT* algorithm.

Table 5. Experimental results, mean and standard deviation of the run-time of each algorithm in seconds.

Algorithm		Map 1	Map 2	Map 3	Map 4
TLBO	mean	77.1916	221.7160	98.1027	100.3328
	STD	9.1466	145.9610	9.8856	35.7067
DE	mean	57.8452	110.2755	66.7537	71.6009
	STD	10.3801	52.5747	8.0530	19.4613
PSO	mean	107.8372	196.9315	111.1351	114.3043
	STD	24.4556	15.5697	9.4505	37.8680
FF	mean	130.9127	257.07965	153.2906	151.7518
	STD	19.7207	118.1890	13.2743	30.2673
RRT*	mean	5.3038	2.4780	5.8014	4.8056
	STD	0.4246	1.0391	0.9550	0.3053

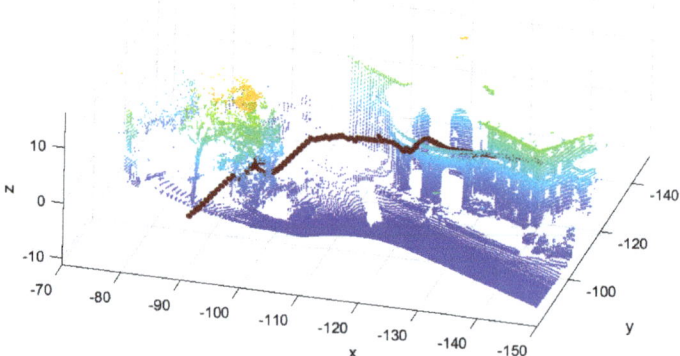

Figure 15. Path planning in a real ellipsoidal map, we show the point cloud for a better understanding of the image. The cloud point has 100,000 points but the map only has 700 ellipsoids.

5. Conclusions and Future Work

In this work we presented a geometrically explicit and simple algorithm that takes advantage of the ellipsoidal representation of maps generated to plan collision-free and smooth paths regardless of the concavity of the obstacles or whether the environment is indoor or outdoor.

Our method solves the non-trivial problem of computing the distance between two ellipsoids by using a neural network. To train the neural network, it was necessary to produce a training dataset and design a novel normalization method for these data. So, we obtain an accurate approximation for the distance, which allows the computation of the free-space and occupied-space of an environment, as is shown in Table 2 and Figure 6.

In order to obtain paths and to keep the computational costs of our approach low, a bio-inspired algorithm named TLBO was used. We have chosen TLBO because it has had the best performance in previous comparisons with other techniques [9]. The fitness function was designed taking into account four desired features for the path obtained: to keep a safe distance between obstacles' ellipsoids and the UAV ellipsoid; to avoid collisions; to reduce the total amount of the UAV's proximity range throughout the whole path; and to give the drone the capability to avoid large convex obstacles (walls inside a room, dense and tall vegetation).

It is important to mention that, based on our design of the fitness function, the computed paths are not optimal. Because it was used as a greedy approach, it cannot get the optimal path but is more versatile and can manage dynamical maps without extra computational costs.

We compare the proposed approach with other evolutionary algorithms, DE, PSO, and FF. We also compare with RRT*, and we constructed the collision detection function for the ellipsoidal map. In most cases, evolutionary techniques with the presented fitness function obtained a better performance than RRT*, but clearly RRT* has a better performance on time. Furthermore, the evolutionary methods also calculate the UAV orientation and not just the (x, y, z) position.

Future Work

The proposed algorithm uses a greedy strategy to find a nearby optimal position. Therefore, the algorithm is locally optimal. To compare different path planning algorithms, a cost function must be developed, which has non dependency on the map abstraction.

We are working on substituting the greedy politic used to compute the path as well as the bio-inspired algorithm by a reinforcement learning algorithm so the system can learn policies of navigation instead of computing paths.

Furthermore, we are designing an intelligent low-level control algorithm that considers the dynamical model of the UAV to follow the planned path.

Author Contributions: Conceptualization, C.V. and J.H.-B.; methodology, C.V. and A.A.G.; software, A.A.G.; validation, G.L.-G. and J.G.-A.; writing—original draft preparation, J.G.-A.; writing—review and editing, G.L.-G.; visualization, J.H.-B.; supervision, N.A.-D.; project administration, C.V. and N.A.-D. All authors have read and agreed to the published version of the manuscript.

Funding: This research was funded by CONACYT México grants numbers CB256769, CB258068, and PN-4107.

Institutional Review Board Statement: Not applicable.

Informed Consent Statement: Not applicable.

Data Availability Statement: No applicable.

Conflicts of Interest: The authors declare no conflict of interest. The founders had no role in the design of the study; in the collection, analyses, or interpretation of data; in the writing of the manuscript, or in the decision to publish the results.

References

1. Zhou, X.; Gao, F.; Fang, X.; Lan, Z. Improved Bat Algorithm for UAV Path Planning in Three-Dimensional Space. *IEEE Access* **2021**, *9*, 20100–20116. [CrossRef]
2. Bolourian, N.; Hammad, A. LiDAR-equipped UAV path planning considering potential locations of defects for bridge inspection. *Autom. Constr.* **2020**, *117*, 103250. [CrossRef]
3. Roberge, V.; Tarbouchi, M.; Labonté, G. Comparison of parallel genetic algorithm and particle swarm optimization for real-time UAV path planning. *IEEE Trans. Ind. Inform.* **2012**, *9*, 132–141. [CrossRef]
4. Fan, M.; Akhter, Y. A Time-Varying Adaptive Inertia Weight based Modified PSO Algorithm for UAV Path Planning. In Proceedings of the 2021 2nd International Conference on Robotics, Electrical and Signal Processing Techniques (ICREST), Dhaka, Bangladesh, 5–7 January 2021; pp. 573–576.
5. Shao, S.; Peng, Y.; He, C.; Du, Y. Efficient path planning for UAV formation via comprehensively improved particle swarm optimization. *ISA Trans.* **2020**, *97*, 415–430. [CrossRef]
6. Ever, Y.K. Using simplified swarm optimization on path planning for intelligent mobile robot. *Procedia Comput. Sci.* **2017**, *120*, 83–9 . [CrossRef]
7. Arana-Daniel, N.; Gallegos, A.A.; López-Franco, C.; Alanis, A.Y. Smooth global and local path planning for mobile robot using particle swarm optimization, radial basis functions, splines and Bézier curves. In Proceedings of the 2014 IEEE Congress on Evolutionary Computation (CEC), Beijing, China, 6–11 July 2014; pp. 175–182.
8. Arana-Daniel, N.; Gallegos, A.A.; López-Franco, C.; Alanis, A.Y. Smooth path planning for mobile robot using particle swarm optimization and radial basis functions. In Proceedings of the International Conference on Genetic and Evolutionary Methods (GEM), Las Vegas, NV, USA, 16–19 July 2012; p. 1.

9. Hernandez-Barragan, J. Mobile Robot Path Planning based on Conformal Geometric Algebra and Teaching-Learning Based Optimization. *IFAC-PapersOnLine* **2018**, *51*, 338–343. [CrossRef]
10. Villaseñor, C.; Arana-Daniel, N.; Alanis, A.Y.; Lopez-Franco, C.; Gomez-Avila, J. Multiellipsoidal Mapping Algorithm. *Appl. Sci.* **2018**, *8*, 1239. [CrossRef]
11. Thrun, S. Robotic Mapping: A Survey. In *Exploring Artificial Intelligence in the New Millennium*; Morgan Kaufmann Publishers Inc.: San Francisco, CA, USA, 2003; pp. 1–35.
12. Collins, T.; Collins, J.; Ryan, D. Occupancy grid mapping: An empirical evaluation. In Proceedings of the 2007 Mediterranean Conference on Control & Automation, Athens, Greece, 27–29 June 2007; pp. 1–6.
13. O'Meadhra, C.; Tabib, W.; Michael, N. Variable resolution occupancy mapping using gaussian mixture models. *IEEE Robot. Autom. Lett.* **2018**, *4*, 2015–2022. [CrossRef]
14. Meyer-Delius, D.; Beinhofer, M.; Burgard, W. Occupancy grid models for robot mapping in changing environments. In Proceedings of the Twenty-Sixth AAAI Conference on Artificial Intelligence, Toronto, ON, Canada, 22–26 July 2012.
15. Thrun, S.; Burgard, W.; Chakrabarti, D.; Emery, R.; Liu, Y.; Martin, C. A real-time algorithm for acquiring multi-planar volumetric models with mobile robots. In *Robotics Research*; Springer: Berlin/Heidelberg, Germany, 2003; pp. 21–35.
16. Sola, J. Simulataneous Localization and Mapping with the Extended Kalman Filter. Avery Quick Guide with MATLAB Code. 2013. Available online: https://www.iri.upc.edu/people/jsola/JoanSola/objectes/curs_SLAM/SLAM2D/SLAM%20course.pdf (accessed on 25 August 2021).
17. Hornung, A.; Wurm, K.M.; Bennewitz, M.; Stachniss, C.; Burgard, W. OctoMap: An efficient probabilistic 3D mapping framework based on octrees. *Auton. Robot.* **2013**, *34*, 189. [CrossRef]
18. Wurm, K.M.; Hornung, A.; Bennewitz, M.; Stachniss, C.; Burgard, W. OctoMap: A probabilistic, flexible, and compact 3D map representation for robotic systems. In Proceedings of the ICRA 2010 Workshop on Best Practice in 3D Perception and Modeling for Mobile Manipulation, Anchorage, AK, USA, 7 May 2010; Volume 2.
19. Munoz, D.; Bagnell, J.A.; Vandapel, N.; Hebert, M. Contextual classification with functional max-margin markov networks. In Proceedings of the 2009 IEEE Conference on Computer Vision and Pattern Recognition, Miami, FL, USA, 20–25 June 2009; pp. 975–982.
20. Kumar, M.S.; Gayathri, G. A short survey on teaching learning based optimization. In *Emerging ICT for Bridging the Future-Proceedings of the 49th Annual Convention of the Computer Society of India CSI Volume 2*; Springer: Berlin/Heidelberg, Germany, 2015; pp. 173–182.
21. Rao, R.; Savsani, V.; Vakharia, D. Teaching–learning-based optimization: A novel method for constrained mechanical design optimization problems. *Comput.-Aided Des.* **2011**, *43*, 303–315. [CrossRef]
22. Mummareddy, P.K.; Satapaty, S.C. An hybrid approach for data clustering using K-means and teaching learning based optimization. In *Emerging ICT for Bridging the Future-Proceedings of the 49th Annual Convention of the Computer Society of India CSI Volume 2*; Springer: Berlin/Heidelberg, Germany, 2015; pp. 165–171.
23. Das, A.; Lewis, F.; Subbarao, K. Backstepping approach for controlling a quadrotor using lagrange form dynamics. *J. Intell. Robot. Syst.* **2009**, *56*, 127–151. [CrossRef]
24. Antonio-Toledo, M.E.; Sanchez, E.N.; Alanis, A.Y.; Flórez, J.; Perez-Cisneros, M.A. Real-time integral backstepping with sliding mode control for a quadrotor UAV. *IFAC-PapersOnLine* **2018**, *51*, 549–554. [CrossRef]
25. Lee, K.U.; Choi, Y.H.; Park, J.B. Inverse optimal design for position control of a quadrotor. *Appl. Sci.* **2017**, *7*, 907. [CrossRef]
26. Noreen, I.; Khan, A.; Habib, Z. Optimal path planning using RRT* based approaches: A survey and future directions. *Int. J. Adv. Comput. Sci. Appl.* **2016**, *7*, 97–107. [CrossRef]
27. Price, K.V. Differential evolution. In *Handbook of Optimization*; Springer: Berlin/Heidelberg, Germany, 2013; pp. 187–214.
28. Poli, R.; Kennedy, J.; Blackwell, T. Particle swarm optimization. *Swarm Intell.* **2007**, *1*, 33–57. [CrossRef]
29. Yang, X.S.; He, X. Firefly algorithm: Recent advances and applications. *Int. J. Swarm Intell.* **2013**, *1*, 36–50. [CrossRef]

Article

Finger-Gesture Recognition for Visible Light Communication Systems Using Machine Learning

Julian Webber [1,*], Abolfazl Mehbodniya [2], Rui Teng [3], Ahmed Arafa [2] and Ahmed Alwakeel [2]

[1] Graduate School of Engineering Science, Osaka University, Toyonaka 560-8531, Japan
[2] Department of Electronics and Communication Engineering, Kuwait College of Science and Technology, 7th Ring Road, Doha 20185145, Kuwait; a.niya@kcst.edu.kw (A.M.); a.arafa@kcst.edu.kw (A.A.); a.alwakeel@kcst.edu.kw (A.A.)
[3] Organization for Research Initiatives and Development, Doshisha University, Kyoto 610-0394, Japan; dr.r.teng@ieee.org
* Correspondence: webber@ee.es.osaka-u.ac.jp

Abstract: Gesture recognition (GR) has many applications for human-computer interaction (HCI) in the healthcare, home, and business arenas. However, the common techniques to realize gesture recognition using video processing are computationally intensive and expensive. In this work, we propose to task existing visible light communications (VLC) systems with gesture recognition. Different finger movements are identified by training on the light transitions between fingers using the long short-term memory (LSTM) neural network. This paper describes the design and implementation of the gesture recognition technique for a practical VLC system operating over a distance of 48 cm. The platform uses a single low-cost light-emitting diode (LED) and photo-diode sensor at the receiver side. The system recognizes gestures from interruptions in the direct light transmission, and is therefore suitable for high-speed communication. Gesture recognition accuracies were conducted for five gestures, and results demonstrate that the proposed system is able to accurately identify the gestures in up to 88% of cases.

Keywords: visible light communications (VLC); gesture recognition (GR); human-computer interaction (HCI); human activity recognition (HAR); machine learning (ML); neural network; long short-term memory (LSTM); photo-diode (PD)

Citation: Webber, J.; Mehbodniya, A.; Teng, R.; Arafa, A.; Alwakeel, A. Finger-Gesture Recognition for Visible Light Communication Systems Using Machine Learning. *Appl. Sci.* **2021**, *11*, 11582. https://doi.org/10.3390/app112411582

Academic Editor: Grzegorz Dudek

Received: 2 November 2021
Accepted: 2 December 2021
Published: 7 December 2021

Publisher's Note: MDPI stays neutral with regard to jurisdictional claims in published maps and institutional affiliations.

Copyright: © 2021 by the authors. Licensee MDPI, Basel, Switzerland. This article is an open access article distributed under the terms and conditions of the Creative Commons Attribution (CC BY) license (https://creativecommons.org/licenses/by/4.0/).

1. Introduction

Gesture recognition (GR) systems can greatly assist the elderly or infirm as well as persons unable to control equipment through speech. Meanwhile the growth of Internet of Things (IoT) propelled the need for improved human-computer interaction (HCI) to enable control of devices inthe areas of work, play, health, communication, and education. For real-world application, a GR system should require modest computing resources and be implementable with low-cost. While proprietary GR systems are emerging, they tend to be expensive, single-task oriented, and application-specific.

Gesture recognition systems can be classified into contact or contactless types. The most common contact type is the accelerometer or inertial sensor, while the contactless types include (i) ultrasound-, (ii) mm-wave radar-, (iii) video camera-, and (iv) photo-diode (PD)-based units. An accelerometer consists of multiple motion sensors in order to detect movement in the three cardinal directions. A wrist-strapped accelerometer is a low-cost GR solution in which the sensor directly tracks the hand gesture. Although research benefited from analysis of accelerometer data collected by smartphones, such systems are still impractical. Short-range frequency-modulated continuous wave (FMCW) radar was recently used in movement and gesture detection, as well as monitoring vital-signs (breathing and heart rates), based on measuring the Doppler shifts. Similarly, GR can also be achieved by measuring the Doppler from ultrasonic waves reflected by limb movement. However, these approaches are prone to clutter between the Tx and Rx reducing the resolution, and ultrasounds can also cause stress to pets and infants who can hear the low-frequency waves. Unlike visible light, some radio-frequency systems are precluded from use in hospitals, aircraft, or mines due to electromagnetic compatibility issues. One issue with video-based GR is that the foreground limb image needs to be distinguished from nearby clutter and background objects. As deep-learning algorithms became more powerful, the ability to delineate these images increased. However, deep learning often necessitates a high degree of storage and processing power, such as from a desktop computer. Although recent development kits including the Nvidia Jetson and Microsoft Kinect [1] greatly facilitated AI-based image processing, the hardware and computational costs can still be prohibitive. Another disadvantage of using video cameras for GR is due to privacy concerns and laws. Meanwhile, interest in photo-diode (PD)-based GR will increase with the emerging visible light communication (VLC) systems, which can be made with light emitting diodes (LEDs) at a fraction of the cost.

Gesture recognition is a related field of human activity recognition (HAR), and recent developments are briefly described here. Two common methods for HAR are those based on video scene extraction and that of indirect sensing using wireless signals. Indirect sensing involves the analysis of the received signal strength signature from Wi-Fi signals that are blocked or reflected by human movement. Researchers demonstrated accuracies above 90% using support vector machines (SVM) machine learning (ML) [2–4]. However, it is currently very difficult to classify the subtle finger gestures using the wireless signals in a practical setting with a wall-mounted access-point, and it becomes harder with several people in the room. Physical activity recognition system using wrist-band based sensors were designed for wheelchair-bound patients with spinal cord injuries [5]. Smart healthcare systems are increasingly employing neural networks to categorize and automate functions [6]. Estimation of the number of people in a room was made through an analysis of reflection and blocking of visible light [7]. The long short-term memory (LSTM) algorithm is a type of recurrent neural network that can efficiently learn time-series sequences that are increasingly used in ML-based HAR systems, such as [8], for wearable activity recognition [9] and sign language translation [10].

Meanwhile, visible light communication systems exploit the existing lighting infrastructure to provide high-speed and secure data communication [11–13] and are expected to become commonplace in homes and office following the release of the IEEE 802.11bb [14] Standardization currently scheduled for 2022. VLC leverages the huge bandwidth available in the nonionizing visible electromagnetic spectrum [15]. Light is a suitable communication medium in medical environments [16–18] where there are strict electromagnetic compatibility conformance standards. VLC-based health monitoring [19] and notification systems were developed for the blind [20]. VLC systems can be built with very low-cost [21] using standard light emitting diodes (LEDs) and photodiodes (PDs), such as those commonly used in DVD players. High-speed VLC systems direct the transmission of focused light between the transmitter (Tx) LED and receiver (Rx) PD. On the other hand, currently, most GR systems for visible light operate on reflected light captured by multiple PDs. A non-ML-based motion detection system using VL comprising multiple PDs was proposed in [22]. The work focused on communications performance, and there were no gesture classification accuracy results.

Gesture patterns are statistically repeatable and can be learned by repeated sampling using ML. A summary of recent hand GR research using ML is tabulated in Table 1. Infrared (IR) systems are less affected by ambient light and can generally achieve higher classification accuracies. However, most IR systems do not achieve the high visible light (VL) data-rates and at the same price-point. Using the decision-trees algorithm, authors reported a 98% classification accuracy using IR proximity sensors [23]. Feature extraction using SVM achieved 95% accuracy on data collected from an accelerometer [24]. Back-propagation was used to track hand trajectories using an inertial sensor with 89% accuracy [25]. A smart electronic-skin comprising an array of detectors and LSTM processing was proposed [26].

By tracking the shape of shadows cast through hand-blocking using a 32-sensor array, researchers achieved 96% accuracy [27]. Although the system achieved good performance, the large 6 × 6 ft array is rather impractical, and additionally, not aimed at communications. Classification performance is generally improved by deploying multiple PDs on the ceiling and floor. As the cost and computational complexity generally scale with the number of detection chains, these should be kept to a minimum. K-nearest neighbors (KNN) is a low-complexity, nonparametric algorithm that can distinguish gesture classes based on the Euclidean distances between samples. An accuracy of 48% was achieved using KNN with a single PD and increased to 83% by employing two PDs [28]. Classification of reflected IR waves was achieved using a hybrid KNN and SVM [29]. The researchers used the THORLABS PDA100 PD module (currently cost about $430) to capture a wide range of wavelengths with design ease. When the separation was 20 cm, the average denoised accuracy was 96% for IR and 85% for VL. The performance decreased with increasing Tx-Rx distance due to the lower received light intensity. When the separation increased to 35 cm, the performance decreased to 91% for IR and 73% for VL. The use of reflected light generally requires additional postprocessing to remove artifacts generated by multipath reflections from surrounding clutter and is sensitive to thresholding. This makes building a practical low-cost system challenging, and these systems offer lower data rates. The FingerLight system employs 8 spatially separated PDs and a recurrent neural network to learn the gestures from measured light intensities. When a hand is carefully positioned in front of the sensor array, a 99% classification accuracy was reported possible [30]. Short-range millimeter wave radar has provided a 98% classification accuracy for hand gesture recognition using LSTM [31]. Image processing-based techniques generally exhibit the highest performance but require very high computing resources, and hence, are less suitable for low-cost, portable-use cases. GR using captured video is often implemented using CNNs, and researchers reported a 97% classification accuracy using this technique [32]. Recurrent neural networks are able to extract auto-correlations in sequential data and were particularly successful with speech- and hand-writing recognition. The LSTM recurrent network contains gates that allow it to operate on relatively long time sequences. Multimodal gesture recognition using 3D convolution and convolutional LSTM was described in [33]. Tracking of hand-joint movements using the unscented Kalman filter [34] with LSTM and dynamic probabilities [35] was reported.

Our proposed GR solution is part of a wider VLC-capable system, and therefore the GR capability comes at almost no additional cost. The system learns to associate finger movements with the pattern of light directly impinging on the PD in the absence of obstruction by fingers. This method is unaffected by nearby clutter or by the light-reflecting properties of a subjects skin, which can depend on their age and gender. This enables us to employ a low-cost PD (about $8 in small volumes) and the approach is compatible with high-speed VLC systems targeted for communications. We employ the LSTM algorithm for the gesture classification which requires considerably lower complexity than than that of the CNN algorithm for video processing. Despite the modest complexity, the gesture recognition performs well (88%) and can be used within a communications-based VLC system.

Our contributions can be summarized as follows:

1. Provided a review of contemporary gesture recognition systems.
2. Developed a practical GR methodology that can be integrated with a VLC system. The technique uses common off-the-shelf components with full part numbers provided.
3. Developed a system using a single PD that receives direct light from the transmitting LED.
4. Demonstrated an efficient LSTM-based GR system with limited computational complexity.
5. Achieved high classification accuracy under natural settings: gestures made at natural speed and visible light.
6. Confirmed the system performance at different sampling rates and complexities.

In this paper, we focus on describing the operation of the GR module, which uses the same components as the VLC system for compatibility. The scope of this paper is limited to the gesture recognition system, and a full description of the communication operation will be described separately. The context switching between the sensing and communications systems is an implementation issue and outside the scope of this paper. However, we considered a method based on halting the communications as soon as the hand is inserted between the Tx and Rx. This would be detected by a significant dip in the received signal power. Communications would then resume a short period after the signal blocking finishes.

The organization of this paper is as follows. Section 2 describes the VLC channel model, and Section 3 discusses the activity recognition concept and our proposed solutions for a VLC system. Section 4 details the system implementation and experiment setup, while Section 5 describes the performance results. Discussions on areas for future work and a conclusion is drawn in Sections 6 and 7, respectively.

Table 1. Gesture recognition systems using machine learning.

Reference	Processing	Sensor	Accuracy (%)	VLC
[23]	Decision-trees	IR proximity	98	No
[24]	SVM	Accelerometer	95	No
[25]	BP-NN	Inertial sensor	89	No
[26]	LSTM	5 × 7 sensor array	85	No
[27]	PCA	32 PDs	96	No
[28]	KNN	3 × 3 PD array	48 (single PD)	No
[29]	KNN/SVM	IR/VL (PDA100A)	73(VL@35 cm)	No
[30]	RNN	8 PDs	99 (10 cm)	No
[31]	LSTM	FMCW radar	98	No
[32]	CNN	RGB Camera	97	No
[33]	LSTM	RGB/depth Camera	98	No
[34]	LSTM	RGB Camera (dataset)	85	No
[35]	DP-LSTM	RGB Camera	83	No
This work	LSTM	Single PD (low-cost)	88	Yes

2. VLC Channel Model

Assume a channel model between a Tx (LED) and an Rx (PD), and consider only the line-of-sight (LOS) path. The channel impulse response of this LOS component is deterministic and given by Equation (1) [36].

$$h^{LOS}(t) = I(\phi)\frac{g(\psi)A_{PD}}{d^2}\delta(t - d/c), \tag{1}$$

where A_{PD} is the photo-diode surface area, ϕ is the angle from the Tx to Rx, ψ is is the angle of incidence with respect to the axis normal to the receiver surface, d is distance between Tx and Rx, c is the speed of light, $g(\psi)$ is the Rx optical gain function, and $I(\phi)$ is the luminous intensity.

At the Rx, the received optical power can be expressed as (2).

$$P_R = H(0)P_E, \tag{2}$$

where $H(0)$ is the channel DC gain, and P_E is the emitted optical intensity.

It is common to model the emitted signal by a generalized Lambertian pattern, and the DC channel gain can be expressed as [37].

$$H(0) = \frac{(m+1)A_{PD}}{2\pi d^2}\cos^m(\phi)T_s(\psi)g(\psi)\cos(\psi), \tag{3}$$

for $0 \leq \psi \leq \Psi_c$ where Lambertian order is denoted by (4)

$$m = \frac{-\ln(2)}{\ln(\cos(\Phi_{1/2}))}, \tag{4}$$

where $\Phi_{1/2}$ is the semiangle at half-illuminance of the Tx. $T_s(\psi)$ is the optical filter gain, Ψ_c is the Rx field of view (FOV) semi-angle.

The illuminance at a point on the receiving plane is described by $I(\psi)\cos(\psi)/d^2$ [38]. The total received power with lens is plotted in Figure 1. This figure shows that the power is greatest directly below the LED and falls off greatest at the corners. The Rx power is sufficiently high in all directions within 2 m of the center, and therefore photo-detectors receive sufficient illuminance in a typical small room or office setting.

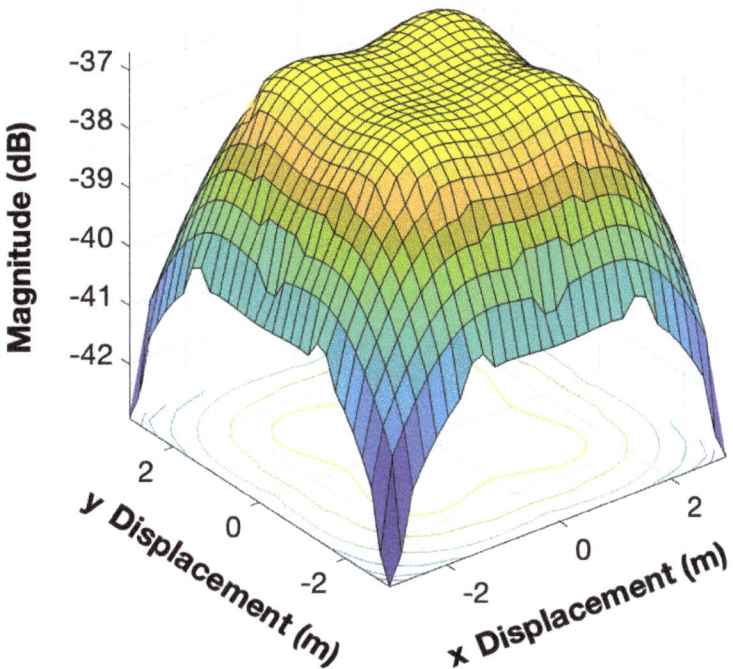

Figure 1. Lambertian simulation for total Rx power for $\phi = 30°, \psi = 30°$ FOV.

3. Gesture Recognition System with LSTM Network

A typical HAR system comprises data acquisition, segmentation, feature extraction, and classification stages. The categorization is based on an analysis of the pattern activity sensed on each PD. Through training, the system learns to associate the sequences with each activity.

The concept of the hand movement recognition system is shown in Figure 2. The identification activity takes place between the LED and PD. Unobstructed light from the LED is incident on the photo-diode sensor and, as an object moves in between the two, light can become blocked. The task is to associate the sequence of incident light with the particular gesture. Typically, a hand may move at about 1 m/s or 1000 mm/s. The distance between fingers is up to about 10 mm, and therefore periods of activity and inactivity will typically last for about 10 ms. To reliably capture these movements the symbol sensing slot-time should be at least 0.1 ms. The slot time depends on the underlying use of the VLC system and is a trade-off between VLC data rate requirements, prediction accuracy, and computational complexity. The signaling rate is typically easily satisfied by modern VLC systems that operate above 1 Mbit/s.

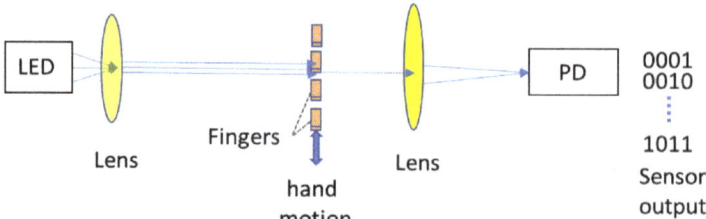

Figure 2. Concept of finger movement recognition system based on received patterns of light on a photo-diode sensor.

LSTM is a type of recurrent network that learns patterns embedded in time-series data [39] and has complexity proportional to the number of time-steps. The network is applied here to predict the finger gesture on a per time-step basis. The network comprises a sequence layer for handling the series input data, an LSTM layer for computing the learning, a fully-connected layer, a softmax layer, and finally, a classification layer. The size of the fully connected layer determines how well the network can learn the dependencies but care is required to avoid problems associated with over-fitting. The LSTM block diagram is shown in Figure 3 in which x_t represents the input data. The hidden-state and cell-states at time t are termed $\mathbf{h}_t$ and $\mathbf{c}_t$, respectively. The current state and the next sequence data samples will determine the output and updated cell state. The cell state is given by Equation (5)

$$\mathbf{c}_t = f_t \odot \mathbf{c}_{t-1} + i_t \odot g_t \qquad (5)$$

The hidden-state is given by Equation (6)

$$\mathbf{h}_t = o_t \odot \sigma_c(\mathbf{c}_t), \qquad (6)$$

where σ_c represents the state activation function. Control gates allow data to be forgotten or remembered at each iteration.

The forget, cell-candidate, input, and output-states at time step t are given by Equations (7)–(10) respectively:

$$f_t = \sigma_c(W_f \mathbf{x}_t + R_f \mathbf{h}_{t-1} + b_f), \qquad (7)$$
$$g_t = \sigma_c(W_g \mathbf{x}_t + R_g \mathbf{h}_{t-1} + b_g), \qquad (8)$$
$$i_t = \sigma_c(W_i \mathbf{x}_t + R_i \mathbf{h}_{t-1} + b_i), \qquad (9)$$
$$o_t = \sigma_c(W_o \mathbf{x}_t + R_o \mathbf{h}_{t-1} + b_o), \qquad (10)$$

where W_f, W_g, W_i, W_o represent the forget, cell-candidate, input, and output weights. R_f, R_g, R_i, and R_o are the forget, cell-candidate, input, and output recurrent weights. b_f, b_g, b_i, and b_o are the forget, cell-candidate, input, and output biases.

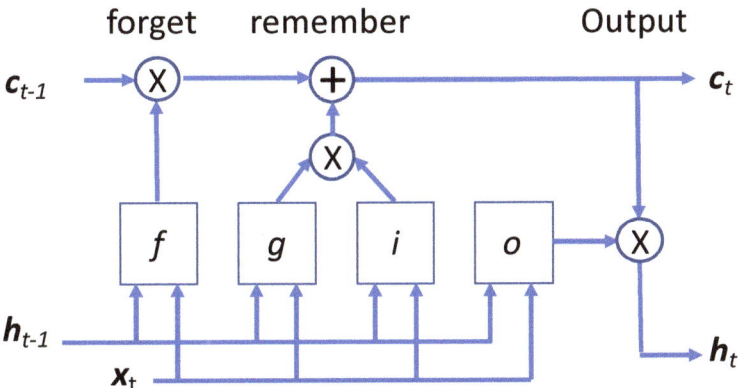

Figure 3. LSTM algorithm unit structure.

4. System Implementation

4.1. Design Approach

Two design approaches were considered for the gesture sensing operation. Approach (i): the mark-space waveform generated by all fingers is encoded. As a finger cuts the light beam, it results in a space period where the received light intensity on the PD sensor is low. In the period where light can pass between the fingers, the received intensity is high. Approach (ii): the PD output is summed over the duration of the whole gesture. The total light incident on the PD from the first to last finger cutting the light beam is recorded. The first approach was selected after an initial study showed it was more reliable, and in particular, is less dependent on the hand-speed. A minimum and maximum threshold is set, and the on-off signal is passed to the LSTM algorithm.

4.2. VLC Transceiver

The VLC system is implemented with real-time transmission and reception of symbols using an arbitrary waveform generator (AWG) and digital storage oscilloscope (DSO) as depicted in Figure 4. VLC data modulation/demodulation and activity recognition tasks are computed off-line using a personal computer with Matlab software.

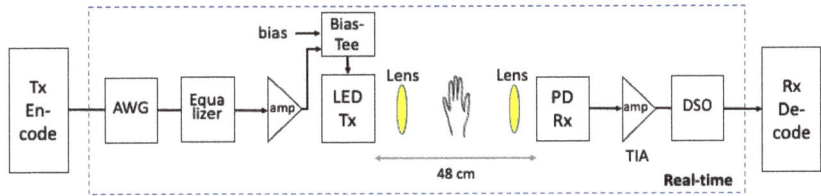

Figure 4. VLC for HAR system block diagram.

The Tx signal was generated with amplitude 1.80 V at 100 kHz in real-time using an arbitrary waveform generator Tektronix AWG 710B (max. 2.1 GHz bandwidth, 4.2 Gsa/s). An amplitude equalizer was inserted to counteract the low-pass frequency response of the LED. The amplitude equalizer provides about 7 dB loss at DC and the normalized gain rises to unity in the high-pass region at around 100 MHz. A Mini-Circuits ZHL-500 (0.1 MHz to 500 MHz) 17-dB gain-block is employed as a preamplifier to increase the small signal-level. The amplified data signal is added to a LED bias voltage of 4.2 v using a Mini-Circuits Bias-T ZFBT-4R2GW-FT+ (0.1–6000 MHz bandwidth) and the output connected to a Luxeon Rebel LED via a standard SMA connector. The LED was selected as it is capable of supporting a data-rate in the order of 100 Mbit/s for communications. However, many other LEDs can also be used for the purpose of gesture recognition. The bias-T and amplifier had minimum operating frequency around 50 kHz. The bias voltage is adjusted to maximize the amplifier output power but backed off to avoid distortion. The amplifier, bias-T and LED were mounted onto a movable micro-stage platform to facilitate the alignment of the Tx.

To increase the communication distance, a focusing-lens of diameter 40 mm was placed at both the Tx and Rx sides with a separation of 30 cm as shown in Figure 5. The focusing lens produces a narrow beam with optimum focus at the region where the hand is placed which is at the half-distance between Tx LED and RX PD. The required distance can be easily adjusted by increasing or decreasing the lens focal-range. In the current set-up if the hand is positioned away from the center-point then the signal-to-noise ratio (SNR) is reduced and therefore estimation accuracy will be degraded. A focusing lens is also an integral and necessary component in all VLC systems and so is not an additional cost. A consumer VLC system may likely employ directional Tx/Rx or an adaptive lens mechanism.

A standard PD (Hamamatsu S10784 commonly used in DVD laser-discs) was employed at the receiver. The PD output was amplified by an OPA 2356 based low-noise amplifier (LNA) circuit that has a BW of about 200 MHz and was used here as a trans-impedance amplifier (TIA). The Rx waveform is detected by a PD and amplified by the LNA. LEDs generate incoherent light, which can be detected using simple direct or envelope detection circuitry. The Rx DSO was set at 2 Msa/s with a total 3.2 Mpoints stored after peak sampling.

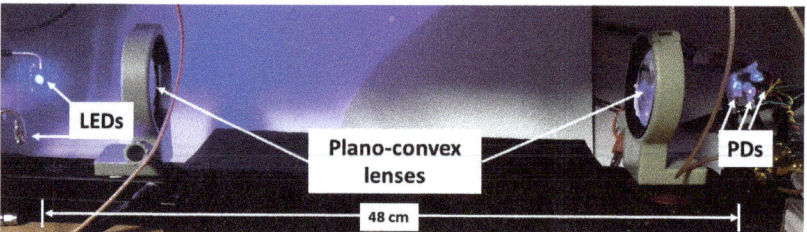

Figure 5. Photograph of optical component section.

4.3. Gesture Waveform Capture

As a proof of concept, the system was trained with five gestures with an increasing number of fingers as follows:

- Reference Rx signal (absence of movement),
- pointing up-down with 1 finger,
- pointing up-down with 2 fingers,
- pointing up-down with 3 fingers, and
- pointing up-down with 4 fingers.

The hand was moved up and down over a period of two seconds at a steady-rate corresponding to a natural hand gesture. As the separation between each finger is only about 3–5 mm, the sampling rate needs to be sufficiently high to capture the correspondingly short duration of light. The Rx signal is first down-sampled as the sampling rate is higher than the modulated light signal. The modulation is removed by finding the signal maxima and the resultant signal corresponding to 1–4 fingers present is shown in Figure 6 (top) to (bottom). The small peaks at the start of each cycle are due to the combined filtering response of the analogue and sample and hold circuitry in the digital storage oscilloscope. The response quickly decays and does not affect the operation of the system. The blocking of light by each finger results in low amplitudes and can be seen in each capture. In part, the accuracy can decrease as the number of fingers increase due to the reduced clarity of the raw signal. This reduction is partly offset however as classification improves when a signal has more unique features.

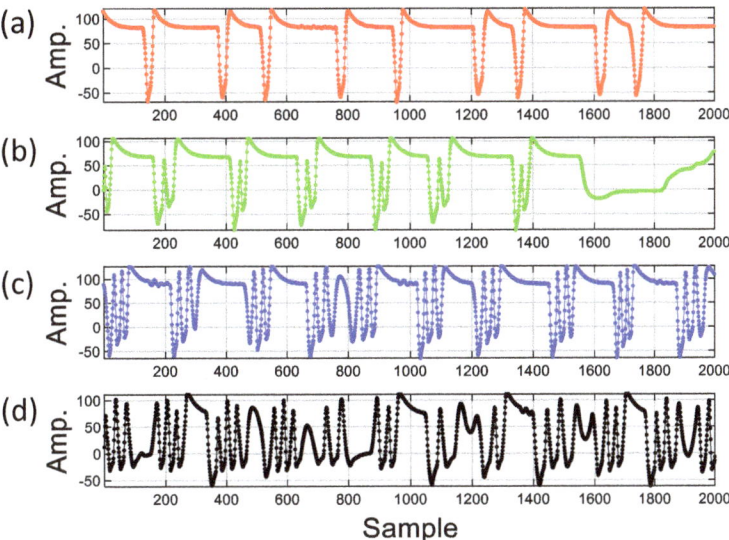

Figure 6. Received signal captured on VLC photodiode corresponding to (from top): (**a**) 1 finger; (**b**) 2 fingers; (**c**) 3 fingers; and (**d**) 4 fingers gestures.

4.4. Process Flow

There are three processing stages: signal-conditioning, training, and classification. Signal conditioning: The waveform sampled by the photo-diode undergoes signal conditioning prior to the identification. The signal magnitude is normalized so that the maximum value for each gesture is one. Gesture training: Data are collected for each of the 5 gestures. For each gesture, multiple frames are collected by repeating the movement over a period of two seconds. The data are then randomly split into two sets one for training and one for classification. This needs to be performed once on first use for each user, as they may have different movement styles and speed for the same gesture type. Gesture classification: The gestures are classified by ML. A practical gesture recognition system should be able to operate in real-time. Therefore a trade-off can be met between computational complexity and accuracy. We selected the LSTM algorithm as it offers a good performance to complexity ratio and is suitable for the repetitive sequential waveforms generated by hand gestures.

4.5. Signal Conditioning

The signal for training and categorization should encode the finger gesture and the performance should be relatively unaffected by the level of ambient light. Any reflected light from an object near to the PD should not result in a high amplitude signal that cannot be recognized from the same motion without reflection. Therefore, the signal should be normalized such that all signals have the same amplitude regardless of the ambient light intensity. The normalization scales the signal according to the minimum and peak signal level recorded over the measurement period. As the ambient light changes more slowly than the direct LED light across a measurement frame, this is a simple and efficient step. The recorded gesture features may vary slightly between each motion and also due to environment. Each user also presents their hands at a slightly different angle and moves them at a variable speed, and there will be temporal variations and potentially irregular random reflex movements. The natural light present in the morning will be different to the artificial light in the evening and can vary if it is cloudy or sunny. All PDs exhibit a noise floor, and the TIA has a noise figure which contributes to a lowering of the signal integrity. Signal conditioning is required to manage these effects and to provide a clean representative signal which contains the essential features of each gesture to the ML algorithm. After conditioning, the Rx signal has range $-1/+1$ and is processed by the LSTM algorithm.

4.6. Training and Evaluation

As a proof of concept, data were collected for four different hands. The smallest span (from extended little finger to thumb) was measured as 16.3 cm and the largest hand had a span of 21.4 cm. Data were collected for the four hands on two separate measurement campaigns. During a first session, data were collected for training the neural network algorithm. A second validation session was conducted on the same day for evaluating the performance of the trained neural network. The data were divided equally into training and verification sets; that is, the training to verification ratio was 50% of all data. This figure is common in ML research and some systems use higher amounts of training to achieve high accuracies. Over-fitting can occur if the system is trained with too much data, and conversely, under-fitting if the training ratio is too low. The LSTM algorithm predicts the next sample in a sequence, and hence the most likely gesture classification, subject to the noise, variation, and irregularities present in human movement. The LSTM was trained using the stochastic gradient descent with momentum (SGDM) optimizer. This is a commonly applied solver with accelerated gradients to reduce the solving time [40]. After training, the LSTM was switched to validation mode in which a section from the nontraining set is evaluated. The output of the stochastic gradient solver can be sensitive to the initial random seed used and, therefore, a Monte Carlo type simulation was set-up averaging results over 50 cycles each with a different random seed. The accuracy and loss versus iteration performance for one of the random seed settings is shown in Figure 7.

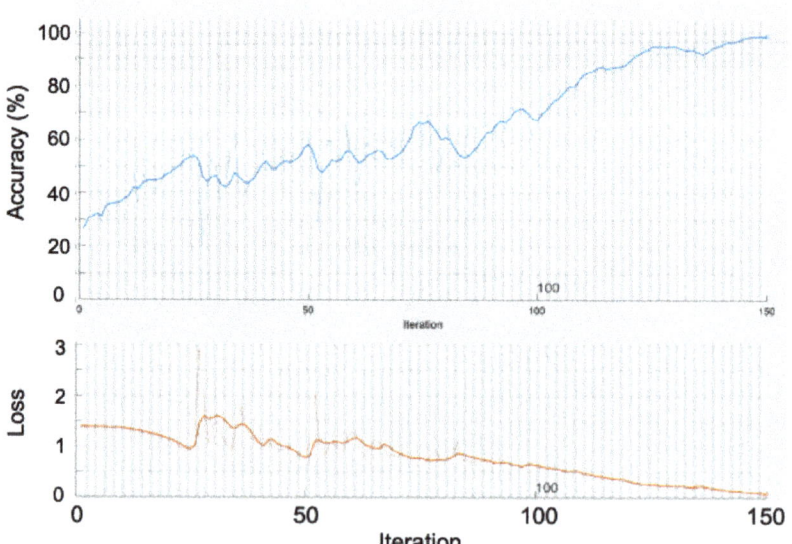

Figure 7. Performance of LSTM algorithm (**top**) Accuracy versus iteration and (**bottom**) Loss versus iteration.

5. Performance Evaluation

The VLC testbed was positioned square to a window with center at a diagonal distance of 4.65 m. The light through the window would enter the room in the direction of the VLC receiver unit. There was no direct sunlight impinging on the Rx in this experiment due to an office-divider positioned between the window and the Tx unit.

A correct classification is determined when the actual and estimated gesture is identical. An average accuracy is computed for all gestures, users and tests per user. An example of predicted versus actual gesture accuracy is shown in Figure 8, for the case of a low number of iterations and sample-rate and demonstrates the frequency and duration of observed errors. There is good agreement between the actual and estimated gesture, and in this example, most errors occurred between the transition from two to three fingers.

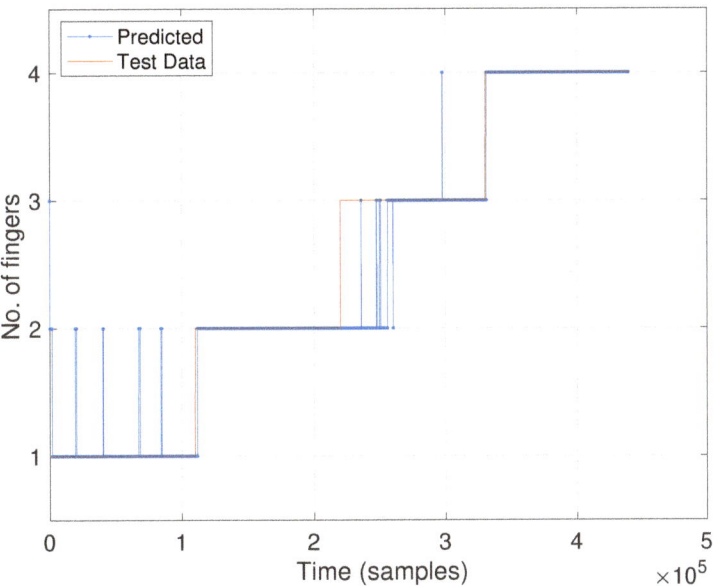

Figure 8. Predicted versus actual number of fingers in gesture.

Classification accuracy versus number of LSTM hidden-units is tabulated in Table 2 and plotted in Figure 9. The performance peaked at 75% accuracy for 50 hidden-units and gradually decreased as the number of units increased. The number of units should not be too large to avoid over-fitting. The performance is limited by the resolution of the input waveforms but can be improved by over-sampling the Rx signal in the presence of sampling and receiver noise. The classification accuracy increased to 88% when the number of samples per symbol increased by a factor of two and is due to the reduction in noise through averaging. We can compare this performance with other GR systems employing visible light using a single PD. Classification accuracies of 85% and 73% were achieved when the Tx-Rx separation was 20 cm and 35 cm, respectively, ref [29] with reflected light. Our accuracy could be further improved by employing a moving-average filter or wavelet denoising. Our performance may also increase by shortening the Tx-Rx separation from 48 cm. However, this is considered a realistic separation for a practical VLC system.

Table 2. Accuracy versus number of LSTM hidden-units.

Hidden-Units	Accuracy (%)
25	72
50	75
75	72
100	71
125	69
150	68
175	70
200	64
225	62

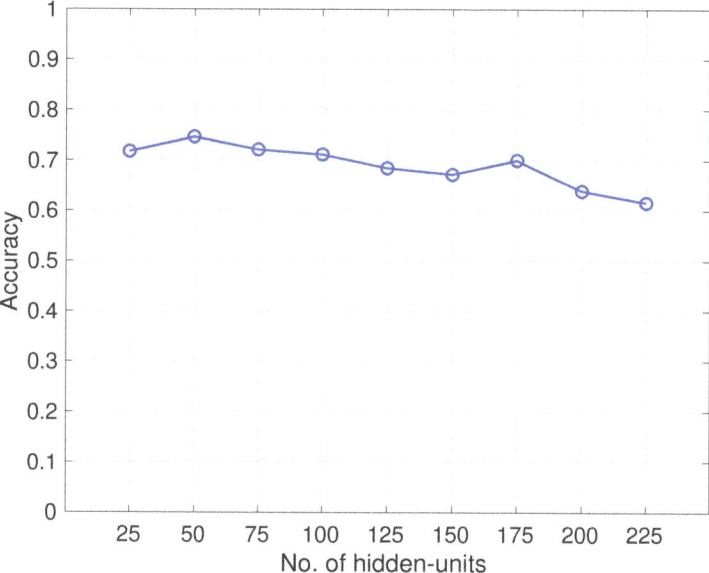

Figure 9. Accuracy versus number of LSTM hidden-units.

The speed of making a hand gesture depends on each individual. If the Rx is tracking, say, a robot arm, one could expect a highly regular pattern with near constant time intervals between blocking. However, there is a relatively large time variation with human gestures. Hand movements, even by the same person, move at a slightly different angle, speed, and position relative to the sensor. Therefore, the performance can depend on the sample-rate, and a system should be capable of increasing this to capture patterns from subjects who make very fast hand movements. Figure 10 shows the normalized performance figure-of-merit versus the sensor sample-rate. The normalized performance figure-of-merit in Figure 10 is computed by dividing the classification accuracy by the processing time and normalized to the highest value. From this result, we could select 0.25 MHz sampling-rate as providing a good performance to processing-time ratio. These results show that there are diminishing performance benefits from over-sampling when considering the added processing complexity. There are a number of VLC parameters that can affect the overall accuracy of the GR system. In particular, performance is sensitive to LED bias-voltage, which should be set high enough to enable communication over the required distance but not so high as to distort the waveform.

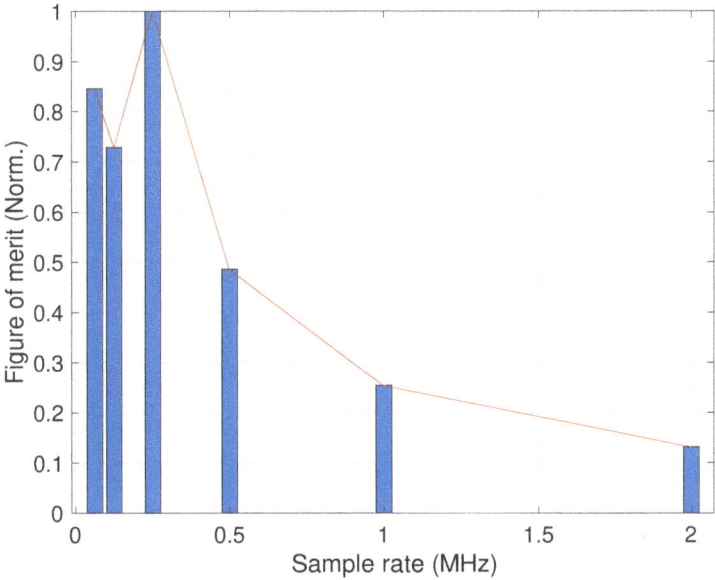

Figure 10. Normalized figure-of-merit versus sensor sample-rate.

6. Discussion

Human limbs generally do not move with a constant velocity, and different users may move their hands at a different speed. Depending on the point of capture, the finger may be accelerating or decelerating. To compensate, the signal can be time-scaled as a function of the finger velocity. For example, a person who moves their hand at half the speed of another person would have their signal sampled at half the rate. The duration of shadows generated by their fingers should then be approximately the same. Hand-speed could be determined by a variety of means offline or during a calibration, such as by mm-wave radar. It would also be possible to identify an individual from their unique finger signature, and this is an interesting area for future work.

6.1. Calibration

Light-intensity distribution may vary at different locations within a room. The natural changes in the ambient light level within limits should be managed by the amplitude normalization step. For optimized performance, a calibration should be made if the system is moved to a new location where the ambient light range may be different. The calibration routine which could quickly cycle through parameters such as Tx LED amplitude, equalizer coefficients, Tx-amp bias, and Rx TIA tuning to find optimized values. Alternatively, a look-up table can supply the coefficients based on the location, time of day, and season. Aging of components and heating may also result in drift, which can be resolved by a relatively in-frequent calibration once a week. The calibration routine could also be executed automatically once the system is first switched on.

6.2. Sensitivity to Hand Movement

Practical VLC systems require lenses to focus beams of light on the small photo-diode. If the hand is placed off-center, the Rx beam will be slightly off-focus and the accuracy may be reduced. This issue can be solved using an automatic lens or by employing multiple spatially separated PDs. An interesting alternative solution would be to employ the neural network to learn and predict gestures in cases where the beam is defocused. A study on the performance as a function of hand-offset position is considered as part of the future work.

6.3. Competing Systems and Cost

Assuming that a VLC infrastructure was established, the additional cost for the GR subsystem would mainly be due to the software development time. The cost of a dedicated gesture system is worth consideration. In our work, we employed relatively expensive and bulky AWG and DSO. The off-line processing could be conducted in real-time using a low-power microprocessor, such as the MSP430 from Texas Instruments, which includes built-in signal converters. One competitor to the optical system is an accelerometer based design that could be positioned on the wrist by a strap or as part of a smartwatch. However, a wrist-based transmitter unit would also be needed for relaying the accelerometer data to a receiving unit for further processing. A VLC-based system is still preferable in a hospital environment or for the elderly who may not own a smartwatch or smartphone.

6.4. Areas for Future Work

The number of recognizable gestures could be increased to include common sign-language ones. The system could be developed for general human activity recognition by extending the distance between LEDs and PD with their placement on the ceiling and/or wall. The duration of each shadow cast could be encoded as a binary sequence, and this could enable a probabilistic neural network to be employed for gesture pattern recognition, applying a similar approach to [41], where binary bits encoded a communications busy-idle state. We will investigate if there is any variability in the performance with different directions of sunlight and placement. However, this should not impact the system design. Finally, an automated VLC system should include an initial detection block which would be intermittently polled to recognize when a finger gesture is deliberately being performed.

7. Conclusions

This work described the design and implementation of a finger-gesture recognition system for visible light communication systems. The system employs a single low-cost LED at the Tx and a single photo-diode at the Rx and operates on the patterns of blocking of direct light by the finger motion. The LSTM algorithm can correctly categorize the finger gestures with an average accuracy of 88%, and the optimized number of hidden units was 50. A good performance-to-complexity state could be achieved by sampling the light at 250 kHz. The system has many applications in human-computer interaction, including health-care, commerce, and in the home. Our further work will focus on increasing the number of gestures and tasking the system with recognizing individuals from their gesture signatures.

Author Contributions: All authors contributed to the paper. Conceptualization & methodology, J.W., A.M. and R.T.; software, J.W.; validation, investigation, formal analysis, all authors; writing—original draft preparation, J.W., A.M. and R.T.; writing—review and editing, all authors; funding acquisition, A.M. All authors have read and agreed to the published version of the manuscript.

Funding: This work was partially supported by the Kuwait Foundation for Advancement of Sciences (KFAS) under Grant PR19-13NH-04.

Institutional Review Board Statement: Not applicable.

Informed Consent Statement: Not applicable.

Data Availability Statement: Not applicable.

Acknowledgments: The authors would like to thank anonymous reviewers for their constructive comments, which helped in improving this manuscript.

Conflicts of Interest: The authors declare that there are no conflict of interest regarding the publication of this paper.

References

1. Wang, C.; Liu, Z.; Chan, S. Superpixel-based hand gesture recognition with Kinect depth camera. *IEEE Trans. Multimed.* **2015**, *17*, 29–39. [CrossRef]
2. Li, W.; Xu, Y.; Tan, B.; Piechocki, R. Passive wireless sensing for unsupervised human activity recognition in healthcare. In Proceedings of the International Wireless Communications and Mobile Computing Conference (IWCMC), Valencia, Spain, 26–30 June 2017; pp. 1528–1533.
3. Bhat, S.; Mehbodniya, A.; Alwakeel, A.; Webber, J.; Al-Begain, K. Human Motion Patterns Recognition based on RSS and Support Vector Machines. In Proceedings of the IEEE Wireless Communications and Networking Conference (WCNC), Seoul, Korea, 25–28 May 2020; pp. 1–6.
4. Bhat, S.; Mehbodniya, A.; Alwakeel, A.; Webber, J.; Al-Begain, K. Human Recognition using Single-Input-Single-Output Channel Model and Support Vector Machines. *Int. J. Adv. Comput. Sci. Appl. (IJACSA)* **2021**, *12*, 811–823. [CrossRef]
5. Alhammad, N.; Al-Dossari, H. Dynamic Segmentation for Physical Activity Recognition Using a Single Wearable Sensor. *Appl. Sci.* **2021**, *11*, 2633. [CrossRef]
6. Mucchi, L.; Jayousi, S.; Caputo, S.; Paoletti, E.; Zoppi, P.; Geli, S.; Dioniso, P. How 6G Technology Can Change the Future Wireless Healthcare. In Proceedings of the IEEE 2nd 6G Wireless Summit (6G SUMMIT), Levi, Finland, 17–20 March 2020; pp. 1–5.
7. Yang, Y.; Hao, J.; Luo, J.; Pan, S.J. Ceilingsee: Device-free occupancy inference through lighting infrastructure based led sensing. In Proceedings of the IEEE International Conference on Pervasive Computing and Communication (PerComs), Kona, HI, USA, 13–17 March 2017; pp. 247–256.
8. Xia, K.; Huang, J.; Wang, H. LSTM-CNN architecture for human activity recognition. *IEEE Access* **2020**, *8*, 56855–56866. [CrossRef]
9. Ordóñez, F.J.; Roggen, D. Deep convolutional and lstm recurrent neural networks for multimodal wearable activity recognition. *Sensors* **2016**, *16*, 115. [CrossRef] [PubMed]
10. Guo, D.; Zhou, W.; Li, H.; Wang, M. Hierarchical lstm for sign language translation. In Proceedings of the AAAI Conference on Artificial Intelligence, New Orleans, LA, USA, 2–7 February 2018; Volume 32.
11. Du, C.; Ma, S.; He, Y.; Lu, S.; Li, H.; Zhang, H.; Li, S. Nonorthogonal Multiple Access for Visible Light Communication IoT Networks. *Hindawi Wirel. Commun. Mob. Comput.* **2020**, *2020*, 5791436. [CrossRef]
12. Kim, B.W. Secrecy Dimming Capacity in Multi-LED PAM-Based Visible Light Communications. *Hindawi Wirel. Commun. Mob. Comput.* **2017**, *2017*, 4094096. [CrossRef]
13. Wang, Z.; Chen, S. A chaos-based encryption scheme for DCT precoded OFDM-based visible light communication systems. *Hindawi J. Electr. Comput. Eng.* **2016**, *2016*, 2326563. [CrossRef]
14. Purwita, A.A.; Haas, H. Studies of Flatness of LiFi Channel for IEEE 802.11 bb. In Proceedings of the IEEE Wireless Communications and Networking Conference (WCNC), Seoul, Korea, 25–28 May 2020; pp. 1–6.
15. Ghassemlooy, Z.; Alves, L.; Zvanovec, S.; Khalighi, M. (Eds.) *Visible Light Communications: Theory and Applications*; CRC Press: Boca Raton, FL, USA, 2017.
16. Ding, W.; Yang, F.; Yang, H.; Wang, J.; Wang, X.; Zhang, X.; Song, J. A hybrid power line and visible light communication system for indoor hospital applications. *Comput. Ind.* **2015**, *68*, 170–178. [CrossRef]
17. An, J.; Chung, W. A novel indoor healthcare with time hopping-based visible light communication. In Proceedings of the IEEE 3rd World Forum on Internet of Things (WF-IoT), Reston, VA, USA, 12–14 December 2016; pp. 19–23.
18. Lim, K.; Lee, H.; Chung, W. Multichannel visible light communication with wavelength division for medical data transmission. *J. Med. Imaging Health Inform.* **2015**, *5*, 1947–1951. [CrossRef]
19. Tan, Y.; Chung, W. Mobile health–monitoring system through visible light communication. *Bio-Med. Mater. Eng.* **2014**, *24*, 3529–3538. [CrossRef] [PubMed]
20. Jerry Chong, J.; Saon, S.; Mahamad, A.; Othman, M.; Rasidi, N.; Setiawan, M. Visible Light Communication-Based Indoor Notification System for Blind People. In *Embracing Industry 4.0*; Springer: Berlin/Heidelberg, Germany, 2020; pp. 93–103.
21. Zhang, C.; Tabor, J.; Zhang, J.; Zhang, X. Extending mobile interaction through near-field visible light sensing. In Proceedings of the ACM International Conference on Mobile Computing and Networking, MobiCom '15, Paris, France, 7–11 September 2015; pp. 345–357.
22. Sewaiwar, A.; Vikramaditya, S.; Chung, Y.-H. Visible light communication based motion detection. *Opt. Express* **2015**, *23*, 18769–18776. [CrossRef] [PubMed]
23. Cheng, H.; Chen, A.M.; Razdan, A.; Buller, E. Contactless gesture recognition system using proximity sensors. In Proceedings of the IEEE International Conference on Consumer Electronics (ICCE), Berlin, Germany, 6–8 September 2011; pp. 149–150.
24. Wu, Y.; Pan, G.; Zhang, D.; Qi, G.; Li, S. Gesture recognition with a 3-d accelerometer. In *Proceedings of the International Conference on Ubiquitous Intelligence and Computing*; Springer: Berlin/Heidelberg, Germany, 2009; pp. 25–38.
25. Wang, Z.; Chen, B.; Wu, J. Effective inertial hand gesture recognition using particle filtering based trajectory matching. *Hindawi Wirel. Commun. Mob. Comput.* **2018**, *1*, 1–9. [CrossRef]
26. Liu, G.; Kong, D.; Hu, S; Yu, Q.; Liu, Z.; Chen, T. Smart electronic skin having gesture recognition function by LSTM neural network. *Appl. Phys. Lett.* **2018**, *113*, 084102. [CrossRef]
27. Venkatnarayan, R.H.; Shahzad, M. Gesture recognition using ambient light. *ACM Interact. Mob. Wearable Ubiquitous Technol.* **2018**, *2*, 1–28. [CrossRef]

28. Kaholokula, M.D.A. Reusing Ambient Light to Recognize Hand Gestures. Undergraduate Thesis, Dartmouth College, Hanover, NH, USA, 2016.
29. Yu, L.; Abuella, H.; Islam, M.; O'Hara, J.; Crick, C.; Ekin, S. Gesture Recognition using Reflected Visible and Infrared Light Wave Signals. *arXiv* **2020**, arXiv:2007.08178.
30. Huang, M.; Duan, H.; Chen, Y.; Yang, Y.; Hao, J.; Chen, L. Demo Abstract: FingerLite: Finger Gesture Recognition Using Ambient Light. In Proceedings of the INFOCOM 2020-IEEE Conference on Computer Communications Workshops (INFOCOM WKSHPS), Toronto, ON, Canada, 6 July 2020; pp. 1268–1269.
31. Choi, J.W.; Ryu, S.J.; Kim, J.H. Short-range radar based real-time hand gesture recognition using LSTM encoder. *IEEE Access* **2019**, *7*, 33610–33618. [CrossRef]
32. Pinto, R.F.; Borges, C.D.; Almeida, A.; Paula, I.C. Static hand gesture recognition based on convolutional neural networks. *Hindawi Wirel. Commun. Mob. Comput.* **2019**, *2019*, 4167890. [CrossRef]
33. Zhu, G.; Zhang, L.; Shen, P.; Song, J. Multimodal gesture recognition using 3-D convolution and convolutional LSTM. *IEEE Access* **2017**, *5*, 4517–4524. [CrossRef]
34. Ma, C.; Wang, A.; Chen, G.; Xu, C. Hand joints-based gesture recognition for noisy dataset using nested interval unscented Kalman filter with LSTM network. *Vis. Comput.* **2018**, *34*, 1053–1063. [CrossRef]
35. Jian, C.; Li, J.; Zhang, M. LSTM-based dynamic probability continuous hand gesture trajectory recognition. *IET Image Process.* **2019**, *13*, 2314–2320. [CrossRef]
36. Barry, J.R. *Wireless Infrared Communications*; Kluwer Academic Publishers: Norwell, MA, USA, 1994.
37. Komine, T.; Nakagawa, M. Fundamental analysis for visible-light communication system using LED lights. *IEEE Trans. Consum. Electron.* **2004**, *50*, 100–107. [CrossRef]
38. Do, T.; Junho, H.; Souhwan, J.; Yoan, S.; Myungsik, Y. Modeling and analysis of the wireless channel formed by LED angle in visible light communication. In Proceedings of the International Conference on Information Networking (ICOIN2012), Bali, Indonesia, 1–3 February 2012; pp. 354–357.
39. Greff, K.; Srivastava, R.; Koutník, J.; Steunebrink, B.; Schmidhuber, J. LSTM: A search space odyssey. *IEEE Trans. Neural Netw. Learn. Syst.* **2016**, *28*, 2222–2232. [CrossRef] [PubMed]
40. Postalcıoğlu, S. Performance analysis of different optimizers for deep learning-based image recognition. *Int. J. Pattern Recognit. Artif. Intell.* **2020**, *34*, 2051003. [CrossRef]
41. Webber, J.; Mehbodniya, A.; Hou, Y.; Yano, K.; Kumagai, T. Study on Idle Slot Availability Prediction for WLAN using a Probabilistic Neural Network. In Proceedings of the IEEE Asia Pacific Conference on Communications (APCC'17), Perth, Australia, 11–13 December 2017.

Article

Comparative Study of Machine Learning Classifiers for Modelling Road Traffic Accidents

Tebogo Bokaba [1,*], Wesley Doorsamy [2] and Babu Sena Paul [2]

[1] Department of Applied Information Systems, University of Johannesburg, Johannesburg 2006, South Africa
[2] Institute for Intelligent Systems, University of Johannesburg, Johannesburg 2006, South Africa; wdoorsamy@uj.ac.za (W.D.); bspaul@uj.ac.za (B.S.P.)
* Correspondence: tbokaba@uj.ac.za

Abstract: Road traffic accidents (RTAs) are a major cause of injuries and fatalities worldwide. In recent years, there has been a growing global interest in analysing RTAs, specifically concerned with analysing and modelling accident data to better understand and assess the causes and effects of accidents. This study analysed the performance of widely used machine learning classifiers using a real-life RTA dataset from Gauteng, South Africa. The study aimed to assess prediction model designs for RTAs to assist transport authorities and policymakers. It considered classifiers such as naïve Bayes, logistic regression, k-nearest neighbour, AdaBoost, support vector machine, random forest, and five missing data methods. These classifiers were evaluated using five evaluation metrics: accuracy, root-mean-square error, precision, recall, and receiver operating characteristic curves. Furthermore, the assessment involved parameter adjustment and incorporated dimensionality reduction techniques. The empirical results and analyses show that the RF classifier, combined with multiple imputations by chained equations, yielded the best performance when compared with the other combinations.

Keywords: machine learning; road traffic accidents; data analysis; missing data; dimensionality reduction

1. Introduction

The rapidly increasing number of road traffic accidents (RTAs) has negatively affected different countries by resulting in a high number of injuries and fatalities. The World Economic Forum [1] estimates that the number of vehicles worldwide is expected to double by 2040, putting more pressure on the transport infrastructure. According to the World Health Organisation (WHO) [2,3], RTAs are likely to be the seventh leading cause of death by 2030. The WHO further stipulated that RTAs cause death to vulnerable road users because more than half (54%) of the individuals killed on the roads are cyclists, motorcyclists, and pedestrians. An RTA can be described as an accident that occurs when at least one road vehicle is involved in an accident which happens on an open public road, and at least one person ends up being killed or injured [4]. The leading recorded causes of RTAs are speeding, driving under the influence of alcohol, and distractions when using mobile phones while driving. In 2015, the WHO reported that RTA deaths affect countries differently: low-income countries had 24.1 deaths per 100,000 of the population; middle-income countries had 18.4 deaths per 100,000; and high-income countries had 9.2 deaths per 100,000 [2]. The figures thus reveal that low- and middle-income countries contribute more than double the number of deaths than high-income countries.

RTAs remain the main source of travelling uncertainty and impose a high cost on the transportation infrastructure [5]. Primary road accidents can result in multiple road accidents, which are referred to as secondary accidents. In some cases, secondary road accidents add to more lives being lost. Primary road accidents result in secondary accidents due to delayed primary accident clearance, poor road surface and light conditions, traffic volume, and travel time. Furthermore, secondary accidents that occur after the initial road accident can escalate traffic congestion, travel delays, and safety issues [3,6,7]. Secondary accidents may account for a lower ratio as compared with initial or primary accidents. However, despite this, they account for risks that are estimated to be six times greater than the initial accident, resulting in multiple traumas, serious and complex injuries, as well as overlapping injuries. The prevention of RTAs has become a priority in transportation management. Initial and secondary accidents can be identified and investigated using different data mining techniques that can help support transport authorities and contribute to reducing the high number of road injuries and fatalities [6,8–11].

Data mining techniques can be globally applied in road safety to improve life-threatening problems on the roads. Applications of data mining techniques in RTAs can help in the modelling and better understanding of RTA data records. These records contain important hidden patterns that RTA stakeholders and decision-makers can use to introduce better safety policies [12,13]. Data mining techniques are available in data science and can be used to achieve numerous outcomes such as classification, prediction, outlier analysis, and clustering analysis. According to [12], data mining techniques are machine learning (ML) processes. ML is described as a method that can be used to make provisions for data analysis, decision making, and data preparation for real-life problems, and that allow self-learning for computers without any complex coding involved [14,15]. Additionally, ref. [16] describes ML as an approach that focuses mainly on improving computer programs' capability of accessing data and using the data to learn for themselves. The learning begins with the data to look for any patterns in the dataset and make future decisions involving societal problems. ML methods are categorised as supervised, unsupervised, and semi-supervised. ML have successfully been implemented in automated stock trading, computer vision, health care, speech recognition, and customer services.

This study investigated widely used supervised ML methods to perform comparative analysis using a real-life RTA dataset to present the best predictive model. The study used data collected from Gauteng province, South Africa. The study aimed to align with the Sustainable Development Goals (SDGs) document regarding road safety to reduce the high number of fatalities and injuries [17,18]. The objectives of the study were as follows:

(1) To employ six traditional ML methods: naïve Bayes (NB), logistic regression (LR), k-nearest neighbour (k-NN), AdaBoost, support vector machine (SVM), and random forest (RF) on a real-life dataset containing primary and secondary RTA features. The main reasons for using these specific ML classifiers are their unique characteristics and their popularity in the literature;

(2) To include dimensionality reduction techniques, principal component analysis (PCA) and linear discriminant analysis (LDA) were utilised to identify the relationship between the RTA variables to improve the performance of the proposed models. The study further implemented various missing data methods such as the mean, median, k-NN, and multiple imputations by chained equations (MICE) to handle missing values in the RTA dataset;

(3) To further use well-established evaluation metrics such as accuracy, root-mean-square error (RMSE), precision, recall, and the area under the receiver operating characteristic (ROC) curve (also referred to as the AUC—the area under the ROC) to evaluate the performance of the classification models.

The remainder of the paper is structured as follows: Section 2, the literature review, discusses classification and then focuses on RTA studies; Section 3 comprises the study's methodology; the study's dimensionality reduction techniques are presented in Section 4; Section 5 presents the experimental results, their discussion and comments on findings relating to the AUC; and Section 6 provides a conclusion to the paper.

2. Literature Review

This section covers the related RTA studies conducted using both primary and secondary accident datasets. To begin with, classification is discussed.

2.1. Classification

In statistics or ML, classification is a supervised learning method that predicts a class of given datasets. In addition, classification modelling can approximate the mapping of a function *(f)* from a given input value *(x)* and its discrete output value *(y)*, as shown in Equation (1) below [19]. According to [20], classification is a process that categorises a given set of data into classes (also referred to as targets). Classification can be executed on both structured and unstructured datasets. The process begins by predicting the target of a given data point. The main idea behind classification is identifying into which of the available classes or targets the data point will fall [21]. The most common areas in which classification is applied include facial expression detection, image and document classification, sentiment analysis, and speech recognition. There are famously four types of classification, namely, binary, multi-label, multi-class, and imbalanced. Multi-class classification is employed in studies in which the variable *(y)* consists of more than two targets or classes.

$$y = f(x), \text{ where } y = \text{class or target output} \qquad (1)$$

2.2. Related Studies

The related studies show an increasing interest in RTAs. This section reviews some prediction models which have incorporated traditional ML methods. The benefits of the various prediction models are taken into consideration.

ML methods have been employed for road accident prediction using primary and secondary road accident datasets. The most considered among these methods are SVM, decision trees (J48 or C4.5), RF, least squares support vector machine (LSSVM) and LR. A study by [6] modelled the occurrence of secondary accidents using LSSVM and back-propagation neural networks (BPNNs); the investigation revealed that BPNNs performed best in terms of the correlation coefficient (CORR) and mean squared error (MSE). A study by [22] presented a comparative analysis of sequential minimal optimisation (SMO), J48, and instance-based learning with k-parameter methods. The study's findings discovered that the SMO algorithm accurately compared with the other methods. Another study [23] predicted traffic accident severity using supervised ML methods such as LR, NB, RF, and AdaBoost. The study considered the freeway crash dataset, with the RF performing best with high accuracy of 75.5%. Ref. [24] investigated road accident analysis and predicted accident severity by considering four supervised methods: k-NN, DT, AdaBoost, and NB. The results of the study revealed that AdaBoost outperformed the other methods. Furthermore, in [25–27], the authors investigated road accidents using real-life data considering methods such as J48, LSSVM, and RF. Other studies used probabilistic reasoning models such as Bayesian networks, or BNs, [28–32], with [28] performing a comparison between BNs and regression models. The study's results showed that BN achieved the best performance. Artificial neural networks (ANNs), BPNNs, and multilayer perceptron (MLP) methods were applied during road accident predictions [31,33–35]. In [33], the authors used ML methods to compare models for incident duration prediction, obtaining promising results. Another study [35] presented road accident detection by comparing the performance of three methods: SVM, RF and ANN. The study showed that RF achieved the best results. Other studies [22,24,30,32] considered k-NN and classification and regression trees (CARTs) to predict road accidents. It was observed from the literature that there are various reasons why a study uses a specific method. One such reason is the data type, which can be categorised into primary and secondary datasets. Studies that designed a predictive model using secondary road accident data were those of [6,29]. A study by [34] considered using primary and secondary RTA datasets. In this study, MLP performed best during the modelling of the traffic risk of secondary incidents.

Another study [36] proposed the importance of performing exploratory data analysis on the road traffic accident dataset. The authors revealed which features affect road accidents and their negative impact during the investigation. A study by [37] presented a method of modelling and characterising traffic flow. The study employed regression and clustering methods, which achieved very promising results. A Bayesian network-based framework was developed for assessing the cost of road traffic accidents [38]. This study managed to identify which features can be incorporated into the framework to assess different negative impacts on road accidents. The framework presented promising results. Lastly, [39] presented a study using adaptive Kalman filtering to predict urban road networks. The study revealed that the proposed model is capable of predicting traffic correctly.

Most ML classifiers are influenced by the size of the dataset and capabilities to handle overfitting problems and are being implemented in different environments such as urban and rural settings and on freeways and highways. Evidence from a study by [25] demonstrated promising results when the RF method was compared with other classifiers. The study evaluated models using an out-of-bag (OOB) estimate of error rate, mean square error (MSE) and RMSE. The RF method aims to reduce overfitting and is capable of improving model accuracy. Other performance evaluation methods used in different studies are precision, recall, f1 score, ROC curve, true positive rate (TPR), and false positive rate (FPR) [27,30,33,35,36,38]. The LDA approach was implemented by [32]. This study employed SVM, RF, LR, NB, and k-NN during the comparative analysis due, as mentioned, to their popularity and demonstrated capabilities in the literature. Furthermore, AdaBoost was considered even though there is no evidence of it tackling road accident problems. AdaBoost is perceived as improving the performance of weak classifiers. It can also handle image and text problems well.

Overall, the literature review revealed that there is no such thing as a perfect method. Thus, with RTAs, the most appropriate approach to finding the best performing method is to continue constantly combining and comparing various methods.

3. Methodology

This section covers ML classifiers, experimental settings, the RTA dataset, model evaluation methods, and the study's statistical analysis.

3.1. Machine Learning Classifiers

The ML classifiers employed during the comparative analysis are described below. Six classifiers were used in the study: the aforementioned NB, LR, k-NN, AdaBoost, RF, and SVM. The classifiers were considered due to their regular usage by other researchers in the RTA domain (as highlighted in Section 2.2) to construct robust models.

3.1.1. Naïve Bayes

The NB classifier is a simple probabilistic classifier based on applying Bayes' theorem with strong independence assumptions among variables. The classifier uses prior knowledge to compute the probabilities of sample data. NB can be easily implemented [40]. Two algorithms were used during the model design, namely, *GaussianNB* and *BernoulliNB*, both with their default settings.

3.1.2. Logistic Regression

LR is well-known as a classification method with mapping results of the linear functions to the sigmoid functions [41,42]. Similarly to NB, implementation of the method is easy and it can effortlessly be extended to multi-class problems. LR is well-known as one of the simplest ML methods. The default parameter, *ovr*, and *multinomial* parameter tuning were applied during implementation of the LR model.

3.1.3. k-Nearest Neighbour

k-NN classifiers, also known as lazy learners, are a form of instance-based method and are among the simplest classifiers that can handle classification problems well. The algorithm is a supervised method that employs both regression and classification. The *k* refers to the number of the nearest neighbours a model can consider [43,44]. The algorithm works on similarity measures between new data and categorises the new data into groups related to the available classes. One of the advantages of the algorithm is that it is straightforward to implement. During the analysis, k values of 5 and 10 were used.

3.1.4. AdaBoost

AdaBoost, or meta-learning, is known to be one of the best boosting algorithms. It uses the iterative concept to study errors of weak algorithms and turn them into robust ones. The weak classifiers can be referred to as algorithms that perform poorly. The classifier can assist in joining two or more classifiers into one strong classifier. The AdaBoost classifier can be used to solve classification and regression problems [24,45]. It can also benefit poor classifiers by improving their performance. In this study, the default parameters *learning_rate* −1 and *algorithm* –*SAMME.R* were initially applied and later optimised to *SAMME*.

3.1.5. Random Forest

The RF model is ensemble learning and tree-based, which are employed to construct predictive models. In line with its name, the classifier creates a forest that is made up of trees; more trees mean a more robust forest. RF uses the data samples to create decision trees to calculate each tree and select the best result using the voting approach [46,47]. The algorithm can best identify the significance of features from a set of datasets. The parameters were set to default and later optimised to *n_estimators* –10 and *criterion* –*entropy*.

3.1.6. Support Vector Machine

SVM is a supervised classifier that addresses the computational problem of predicting using kernels. SVMs can be used for classification and regression problems [48,49]. In SVMs, data items are plotted as points in a dimensional space, with the values of each variable being the value of specific coordinates. SVMs can be applied for variable selection, prediction, and detection of an outlier. In this study, the *Linear Support Vector Classifier (LinearSVC)* was applied because it can handle multi-class problems well. The default setting was used for the first set of results and, later on, the multi-class parameter was optimised to *crammer_singer*.

3.2. Missing Data Strategies

Handling missing data is an essential part of the pre-processing data stage that helps ensure that absent values are dealt with sufficiently. Missing values are common problems in RTAs and result from, for example, human error, incomplete data capturing, and system failure [13,50]. The data were missing some random values that were dealt with using several missing methods. In this study, missing data methods for single and multiple imputation methods were used.

3.2.1. Mean and Median

Some methodological strategies replace the missing values for given data with the mean or median of all the known values by adding available values and dividing their sum with by the average [51].

3.2.2. k-Nearest Neighbour

This method uses a set of given k-NNs for each sample and then replaces the missing data for a given variable derived by averaging through non-missing values in the neighbours. The sample's missing values are dealt with using the mean value of the k-neighbour from the data. The k-NN imputation method assists in handling missing values present in the dataset by finding the NN using the Euclidean distance matrix [52,53].

3.2.3. Multiple Imputations by Chained Equations (MICE)

MICE is a well-known multiple imputation method that can, in practice, be implemented to generate imputations based on different sets of imputation models. Initially, the missing values are filled in by replacing the observed values using the missing-at-random mechanism [51,54]. This method works better on a numerical dataset. These imputation methods were chosen due to their traits and frequent use in related studies.

3.3. Experimental Setup

The experiments performed were comparative analyses to evaluate the performance of the six ML classifiers described above using five performance metrics, four missing data methods to handle missingness in the dataset, and incorporating three-dimensionality reduction methods to reduce the feature scope of the RTA dataset. The experiments were conducted using the Python platform. During the investigation, the results were generated using the default setting and parameter tuning. The experiments were performed using a real-life RTA dataset that contained primary and secondary accident parameters. As outlined above, the applied ML classifiers were NB, LR, k-NN, AdaBoost, RF, and SVM, and the missing data methods applied to the dataset were the mean and median, k-NN, and MICE. The LDA and PCA were the dimensional reduction techniques used. Additionally, as outlined, the abovementioned methods were employed in the study due to their frequent use in related studies. The introduction of LDA and PCA methods to the study was to observe whether they could contribute positive outcomes to constructing the RTA model.

RTA Experimental Process

This section depicts the stages of the experimental process that were followed during the construction of the RTA model. The process consisted of five layers: type of dataset; data pre-processing, which involved data cleaning, dimensionality reduction, and preparation; data pre-processing was followed by sub-processes, namely, data training and testing; comparison analysis of the ML methods; and finally, the predicted RTA model evaluated. The process is illustrated in Figure 1 below.

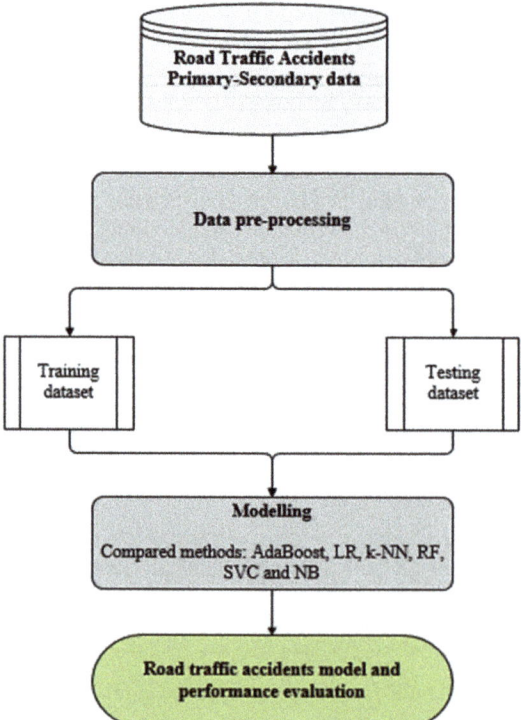

Figure 1. RTAs experimental procedure.

Table 1. RTA features and events.

No.	Features	Data Type	Events
1.	Primary Cause	Categorical	Major
2.	Primary Sub Cause	Categorical	Minor
3.	Secondary Cause	Categorical	Natural disaster
4.	Wet Road	Categorical	None
5.	No. of Travel Lanes	Numeric	Unknown
6.	No. of Vehicles Involved	Numeric	-
7.	Roadway Name	Categorical	-
8.	Date Time	Date time	-

3.4. Dataset and Statistical Analysis

Experiments were conducted using real-life data obtained from the Gauteng Department of Community Safety (GDCS). The collected dataset was compiled over a four-year duration. Ethical clearance was obtained from the ethics committee and the department to collect the historical dataset (Ref: 2020SCiiS04). The dataset included recordings of road traffic accidents over major highways in Gauteng province. Some features were omitted during data preparation because they contained insufficient entries. Then, features with 5% missing values were used during the analysis and handled using missing data strategies. Extensive data pre-processing was performed, resulting in a cleaned dataset containing 46,692 instances and 8 attributes, as shown in Table 1. The data had missing values that were handled using several missing value methods, as discussed in Section 3.2 above.

RTA Dataset

Table 1 contains a list of features and events employed for the study. The Events column shows that there are four classes. Due to the kind of dataset, the study was solving a multi-class problem. Multi-class classification refers to a classification task that contains more than two classes; it makes assumptions that each sample is assigned to only one label [53].

During data exploration, different numbers of parameters (features) were chosen to compute the classification model. This section of the paper statistically summarises the dataset to observe how data were distributed among the parameters/features. Figure 2a shows a distribution of road traffic accidents based on the *Primary Cause*. Stationary vehicles were the main contributors to causing primary accidents and were followed by crashes. This means that if the transport authorities or emergency authorities should prioritise clearing stationary vehicles on the roads, this may significantly reduce the high number of initial incidents. Figure 2b shows that five lanes were open when *minor* accidents occurred, followed by four lanes, which mean most incidents occur when most lanes are unavailable. The numbers in the figure are ordered according to the high number of vehicles or incidents. This figure reveals that accidents occur when fewer lanes are open on the freeway.

Figure 2c shows that when the roads were wet, fewer accidents were recorded. The wet road feature consists of *No* and *Yes* variables, with the *No* wet roads contributing significantly more to the road accident records when compared with the *Yes* variable. This means that from the obtained dataset, most of the accidents are not affected by wet roads. Figure 2d shows the data distribution for *secondary accidents*. The secondary accident's cause is made up of seven variables, i.e., *Crash, Stationary Vehicle, Road Construction, Load Lost, Routine Road Maintenance, Police and Military,* and *Fire*. It is observed that *Crash* accidents contribute more to secondary accidents, which can be due to delayed clearance of the initial accidents. An overall observation is that if initial accidents are cleared on time, this could reduce the number of secondary accidents.

Figure 3 shows the distribution of the dependent (events) variables. It demonstrates that *Minor* events contribute more than *None, Major* and *Natural Disaster* events. This means that most of the contributing RTAs happen during *Minor* accidents. In addition, it means *Minor* accidents are those which contribute to the high number of road accidents, and they can result in lane closures, an increase in the number of stationary vehicles, and delayed clearance. In terms of the *None* event, the dataset containing this class was originally the resulting label or class. Furthermore, the data also contained unknown or unlabelled instances, which could be the result of capturing errors or the system being offline to capture real-time information with labels.

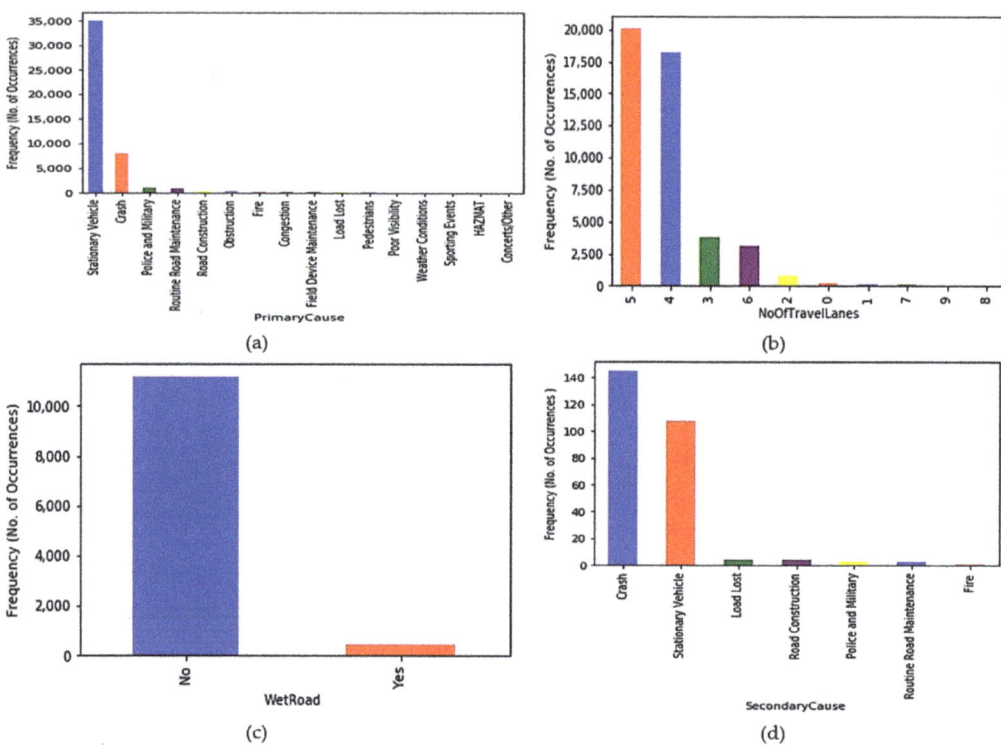

Figure 2. RTA data distribution over different features: (**a**) primary cause; (**b**) no. of travel lanes; (**c**) wet road; and (**d**) secondary cause.

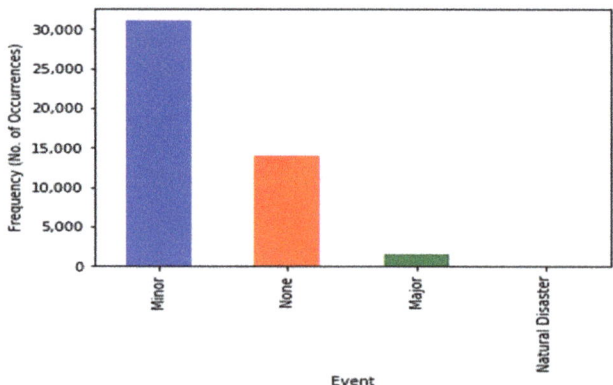

Figure 3. RTA events data distribution.

3.5. Model Evaluation

The study evaluated the performance of the classification model using accuracy, RMSE, precision, recall, and area under the ROC curve based on the confusion matrix. A low value for RMSE indicates that the predicted model can be considered, whereas a higher accuracy value indicates outstanding performance [55]. Formulas for calculating the evaluation metrics are shown in Equations (2)–(6):

The accuracy evaluation metrics in Equation (1) are calculated using the following: true positive (*TP*), true negative (*TN*), false negative (*FN*), and false positive (*FP*). The metrics correspond to the instances that are correctly classified [56].

$$Accuracy = \frac{TP + TN}{TP + TN + FN + FP} \quad (2)$$

Precision and recall represent the ratio of positive instances (*TP*) that are correct in the RTA dataset. High values of precision and recall indicate that the returned results are significant. The computation formulas are captured in Equations (3) and (4):

$$Precision = \frac{TP}{TP + FP} \quad (3)$$

$$Recall = \frac{TP}{TP + FN} \quad (4)$$

Model validation was carried out using the area under the ROC curve, as defined by Equation (5). The ROC curve can assist in determining the best threshold values produced by plotting sensitivity (*TPR*—true positive rate) against the specificity (*FPR*—false positive rate), indicating the proportion of RTAs. The study computed the AUC, the purpose of which is to deal with problems that contain a skewed data distribution to avoid over-fitting to a single class. An outstanding model will achieve an AUC near 1, which means good performance; a poor model will achieve an AUC near 0.5, which means poor performance [57]. The AUC can be defined using Equation (5), representing the average overall sensitivity values of *FPR* and *TPR*.

$$FPR = \frac{FP}{TN + FP} \text{ and } TPR = \frac{TP}{TP + FN} \quad (5)$$

Equation (6) shows how the *RMSE* formulation, which determines the difference between the predicted and actual values, is computed as $X_{obs,i} - X_{model,i}$, with $X_{obs,i}$ being the observed value for *ith* and $X_{model,i}$ being the model's predicted value.

$$RMSE = \sqrt{\frac{\sum_{i=1}^{n}(X_{obs,i} - X_{model,i})^2}{n}} \quad (6)$$

4. Dimensionality Reduction

In this section of the study, dimensionality reduction techniques, PCA and LDA, were applied to the dataset. PCA was applied to the dataset to reduce its dimensionality by identifying the most important and best-contributing features. PCA can be used as an exploratory data analysis technique, with PC1 describing the highest variance in the RTA data. Four datasets were used to construct Figure 4: mean, median, k-NN, and MICE. Missing data methods were applied to the original data to handle the missingness. For the four augmented datasets, three principal components (PCs) and linear discriminants (LDs) were used during the experiments discussed in Section 5 and in designing the 3D graphs in Figure 5. LDA mainly considers the response/state variable chosen by the classifier. Linear discriminant analysis was used to reduce the different feature sets and predict RTA states by using different features in this paper. Overall, the PC results captured the following percentages for the datasets:

(1) Mean missing data method: PC1—20%, PC2—17%, and PC3—13%, which explained 50% of the overall dataset;
(2) Median method: PC1—20%, PC2—16%, and PC3—14%, which explained 50%;
(3) k-NN method: PC1—27%, PC2—17%, and PC3—14%, which explained 58%;
(4) MICE method: PC1—30%, PC2—23%, and PC3—14%, which explained 67% (of the overall dataset).

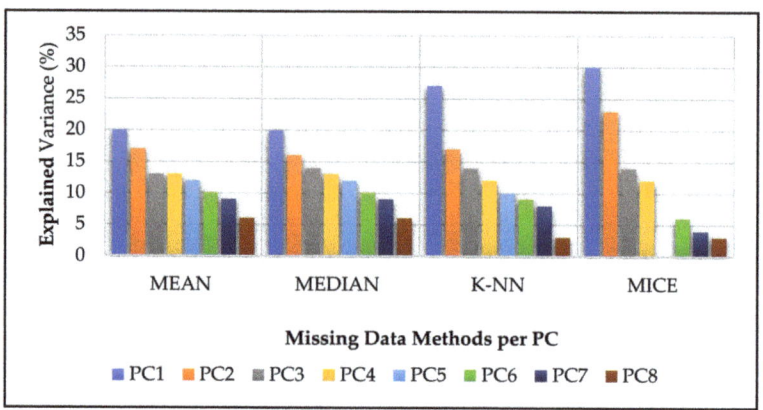

Figure 4. The proportions of variance explained for the RTA dataset.

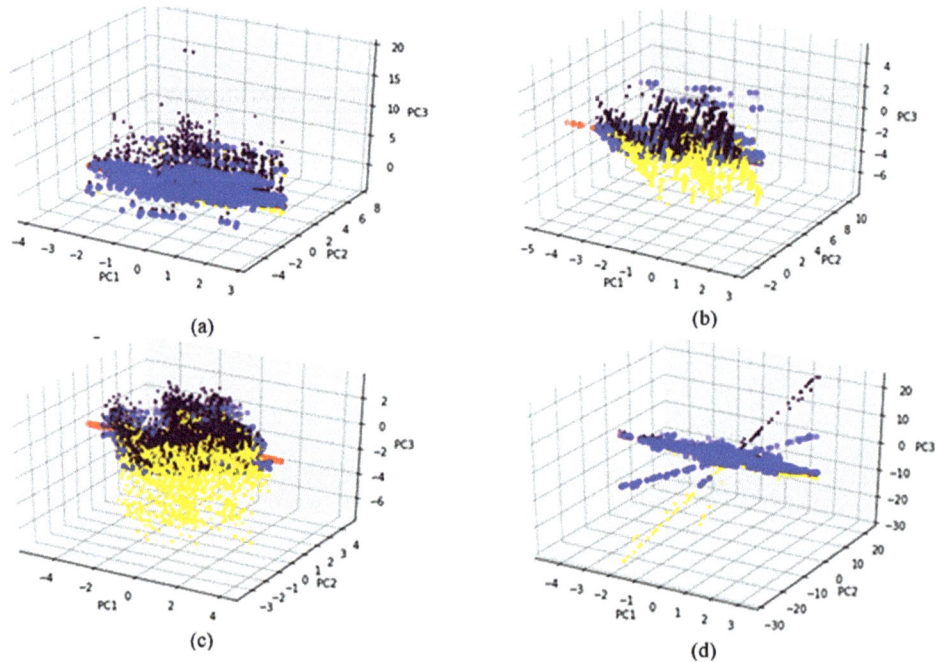

Figure 5. Three-dimensional principle component plots using the four missing data methods: (**a**) mean, (**b**) median, (**c**) k-NN, and (**d**) MICE.

The MICE dataset explained more of the PCs when compared with the other PCs. In this study, the main idea behind PCA was to identify the correlation between the RTA features.

Figure 5 shows the 3D scatter plots for PC1, PC2, and PC3 components against four events to better understand the data distribution. The distributions of PC1, PC2, and PC3 are represented by the colours yellow, blue and viridis, respectively. Figure 5 presents the data variance distribution for the RTA dataset.

Figure 5a shows that PC2 was distributed more than PC1 and PC3. On the other hand, some outliers were observed from PC3. Outliers can affect the final results of the analysis of the study.

Figure 5b shows that PC1 and PC2 contributed most of the variance in the data distribution, when compared with PC3. Some outliers are observed from PC2, which were moving towards PC3 using the median RTA dataset.

Figure 5c shows that PC1 and PC3 were moving more towards PC3, which appeared to be overlapping with PC2. It can also be observed that PC1 was moving away from PC2 and PC3, with some outliers from PC1. The figure shows some correlation between PC2 and PC3.

In Figure 5d, it can be observed that PC2 contributed more to the data points when compared with the other PCs. PC1 shows fewer data points moving towards PC3.

5. Results and Discussion

This section discusses and presents the results of the six classifiers, namely, NB, LR, k-NN, AdaBoost, RF, and SVM. The classification comparisons are discussed in detail to observe which methods/algorithms best predict RTAs.

5.1. Comparison Results

Figures 6 and 7 show the results for the default and optimised model settings. The results report the performance of the observed classifiers based on different missing data methods. The following can be observed: the results obtained using default Figure 6a settings for the six classifiers did not perform well across the different missing data methods applied to the RTA dataset. However, RF (97%) performed much better in terms of all the model evaluations. These results could be due to RF offering efficient test error estimates without experiencing any cost and offering reliable feature importance approximation. The AdaBoost classifier showed the lowest performance across all evaluation methods. AdaBoost could have performed poorly because it cannot handle data with outliers well. Figure 6b shows results obtained for RMSE where the RF model obtained the lowest value of 0.01, which means the model had lower errors when compared to the other methods. In terms of precision, the RF model achieved the best value of 93% when the mean and kNN missing value methods data was used in Figure 6c. Then results presented in Figure 6d for recall show that RF model obtained a high value of 89% when the mean missing value data method was utilised. In addition, MICE performed well across the used classifiers compared with the mean, k-NN, and median missing value methods.

Concerning the Figure 7 model optimisation results, the following can be observed: Figure 7a RF performed slightly better overall than the other classifiers across all the evaluation methods with an accuracy of 97%. One possible reason is that RF can handle thousands of inputs without deleting any variables. The RF settings were tuned to entropy and n_estimators = 10. The RF results show that parameter tuning did not improve the results, as shown in Figure 7a. Furthermore, LR and SVC performed poorly when compared with the other classifiers. In terms of RMSE in Figure 7b, RF model obtained 0.12, which mean the model has low errors compared to the others. Figure 7c shows precision results, which revealed that the RF performed well by obtaining 93% when mean missing value data was considered. Finally, Figure 7d shows that RF achieved the best value of 89% compared with the other methods such as SVC, NB, kNN, LR and AdaBoost. In general,

RF obtained promising results when compared with the other classifiers. The following graphs present results for PCA and LDA.

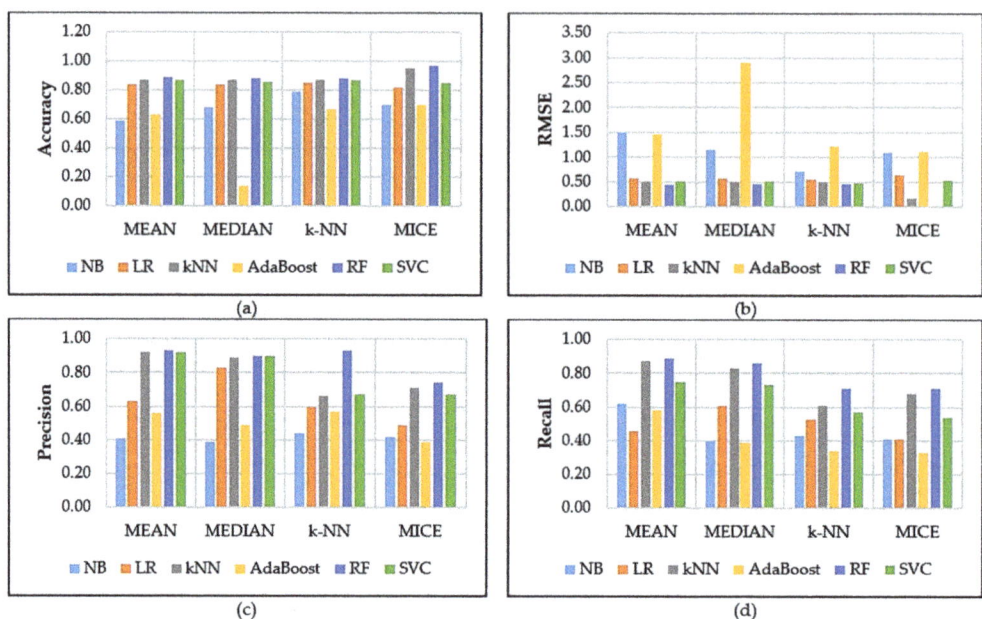

Figure 6. Default settings performance results.

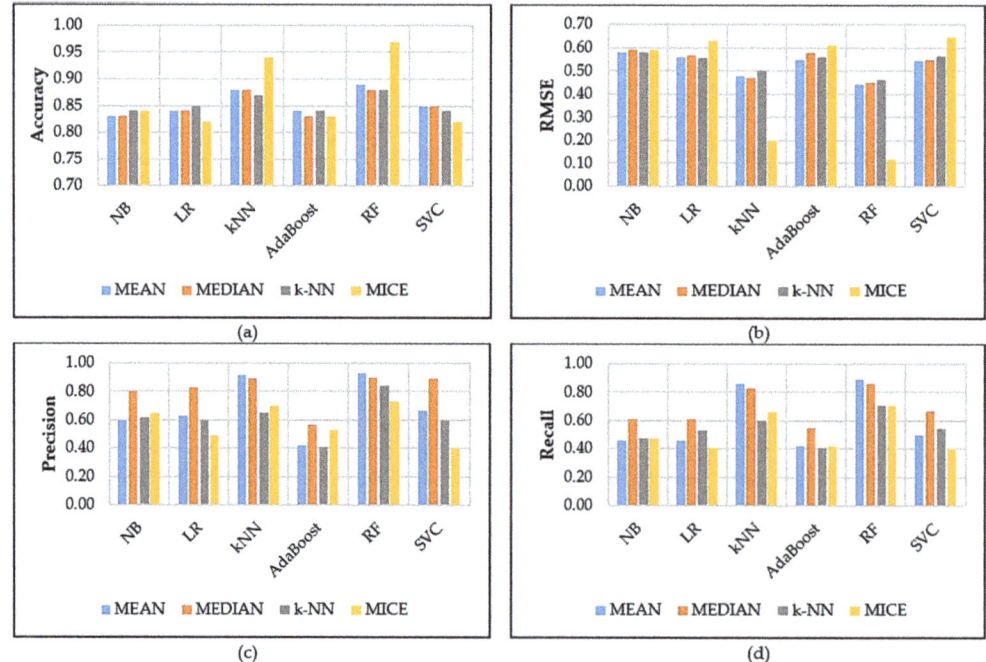

Figure 7. Model optimisation performance results.

Figures 8 and 9 contain graphical results computed using the RTA dataset. They include PCA and LDA dimensionality reduction techniques, which means reducing a large number of features to a smaller number of PCs. The results report the performance of the six classifiers based on four different missing data methods. The following is observed from the results: in the PCA results in Figure 8a, the RF classifier performed reliably and much better with accuracy (93%), precision and recall performance metrics when using MICE data. The MICE imputation method performed better compared with the other missing value methods because, as pointed out in Section 4, it captured 67% of the overall dataset. With a high RMSE, the AdaBoost classifier is the most poorly performing classifier. Figure 8b shows the results of the RMSE for all the augmented datasets and the results revealed that RF obtained a very low RMSE value of 0.27 compared to the other methods. Figure 8c show that the RF models achieved the best results in terms of precision, with MICE imputation methods achieving 93%. Then in Figure 8d, the graph presents recall results, which revealed that RF in terms of mean and median obtained 84%.

The LDA results in Figure 9a indicate that the RF (94%) and k-NN (94%) classifiers performed comparatively better than the other classifiers and the PCA results. AdaBoost (82%) was the classifier with the lowest performance results across all the evaluation metrics. In Figure 9b, the results show that kNN and RF methods best performed by achieving 0.22; in terms of the RMSE metric, the lowest values were obtained by RF and kNN when MICE imputation data is utilised. Figure 9c presents precision results with RF obtaining the best performance across all missing value methods compared to the others. Lastly, the Recall results graph in Figure 9d shows that RF, in terms of the mean missing value method, achieved the best value of 86%. The results mean that the LDA reduction method dataset obtained much better results when compared with the PCA technique. Furthermore, LDA performed best in multi-class classification problems. The LDA technique, when compared with the PCA, considers dependent variables during the creation of the LDs.

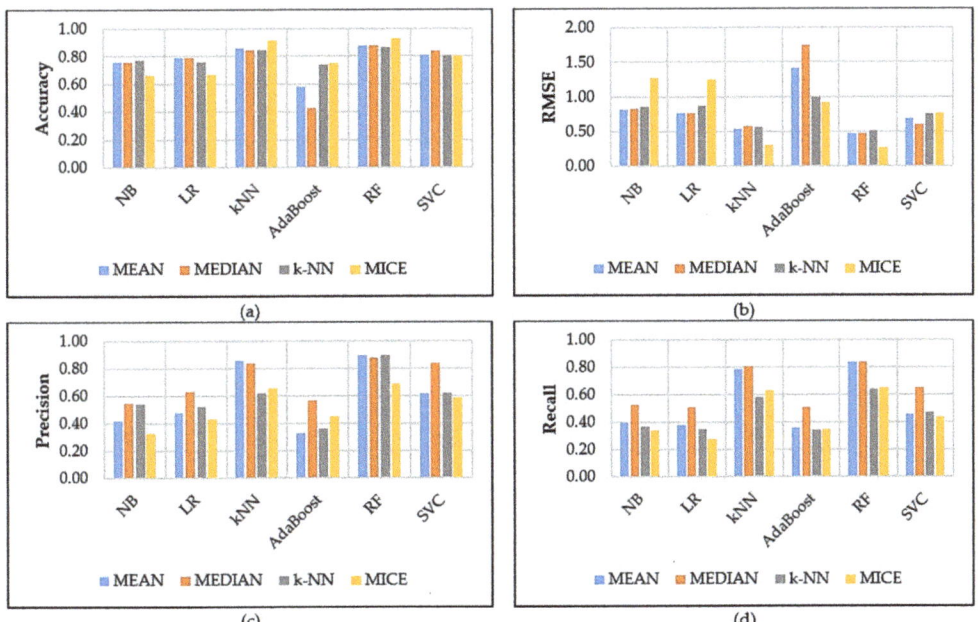

Figure 8. PCA performance results.

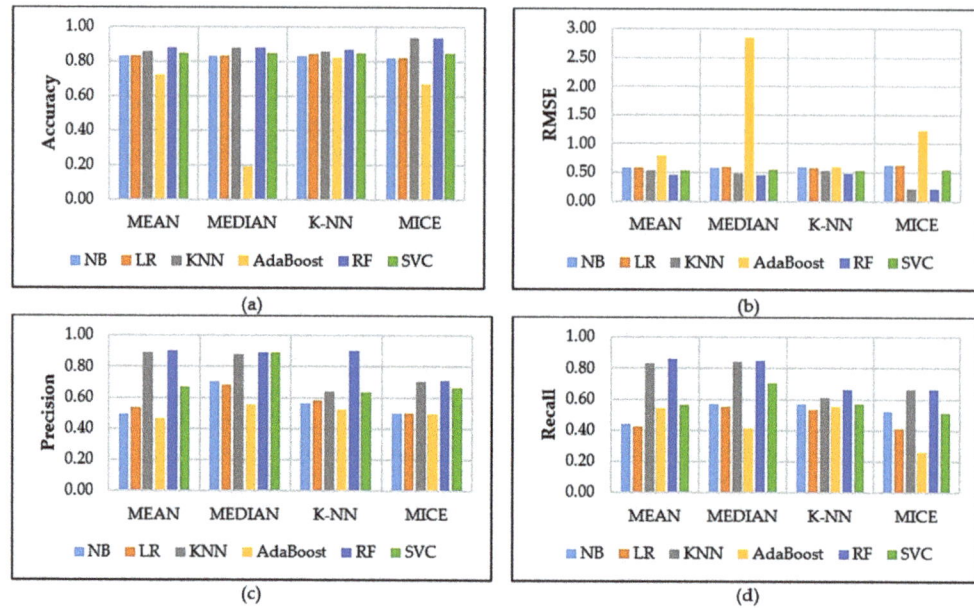

Figure 9. LDA performance results.

The results in Figures 8 and 9 show that the application of PCA and LDA positively changed the performance of the classifiers. The RF model remained the best performing in terms of the overall results. This is in addition to the fact that Figures 6 and 7 present a lower RMSE when compared with the Figure 8 and 9 results.

5.2. ROC Curve (AUC)

The area under the ROC curve is the ratio between 0.5 and 1, where values close to 0.5 indicate poor results, whereas values of 1 mean the best performance. The AUC is mainly implemented to evaluate and validate how robust the ML model is. In this study, the AUC for the MICE data performed better throughout the investigation compared with other missing data methods. The RF model, as seen in Figure 10, showed a performance of 99%; better than the other classifiers. Additionally, as shown in Figure 10, the AUC gives certainties of excellent classifications of the RF model.

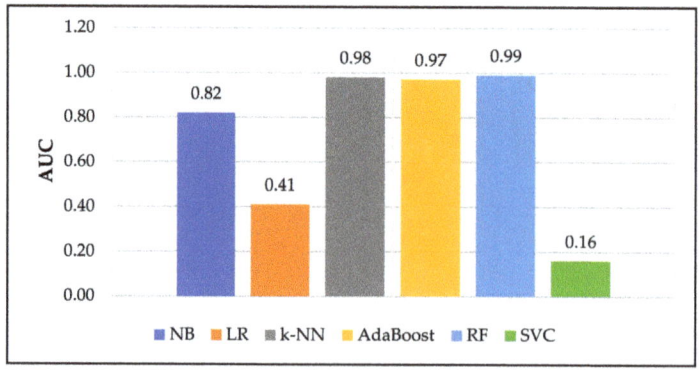

Figure 10. Comparison of the AUC results.

6. Conclusions

This study investigated the strength of widely used ML classifiers for road traffic accident problems. The classifiers were NB, k-NN, AdaBoost, SVM, LR, and NB. These were evaluated with four missing data methods: MICE, k-NN, mean and median, and two-dimensionality reduction methods: PCA and LDA. Accuracy, RMSE, precision, recall, and the ROC curve (AUC) were the five performance metrics used to evaluate the ML models. The overall results revealed that RF performed marginally better across the experiments in terms of accuracy, precision, recall, and ROC (AUC) when compared with the other classifiers. RF had the lowest RMSE compared with all the other classifiers, indicating a better fit for the RF model. Overall findings of the study on this particular RTA dataset are as follows:

(1) Statistical analysis included two-dimensionality reduction methods, with LDA obtaining promising results compared with PCA. In terms of missing data methods, MICE achieved good results;
(2) A wide range of ML methods was applied due to their popularity and characteristics. It was observed from the empirical analysis that RF performed best when compared with the rest;
(3) Furthermore, the AUC evaluation method was introduced to validate the classification results once the evaluation performance was assessed using accuracy, precision, and recall.

Some apparent limitations of the study are as follows: only a dataset from Gauteng province was utilised during the comparative analysis. The dataset contained a certain number of features for the specific area of interest, excluding other features that could have been beneficial to improving the model's performance. The data only contained four events/targets for possible scenarios to incorporate subclasses into the data.

For future work, further hyperparameter tuning could improve the SVC model results because the classifier is more strongly influenced by proper parameter tuning. Future research could test other ML classifiers such as artificial neural networks and deep learning, testing similar methods with different datasets or provincial metro and expanding the data in years. The approach itself is a contribution that benefits RTA stakeholders such as model developers and researchers, and inform policymakers and transportation safety designers in terms of actions relating to modern traffic safety control and actual predictive models, which will help develop the field of transportation.

Author Contributions: T.B.: conceptualisation, data curation, formal analysis, methodology, experiments, writing—review and editing, and result validation. W.D. and B.S.P. project administration, supervision, conceptualisation, and critical revision. All authors have read and agreed to the published version of the manuscript.

Funding: This research did not receive external funding.

Institutional Review Board Statement: Not applicable.

Informed Consent Statement: Informed consent was obtained from all subjects involved in the study.

Data Availability Statement: The data are not publicly available due to restrictions from the subject's agreement.

Acknowledgments: The Department of Applied Information Systems, the Institute for Intelligent Systems, and the University of Johannesburg supported this research. The authors would also like to thank the Gauteng Department of Community Safety, South Africa, for permitting the use of the RTA dataset.

Conflicts of Interest: The authors do not have any conflict of interest with other entities or researchers.

References

1. World Economic Forum. The Number of Cars Worldwide Is Set to Double by 2040. 2016. Available online: https://www.weforum.org/agenda/2016/04/the-number-of-cars-worldwide-is-set-to-double-by-2040 (accessed on 8 February 2021).
2. World Health Organisation. Global Status Report on Road Safety. 2015. Available online: https://www.who.int/violence_injury_prevention/road_safety_status/2015/en/ (accessed on 25 January 2021).
3. World Health Organisation. Global Status Report on Road Safety. 2018. Available online: https://www.who.int/violence_injury_prevention/road_safety_status/2018/en/ (accessed on 25 January 2021).
4. National Institute of Statistics and Economic Studies (INSEE). Road Accidents. 2020. Available online: https://www.insee.fr/en/metadonnees/definition/c1116 (accessed on 25 January 2021).
5. Wesson, H.K.; Boikhutso, N.; Hyder, A.A.; Bertram, M.; Hofman, K.J. Informing road traffic intervention choices in South Africa: The role of economic evaluations. *Global Health Action.* **2016**, *9*, 30728. [CrossRef] [PubMed]
6. Wang, J.; Liu, B.; Fu, T.; Liu, S.; Stipancic, J. Modelling when and where a secondary accident occurs. *Accid. Anal. Prev.* **2019**, *130*, 160–166. [CrossRef]
7. World Health Organisation. Global Status Report on Road Safety. 2019. Available online: https://www.who.int/violence_injury_prevention/road_safety_status/2019/en/ (accessed on 8 January 2021).
8. Makaba, T.; Gatsheni, B. A decade bibliometric review of road traffic accidents and incidents: A computational perspective. In Proceedings of the 2019 International Conference on Computational Science and Computational Intelligence (CSCI), Las Vegas, NV, USA, 5–7 December 2019; IEEE: New York, NY, USA, 2019; pp. 510–516.
9. Sánchez González, S.; Bedoya-Maya, F.; Calatayud, A. Understanding the Effect of Traffic Congestion on Accidents Using Big Data. *Sustainability* **2021**, *13*, 7500. [CrossRef]
10. Zhang, H.; Khattak, A. What is the role of multiple secondary incidents in traffic operations? *J. Transp. Eng.* **2010**, *136*, 986–997. [CrossRef]
11. Zhan, C.; Shen, L.; Hadi, M.A.; Gan, A. *Understanding the Characteristics of Secondary Crashes on Freeways*; No. 08-1835; Transportation Research Board: Washington, DC, USA, 2008.
12. Ramageri, B.M. Data mining techniques and applications. *Indian J. Comput. Sci. Eng.* **2010**, *1*, 301–305.
13. Li, L.; Shrestha, S.; Hu, G. Analysis of road traffic fatal accidents using data mining techniques. In Proceedings of the 2017 IEEE 15th International Conference on Software Engineering Research, Management and Applications (SERA), London, UK, 7–9 June 2017; IEEE: New York, NY, USA, 2017; pp. 363–370.
14. Alpaydin, E. *Introduction to Machine Learning*; MIT Press: Cambridge, MA, USA, 2020.
15. Mohri, M.; Rostamizadeh, A.; Talwalkar, A. *Foundations of Machine Learning*; MIT Press: Cambridge, MA, USA, 2018.
16. Expert AI. What Is Machine Learning? A Definition. 2020. Available online: https://www.expert.ai/blog/machine-learning-definition/ (accessed on 20 March 2021).
17. Costanza, R.; Daly, L.; Fioramonti, L.; Giovannini, E.; Kubiszewski, I.; Mortensen, L.F.; Pickett, K.E.; Ragnarsdottir, K.V.; De Vogli, R.; Wilkinson, R. Modelling and measuring sustainable wellbeing in connection with the UN Sustainable Development Goals. *Ecol. Econ.* **2016**, *130*, 350–355. [CrossRef]
18. Sachs, J.D.; Kroll, C.; Lafortune, G.; Fuller, G.; Woelm, F. Sustainable Development Report: The Decade of Action for the Sustainable Development Goals. 2021. Available online: https://s3.amazonaws.com/sustainabledevelopment.report/2021/2021-sustainable-development-report.pdf (accessed on 21 March 2021).
19. Asiri, S. Machine Learning Classification, towards Data Science. 2018. Available online: https://towardsdatascience.com/machine-learning-classifiers-a5cc4e1b0423 (accessed on 20 December 2020).
20. Waseem, M. How to Implement Classification in Machine Learning, Data Science with Python. 2021. Available online: https://www.edureka.co/blog/classification-in-machine-learning/#classification (accessed on 5 April 2021).
21. Sarangam, A. Classification in Machine Learning: A Comprehensive Guide, Jigsaw. 2021. Available online: https://www.jigsawacademy.com/blogs/ai-ml/classification-in-machine-learning (accessed on 8 August 2021).
22. Priyanka, A.; Sathiyakumari, K. A comparative study of classification algorithm using accident data. *Int. J. Comput. Sci. Eng. Technol.* **2014**, *5*, 1018–1023.
23. AlMamlook, R.E.; Kwayu, K.M.; Alkasisbeh, M.R.; Frefer, A.A. Comparison of machine learning algorithms for predicting traffic accident severity. In Proceedings of the 2019 IEEE Jordan International Joint Conference on Electrical Engineering and Information Technology (JEEIT), Amman, Jordan, 9–11 April 2019; IEEE: New York, NY, USA, 2019; pp. 272–276.
24. Labib, M.F.; Rifat, A.S.; Hossain, M.M.; Das, A.K.; Nawrine, F. Road accident analysis and prediction of accident severity by using machine learning in Bangladesh. In Proceedings of the 2019 7th International Conference on Smart Computing & Communications (ICSCC), Miri, Malaysia, 28–30 June 2019; IEEE: New York, NY, USA, 2019; pp. 1–5.
25. Lee, J.; Yoon, T.; Kwon, S.; Lee, J. Model evaluation for forecasting traffic accident severity in rainy seasons using machine learning algorithms: Seoul City study. *Appl. Sci.* **2020**, *10*, 129. [CrossRef]
26. Ijaz, M.; Zahid, M.; Jamal, A. A comparative study of machine learning classifiers for injury severity prediction of crashes involving three-wheeled motorised rickshaw. *Accid. Anal. Prev.* **2021**, *154*, 106094. [CrossRef] [PubMed]
27. Sangare, M.; Gupta, S.; Bouzefrane, S.; Banerjee, S.; Muhlethaler, P. Exploring the forecasting approach for road accidents: Analytical measures with hybrid machine learning. *Expert Syst. Appl.* **2021**, *167*, 113855. [CrossRef]

28. Zong, F.; Xu, H.; Zhang, H. Prediction for traffic accident severity: Comparing the Bayesian network and regression models. *Math. Probl. Eng.* **2013**, *2013*, 475194. [CrossRef]
29. Park, H.; Haghani, A. Real-time prediction of secondary incident occurrences using vehicle probe data. *Transportation Research Part C Emerg. Technol.* **2016**, *70*, 69–85. [CrossRef]
30. Bahiru, T.K.; Singh, D.K.; Tessfaw, E.A. Comparative study on data mining classification algorithms for predicting road traffic accident severity. In Proceedings of the 2018 Second International Conference on Inventive Communication and Computational Technologies (ICICCT), Coimbatore, India, 20–21 April 2018; IEEE: New York, NY, USA, 2018; pp. 1655–1660.
31. Kumeda, B.; Zhang, F.; Zhou, F.; Hussain, S.; Almasri, A.; Assefa, M. Classification of road traffic accident data using machine learning algorithms. In Proceedings of the 2019 IEEE 11th International Conference on Communication Software and Networks (ICCSN), Chongqing, China, 12–15 June 2019; IEEE: New York, NY, USA, 2019; pp. 682–687.
32. Jha, A.N.; Chatterjee, N.; Tiwari, G. A performance analysis of prediction techniques for impacting vehicles in hit-and-run road accidents. *Accid. Anal. Prev.* **2021**, *157*, 106164. [CrossRef] [PubMed]
33. Valenti, G.; Lelli, M.; Cucina, D. A comparative study of models for the incident duration prediction. *Eur. Transp. Res. Rev.* **2010**, *2*, 103–111. [CrossRef]
34. Vlahogianni, E.I.; Karlaftis, M.G.; Orfanou, F.P. Modelling the effects of weather and traffic on the risk of secondary incidents. *J. Intell. Transp. Syst.* **2012**, *16*, 109–117. [CrossRef]
35. Dogru, N.; Subasi, A. Traffic accident detection using random forest classifier. In Proceedings of the 2018 15th learning and technology conference (L&T), Jeddah, Saudi Arabia, 26–28 February 2018; IEEE: New York, NY, USA, 2018; pp. 40–45.
36. Makaba, T.; Doorsamy, W.; Paul, B.S. Exploratory framework for analysing road traffic accident data with validation on Gauteng province data. *Cogent Eng.* **2020**, *7*, 1834659. [CrossRef]
37. Zambrano-Martinez, J.L.; Calafate, C.T.; Soler, D.; Cano, J.C.; Manzoni, P. Modeling and characterisation of traffic flows in urban environments. *Sensors* **2018**, *18*, 2020. [CrossRef]
38. Makaba, T.; Doorsamy, W.; Paul, B.S. Bayesian Network-Based Framework for Cost-Implication Assessment of Road Traffic Collisions. *Int. J. Intell. Transp. Syst. Res.* **2021**, *19*, 240–253. [CrossRef]
39. Mir, Z.H.; Filali, F. An adaptive Kalman filter based traffic prediction algorithm for urban road network. In Proceedings of the 2016 12th International Conference on Innovations in Information Technology, Al-Ain, United Arab Emirates, 28–30 November 2016; IEEE: New York, NY, USA, 2016; pp. 1–6.
40. Budiawan, W.; Saptadi, S.; Tjioe, C.; Phommachak, T. Traffic accident severity prediction using Naive Bayes algorithm—A case study of Semarang Toll Road. *IOP Conf. Ser. Mater. Sci. Eng.* **2019**, *598*, 012089. [CrossRef]
41. Kim, D.; Jung, S.; Yoon, S. Risk Prediction for Winter Road Accidents on Expressways. *Appl. Sci.* **2021**, *11*, 9534. [CrossRef]
42. Li, P.; Abdel-Aty, M.; Yuan, J. Real-time crash risk prediction on arterials based on LSTM-CNN. *Accid. Anal. Prev.* **2020**, *135*, 105371. [CrossRef] [PubMed]
43. Twala, B. Dancing with dirty road traffic accidents data: The case of Gauteng Province in South Africa. *J. Transp. Saf. Secur.* **2012**, *4*, 323–335. [CrossRef]
44. Yu, H.; Ji, N.; Ren, Y.; Yang, C. A special event-based K-nearest neighbor model for short-term traffic state prediction. *IEEE Access.* **2019**, *7*, 81717–81729. [CrossRef]
45. Zhang, X.; Waller, S.T.; Jiang, P. An ensemble machine learning-based modelling framework for analysis of traffic crash frequency. *Comput. -Aided Civ. Infrastruct. Eng.* **2020**, *35*, 258–276. [CrossRef]
46. Chen, M.M.; Chen, M.C. Modelling road accident severity with Comparisons of Logistic Regression, Decision Tree and Random Forest. *Information* **2020**, *11*, 270. [CrossRef]
47. Lin, Y.; Li, R. Real-time traffic accidents post-impact prediction: Based on crowdsourcing data. *Accid. Anal. Prev.* **2020**, *145*, 105696. [CrossRef] [PubMed]
48. Parsa, A.B.; Taghipour, H.; Derrible, S.; Mohammadian, A.K. Real-time accident detection: Coping with imbalanced data. *Accid. Anal. Prev.* **2019**, *129*, 202–210. [CrossRef]
49. Tang, J.; Liang, J.; Han, C.; Li, Z.; Huang, H. Crash injury severity analysis using a two-layer stacking framework. *Accid. Anal. Prev.* **2019**, *122*, 226–238. [CrossRef] [PubMed]
50. Makaba, T.; Dogo, E. A comparison of strategies for missing values in data on machine learning classification algorithms. In Proceedings of the 2019 International Multidisciplinary Information Technology and Engineering Conference (IMITEC), Vanderbijyl Park, South Africa, 21–22 November 2019; IEEE: New York, NY, USA, 2019; pp. 1–7.
51. Liu, Y.; Brown, S.D. Comparison of five iterative imputation methods for multivariate classification. *Chemom. Intell. Lab. Syst.* **2013**, *120*, 106–115. [CrossRef]
52. Chowdhury, K.R. KNN Imputer: A Robust Way to Impute Missing Values Using Scikit-Learn. 2020. Available online: https://www.analyticsvidhya.com/blog/2020/07/knnimputer-a-robust-way-to-impute-missing-values-using-scikit-learn/ (accessed on 22 December 2020).
53. Mokoatle, M.; Marivate, V.; Bukohwo, M.E. Predicting road traffic accident severity using accident report data in South Africa. In Proceedings of the 20th Annual International Conference on Digital Government Research, Dubai, United Arab Emirates, 18–20 June 2019; ACM: New York, NY, USA, 2019; pp. 11–17.
54. Buuren, S.V.; Groothuis-Oudshoorn, K. Mice: Multivariate imputation by chained equations in R. *J. Stat. Softw.* **2010**, *45*, 1–68.

55. Ramani, R.G.; Shanthi, S. Classifier prediction evaluation in modelling road traffic accident data. In Proceedings of the 2012 IEEE International Conference on Computational Intelligence and Computing Research, Coimbatore, India, 18–20 December 2012; IEEE: New York, NY, USA, 2012; pp. 1–4.
56. Gutierrez-Osorio, C.; Pedraza, C. Modern data sources and techniques for analysis and forecast of road accidents: A review. *J. Traffic Transp. Eng.* **2020**, *7*, 432–446. [CrossRef]
57. Cigdem, A.; Ozden, C. Predicting the severity of motor vehicle accident injuries in Adana-turkey using machine learning methods and detailed meteorological data. *Int. J. Intell. Syst. Appl. Eng.* **2018**, *6*, 72–79.

Article

Textual Emotional Tone and Financial Crisis Identification in Chinese Companies: A Multi-Source Data Analysis Based on Machine Learning

Zhishuo Zhang, Manting Luo, Zhaoting Hu and Huayong Niu *

International Business School, Beijing Foreign Studies University, Beijing 100089, China;
zhangzhishuo@bfsu.edu.cn (Z.Z.); manting@bfsu.edu.cn (M.L.); 18900024@bfsu.edu.cn (Z.H.)
* Correspondence: bfsuniuhy@163.com

Abstract: Nowadays, China is faced with increasing downward pressure on its economy, along with an expanding business risk on listed companies in China. Listed companies, as the solid foundation of the national economy, once they face a financial crisis, will experience hazards from multiple perspectives. Therefore, the construction of an effective financial crisis early warning model can help listed companies predict, control and resolve their risks. Based on textual data, this paper proposes a web crawler and textual analysis, to assess the sentiment and tone of financial news texts and that of the management discussion and analysis (MD&A) section in annual financial reports of listed companies. The emotional tones of the two texts are used as external and internal information sources for listed companies, respectively, to measure whether they can improve the prediction accuracy of a financial crisis early warning model based on traditional financial indicators. By comparing the early warning effects of thirteen machine learning models, this paper finds that financial news, as external texts, can provide more incremental information for prediction models. In contrast, the emotional tone of MD&A, which can be easily modified by the management, will distort predictions. Comparing the early warning effect of machine learning models with different input feature variables, this paper also finds that DBGT, AdaBoost, random forest and Bagging models maintain stable and accurate sample recognition ability. This paper quantifies financial news texts, unraveling implied information hiding behind the surface, to further improve the accuracy of the financial crisis early warning model. Thus, it provides a new research perspective for related research in the field of financial crisis warnings for listed companies.

Keywords: textual analysis; emotional tone; machine learning; financial crisis early warning

Citation: Zhang, Z.; Luo, M.; Hu, Z.; Niu, H. Textual Emotional Tone and Financial Crisis Identification in Chinese Companies: A Multi-Source Data Analysis Based on Machine Learning. *Appl. Sci.* **2022**, *12*, 6662. https://doi.org/10.3390/app12136662

Academic Editors: Grzegorz Dudek and Antonio Fernández

Received: 6 June 2022
Accepted: 29 June 2022
Published: 30 June 2022

Publisher's Note: MDPI stays neutral with regard to jurisdictional claims in published maps and institutional affiliations.

Copyright: © 2022 by the authors. Licensee MDPI, Basel, Switzerland. This article is an open access article distributed under the terms and conditions of the Creative Commons Attribution (CC BY) license (https://creativecommons.org/licenses/by/4.0/).

1. Introduction

The financial situation of listed companies has attracted the attention of government departments, shareholders, business operators, creditors and other stakeholders in pace with the development of the capital market. Academics have also been committed to exploring effective financial crisis recognition indicators and constructing a more accurate financial crisis warning model to improve the predictive capability of listed companies' financial crises. In terms of the selection of crisis recognition indicators, most scholars focus more on standardized financial data and less on non-standardized textual information. Textual information, as a newer data element, contains richer emotions. Thus, the sentiment analysis of textual information turns out to be an effective supplement to financial indicators. This paper quantifies the sentiment and tone of MD&A sections in the annual financial reports of listed companies and financial news texts, combining them with traditional financial indicators, respectively, to form new input feature variables. Furthermore, it constructs different financial crisis early-warning models based on thirteen representative machine learning methods. The study puts textual information and traditional financial indicators together for financial crisis identification, which has a significant positive effect on the sustainable growth of Chinese listed companies and the capital market.

Based on the emotional tone of texts and machine learning models, this paper mainly focuses on four questions as follows:

RQ1: Whether the combination of the emotional tone of MD&A texts and traditional financial indicators can improve the identification of financial crises of listed companies.
RQ2: Whether the combination of the emotional tone of financial news texts and traditional financial indicators can improve the identification of financial crises of listed companies.
RQ3: A comparative study of the effect of the emotional tone of internal texts (MD&A) and external texts (financial news) on early warning of financial crises in listed companies.
RQ4: A comparative study of the early warning effects of thirteen machine learning models.

Based on the above research questions, this paper selects 1082 Chinese A-share (RMB-denominated common shares) listed companies from 2012 to 2021 as the sample. This paper takes the year of the sample as T and selects the traditional financial indicators in T-3 years as the benchmark. This study compares the financial crisis early warning effect incorporated with the emotional tone of MD&A texts and financial news texts, respectively, and then compares the recognition performance of thirteen machine learning models. Finally, in this paper, we find the emotional tone of the text that can improve the financial crisis recognition performance of listed companies, along with the financial crisis early warning model with greater accuracy.

In summary, the contributions of this paper are mainly: (1) This paper quantifies textual information and uses the information as a new prediction indicator to measure the financial crisis of listed companies, which expands the choice of financial crisis prediction indicators. (2) This paper covers universal machine learning models. By comparing the effects of different models based on different combinations of prediction indicators, this paper finds models with better and more stable early warning effects, which provide references for model users. (3) This paper investigates the effectiveness of the emotional tone indicator of financial news texts on the early warning models for financial crises and finds that this indicator helps enhance the accuracy of these early-warning financial crisis models for listed companies. (4) This study expands on the differences between the emotional tone indicator of MD&A and that of financial news in enhancing financial crisis warning capability, from the perspective of the internal and external texts of companies. Moreover, it expands the relevant research in the field of research concerning financial crisis early warning models for listed companies.

This paper is structured as follows. The second part introduces related studies. The third part gives an introduction to the basic models and methods involved in this study. The fourth part describes the selection of traditional financial indicators and the process of emotional tone indicators and conducts an empirical study and analysis based on the data of Chinese listed companies. The fifth part further discusses the empirical results. Finally, the paper concludes with an outlook on future research directions.

2. Related Studies

2.1. Theoretical and Empirical Definition of the Concept of Financial Crisis

There is no uniform theoretical definition of the concept of the financial crisis. Two mainstream views exist on the current definition. Beaver [1] took the company's inability to pay its debts as the main measure of a financial crisis and summarized four elements of financial crises: bank overdrafts, unpaid preferred stock dividends, bond defaults and declaration of bankruptcy. A company would be considered to be in financial crisis if it meets one of these conditions, only the severity of the crisis varies. Another view equated a financial crisis with the situation where the company collapses into bankruptcy, claiming that a company in financial crisis referred to the act of filing a legal bankruptcy petition under the bankruptcy law [2]. From the perspective of defining financial crises empirically, the researchers usually define the listed companies undergoing financial crises as those under special treatment (ST) [3–7]. A stock identified as ST represents that the listed company has an abnormal financial condition, and this abnormality mainly includes one of two cases: one is that the listed company has lost money for two consecutive years, and the other is that the net assets of the listed company are lower than the par value of the stock. In this paper, the research object is Chinese listed companies. It is difficult to apply the standards of other countries to meet the actual situation and to define whether a listed company has a financial crisis or not. Therefore, the financial crisis in this study is defined as the listed companies marked with ST, which is more in line with objective reality.

2.2. Financial Crisis Early Warning Indicators and Methodological Techniques

In terms of the selection of early warning indicators for financial crises, existing studies have mainly used traditional financial indicators as the basis for early warning of financial crises, with the indicators mainly reflecting solvency, operating performance and cash flow [8–14]. However, little literature considered other sources of information that interact with financial data, where textual information is an important form. There was a small proportion of literature that used the tone of texts such as company annual reports to predict corporate financial crises and confirmed that non-standardized financial information can be used for financial crisis early warning [15–18]. Referring to existing literature [19,20], this paper considers the following five perspectives which measure the performance of listed companies as profitability, solvency, asset operating efficiency, cash flow quality and development quality, choosing ten traditional financial indicators as benchmarks. For the textual information, this paper selects both internal (MD&A) and external (financial news) texts and calculates the emotional tone to complement traditional financial indicators.

In terms of the use of early warning models, related research presents a transition from univariate analysis to multivariate analysis, and then to the machine learning method which is broadly used nowadays. At the very beginning, researchers mainly focused on univariate analysis methods, using two ratios, net income/shareholders' equity and shareholders' equity/debt, for early warning of the financial crisis of the company [21]. Some researchers selected fourteen financial ratios from company financial statements for comparative studies and found that the ratio of cash flow to total liabilities is a better predictor of financial crisis in a company [1]. For bridging the limitation of the univariate analysis method, researchers used the Z-score model as the introduction of multivariate discriminant analysis into financial crisis warning. Some researchers chose their five most significant indicators among the beginning twenty-two financial indicators to construct the Z-score model. They used the magnitude of the Z-value to reflect the bankruptcy risk a company faces and found it more accurate than the univariate warning model [2]. However, in practice, it was found that the Z-score model is especially suitable for short-term prediction, so the ZETA model was subsequently proposed as a complement to this model. The modified model had a significantly better long-term warning effect [22]. Other scholars used logistic models for financial crisis prediction. With the help of this model, they overcame the strict requirements for the distribution of independent variables in the analysis and confirmed its high accuracy in predicting studies of listed companies [23]. As a result, this method has gradually replaced discriminant analysis as the mainstream method in this field.

Machine learning began to be introduced into the field of financial crisis early warning with the development of information technology. Some scholars applied neural network techniques to crisis early warning models and found that this method could better predict samples [24]. Random forest was also applied in the risk prediction of listed companies. Compared to the AdaBoost algorithm, the result of the random forest exercise showed a decreasing error rate [25]. Researchers also applied the model of support vector machine (SVM), which works well for nonlinear and high-dimensional samples. In the prediction results of 944 manufacturing companies, they found that the SVM has a better early warning effect than the Back Propagation (BP) neural network, logistic regression and multiple linear regression models [26]. Furthermore, some researchers conducted a comparative study, by using several methods to construct financial early warning models. Wang et al. [27] used three decision tree models to build a financial crisis early warning model and found that the random forest model has the best classification and prediction capabilities.

The existing research mainly used a single model or several models but paid little attention to the comparative study of different machine learning models. This paper proposes to use thirteen mainstream machine learning methods, including logistic regression, ridge regression, lasso regression, GBDT, CatBoost, XGBoost, LightGBM, AdaBoost, SVM, BPNN, decision tree, random forest and Bagging, to build early warning models for corporate financial crises. Each type of machine learning is based on different theoretical backgrounds, and its applicability can be fully exploited for different data. The empirical study demonstrates the financial crisis recognition effect of each model to provide a basis for enterprises' decision-making.

2.3. The Emotional Tone of Text and Financial Crisis Early Warning

Textual information, as a new type of data factor, contains more emotions than standardized financial data and is characterized by containing both negative and positive emotions. Some researchers have studied the tone of textual information disclosed by companies. They found that the tone of management in the disclosure of annual reports, management discussion, analysis and prospectuses has a predictive effect on the future performance of the company [28–32]. Chinese listed companies have begun to add management discussion and analysis to their annual reports since 2005, which is an effective supplement to the annual reports. This section includes further explanations of important events in the earning calendar and descriptions of business plans, possible challenges and difficulties in the next year. Existing literature has suggested that when listed companies are trapped in financial trouble in the current year, the appearance of negative words in the MD&A section will increase, along with the level of uncertainty [33,34]. By analyzing the tone of earning calendars some researchers predicted the financial crisis of listed companies and verified the availability of non-standardized financial information in financial crisis recognition [35–38]. However, the textual tone seems to fail to perform as a definite and true reflection of the situation of the company all the time. Compared to numerical information, textual information can be more easily manipulated, which even costs less [39]. Some researchers have pointed out that management can manipulate their tone for the purpose of whitewashing corporate earnings, which further leads to irrational trading and poses greater risks to business operations [40,41]. The positive tone formed by this manipulative behavior affected the assessment of the firm's operating conditions, so it did not necessarily improve the early warning effect of the model [42,43]. Yang et al. [44] also pointed out that company management may release positive information by modifying the text, and it would in turn reduce the accuracy of the early warning model of a company's financial crisis by adding emotional tone.

It can be seen that in some relevant papers, research mainly focused on the internal texts of companies, including MD&A and annual reports, but seldom noticed the external texts. This paper will study the emotional tone of financial news texts relating to listed companies and compare the effect of internal and external texts on the improvement of prediction accuracy of the financial crisis early warning model. In addition, the literature showed that research on internal textual tone and the effect of early warning of a financial crisis in listed companies presented two views. This paper will also use sample data for a 10-year period from 2012 to 2021 to explore these two views empirically.

3. Machine Learning Models

Machine learning methods are widely used to solve complex problems in engineering applications and scientific fields [45–51]. Based on the classification problem, this paper chooses thirteen mainstream machine learning models to study the effect of crisis warning. These models include traditional machine learning models, tree-based machine learning models and integrated machine learning models. This section introduces the main contents of the models.

3.1. Logistic Regression, Ridge Regression, Lasso Regression

Logistic regression (LR) is well-known as a machine learning method for solving binary classification problems by mapping the results of sigmoid functions. It maps any real value to a value between zero and one but does not take zero or one. A threshold classifier is then used to convert the value in the interval of (0, 1) to the value of zero or one. The Sigmoid function plays the role of a threshold classifier, and the functional formula is shown in Equation (1).

$$sigmoid(x) = \frac{1}{1 + e^{-x}} \quad (1)$$

Overfitting problem always exists when fitting a model, and so is the case with the logistic regression model. One solution to this problem is regularization, which can be divided into L1 regularization and L2 regularization. The objective function of the ridge regression is the sum of the average loss function and L2 regularization. The objective function of the Lasso regression is the sum of the average loss function and L1 regularization. The key difference between these two is the penalty term. L1 regularization adds the L1 norm as a penalty term to the average loss function, making it easier to obtain a sparse solution. L2 regularization adds a squared magnitude of the L2 norm as a penalty term to the loss function. Compared with L1 regularization, L2 regularization provides a smoother solution that can reduce the complexity of the model.

3.2. Support Vector Machine

Support vector machine (SVM) is a binary classification model and a linear classifier that finds the partitioned hyperplane with the maximum interval. Its learning strategy is interval maximization, which can eventually be translated into the solution of a convex quadratic programming problem. Vapnik first proposed the SVM model in 1995 [52], and this model has shown many unique advantages in solving problems such as small samples, non-linear and high-dimensional pattern recognition. Its excellent performance in classification becomes a major technique in machine learning and has been extended to other machine learning applications such as function fitting. In real situations, the sample data are mostly nonlinearly separable. When dealing with nonlinear problems, they need to be transformed into linear problems. By introducing a suitable kernel function, an optimal classification hyperplane can be constructed to achieve fast processing of high-dimensional inputs. This paper adopts the current mainstream radial basis kernel function, as shown in Equation (2). x_i and x_j represent the feature vectors of the ith sample and jth sample, respectively. σ represents the parameter of the radial basis kernel function.

$$\kappa(x_i, x_j) = \exp\left(-\frac{\|x_i - x_j\|^2}{2\sigma^2}\right) \quad (2)$$

3.3. Back Propagation Neural Network

Back propagation neural network (BPNN) was proposed by Rumelhart et al. [53]. The BPNN is a widely used neural network model, consisting of an input layer, an implicit layer and an output layer. Through the training of sample data, researchers continuously modify and iterate the network weights and thresholds until they reach the minimum sum of squared errors of the network, where the desired output is approximated. The neural network model needs the participation of the activation function, which could make the sparse model better able to mine relevant features to fit the training data, as a source of nonlinearity in neural networks. The commonly used activation functions are the Sigmoid function, Tanh function and ReLU function. This paper uses the ReLU function, which is a sparse activation function that enables the sparse model to better mine the relevant features and fit the training data. Concurrently, compared with the Sigmoid function and Tanh function, the ReLU function is faster and overcomes the problem of gradient saturation and gradient disappearance. The formula of the ReLU function is shown in Equation (3).

$$f(x) = \max(0, x) \tag{3}$$

3.4. Decision Tree and Random Forest

Decision tree (DT) model is a tree structure for classifying samples based on features, with each of its leaf nodes corresponding to a classification, and non-leaf nodes corresponding to a division of a certain attribute. The models constructed by decision trees are readable, and common DT algorithms are ID3, C4.5 and CART (Classification and Regression Tree) [54–56]. This paper adopts the Gini index to classify the attributes of the CART decision tree, and the $Gini(D)$ reflects the probability that two randomly selected samples with inconsistent category labels in the data set D. The smaller the $Gini(D)$, the higher the purity of the dataset. The higher the purity of a decision tree node means that the samples contained in the branch nodes of the decision tree are most likely to belong to the same category. The Gini index of attribute α is defined by Equation (4), where V is the number of possible values of attribute α.

$$Gini(D, \alpha) = \sum_{v=1}^{v} \frac{|D^v|}{|D|} Gini(D^v) \tag{4}$$

Random forest (RF) is an integrated machine learning model. It consists of several decision trees and selects the majority of classification results as the final result, resulting in an overall model with high accuracy and generalization performance.

3.5. Gradient Boosted Decision Tree

Proposed by Friedman [57], Gradient boosted decision tree (GBDT) is an iterative decision tree algorithm, which is composed of multiple decision trees. The main idea of the algorithm is as follows. (1) The initialization of the first base learner. (2) The construction of M base learners. (3) The calculation of the value of the negative gradient of the loss function in the current model, then using it as an estimate of the residual. (4) Building a CART regression tree to fit this residual and finding a value that reduces the loss as much as possible at the leaf nodes of the fitted tree. (5) Updating the learner. The method can do both regression and classification. The loss function chosen in the regression algorithm is generally the mean squared error or absolute value error, while the loss function chosen in the classification algorithm is generally a logarithmic function. The core of GBDT is that in each iteration, the latter decision tree is trained using the residuals of the previous decision trees following the negative gradient. The negative gradient residuals can be calculated by Equation (5).

$$r_{ti} = -\left[\frac{\partial L(y, f(x_i))}{\partial f(x_i)}\right]_{f(x) = f_{t-1}(x)} \tag{5}$$

where r_{ti} denotes the negative gradient of sample i at the iteration of tth times. $L(y, f(x_i))$ represents the loss function, which can be expressed as Equation (6).

$$L(y, f(x)) = \log(1 + \exp(-yf(x))) \tag{6}$$

3.6. CatBoost, XGBoost and LightGBM

CatBoost, XGBoost and LightGBM share basically the same principle, and can be categorized into the family of gradient boosting decision tree algorithms. The characteristics of these three models are described below.

CatBoost takes a symmetric decision tree as a base model, having only a few parameters. CatBoost combines category features to construct new features, which enriches the feature dimension and facilitates the model to find important features. CatBoost is very flexible in handling category-based features, and the processing process is as follows:

(1) Randomly sort the input sample set and generate multiple sets of random permutations. (2) Convert floating point or attribute value token to integers. (3) All the category-based feature results are converted into numerical results according to Equation (7). Where, φ represents the indicator function. The function value takes 1 if it satisfy the condition $\left(x_j^i = x_k^i\right)$, otherwise takes 0. p is the a priori value, and α is the weight of the a priori value.

$$\hat{x}_k^i = \frac{\sum_{j=1}^{n} \varphi\left(x_j^i = x_k^j\right)^{y_j + \alpha p}}{\sum_{j=1}^{n} \varphi\left(x_j^i = x_k^j\right)^{y_j}} \tag{7}$$

XGBoost adds the complexity of the tree model into the regularization to avoid overfitting. The model performs well in generalization and supports training and prediction for data containing the missing value. The essence of XGBoost is integrated from decision trees, so the model can be written as Equation (8), where k is the number of decision trees in the model, X_i is the ith input sample, $\hat{y}_i$ denotes the predicted value of the model after the kth iteration, $f_k(X_i)$ denotes the predicted value of the kth tree and F is the set of all decision trees.

$$\hat{y}_i = \sum_{k=1}^{K} f_k(X_i), \ f_k \in F \tag{8}$$

GBDT requires multiple training of the entire training data at each iteration. With a higher training efficiency, LihghtGBM takes GBDT as its core and makes essential improvements in many aspects, including second-order Taylor expansion for objective function optimization, a histogram algorithm and an optimized leaf growth strategy. It also makes the algorithm more adaptable to high-dimensional data. LightGBM uses the Gradient-based One-Side Sampling algorithm, which maintains the accuracy of the information gain estimation. The information gain is measured using the variance gain after splitting, keeping only those samples with larger contributions. The formula of variance gain is given in Equation (9), where j is the split feature used, d is the split point of the sample feature and n is the number of samples. A and B are samples with large and small gradients, respectively. l and r are the left and right subtrees, respectively, and g is the sample gradient.

$$\widetilde{V}_j(d) = \frac{1}{n}\left(\frac{\left(\sum_{x_i \in A_l} g_i + \frac{1-a}{b}\sum_{x_i \in B_l} g_i\right)^2}{n_l^j(d)} + \frac{\left(\sum_{x_i \in A_r} g_i + \frac{1-a}{b}\sum_{x_i \in B_r} g_i\right)^2}{n_r^j(d)}\right) \tag{9}$$

3.7. AdaBoost and Bagging

Freund and Schapire first proposed the AdaBoost algorithm in 1995 [58]. The algorithm learns a series of weak classifiers from the training data and then accumulates them by certain weights to obtain strong classifiers. It first assigns an initial weight value to each sample and then updates the sample weight with each iteration. The sample with a small error rate will have a reduced weight value in the next iteration, while the sample with a significant error rate will increase the weight value in the next iteration. This algorithm belongs to a typical integrated learning method. Finally, M weak classifiers are combined into a strong classifier according to their respective weights, as detailed in Equation (10). Where, $G_m(x)$ is the mth base classifier, and α_m is the weight of this base classifier in the strong classifier.

$$G(x) = sign(f(x)) = sign\left(\sum_{i=1}^{M} \alpha_m G_m(x)\right) \tag{10}$$

Bagging is another sort of integrated learning method. The main idea is to train multiple classifiers by sampling the training set several times and then vote on the test set, in which each classifier is equally weighted. The given winning result is the final classification result. The final classifier is shown in Equation (11), where M is the number of classifiers, and $a_i(x)$ is the individual classifiers trained. The main difference with AdaBoost is that its training set is selected with put-back in the original set, and the training set selected from the original set are independent of each other for each round. In addition, AdaBoost determines its weight values based on the error rate situation, while Bagging uses uniform sampling with equal weights for each sample. Finally, Bagging can generate the individual prediction functions in parallel, while AdaBoost can only generate them sequentially because the latter model parameters require the results of the previous model round.

$$a(x) = \frac{1}{M}\sum_{i=1}^{M} a_i(x) \qquad (11)$$

4. Empirical Analysis

4.1. Design of the Empirical Analysis Process

As shown in Figure 1, the steps of the empirical process of financial crisis warning in listed companies based on thirteen machine learning models are as follows.

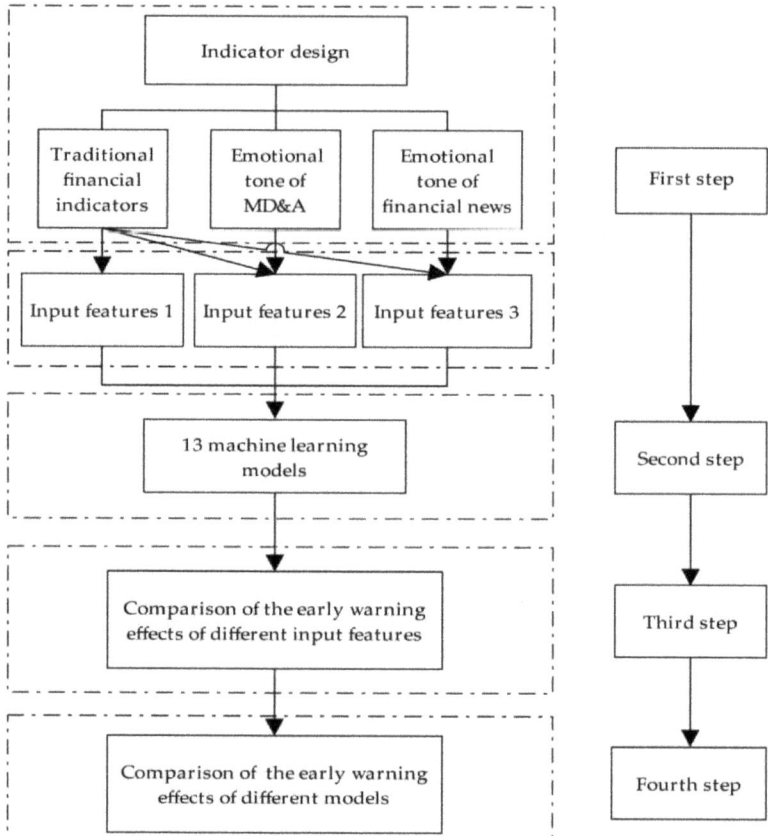

Figure 1. Flow chart of empirical analysis.

In the first step, this paper carries out the indicator design, including the selection of traditional financial indicators, the construction of the emotional tone indicators of both the MD&A section and financial news. Traditional financial indicators constitute input feature 1. Traditional financial indicators and the emotional tone indicators of MD&A constitute input feature 2, and traditional financial indicators and emotional tone indicators of financial news constitute input feature 3.

In the second step, this paper uses thirteen mainstream machine learning models, including logistic regression, ridge regression, lasso regression, GBDT, CatBoost, XGBoost, LightGBM, AdaBoost, SVM, BPNN, decision tree, random forest and Bagging, to establish a financial crisis early warning model for companies. The three sets of input feature variables formed in the first step are sequentially substituted into the model, and the output feature variables are binary values, which implies whether the company is a listed company marked ST or not. All machine learning models in this paper are supervised learning models. The code of machine learning models is written and run using PyCharm.

In the third step, this paper compares the effect of different input feature variables for the identification of financial crises of listed companies.

In the fourth step, the early warning effects of thirteen machine learning models are compared based on a combination of different input feature variables.

4.2. Evaluation Index System Construction

Based on traditional financial indicators, this paper compares the warning effect of the financial crisis early warning model merged with different textual emotional tone indicators. In this section, this paper explains the selection of traditional financial indicators and the process of textual emotional tone indicators.

4.2.1. Traditional Financial Indicators

The selection of traditional financial indicators has a direct influence on the accuracy of the early warning model. This paper follows the principles below in terms of selecting indicators.

1. Principle of importance: It is necessary to select important indicators, instead of picking all traditional financial indicators indiscriminately.
2. Principle of accessibility: The selection of traditional financial indicators should consider the accessibility of data and try to select data that are easy to collect.
3. Principle of objective relevance: The selection of traditional financial indicators needs to be highly relevant to the purpose of use, and a financial crisis warning requires that the selected indicators are highly relevant to the financial situation of the listed company.

Since there is no accepted standard for the financial indicators used in the financial crisis early warning model, based on the relevant category literature, this paper selects five aspects of traditional financial indicators according to the principles of selection [8–14,19,20]. The financial status of listed companies depends mainly on the profitability, solvency, asset operating efficiency, cash flow quality and development quality of listed companies in these five aspects, which contain a total of ten specific indicators. The traditional financial indicators selection and calculation formula are shown in Table 1.

4.2.2. Textual Emotional Tone Indicators

For the emotional tone indicators of MD&A, this paper first uses Python to write a web crawler program to crawl from CNINFO (see www.cninfo.com.cn, accessed on 17 April 2022), which is the information disclosure website of listed companies designated by the China Securities Regulatory Commission. After data cleaning and making Chinese word separation with the raw text data crawled, based on the financial emotional English words list provided by Loughran and McDonald [28], this study obtains an emotional dictionary translated from English to Chinese, and then counts positive and negative emotion words.

Table 1. The selection of traditional financial indicators and formulas.

First Level Indicators	Specific Financial Indicators	Formulas
Profitability indicator	Operating profit ratio (%)	Operating profit/Operating income × 100%
	Earnings per share (yuan)	An enterprise shall calculate basic earnings per share by dividing the net profit for the period attributable to common shareholders by the weighted average number of common shares outstanding
Solvency indicator	Current ratio (time)	Current assets/Current debts
	Oper-cash into current debt (%)	Net cash flow from operating activities/Current debts × 100%
	Debt assets ratio (%)	Total debts/Total assets × 100%
	Interest cover (time)	(Net income + Income tax expense + Finance costs)/Finance costs
Asset operating efficiency indicator	Accounts receivable turnover rate (time)	Operating revenues/Accounts receivable ending balance
Cash flow quality indicator	Operating cash per share (yuan)	Net cash flow from operating activities/Total common share capital at the end of the year
	Cash rate of sales (time)	Cash received from sales of goods and services/Operating income
Development capacity indicator	Net profit growth rate (%)	Additional net profit in this year/Net profit in the previous year

There are two main methods in terms of measuring the textual emotional tone. The first is to measure emotional tone by the ratio of the difference between positive words and negative words to the total words [59,60]. The second is to use the ratio of the difference between positive words and negative words to the sum of positive words and negative words [61–66]. The second method is adopted in this paper, and the formula is shown in Equation (12).

$$\text{Tone} = \frac{\text{Pos} - \text{Neg}}{\text{Pos} + \text{Neg}} \qquad (12)$$

Tone presents the value of emotional tone, and the range of values is $[-1, 1]$. Pos is the number of words with a positive tone in the text, and Neg is the number of words with a negative tone in the text.

For the emotional tone indicators of financial news, the study uses the data from the Chinese research data Services Platform, which has a database of financial news of Chinese listed companies. The database collects financial news of listed companies from more than 400 online media and 500 newspaper publications. It also counts the amount of positive and negative news for each listed company. The same Formula (1) is used to calculate the value of the emotional tone of financial news based on the number of positive and negative news.

4.3. Sample Selection and the Source of Data

Whether a company is marked as ST (an indicator of delisting risk) is taken as the identifier of financial crisis for Chinese listed companies, and the year in which a financial crisis occurs is defined as year T. This paper chooses listed companies that are newly labeled as ST in year T as the sample of ST listed companies, with a time interval from 2012 to 2021. The number of listed companies labeled as ST in 2012–2021 and the ratio of listed companies marked as ST to all A-share listed companies in that year are shown in Table 2. The number of listed companies labeled as ST in each of the 10 years is 550, and we finally obtained 541 listed companies labeled as ST by excluding 9 companies that had no traditional financial indicators data in year T-3. It can be found in this table that the total number of listed companies labeled as ST is very limited, which will lead to the imbalance of data between ST and non-ST listed companies. Therefore, this paper will explain how to solve the imbalance data problem in Section 4.4. Finally, this paper chooses 541 non-ST listed companies, the same number as the selected ST listed companies. It forms a total of 1082 samples, of which ST listed companies are in the positive category and non-ST listed companies are in the negative category.

Table 2. Number and share of ST companies and all listed companies.

Year	Number of ST Companies	Total Number of Listed Companies	Ratio
2012	16	2494	0.0064
2013	23	2489	0.0092
2014	35	2613	0.0134
2015	42	2827	0.0149
2016	58	3052	0.0190
2017	55	3485	0.0158
2018	52	3584	0.0145
2019	84	3777	0.0222
2020	101	4154	0.0243
2021	75	4682	0.0160

ST listed companies are companies that have been given special treatment for two consecutive years of losses, so the financial indicator data of T-2 years have already shown the financial crisis. In order to reflect the effect of early warning, this paper uses the financial indicator data of T-3 years. For instance, financial indicator data in 2017 are used, which were actually published in 2018, for the early warning analysis of listed companies labeled as ST in 2021. The traditional financial indicator data used in this paper are obtained from the China Stock Market and Accounting Research Database. MD&A text is crawled from CNINFO, which is processed as an emotional tone indicator through natural language. The financial news text data are obtained from the Chinese Research Data Services Platform, with the tone values calculated according to the emotional tone formula.

4.4. Data Processing

To solve the problem of imbalanced data, this paper follows the practice of many previous researchers, adopting the random under-sampling method [67–69]. By selecting the number of listed companies labeled as ST as the number of non-ST listed companies and form a balanced data set.

Considering the effect of extreme values of the data, this paper winsorizes all continuous variables by 1% up and down.

This paper uses gradient descent for loss function optimization, and the use of feature normalization helps the model converge faster and the gradient descent process is straighter and more stable. The use of Lasso regression and ridge regression will make coefficients smaller for features with large dimensions, leading to an omission of this feature. The coefficient changes have a very small degree of influence on the change of regularization term values, so the effect of dimension needs to be eliminated by normalization. Although some tree-based models are more concerned with which cut point is optimal in a particular feature, normalizing these features does not affect the result of that model. It is necessary to normalize the feature variables of other models. In summary, this paper normalizes all input feature variables to map the feature variable data to a range of [0, 1], and the normalization formula is given in Equation (13).

$$x_i^* = \frac{x_i - x_{\min}}{x_{\max} - x_{\min}} \quad (13)$$

x_i and x_i^* present the values before and after data normalization, $x_{\min}$ and $x_{\max}$ present the minimum and maximum values of the sample data, respectively.

4.5. Results of Empirical Analysis

In the division of the machine learning model dataset, this paper adopts the 10-fold cross-validation, dividing the dataset into 10 parts, and taking turns to use 9 of them as the training set and 1 as the test set. The process is repeated 10 times, and we use the average of the results as the estimation of the algorithm accuracy. For one thing, it enhances the generalization ability of the model. For another thing, it avoids the overfitting situation.

This paper performs ten times the 10-fold cross-validations and averages the results to reduce the chance and increase the confidence of the results.

As for the evaluation indexes of the early warning effect of machine learning models, this paper selects the average accuracy, the prediction accuracy of non-ST listed companies, the prediction accuracy of ST listed companies and Area Under Curve (AUC) as the evaluation indexes. In the dichotomous classification, the prediction results will appear in the following four cases.

1. True Positive (TP): Positive samples predicted by the model as positive;
2. False Positive (FP): Negative samples predicted by the model as positive;
3. False Negative (FN): Positive samples predicted by the model as negative;
4. True Negative (TN): Negative samples predicted by the model as negative;

According to the four prediction results, this paper calculates the evaluation indicators of the machine learning model. The average accuracy (ACC) is calculated by Equation (14), which represents the share of the number of correctly predicted samples to the total number of the samples.

$$\text{ACC} = \frac{\text{TP} + \text{TN}}{\text{TP} + \text{FP} + \text{FN} + \text{TN}} \tag{14}$$

The prediction accuracy rate of non-ST listed companies, also known as sensitivity (SEN), is calculated by Equation (15), which represents the percentage of samples with correct predictions among all samples that are truly non-ST listed companies.

$$\text{SEN} = \frac{\text{TP}}{\text{TP} + \text{FN}} \tag{15}$$

The prediction accuracy rate of ST listed companies, also known as specificity (SPE), is shown in Equation (16), which represents the percentage of samples with correct predictions among all samples that are truly ST listed companies.

$$\text{SPE} = \frac{\text{TN}}{\text{TN} + \text{FP}} \tag{16}$$

AUC is the area under the line of the Receiver Operating Characteristic (ROC) Curve, the area which is chosen to measure the accuracy of the dichotomous classification model. The larger the value of the AUC area is, the higher the classification accuracy of the model. When the value of the AUC area is less than 0.5, the model will almost lose its predictive effect. the AUC calculation formula is shown in Equation (17).

$$\text{AUC} = \frac{\sum_{i \in \text{positiveClass}} rank_i - \frac{m(1+m)}{2}}{m * n} \tag{17}$$

$rank_i$ represents the serial number of the ith sample. m and n represent the number of positive samples and negative samples, respectively. $\sum_{i \in \text{positiveClass}}$ means the numbers of positive samples are added up.

In this paper, AUC, as well as the value of SPE, will be prioritized when determining the effect of early warning. This is because AUC is used to measure the overall performance of a model in identifying the financial crisis of the sample companies. As the prediction accuracy of the sample of ST listed companies, SPE is more important than the prediction accuracy of the sample of non-ST listed companies, because the goal is the identification of the listed companies in financial crisis.

4.5.1. Analysis of Empirical Results of Financial Crisis Early Warning Based on Traditional Financial Indicators

Using traditional financial indicators as the benchmark, this paper tests the performance effects of thirteen machine learning models based on traditional financial indicators, and the results are shown in Table 3. The ranking is based on the value of AUC, where the five models with the highest value are AdaBoost, random forest, Bagging, DBGT, and CatBoost. Bagging has the highest prediction accuracy of 0.6839 for the sample of ST listed companies, followed by the random forest model and the DBGT model, with a value of 0.6821 and 0.6710, respectively. Among the thirteen machine learning models, the decision tree has the lowest value of AUC and SPE. All thirteen models have an AUC of 0.7 or higher, and the average AUC of the thirteen models is 0.7292. The average score of ACC, SEN and SPE is 0.6647, 0.6707 and 0.6586, respectively.

Table 3. Early warning effects of thirteen machine learning models based on traditional financial indicators.

	AUC	ACC	SEN	SPE	Rank
Logistic regression	0.7149	0.6488	0.6322	0.6654	11
Ridge regression	0.7144	0.6488	0.6322	0.6654	12
Lasso regression	0.7152	0.6497	0.6322	0.6673	10
DBGT	0.7429	0.6784	0.6858	0.6710	4
XGBoost	0.7300	0.6590	0.6599	0.6580	7
LightGBM	0.7230	0.6580	0.6617	0.6543	8
CatBoost	0.7413	0.6728	0.6969	0.6488	5
AdaBoost	0.7462	0.6867	0.7061	0.6673	1
SVM	0.7165	0.6534	0.6488	0.6580	9
BPNN	0.7397	0.6728	0.6913	0.6543	6
Decision tree	0.7065	0.6442	0.7024	0.5860	13
Random forest	0.7455	0.6774	0.6728	0.6821	2
Bagging	0.7431	0.6904	0.6969	0.6839	3
Mean	0.7292	0.6647	0.6707	0.6586	

4.5.2. Analysis of the Empirical Results of Financial Crisis Early Warning Based on Traditional Financial Indicators and Emotional Tone of MD&A

According to the RQ1 proposed by this paper, this section examines the early warning effects of thirteen machine learning models using traditional financial indicators and the emotional tone of MD&A as input feature variables. The results are shown in Table 4, and the ROC curves are detailed in Figure A2 of Appendix A. From the comparison of the values of AUC, it can be found that AdaBoost, random forest, DBGT, and Bagging and CatBoost models are the five models with the best performance.

Table 4. Early warning effects of thirteen machine learning models based on traditional financial indicators and emotional tone of MD&A.

	AUC	ACC	SEN	SPE	Rank
Logistic regression	0.7136	0.6525	0.6359	0.6691	11
Ridge regression	0.7135	0.6525	0.6359	0.6691	12
Lasso regression	0.7141	0.6525	0.6340	0.6710	10
DBGT	0.7434	0.6719	0.6821	0.6617	3
XGBoost	0.7301	0.6571	0.6747	0.6396	7
LightGBM	0.7212	0.6516	0.6636	0.6396	8
CatBoost	0.7355	0.6691	0.6932	0.6451	5
AdaBoost	0.7514	0.6774	0.7006	0.6543	1
SVM	0.7164	0.6599	0.6433	0.6765	9
BPNN	0.7343	0.6811	0.6543	0.7079	6
Decision tree	0.7071	0.6349	0.6913	0.5786	13
Random forest	0.7464	0.6682	0.6691	0.6673	2
Bagging	0.7432	0.6747	0.6839	0.6654	4
Mean	0.7285	0.6618	0.6663	0.6573	

Compared to the warning effect of thirteen machine learning models based on traditional financial indicators, there is a slight decrease in the average value of AUC, ACC, SEN and SPE in thirteen machine learning models merging emotional tone of MD&A,

but the magnitude of decrease was less than 0.01. In addition, there are seven machine learning models with slightly decreasing AUC and six machine learning models with slightly increasing AUC, but the magnitude was less than 0.01. As for these six machine learning models with slightly higher AUC, a further comparison of the value of ACC, SEN and SPE shows that the values of the five models are lower than those only based on traditional financial indicators. Then this paper studies the distribution of emotional tone of MD&A for ST and non-ST listed companies and finds that the distribution is more consistent and does not have significant differentiation. The results are shown in Table 5. Because of the existence of management manipulation and modification of emotional tone in ST listed companies, the emotional tone of MD&A in ST and non-ST listed companies is not as distinguishable as it is expected to be. Through the empirical results, it can be clearly seen that the emotional tone of MD&A does not have a significant effect on the early warning of financial crises of listed companies and even brings some noise.

Table 5. Descriptive statistics of the emotional tone of MD&A for ST and non-ST listed companies.

	ST	Non-ST
Average value	0.4435	0.4548
25th percentile	0.3420	0.3312
Median	0.4725	0.4930
75th percentile	0.5607	0.5885

4.5.3. Analysis of Empirical Results of Financial Crisis Early Warning Based on Traditional Financial Indicators and Emotional Tone of Financial News

Financial news text, as an external text, having a characteristic of objectivity, is not susceptible to manipulation by the companies. Based on this, this paper studies whether the emotional tone of financial news texts can enhance the effect of traditional financial indicators for the identification of financial crises in listed companies. Based on traditional financial indicators and the emotional tone of financial news, the empirical results of financial crisis early warning are shown in Table 6. The ROC curve is detailed in Figure A3 of Appendix A. By comparing the values of AUC, it can be found that CatBoost, AdaBoost, random forest, DBGT and Bagging remain to be the five models with the best performance.

Table 6. Early warning effects of thirteen machine learning models based on traditional financial indicators and the emotional tone of financial news.

	AUC	ACC	SEN	SPE	Rank
Logistic regression	0.7359	0.6765	0.6617	0.6913	11
Ridge regression	0.7349	0.6747	0.6636	0.6858	13
Lasso regression	0.7358	0.6765	0.6599	0.6932	12
DBGT	0.7732	0.7135	0.7190	0.7079	4
XGBoost	0.7648	0.6969	0.7024	0.6913	6
LightGBM	0.7550	0.6839	0.6858	0.6821	8
CatBoost	0.7795	0.7033	0.7375	0.6691	1
AdaBoost	0.7761	0.7098	0.7043	0.7153	2
SVM	0.7368	0.6895	0.6821	0.6969	9
BPNN	0.7587	0.6904	0.6691	0.7116	7
Decision tree	0.7367	0.6765	0.7301	0.6229	10
Random forest	0.7751	0.7107	0.7098	0.7116	3
Bagging	0.7679	0.7043	0.7116	0.6969	5
Mean	0.7562	0.6928	0.6952	0.6905	

Figure 2 is plotted based on the values of the AUC of thirteen machine learning models under three groups of input feature variables. According to Figure 2, the values of the AUC of the group with the emotional tone indicators of financial news are higher than the effects of the other two groups of input feature variables on each machine learning model. Moreover, according to the average value of the four evaluation indexes of the thirteen machine learning models, the prediction effect of the group of input feature variables with the emotional tone indicators of financial news is significantly better than those of the other two groups of input features.

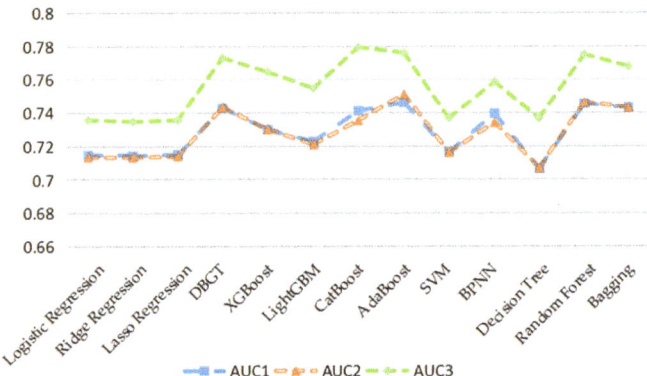

Figure 2. AUC values of 13 machine learning models under three sets of input feature variables.

4.5.4. Comparative Analysis of the Effect of Financial Crisis Early Warning with the Emotional Tone of MD&A and Financial News

According to the rank of AUC, this paper selects five models with the best performance to compare the early warning effect. Based on the values of four evaluation indexes, Figure 3 is plotted, which shows in detail the early warning effect of the five models incorporated with the emotional tone of MD&A and financial news. AdaBoost-MD&A represents the early warning effect of the AdaBoost model based on traditional financial indicators and the emotional tone indicators of MD&A. AdaBoost-News represents the early warning effect of the AdaBoost model based on traditional financial indicators and the emotional tone indicators of financial news. The other four models also use the same rule of labeling. It can be seen from Figure 3 that the five models incorporating the emotional tone of financial news are more effective than the models incorporating the tone of MD&A in all four evaluation indexes. The average value of the AUC of the thirteen models considering the tone of financial news is 0.0277 higher than that of MD&A in terms of warning effect. It is also 0.0310 higher in terms of prediction accuracy, 0.0289 higher in non-ST listed company sample, and 0.0332 higher in ST listed company sample.

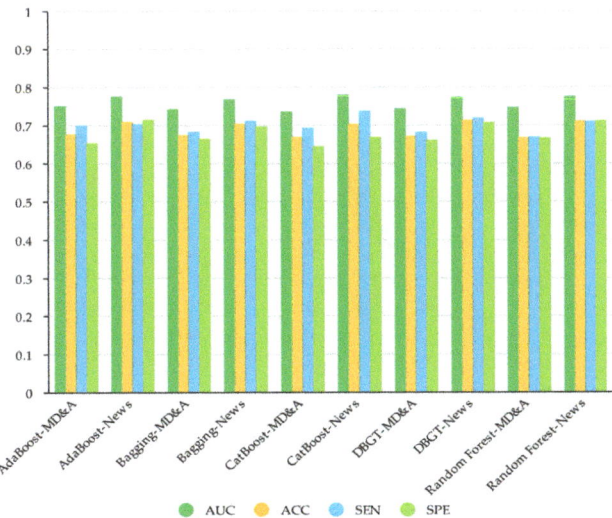

Figure 3. Models warning effects based on different textual emotional tones.

4.5.5. Comparative Analysis of the Performance of Each Machine Learning Model for Sample Recognition

This paper uses the average value of the effect evaluation indexes of the thirteen machine learning models based on three different groups of input feature variables and ranks each effect evaluation index to compare and analyze the performance of each machine learning model for sample recognition. The specific results are shown in Table 7. There are seven models with AUC above the mean, six models with ACC above the mean, seven models with SEN above the mean and nine models with SPE above the mean. There are four models with all four groups of effect evaluation indexes exceeding the mean, namely DBGT, AdaBoost, random forest and Bagging. These four models also rank in the top five in terms of AUC and ACC, and both the rankings of SEN and SPE remain in the top positions with good and smooth forecasting results. In addition, the BPNN model, whose AUC ranks sixth, ranks first in terms of SPE. It means this model has the highest prediction accuracy for ST listed companies. The traditional logistic regression, ridge regression and Lasso regression models have poor performance in identifying samples. Decision tree models rank last in the value of AUC, ACC and SPE, but rank second for identifying non-ST listed companies. The purpose of early warning mainly lies in the identification of ST listed companies, so the decision tree model does not belong to the focus of this paper.

Table 7. Mean values and ranking of early warning effect evaluation indicators of 13 machine learning models based on three different sets of input feature variables.

	AUC	Rank	ACC	Rank	SEN	Rank	SPE	Rank
Logistic regression	0.7215	11	0.6593	11	0.6433	12	0.6753	8
Ridge regression	0.7209	12	0.6587	12	0.6439	11	0.6734	9
Lasso regression	0.7217	10	0.6596	10	0.6420	13	0.6772	6
DBGT	0.7532	3	0.6879	3	0.6956	5	0.6802	4
XGBoost	0.7416	7	0.6710	7	0.6790	7	0.6630	10
LightGBM	0.7331	8	0.6645	9	0.6704	9	0.6587	11
CatBoost	0.7521	4	0.6817	5	0.7092	1	0.6543	12
AdaBoost	0.7579	1	0.6913	1	0.7037	3	0.6790	5
SVM	0.7232	9	0.6676	8	0.6581	10	0.6771	7
BPNN	0.7442	6	0.6814	6	0.6716	8	0.6913	1
Decision tree	0.7168	13	0.6519	13	0.7079	2	0.5958	13
Random forest	0.7557	2	0.6854	4	0.6839	6	0.6870	2
Bagging	0.7514	5	0.6898	2	0.6975	4	0.6821	3
Mean	0.7379		0.6731		0.6774		0.6688	

5. Further Discussion

According to the results of the empirical analysis, it can be found that the introduction of the emotional tone of the MD&A does not provide more incremental information for the identification of financial crises of listed companies. However, it brings a certain amount of noise, which leads to a slight decrease in the overall mean value of AUC, ACC, SEN, and SPE. This is in line with some literature findings that management can manipulate and modify texts to increase the positive level of the emotional tone, which can be very disruptive to the early warning effect [42–44]. It is clear that texts disclosed internally by firms are vulnerable to manipulation by management. This paper further investigates external texts that are difficult for companies to influence, such as financial news texts. The introduction of the emotional tone indicator of financial news to the machine learning model results in a better early warning effect than that of MD&A, which provides a new research idea for financial crisis early warning models from the perspective of feature engineering. On the early warning effects of thirteen machine learning models, DBGT, AdaBoost, random forest and Bagging all have good prediction performance on all three sets of input feature variables, providing an empirical basis for following research and applications.

6. Conclusions

Taking Chinese A-share listed companies as the sample and selecting data from 2012 to 2021, this paper uses a web crawler to obtain the MD&A section in annual reports of listed companies and uses textual analysis technology to quantify this section. Based on the emotional dictionary, this paper calculates the tone of the MD&A and calculates the emotional tone of the financial news by using structured data from the database of the Chinese Research Data Services Platform. The emotional tone of MD&A and the emotional tone of financial news are internal and external texts for listed companies, respectively. This paper further combines them with traditional financial indicators for comparing the early warning effect of financial crises in listed companies, and finally draws the following four conclusions: (1) The introduction of the emotional tone indicators of MD&A text has no significant effect on the improvement of the early warning effect financial crisis in listed companies and even brings some noise, which has a negative influence on the prediction effect of some models. (2) The introduction of the emotional tone indicators of financial news text can improve the early warning effect of financial crises of listed companies. It can be seen that the external text contains incremental information and can objectively reflect the operation and the future development trend of listed companies. (3) The emotional tone indicator of financial news text is not easily influenced by listed companies. However, the emotional tone indicators of MD&A are easily modified and manipulated by the management of listed companies. Adopting the tone of financial news text can exclude the interference of some modification information to the research results, and then improve the accuracy of financial crisis early warning. (4) Under three different sets of input feature variables, DBGT, AdaBoost, random forest and Bagging models still maintain stable and accurate sample recognition ability. The above four models can be used as relatively optimal classifiers for financial crisis early warning for listed companies.

There are still some limitations in this study, which are as follows: (1) There is no research on the early warning effect of linguistic features of texts other than emotional tone. (2) The establishment of a special comprehensive emotional dictionary of financial texts can be a research direction in the future. (3) There is a lack of research on other external texts, such as commentary texts, which represent the emotions of investors, and they may have an enhancing effect on the early warning effect of financial crises.

Owing to low credibility and financial falsification, traditional financial indicators may fail to truly reflect the development of listed companies. This paper focuses on non-financial indicators such as textual data, to quantify the internal and external texts of companies, finding that the emotional tone of financial news texts has an enhancing effect on the early warning effect of models based on traditional financial indicators. This finding will provide a useful supplement to the methods of crisis prediction relying solely on traditional financial indicators. It will also bring important theoretical and practical implications for the financial risk identification of listed companies.

Author Contributions: Conceptualization, H.N., Z.Z.; Methodology, H.N., Z.Z.; Writing—original draft preparation, Z.Z., M.L., Z.H.; Writing—review and editing, Z.Z., M.L., Z.H., H.N. All authors have read and agreed to the published version of the manuscript.

Funding: This research was supported by Beijing Foreign Studies University Double First Class Major Landmark Project (No. 2022SYLZD001) in China, the Fundamental Research Funds for the Central Universities (No. 2022JX031) in China, and Beijing Foreign Studies University G20 Research Center Project (No. G20ZX20223003) in China.

Institutional Review Board Statement: Not applicable.

Informed Consent Statement: Not applicable.

Data Availability Statement: Figures A1–A3 in Appendix A were generated by PyCharm, all other charts and diagrams in the text were exported by WPS Office. The data and code of this study can be downloaded by visiting https://github.com/zzs0216/applsci (accessed on 24 June 2022), or contact the author, email address: bfsuniuhy@163.com.

Conflicts of Interest: The authors declare no conflict of interest.

Appendix A

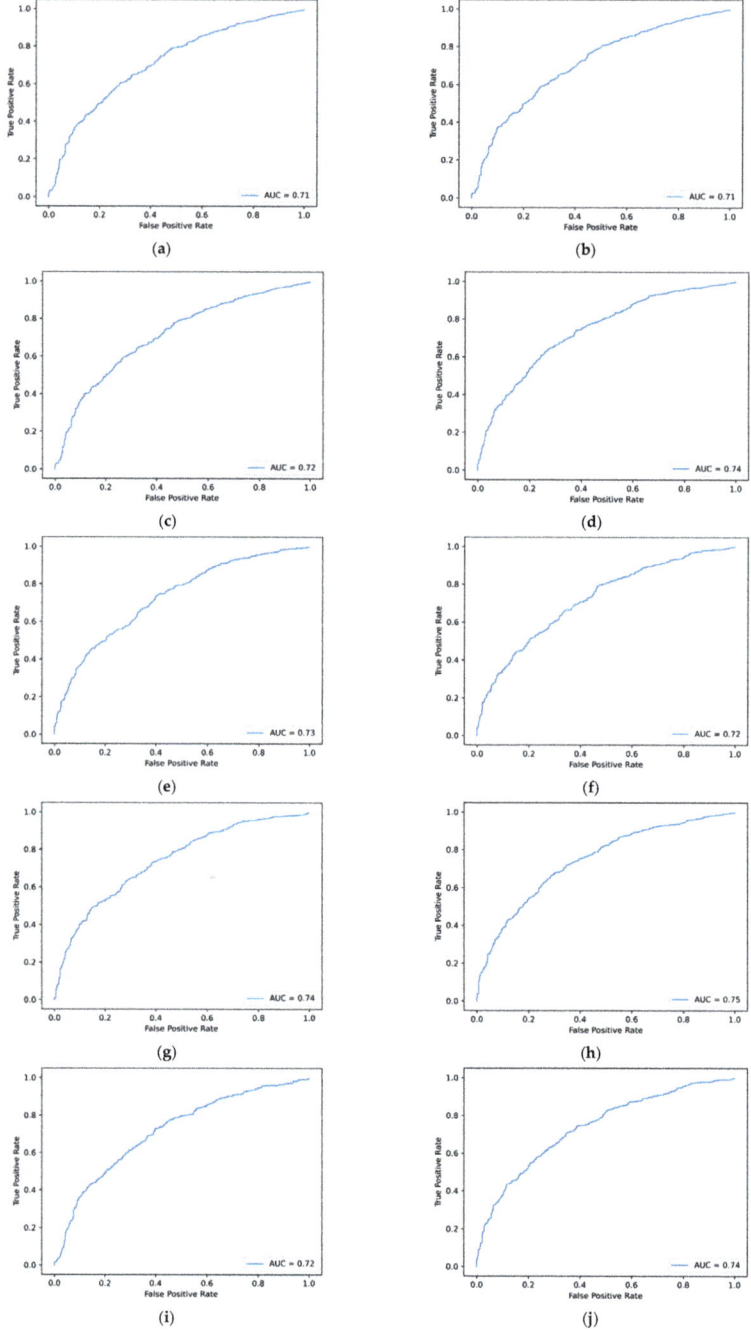

Figure A1. *Cont.*

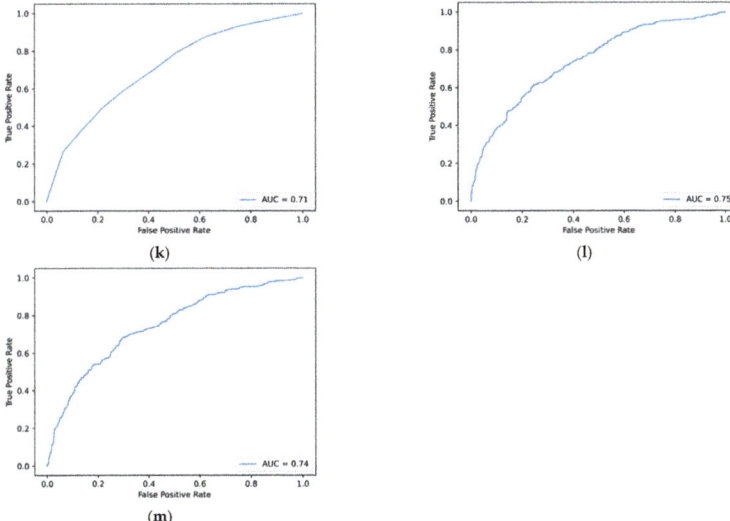

Figure A1. ROC curve of machine learning model based on traditional financial indicators. (**a**) Logistic regression. (**b**) Ridge regression. (**c**) Lasso regression. (**d**) GBDT. (**e**) XGBoost. (**f**) LightGBM. (**g**) CatBoost. (**h**) AdaBoost. (**i**) SVM. (**j**) BPNN. (**k**) Decision tree. (**l**) Random forest. (**m**) Bagging.

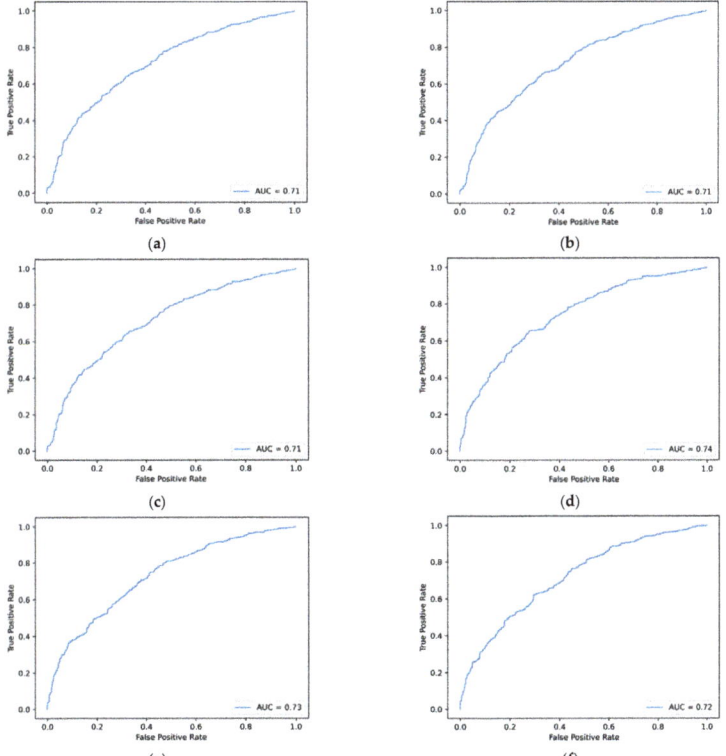

Figure A2. *Cont.*

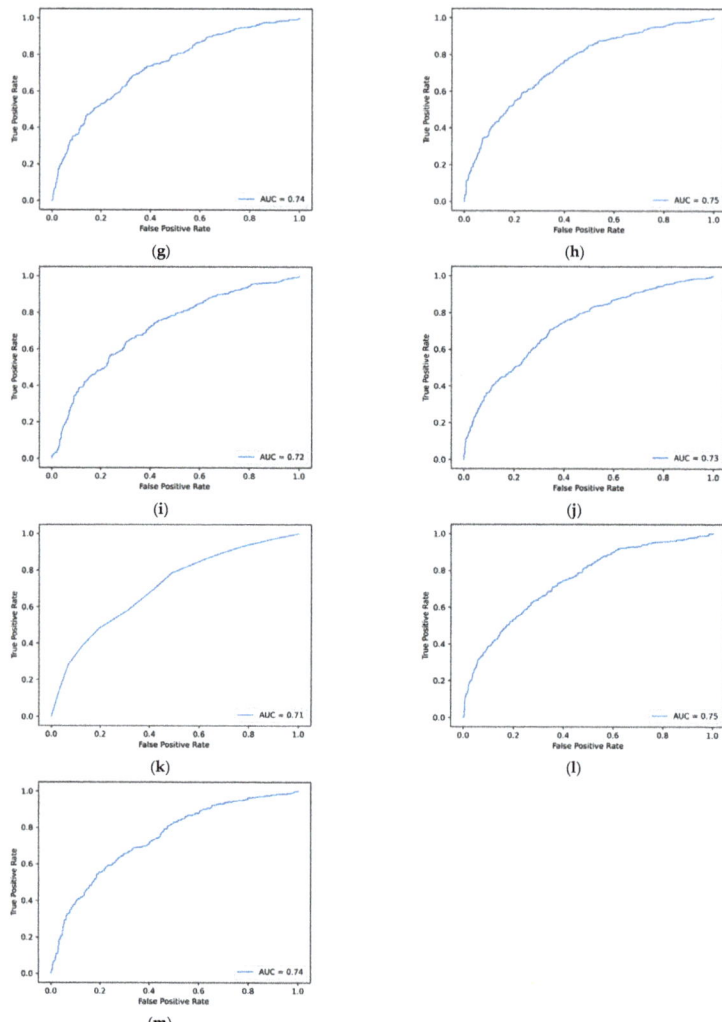

Figure A2. ROC curve of machine learning model based on traditional financial indicators and MD&A emotional tone indicators. (**a**) Logistic regression. (**b**) Ridge regression. (**c**) Lasso regression. (**d**) GBDT. (**e**) XGBoost. (**f**) LightGBM. (**g**) CatBoost. (**h**) AdaBoost. (**i**) SVM. (**j**) BPNN. (**k**) Decision tree. (**l**) Random forest. (**m**) Bagging.

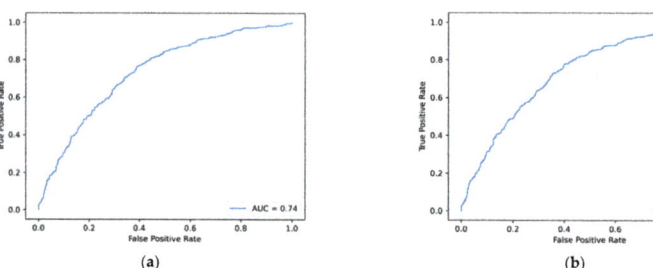

Figure A3. *Cont.*

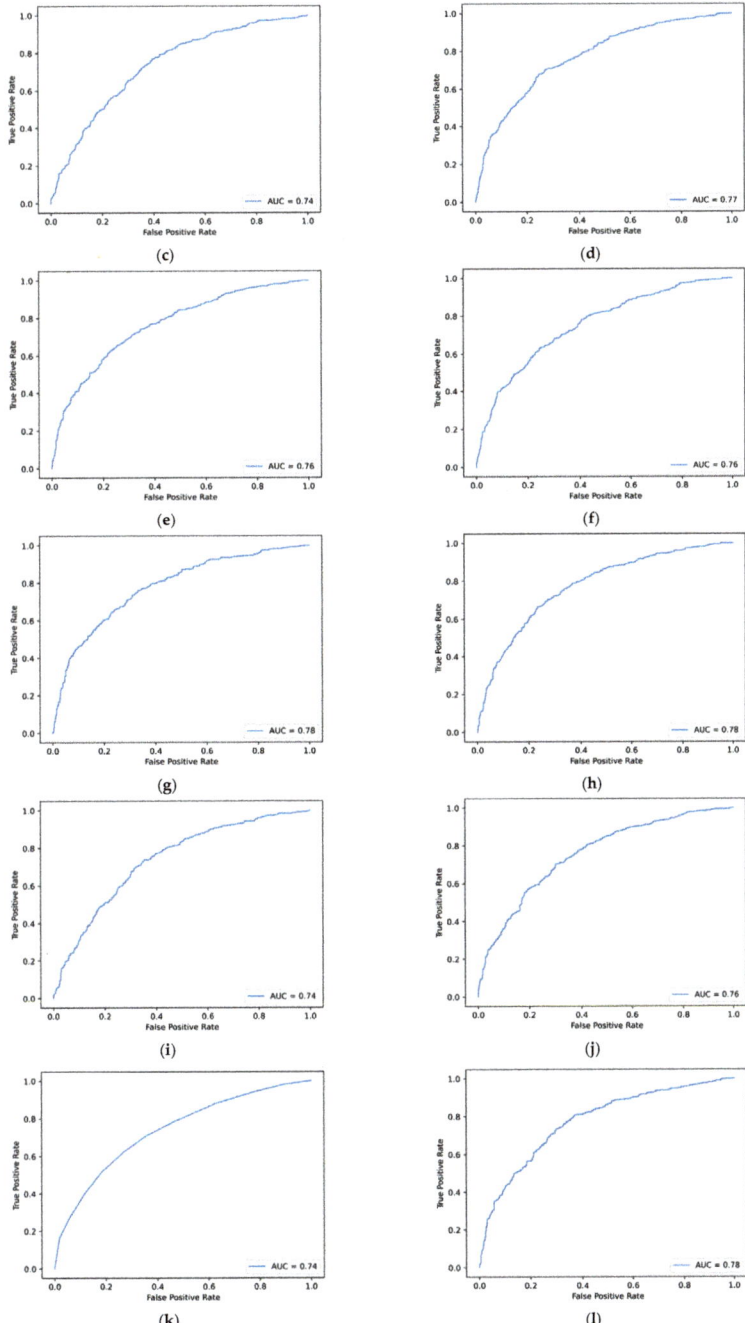

Figure A3. *Cont.*

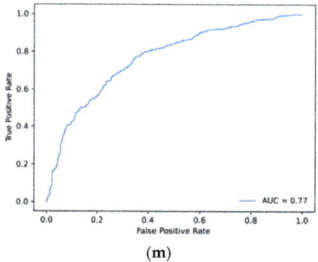

(m)

Figure A3. ROC curve of machine learning model based on traditional financial indicators and financial news emotional tone indicators. (**a**) Logistic regression. (**b**) Ridge regression. (**c**) Lasso regression. (**d**) GBDT. (**e**) XGBoost. (**f**) LightGBM. (**g**) CatBoost. (**h**) AdaBoost. (**i**) SVM. (**j**) BPNN. (**k**) Decision tree. (**l**) Random forest. (**m**) Bagging.

References

1. Beaver, W.H. Financial rations as predictors of failures. *J. Account. Res.* **1966**, *4*, 71–111. [CrossRef]
2. Altman, E.I. Financial ratios, discriminant analysis and the prediction of corporate bankruptcy. *J. Financ.* **1968**, *23*, 589–609. [CrossRef]
3. Chang, H.Y.; Ma, C.A. Financial flexibility, managerial efficiency and firm life cycle on firm performance: An empirical analysis of Chinese listed firms. *J. Adv. Manag. Res.* **2018**, *16*, 168–180. [CrossRef]
4. Li, H.; Chen, Q.X.; Hong, L.Y.; Zhou, Q. Asset restructuring performance prediction for failure firms. *J. Corp. Account. Financ.* **2019**, *30*, 25–42. [CrossRef]
5. Jing, J.; Leung, K.; Ng, J.; Zhang, J.J. Fixing the core, earnings management, and sustainable emergence from financial distress: Evidence from china's special treatment system. *J. Account. Audit. Financ.* **2021**, *36*, 1–26. [CrossRef]
6. Wang, R.; Ma, S.; Xu, X.; Song, P. Heterogeneous shareholders' participation, COVID-19 impact, and innovation decisions of state-owned firms: Evidence from China. *Sustainability* **2021**, *13*, 4406. [CrossRef]
7. Jiang, H.; Xia, J.; Devers, C.E.; Shen, W. Who will board a sinking ship? A firm–director interdependence perspective of mutual selection between declining firms and director candidates. *Acad. Manag. J.* **2021**, *64*, 901–925. [CrossRef]
8. Shumway, T. Forecasting bankruptcy more accurately: A simple hazard model. *J. Bus.* **2001**, *74*, 101–124. [CrossRef]
9. Beaver, W.H.; McNichols, M.F.; Rhie, J.W. Have financial statements become less informative? Evidence from the ability of financial ratios to predict bankruptcy. *Rev. Account. Stud.* **2005**, *10*, 93–122. [CrossRef]
10. Woo, S.H.; Kwon, M.S.; Yuen, K.F. Financial determinants of credit risk in the logistics and shipping industries. *Marit. Econ. Logist.* **2021**, *23*, 268–290. [CrossRef]
11. Cao, Y.; Shao, Y.; Zhang, H. Study on early warning of E-commerce enterprise financial risk based on deep learning algorithm. *Electron. Commer. Res.* **2022**, *22*, 21–36. [CrossRef]
12. Balcaen, S.; Ooghe, H. 35 years of studies on business failure: An overview of the classic statistical methodologies and their related problems. *Br. Account. Rev.* **2006**, *38*, 63–93. [CrossRef]
13. Charalambakis, E.C.; Garrett, I. On the prediction of financial distress in developed and emerging markets: Does the choice of accounting and market information matter? A comparison of UK and Indian firms. *Rev. Quant. Financ. Account.* **2016**, *47*, 1–28. [CrossRef]
14. Canbas, S.; Cabuk, A.; Kilic, S.B. Prediction of commercial bank failure via multivariate statistical analysis of financial structures: The Turkish case. *Eur. J. Oper. Res.* **2005**, *166*, 528–546. [CrossRef]
15. Cecchini, M.; Aytug, H.; Koehler, G.J.; Pathak, P. Making words work: Using financial text as a predictor of financial events. *Decis. Support Syst.* **2010**, *50*, 164–175. [CrossRef]
16. Mayew, W.J.; Sethuraman, M.; Venkatachalam, M. MD&A disclosure and the firm's ability to continue as a going concern. *Account. Rev.* **2015**, *90*, 1621–1651.
17. Ertugrul, M.; Lei, J.; Qiu, J.; Wan, C. Annual report readability, tone ambiguity, and the cost of borrowing. *J. Financ. Quant. Anal.* **2017**, *52*, 811–836. [CrossRef]
18. Iqbal, J.; Riaz, K. Predicting future financial performance of banks from management's tone in the textual disclosures. *Qual. Quant.* **2021**, *53*, 1–31. [CrossRef]
19. Kliestik, T.; Valaskova, K.; Lazaroiu, G.; Kovacova, M.; Vrbka, J. Remaining financially healthy and competitive: The role of financial predictors. *J. Compet.* **2020**, *12*, 74–92. [CrossRef]
20. Bao, Y.; Ke, B.; Li, B.; Yu, Y.J.; Zhang, J. Detecting accounting fraud in publicly traded US firms using a machine learning approach. *J. Account. Res.* **2020**, *58*, 199–235. [CrossRef]
21. Fitzpatrick, F.A. Comparison of ratios of successful industrial enterprises with those of failed Firm. *Certif. Publ. Account.* **1932**, *6*, 727–731.

22. Altman, E.I.; Haldeman, R.G.; Narayanan, P. Zetatm analysis a new model to identify bankruptcy risk of corporations. *J. Bank. Financ.* **1977**, *1*, 29–54. [CrossRef]
23. Ohlson, J.A. Financial ratios and the probabilistic prediction of bankruptcy. *J. Account. Res.* **1980**, *18*, 109–131. [CrossRef]
24. Odom, M.D.; Sharda, R. A neural network model for bankruptcy prediction. In Proceedings of the 1990 IJCNN International Joint Conference on Neural Networks, San Diego, CA, USA, 17–21 July 1990.
25. Breiman, L. Random forests. *Mach. Learn.* **2001**, *45*, 5–32. [CrossRef]
26. Min, J.H.; Lee, Y.C. Bankruptcy prediction using support vector machine with optimal choice of kernel function parameters. *Expert Syst. Appl.* **2005**, *28*, 603–614. [CrossRef]
27. Wang, G.; Wang, K.; Zhou, Y.; Mo, X. Establishment of a financial crisis early warning system for domestic listed companies based on three decision tree models. *Math. Probl. Eng.* **2020**, *2020*, 8036154. [CrossRef]
28. Loughran, T.; McDonald, B. When is a liability not a liability? Textual analysis, dictionaries, and 10-Ks. *J. Financ.* **2011**, *66*, 35–65. [CrossRef]
29. Price, S.M.K.; Doran, J.S.; Peterson, D.R.; Bliss, B.A. Earnings conference calls and stock returns: The incremental informativeness of textual tone. *J. Bank. Financ.* **2012**, *36*, 992–1011. [CrossRef]
30. Davis, A.K.; Piger, J.M.; Sedor, L.M. Beyond the numbers: Measuring the information content of earnings press release language. *Contemp. Account. Res.* **2012**, *29*, 845–868. [CrossRef]
31. Guay, W.; Samuels, D.; Taylor, D. Guiding through the fog: Financial statement complexity and voluntary disclosure. *J. Account. Econ.* **2016**, *62*, 234–269. [CrossRef]
32. Li, S.; Wang, G.; Luo, Y. Tone of language, financial disclosure, and earnings management: A textual analysis of form 20-F. *Financ. Innov.* **2022**, *8*, 43. [CrossRef]
33. Tetlock, P.C.; Saar-Tsechansky, M.; Macskassy, S. More than words: Quantifying language to measure firms' fundamentals. *J. Financ.* **2008**, *63*, 1437–1467. [CrossRef]
34. Berns, J.; Bick, P.; Flugum, R.; Houston, R. Do changes in MD&A section tone predict investment behavior? *Financ. Rev.* **2022**, *57*, 129–153.
35. Tennyson, B.M.; Ingram, R.W.; Dugan, M.T. Assessing the information content of narrative disclosures in explaining bankruptcy. *J. Bus. Finan. Account.* **1990**, *17*, 391–410. [CrossRef]
36. Li, F. The information content of forward-looking statements in corporate filings-a naive bayesian machine learning approach. *J. Account. Res.* **2010**, *48*, 1049–1102. [CrossRef]
37. Kim, C.; Wang, K.; Zhang, L. Readability of 10-K reports and stock price crash risk. *Contemp. Account. Res.* **2019**, *36*, 1184–1216. [CrossRef]
38. Huang, B.; Yao, X.; Luo, Y.; Li, J. Improving financial distress prediction using textual sentiment of annual reports. *Ann. Oper. Res.* **2022**, *310*, 1–28. [CrossRef]
39. Brockman, P.; Cicon, J.E.; Li, X.; Price, S.M. Words versus deeds: Evidence from post-call manager trades. *Financ. Manag.* **2017**, *46*, 965–994. [CrossRef]
40. Huang, X.; Teoh, S.H.; Zhang, Y. Tone management. *Account. Rev.* **2014**, *89*, 1083–1113. [CrossRef]
41. Kang, T.; Park, D.H.; Han, I. Beyond the numbers: The effect of 10-K tone on firms' performance predictions using text analytics. *Telemat. Inform.* **2018**, *35*, 370–381. [CrossRef]
42. Mohseni, A.; Roodposhti, F.R. Financial performance and writing tone management in financial reporting. *Empir. Res. Account.* **2020**, *9*, 29–48.
43. Rose, A.M.; Rose, J.M.; Suh, I.; Thibodeau, J.; Linke, K.; Norman, C.S. Why financial executives do bad things: The effects of the slippery slope and tone at the top on misreporting behavior. *J. Bus. Ethics* **2021**, *174*, 291–309. [CrossRef]
44. Yang, F.; Huang, J.; Cai, Y. Tone of textual information in annual reports and regulatory inquiry letters: Data from China. *Emerg. Mark. Financ. Trade* **2022**, *58*, 417–427. [CrossRef]
45. Vaferi, B.; Rahnama, Y.; Darvishi, P.; Toorani, A.; Lashkarbolooki, M. Phase equilibria modeling of binary systems containing ethanol using optimal feedforward neural network. *J. Supercrit. Fluid.* **2013**, *84*, 80–88. [CrossRef]
46. Khalifeh, A.; Vaferi, B. Intelligent assessment of effect of aggregation on thermal conductivity of nanofluids—comparison by experimental data and empirical correlations. *Thermochim. Acta* **2019**, *681*, 178377. [CrossRef]
47. Roshani, M.; Phan, G.; Roshani, G.H.; Hanus, R.; Nazemi, B.; Corniani, E.; Nazemi, E. Combination of X-ray tube and GMDH neural network as a nondestructive and potential technique for measuring characteristics of gas-oil–water three phase flows. *Measurement* **2021**, *168*, 108427. [CrossRef]
48. Nasr, A.K.; Tavana, M.; Alavi, B.; Mina, H. A novel fuzzy multi-objective circular supplier selection and order allocation model for sustainable closed-loop supply chains. *J. Clean. Prod.* **2021**, *287*, 124994. [CrossRef]
49. Karan, E.; Mansoob, V.K.; Khodabandelu, A.; Asgari, S.; Mohammadpour, A.; Asadi, S. Using Artificial Intelligence to Automate the Quantity Takeoff Process. In Proceedings of the International Conference on Software Business Engineering, Amsterdam, The Netherlands, 13–14 May 2021.
50. Niu, H.; Zhang, Z.; Xiao, Y.; Luo, M.; Chen, Y. A Study of Carbon Emission Efficiency in Chinese Provinces Based on a Three-Stage SBM-Undesirable Model and an LSTM Model. *Int. J. Environ. Res. Public Health* **2022**, *19*, 5395. [CrossRef]
51. Zhang, Z.; Xiao, Y.; Niu, H. DEA and Machine Learning for Performance Prediction. *Mathematics* **2022**, *10*, 1776. [CrossRef]
52. Vapnik, V.N. *The Nature of Statistical Learning Theory*; Springer: New York, NY, USA, 1995; pp. 273–297.

53. Rumelhart, D.E.; Hinton, G.E.; Williams, R.J. Learning representations by back-propagating errors. *Nature* **1986**, *323*, 533–536. [CrossRef]
54. Quinlan, J.R. Introduction of decision trees. *Mach. Learn.* **1986**, *1*, 84–100. [CrossRef]
55. Quinlan, J.R. *C4.5: Programs for Machine Learning*; Morgan Kaufmann Publishers Inc.: San Francisco, CA, USA, 1993; pp. 17–42.
56. Breiman, L.I.; Friedman, J.H.; Olshen, R.A.; Stone, C. Classification and regression trees (CART). *Biometrics* **1984**, *40*, 358–361.
57. Friedman, J.H. Greedy function approximation: A gradient boosting machine. *Ann. Stat.* **2001**, *29*, 1189–1232. [CrossRef]
58. Freund, Y.; Schapire, R.E. A decision-theoretic generalization of on-line learning and an application to boosting. *J. Comput. Syst. Sci.* **1997**, *55*, 119–139. [CrossRef]
59. Loughran, T.; McDonald, B. Measuring readability in financial disclosures. *J. Financ.* **2014**, *69*, 1643–1671. [CrossRef]
60. Davis, A.K.; Ge, W.; Matsumoto, D.; Zhang, J.L. The effect of manager-specific optimism on the tone of earnings conference calls. *Rev. Account. Stud.* **2015**, *20*, 639–673. [CrossRef]
61. Henry, E. Are investors influenced by how earnings press releases are written? *J. Bus. Commun.* **2008**, *45*, 363–407. [CrossRef]
62. Henry, E.; Leone, A.J. Measuring qualitative information in capital markets research: Comparison of alternative methodologies to measure disclosure tone. *Account. Rev.* **2016**, *91*, 153–178. [CrossRef]
63. Brockman, P.; Rui, O.M.; Zou, H. Institutions and the performance of politically connected M&As. *J. Int. Bus. Stud.* **2013**, *44*, 833–852.
64. Bicudo de Castro, V.; Gul, F.A.; Muttakin, M.B.; Mihret, D.G. Optimistic tone and audit fees: Some Australian evidence. *Int. J. Audit.* **2019**, *23*, 352–364. [CrossRef]
65. Barakat, A.; Ashby, S.; Fenn, P.; Bryce, C. Operational risk and reputation in financial institutions: Does media tone make a difference? *J. Bank Financ.* **2019**, *98*, 1–24. [CrossRef]
66. Mousa, G.A.; Elamir, E.A.H.; Hussainey, K. Using machine learning methods to predict financial performance: Does disclosure tone matter? *Int. J. Disclosure Gov.* **2022**, *19*, 93–112. [CrossRef]
67. Akkasi, A.; Varoglu, E. Improvement of chemical named entity recognition through sentence-based random under-sampling and classifier combination. *J. AI Data Min.* **2019**, *7*, 311–319.
68. Sun, L.; Wu, Y.; Shu, B.; Ding, X.; Cai, C.; Huang, Y.; Paisley, J. A dual-domain deep lattice network for rapid MRI reconstruction. *Neurocomputing* **2020**, *397*, 94–107. [CrossRef]
69. Liu, S.; You, S.; Lin, Z.; Zeng, C.; Li, H.; Wang, W.; Liu, Y. Data-driven event identification in the US power systems based on 2D-OLPP and RUS Boosted trees. *IEEE Trans. Power Syst.* **2021**, *37*, 94–105. [CrossRef]

Concept Paper

DNA Computing: Concepts for Medical Applications

Sebastian Sakowski [1,*], Jacek Waldmajer [2], Ireneusz Majsterek [3] and Tomasz Poplawski [4]

1. Faculty of Mathematics and Computer Science, University of Lodz, Banacha 22, 90-238 Lodz, Poland
2. Institute of Computer Science, University of Opole, Oleska 48, 45-052 Opole, Poland; jwaldmajer@uni.opole.pl
3. Department of Clinical Chemistry and Biochemistry, Medical University of Lodz, 90-419 Lodz, Poland; ireneusz.majsterek@umed.lodz.pl
4. Department of Molecular Genetics, Faculty of Biology and Environmental Protection, University of Lodz, 90-236 Lodz, Poland; tomasz.poplawski@biol.uni.lodz.pl
* Correspondence: sebastian.sakowski@wmii.uni.lodz.pl

Abstract: The branch of informatics that deals with construction and operation of computers built of DNA, is one of the research directions which investigates issues related to the use of DNA as hardware and software. This concept assumes the use of DNA computers due to their biological origin mainly for intelligent, personalized and targeted diagnostics frequently related to therapy. Important elements of this concept are (1) the retrieval of unique DNA sequences using machine learning methods and, based on the results of this process, (2) the construction/design of smart diagnostic biochip projects. The authors of this paper propose a new concept of designing diagnostic biochips, the key elements of which are machine-learning methods and the concept of biomolecular queue automata. This approach enables the scheduling of computational tasks at the molecular level by sequential events of cutting and ligating DNA molecules. We also summarize current challenges and perspectives of biomolecular computer application and machine-learning approaches using DNA sequence data mining.

Keywords: machine learning; DNA computer; biochips; queue automata; type IIB endonucleases

1. Introduction

For the last several years, there has been a growing interest in the possibility of computing by means of DNA molecules (called "DNA computing" later in this paper). The different directions of studies in this area include construction of biomolecular computers hardware and software which are based on biochemical components (bioorganic chemical compounds). Such computers are nanodevices built exclusively of organic components. Biomolecular computers may have a number of practical uses in the future, owing to their various properties, such as parallelism of operation or the ability to store information. Importantly, the biomolecular computers may, in the predictable future, fill some gaps in the areas not yet accessible to conventional computers. Particularly interesting is the compatibility between biomolecular computers and the cellular environment via biochemical reactions taking place both in vitro and in vivo.

An important part of DNA computing is involved in the construction of intelligent biochips (meaning decision making in the choice of a diagnosis/treatment direction), as such technological solutions may simplify and automate molecular diagnostics. This paper presents the use of biomolecular computers for constructing diagnostic biochips based on DNA chain cutting and ligating reactions carried out by restriction enzymes. The study was inspired by the concept of the hypothetical enzymatic Turing machine that was built of biomolecules by Charles Bennett in 1982 [1]. It also indicates the feasibility of using only biochemical components for designing computers characterized by high energy efficiency— with low energy consumption for performing calculations scheduled by humans. It should be pointed out that Charles Bennett noticed a similarity between the biochemical processes taking place in live organisms (specifically DNA polymerase) and the operation of the Turing machine—specifically, a model of a programmable universal Turing machine that enables data processing and which is very well known in computer science.

In 1995, Paul W.K. Rothemund published his concept of a Turing machine based on commercially available class IIS restriction enzymes [2]. This concept indicated a theoretical possibility (not requiring laboratory experiments) of encoding, in double-stranded DNA, the transition table of the Turing machine, the idea of which is based on alternate cutting and ligating the double-stranded DNA with the class IIS restriction enzymes and a ligase. Moreover, Paul W.K. Rothemund suggested a method for constructing symbols as well as input words, for instance: the input word $x = 000111$ (built of the symbols 0 or 1), of Turing machines which were designed by recording them as double-stranded DNA. In that approach, encoding the information (the symbol encoded in the input word $x = 000111$) as double-stranded DNA is feasible, as modern laboratories offer production of double-stranded DNA with a preset nucleotide sequence. Paul W.K. Rothemund also proposed a method for encoding the state of the biomolecular Turing machine which, in his approach, was interpreted as a sticking-out, single-stranded DNA (the so-called sticky end), obtained by cutting the double-stranded DNA with class IIS restriction enzymes.

Further studies, including experimental ones, were carried out by our and Ehud Shapiro's teams, and demonstrated the potential of restriction enzymes in developing practical programmable biomolecular nanodevices, functioning in actual laboratory conditions [3–6]. In 2001, Ehud Shapiro's group built biomolecular computers in which double-stranded DNA was employed for encoding processed input data (symbols encoded in the input word). They also used double-stranded DNA for developing molecular software to enable such a biomolecular computer to be programmed. The hardware of such a biomolecular computer consisted of *FokI* restriction enzyme and ligase. They achieved a computational result by alternately cutting and ligating double-stranded DNA, placing in a test tube the double-stranded DNA encoding the input word, the software in the form of double-stranded DNA, and the hardware (*FokI*, ligase). It is worth noting that the entire process was run autonomously in a reaction mixture comprising the appropriate reaction buffers until the final computational result was obtained. This approach showed that it is feasible to practically construct a biomolecular computer, working only in a test tube (without any electronic components), in which the computations are based exclusively on biochemical reactions.

The use of restriction enzymes in typical laboratory conditions requires optimization of reaction conditions [5] and an appropriate approach to encoding various components of biomolecular computers, especially when multiple restriction enzymes are used. A number of laboratory experiments were carried out using multiple restriction enzymes, operating alternately on DNA chains in a single reaction mixture [5,6]. After solving various practical problems, we developed an algorithmic method that enabled an ad hoc addition of more restriction enzymes acting alternately on the appropriately encoded DNA [6]. Understanding the successive properties of the biomolecular computers led us to the formulation of a new mathematical theory involving a base formal apparatus concerning performance of computation by means of a single restriction enzyme and a double-stranded DNA [7]. Other theoretical studies included the fundamentals of designing biomolecular computers with memory and discussed the potential use of type IIB restriction endonucleases for developing a biomolecular push-down automaton [8].

One concern with biochip design is targeting particular specific molecular goals. Typically, these targets are specific DNA or RNA sequences defined and determined by the biochip's application target (infectious agent or pathological protein/sequence). This issue can be solved with machine learning.

Machine learning is an important part of the new concept of designing biochips based on biomolecular computers that has been proposed in this paper. This approach (concept) requires knowledge of unique DNA fragments, which is obtained by using machine-learning methods, such as sequence pattern mining [9]. Knowledge about unique

DNA fragments, the presence of which we want to diagnose, makes it possible to use biomolecular computers to read these DNA fragments. We selected from the various approaches to the application of machine-learning methods in biology those that will be useful for finding unique DNA fragments—important from the point of view of designing biochips based on biomolecular computers.

2. Machine-Learning Approaches in Nucleotide Sequence Data Mining

In recent years, the use of algorithms and mathematical methods has become widespread in biological sciences [10,11]. This is due to a dynamic increase in the number of biological data sets, which prompts the use of various methods typical of exact sciences [12], including artificial intelligence and machine-learning algorithms, for example, recurrent neural networks [13] or convolutional neural networks [14]. This requires using sophisticated methods characteristic of exact sciences to deepen the biological knowledge (see Table 1). The current knowledge on living organisms demonstrates great complexity of processes occurring at the molecular level, e.g., the expression of genetic information is a complex and not fully understood process.

Table 1. Summary of the existing machine-learning approaches for DNA sequence mining.

Paper	Method	Type of Input	Target	Dataset	Result
Luedi et al. (2007) [15]	Multiple classification algorithms	DNA sequence	Imprint status of human genes	Ensembl	156 imprinted genes identified
Chen et al. (2016) [16]	Hierarchical neural networks	cDNA microarrays	Molecular signal transduction	PUMAdb	Novel model for evaluating the machinery regulating gene expression
Kelley et al. (2016) [17]	Convolutional neural networks	Genome sequence	To annotate and interpret the noncoding genome parts	DNaseI-seq peak BED format files for 125 cells	Noncoding genome parts annotated and interpreted
Amin et al. (2018) [18]	Long short-term memory	Genome sequence	Annotate genome sequences	NCBI genomedomek-database	DeepAnnotator algorithms and models
Zeng et al. (2018) [19]	Natural language processing	Gene sequence	Enhancer-promoter interactions	Various databases from TargetFinder	Framework EP2vec
Yuan and Bar-Joseph (2019) [20]	Convolutional neural network	RNA sequences	Gene–gene relationships	scRNA-seq and bulk RNA-seq	Framework CNNC
Fudenberg et al. (2020) [21]	Convolutional neural network	DNA sequences	Genome folding	Five Hi-C anddomekMicro-C datasets	Akita network

A dynamic development of the next-generation sequencing (NGS), which became cheap and available, brought about an increase in the amount of data containing nucleotide sequences. NGS is a sequencing method that makes it possible to determine the order of nucleotides in a sample of nucleic acids and high-throughput whole-genome sequencing. The GenBank database, which collects research results from the sequencing of living organisms, is of particular interest here. Thus, it is possible to quickly find information about the nucleotide sequence in the form of files containing nucleotide sequences, e.g., for a selected group of organisms for which we want to check for differences in nucleotide sequences. This makes it possible to develop new approaches to the analysis of data derived from the sequencing of living organisms. In recent years, many different machine-learning approaches have been used in life sciences. They focus on different aspects related to sequencing data analysis, such as sequence alignment, classification, and pattern finding [22].

To implement the biomolecular computers in medicine, as proposed in this paper, it is crucial to find unique DNA fragments that can be read/identified by biomolecular computers. It is important to find unique patterns for the DNA sequences tested so that genetic differentiation of the investigated organisms is possible. DNA fragments encode various information, e.g., they encode amino acids that make up proteins. Therefore, comparing genomes based on specific DNA fragments makes it possible to find similarities between the tested organisms or to differentiate them with respect to the occurrence of unique nucleotide sequence arrangements. The problem of finding patterns in large sets of biological data that contain genomic sequences [9,23] is a challenge both for computer scientists and mathematicians, but also for biologists. Figure 1 presents the main idea of finding patterns in various nucleotide sequences that are analyzed by applying machine-learning methods to files containing nucleotide sequences. In our approach to the use of biomolecular computers, we amplify the unique DNA fragments by PCR (fragments number 2 and number 4 to be exact); then, we read the amplified DNA fragments using a properly designed biomolecular computer. Thus, the step of finding unique patterns using machine-learning methods is a key stage in the application of biomolecular computers for molecular diagnostics.

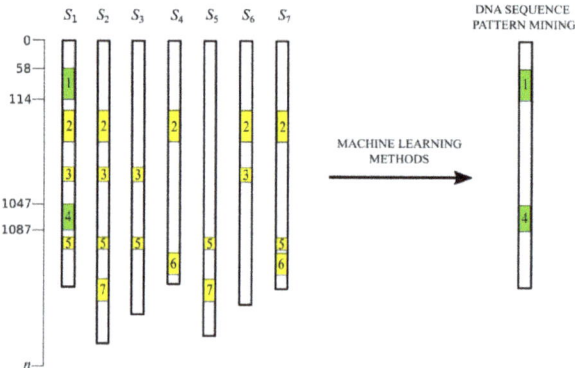

Figure 1. A diagram showing the use of machine-learning methods to find patterns and similarities in nucleotide sequences. By studying different nucleotide sequences with the use of machine-learning methods, unique DNA fragments can be found that are distinctive patterns of a DNA sequence. Two unique sequences (1 and 4) in the S_1 sequence tested are marked green. Abbreviations: $S_1, \ldots, S_7$—denote different genome sequences (different nucleotide sequences in genomes); the numbers 1, 2, 3, 4, 5, 6, 7—denote nucleotide sequences that occur in the sequences tested; the numbers: 58, 114, 1047, 1087—denote the sequence position in the genome; the unique DNA fragments are denoted by green color; the nonunique DNA fragments are denoted by yellow color.

Machine-learning algorithms are of particular interest, as they allow classifying DNA sequences, for example, the use of convolutional neural networks to analyze DNA sequences [14]. The classification of DNA sequences is very useful in understanding the relationship between DNA sequences encoding different proteins, as well as the relationships between proteins [13]. The main problem with these studies is that the functions of DNA fragments are not fully understood and the relationships between DNA fragments are still being discovered. There are many different approaches to finding homology in files containing nucleotide sequences [24], e.g., the use of basic local alignment search tool (BLAST) to find similarities in nucleotide sequences [25]. These problems are similar to those of fast search in text files encountered in computer sciences [26].

The key element of the proposed approach of employing the biomolecular computers is the use of machine-learning methods to find unique and characteristic DNA fragments of the diagnosed organism. These can be unique patterns of DNA fragments that are found by machine learning. Our proposed new approach is a combination of different research results in the field of machine learning and theoretical and practical work in the field of biomolecular computers. This approach requires an interdisciplinary treatment of looking at the problem of molecular diagnostics, which needs to be solved by a joint action of computer science and molecular biology.

3. New Concept of Designing Diagnostic Biochips

Extraction of DNA sequence patterns with the use of machine-learning methods provides the background for the construction of diagnostic biochips based on biomolecular computers. In the proposed concept of designing diagnostic biochips based on biomolecular computers, unique DNA fragments play a special role, as they enable proper programming of a biomolecular computer in such a way that it reads unique DNA nucleotide sequences.

In the previous section, we discussed different machine-learning approaches to nucleotide sequence data mining. In our new concept of designing diagnostic biochips, it is possible to use artificial neural networks, for example, recurrent neural network (RNN) [18], at the stage of machine learning in the sequence data mining. RNNs can be used for data containing ordered strings, e.g., nucleotide sequences. From the point of view of the research methodology involving the RNN, it is important that the nucleotide sequences of the studied living organism genome are the input layer of such a network. RNNs can be used to generate output based on a nucleotide sequence of a given length. For example, RNNs can analyze nucleotide sequences that are characteristic of protein-coding genes and identify promoter sequences [10]. As part of the methodology of working with sequence extraction machine-learning methods, classic elements of machine learning, such as the process of training, validation, and testing, should be distinguished in individual steps. In the first step, it is necessary to well understand the set of input data and then to formulate an appropriate research question. In the next step, the data should be divided into training, testing, and validation sets. The next step is to choose the most suitable model for the research question. At this stage, it is especially important to check assumptions on the possibility of using the model. From the point of view of machine-learning methodology, it is also important to fine-tune the hyperparameters for the methods used. It is worth noting that in recent years, the model called transformers have attracted a lot of interest from researchers, as it allows better accuracy when studying character strings such as nucleotide sequences [27,28].

We propose a new approach to biochip design with biomolecular computing as the hardware and software (Figure 2) to enable DNA-level diagnostics. In this approach, the main mechanism is based on the use of biomolecular computers, built of appropriately encoded DNA chains as the software, and restriction enzymes and ligase as the hardware.

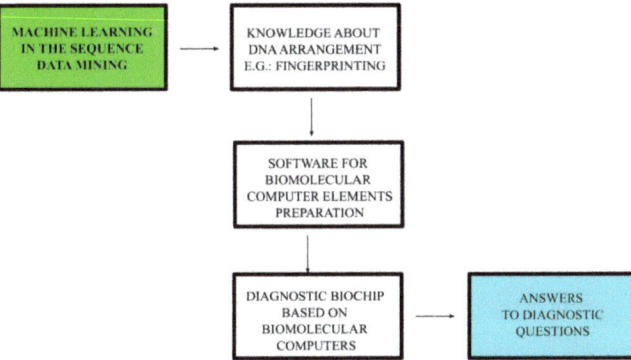

Figure 2. Schematic diagram of the new approach to using biomolecular computers as diagnostic biochips.

In this approach, the DNA fragments, for example, unique to a pathogenic virus, are determined by means of machine-learning methods in the sequence data mining.

Knowledge on unique DNA fragments, e.g., viral genomes, can come from analyzing an open access genetic sequence database, such as the GenBank database. Particularly interesting studies in this area include fingerprinting, which enables detection of the specific DNA fragments (obtained by PCR) characteristic of the investigated organisms. Recent years have also seen the development of methods based on artificial intelligence, which enable an automatic retrieval of information from genetic data. To this end, we propose the development of various machine-learning methods enabling detection of those DNA fragments that are unique with reference to the tested species. An important part of this approach is the software that will enable automatic encoding of the indispensable parts of diagnostic biochips based on biomolecular computers. This type of software will allow highly precise designing of indispensable components of the diagnostic biochips. At the molecular level, the mechanism of action of the diagnostic biochips consists of a sequential (alternate) reading of characteristic genetic features by the programmable biomolecular nanodevices built of a double-stranded DNA and the restriction enzymes. The devices complete their action as soon as they detect the presence of the desired DNA fragments and output signal, e.g., by means of fluorescence. It is worth noting that the so-designed diagnostic biochips can be manufactured commercially as laboratory kits or diagnostic devices.

One of the requirements for the correct and accurate designing of biochips based on biomolecular computers is to develop theoretical fundamentals of the implementation of practical biomolecular computers. In the case of diagnostic biochips, we propose the use of a formal system called queue automata [29] which have a memory that works according to the first in, first out (FIFO) principle—queue memory [30] (Figure 3).

Figure 3. Schematic diagram of the queue memory operation (FIFO principle). A new element added to the queue is placed at the end of the queue, and the first element is removed from the front of the queue. The operation of adding a new element to the queue is called ENQUEUE, while the operation of removing an element from the queue is called DEQUEUE. Abbreviations: 1, 2, 3, 4, 5 denote the positions of the elements that are in the queue.

The queue automata consist of a head (finite control), a type with cells containing an input word created from symbols of a certain finite alphabet and a queue (Figure 3). A finite control reading of the symbols of the input word runs one after another and changes its state according to the transition rules followed. At every step of the queue automaton operation, the first symbol in the queue may be removed or retained, and another symbol may be added at the end of the queue. The transition depends on the current state of the queue automaton and on the symbol read out from the input word. A variant of queue automata is the deterministic input-driven queue automata [31]. In these automata, "input-driven" means that the automata are controlled by the input, i.e., that the input word controls the queue. The deterministic input-driven queue automata are a formal system $M = (Q, \Sigma, \Gamma, q_0, F, \bot, \delta_e, \delta_r, \delta_i)$, where Q is the finite set of internal states; Σ is the finite set of input symbols consisting of the disjoint union of sets Σ_e, Σ_r, Σ_i; Γ is the finite set of queue symbols; $q_0 \in Q$ is the initial state; $F \subseteq Q$ is the set of accepting states; $\bot \notin \Gamma$ is the empty queue symbol; δ_e is the partial transition function mapping $Q \times \Sigma_e \times (\Gamma \cup \{\bot\})$ to $Q \times \Gamma$; δ_r is the partial transition function mapping $Q \times \Sigma_r \times (\Gamma \cup \{\bot\})$ to Q; and δ_i is the partial transition function mapping $Q \times \Sigma_i \times (\Gamma \cup \{\bot\})$ to Q.

The choice of that theoretical model (exactly queue automata) was dictated by the possibility of task scheduling with the use of queue automata, which is required for the controlled genome reading at the molecular level with the use of type IIB restriction endonucleases. The biomolecular implementation of the queue automata (biomolecular queue automata) requires specific encoding of the respective components of the queue automata (Figure 4).

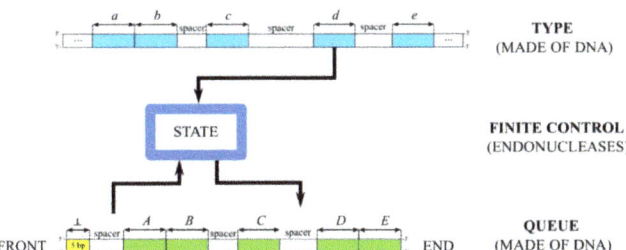

Figure 4. Schematic diagram of a biomolecular queue automaton. Abbreviations: *a, b, c, d, e* denote the symbols of the biomolecular queue automaton; *A, B, C, D, E*—the queue symbols of a biomolecular computer; the empty queue symbol denotes the beginning of the biomolecular queue; the spacer denotes the DNA fragment between the input symbols or the queue symbols of the biomolecular queue automaton; $5'$, $3'$—the DNA chain direction.

We propose that the symbols in the queue automaton should be separated by spacers, that is, the DNA fragments which do not encode the input symbols of a biomolecular computer—similarly to a computing machine made of biomolecules and presented by Ehud Shapiro's group in 2003 [4]. In addition, our proposal is that the spacers between the symbols should be of different length as this provides an opportunity to perceive a genome as a system of different symbols separated by spacers (Figure 5A). In our approach, the spacers can be used as technical DNA fragments encoding additional information at the biological level, but they do not play a significant role in queue automata. From the point of view of queue automata, the spacers are not very important for the calculations, but can be used as carriers of biological information encoded in DNA, e.g., a spacer can be used to store DNA sequences encoding proteins. It is suggested that the input symbols of the queue automata are encoded with same-length DNA chains, for instance: 10 base pairs, since this will enable appropriate encoding of the states of the queue automaton. In this approach, we are able to find the respective DNA fragments in the genome and then read the symbols using type IIB restriction endonucleases. The queue symbols of the biomolecular computer are encoded with DNA chains which have the same encoding lengths and which may contain spacers—just like the symbols of the queue automaton (Figure 5B). The states of the biomolecular queue automata are understood as the cut places of the symbol of a queue automaton within a fragment of the diagnosed genome [7].

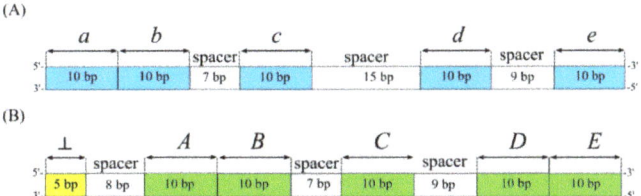

Figure 5. (**A**) An example of the input symbols of a biomolecular queue automaton. (**B**) An example of the queue symbols of a biomolecular queue automaton. Abbreviations: bp—the number of base pairs, encoding information in DNA; 10 bp—the length of a DNA with 10 base pairs (other base pair numbers such as 7 bp are to be understood accordingly); the input symbols of a biomolecular queue automaton are denoted by blue color; the queue symbols of a biomolecular queue automaton are denoted by green color, the empty queue symbol is denoted by yellow color.

The distinguished initial state is the first cut place of a type IIB restriction endonuclease in the appropriate place of the symbol of a genome. The set of accepting states is understood as cut places generated after the last cut with type IIB restriction endonuclease. The empty queue symbol is a separate DNA molecule, encoded with a unique DNA fragment with a sticky end. The queue symbols are encoded within the DNA fragment located in the transition molecule—to the left of the action site of the type IIB restriction endonuclease. The queue symbols are released only after the transition molecule relates to the symbol, encoded in the input word consisting of the symbols of the biomolecular queue automaton. The transitions of the biomolecular queue automaton are encoded with DNA chains which contain the restriction site for a type IIB restriction endonuclease in the middle of the transition. One queue symbol is encoded on the left of the restriction site and on the right, there is the sticky end complementary to the sticky end of the symbol of the biomolecular queue automaton.

Type IIB restriction endonucleases may constitute the hardware for biomolecular computers with queue memory, as they have the ability to simultaneously read and write information by cutting the double-stranded DNA to the right and to the left of the restriction site (Figure 6A). It is also acceptable to use multiple type IIB restriction endonucleases that act alternately in a single reaction mixture as well as to use restriction enzymes of other classes, for instance Class II, which cut the DNA chain only in one direction from the restriction site. This is of interest particularly in the aspect of earlier laboratory studies on the applicability of multiple restriction enzymes [5,6], as well as the concept of a theoretical design of a push-down automaton with the use of multiple restriction enzymes [32].

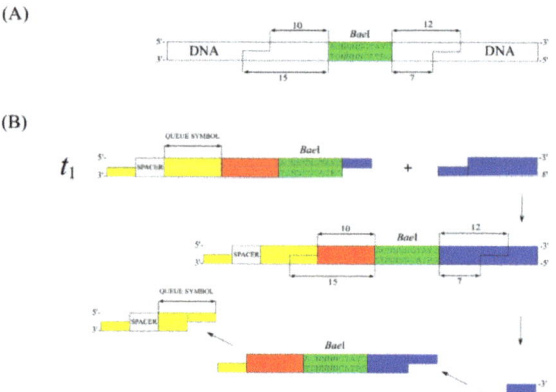

Figure 6. (**A**) The operation of the restriction enzyme *Bae*I. (**B**) The mechanism of writing the queue symbols using the restriction enzyme *Bae*I. Abbreviations: t_1—the transition molecule named t_1.

It is worth mentioning that, in the area of DNA computing, earlier practical solutions based on the use of restriction enzymes, only offered the possibility of reading the information encoded in the DNA, but not that of writing it [3,5]. The type IIB restriction endonucleases enable cutting the DNA chains in two directions and, in addition, they leave relatively long sticky ends, e.g., the length of the sticky ends left by *Bae*I is five nucleotides (Figure 6A). This effect of the type IIB restriction endonucleases enables the biomolecular computer to be programmed so that, after cutting the DNA chain, the enzyme writes information on the read-out DNA fragment (Figure 6B)—this is similar to the case of the biomolecular push-down automaton [8]. It is worth mentioning that a representative of the type IIB restriction endonucleases, *Bae*I, was used in practical experiments aimed at the implementation of the biomolecular computer involving multiple restriction enzymes [6]. This provided an experimental ground in the area of DNA computing for constructing various practical solutions based on type IIB restriction endonucleases.

4. A Concept for PCR Automation by Means of Biomolecular Computers

Biomolecular computers, specifically those with queue memory, which use type IIB restriction endonucleases may be used for automating the PCR method. The proposed new approach (called Queue-PCR) to automating the PCR method consists of the use of biomolecular computers as the hardware and the software for a wide range of PCR solutions. In comparison with the conventional PCR, this approach has the advantage of reading numerous replicated DNA fragments by the appropriately programmed biomolecular computer (Figure 7). The first step involves the replication of selected DNA fragments using the starters and the polymerase—as in the conventional PCR protocol. In the next step, the appropriately programmed biomolecular software in the form of transition molecules (see t_1, t_2, t_3, Figure 8) enables cutting the respective DNA fragments. The transition molecules enable both reading the DNA fragments and writing the read-out DNA fragment at the same time (Figure 8). The key elements in this approach are the appropriately programmed transition molecules that are unique for each transition executed by the biomolecular computer—they have the unique sticky ends and the encoded queue symbols.

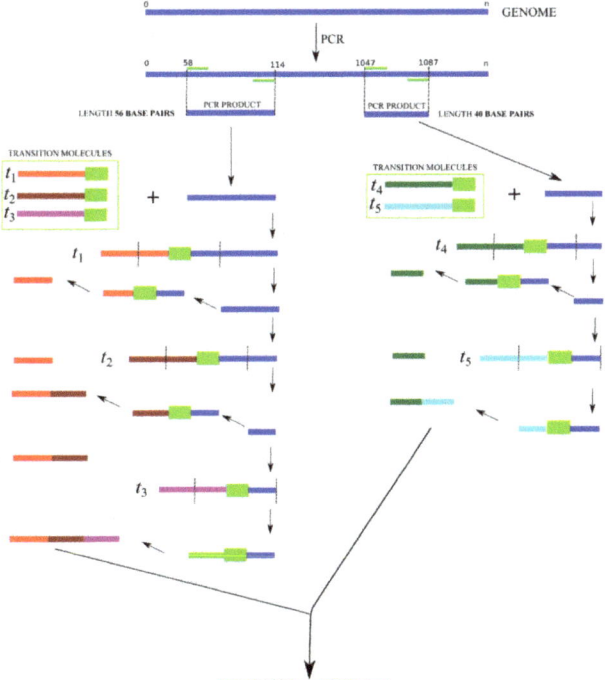

Figure 7. Diagram Queue-PCR of a new PCR automation concept of the use of biomolecular computers with type queue memory based on type IIB restriction endonuclease. The first step of Queue-PCR concept is replication of selected DNA fragments and the next step is sequential cutting and ligating DNA molecules by means of molecular software and hardware. Abbreviations: t_1, t_2, t_3, t_4, t_5—respective transition molecules (molecular software); PCR—conventional PCR method; the numbers: 58, 114, 1047, 1087 denote positions on the genome. The blue line denotes the genome fragment multiplicated by the PCR. The green rectangle denotes the sequence recognized by type IIB restriction endonuclease (molecular hardware). The DNA fragments amplify by PCR are denoted by blue color. The restriction sites are denoted by light green color. The remaining colors schematically illustrate the queue symbols.

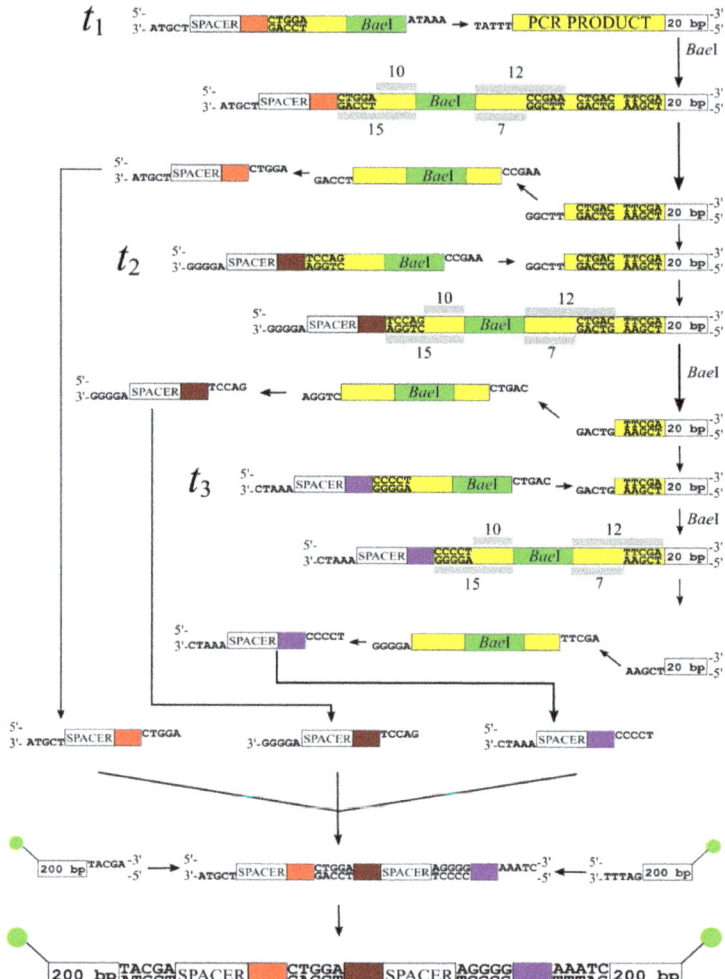

Figure 8. Operation of the restriction enzyme *Bae*I in a system which reads the genome fragment—reading and writing information into the queue. The molecular software (t_1, t_2, t_3) allows alternating and autonomous cleavage of DNA molecules which are genome fragments obtained by the PCR method. The biomolecular computer produces the final DNA fragment, as a standard output, after the cyclic reactions of cutting and ligating the genome fragment obtained by the PCR method. The green circle denotes the factor of fluorescence. The DNA fragments that are cleaved by restriction enzyme (*Bae*I) are denoted in yellow. The restriction sites are denoted by light green color. The other colors schematically illustrate the queue symbols that are placed in the queue.

After reading the DNA fragments (see Appendix A), the appropriately programmed and designed biomolecular computer will return, as the standard output, information on the result of the operation, e.g., in the form of fluorescence (see Appendix B). An important element in the new approach to designing diagnostic biochips is the use of a restriction enzyme cutting DNA in two directions (as described in the previous subsection). This enables designing transition molecules which also comprise writing the information (queue symbols) and reading multiple DNA fragments replicated by the PCR method. In the final phase of DNA reading, a chain is formed that changes the color of the solution due to fluorescence. This approach may additionally be supplemented with DNA sequencing using the restriction enzymes [33,34].

5. Discussion

Searching for unique nucleotide sequences using machine-learning methods is crucial for the proposed applications of biomolecular computing. An important direction of research in this area has been shown to be the discovery of unique patterns in nucleotide sequences [9], as this knowledge enables biomolecular computer programming to read unique patterns in nucleotide sequences.

Current and potential future research directions and an example of the use of biomolecular computers as the hardware and software in technological solutions are presented. Among the vast array of available restriction enzymes, type IIB restriction endonucleases were selected as having a great potential in applications related to biomolecular computers. In addition, the idea of biomolecular queue automata is proposed along with queuing systems and queuing networks based on the use of type IIB restriction endonucleases and appropriate encoding of double-stranded DNA. This approach shows that it is possible to design biomolecular computers with queue memory as well as queuing networks using type IIB restriction endonucleases. The earlier technological solutions included practical laboratory experiments testing biomolecular finite state automata that were computers without memory [3,4]. Moreover, laboratory tests were already run on the functioning of type IIB restriction endonuclease (*Bae*I) in a system of biomolecular computers [6]. This provides practical foundations for creating different technological solutions linked with broadly understood biomolecular computers involving type IIB restriction endonucleases, specifically for creating diagnostic biochips.

The proposed approach to designing biochips with biomolecular computers can incorporate one or more than one type IIB restriction enzyme. The choice of multiple restriction enzymes (type IIB) depends on the possibility of using an appropriate type IIB restriction enzyme to read a genome fragment. If a given DNA fragment cannot be read by a given type IIB restriction enzyme (in use with designed transition molecules), it should be checked whether it is possible to read it using two or more restriction enzymes. When selecting the number of type IIB restriction enzymes, one should be guided by the principle of minimalism and choose the minimum number of restriction enzymes that can read a given DNA fragment. In this regard, attention should be paid to the main advantage of such an approach, namely that the use of more types of IIB restriction enzymes makes it possible to read DNA fragments of greater lengths. Thus, the use of multiple restriction enzymes in the diagnostic biochip (while maintaining the principle of minimalism) allows building more complex biochips.

Additionally, in the case of diagnostic biochips, we propose the use of a formal apparatus available in the theory of queue automata [29,35]. Particularly interesting are the deterministic input-driven queue automata [31]; nevertheless, this approach does not take into account encoding the input data with DNA chains and the action of restriction enzymes. In addition, we used the idea of queue automata—a concept mentioned as early as 1943 by Emil Leon Post [36]. The queue automata were the subject of studies in various areas [31,35,37–39]. From the PCR perspective, especially interesting are the queue automata in the context of scheduling problems [40], as in this method scheduling of the resulting DNA chains is particularly useful. We propose to advance the idea of the deterministic input-driven queue automata [31]. The other theories we used in our paper include the queuing theory [41] and queuing networks [42]. The former was used for modeling biological processes [43].

The use of type IIB restriction endonucleases also makes it possible to implement other models, based on the type of queue memory. Particularly promising seem the queuing systems based on the Erlang queuing theory [44,45]. It is worth noting that queuing systems can be combined to form queuing networks [46], which enable complex systems based on queues to be designed. Biomolecular implementation consists of the appropriate encoding of all elements of the system, where the queue is the hardest element to implement. It should be noted that the idea of biomolecular implementation of a queue is provided in the present paper. For instance, in every queuing system, one can use one type IIB restriction endonuclease and combine it with others so that they form a queuing network.

Theoretical studies on biomolecular computers may provide practical solutions. Such new methods and models may have numerous medical applications, complementing conventional therapies and laboratory diagnostics. Early research on biomolecular computers focused on human-operated, laboratory-scale computers for solving complex computational problems. More recently, simple, autonomous and programmable molecular computers have been presented in which the input and output information can be given in a molecular form. Such computers, using biological molecules as input and biologically active molecules as output, could create a system for the "logical" control of biological processes. An autonomous biomolecular computer is proposed, which, at least in vitro, logically analyzes mRNA levels and responds by producing a molecule capable of affecting gene expression levels. This approach can be applied in vivo for biochemical sensing, genetic engineering, and even medical diagnosis and treatment.

A good example of the use of biomolecular computers is the concept of cancer diagnostics and cancer treatment based on silencing a cancer gene expression [47]. With this approach in mind, Ehud Shapiro's team developed a method for the activation of biomolecular software for cases where the reaction mixture contains typical neoplastic mRNA. For that purpose, they used a simple biomolecular computer, developed in a similar way as in their previous experiments [3,4]: it was built of software (in the form of double-stranded DNA) and hardware (in the form of the *FokI* restriction enzyme), which could only assume one of two states—"yes" or "no". If "cancer mRNA" was present, then the biomolecular computer switched to the "yes" state; otherwise, it was in the "no" state. When all the sought for cancer features in the form of mRNA were present in the reaction mixture, then the biomolecular computer completed its operation and yielded the diagnosis of "yes", confirming the presence of cancer genes. Then, it released a drug capable of silencing the cancer gene expression. A part of that approach was also the proposed new concept of designing the input word, which enabled the release of the drug after the final cutting of the double-stranded DNA encoding the symbols of the biomolecular computer.

Another interesting application of DNA computing is the general concept of designing reconfigurable DNA nanovaults capable of controlling interactions between the enzymes [48]. Of particular interest seem to be issues involving DNA sequencing, where Sanger's sequencing remains the basic method [49]. Interestingly, one of the methods of studying sequencing is based on the use of class IIS restriction enzymes [33,50], and another, similar approach to sequencing is used as well [34,51]. The proposed concept, of which DNA sequencing is the main aim, is based on reading DNA by the restriction enzymes. It is worth noting that the idea of sequencing with the use of the restriction enzymes was shown before the first practical experiment, i.e., implementing biomolecular computers with a single restriction enzyme [3]. It is particularly interesting to study the feasibility of sequencing in the aspect of programming and using biomolecular computers, because the two approaches complement each other. It seems that comprehensive studies on sequencing with the use of biomolecular computers will yield numerous practical solutions in the field of sequencing. Another interesting application of restriction enzymes, regarding type IIB, is fingerprinting with the use of a class of such enzymes [52]. The researchers noted that type IIB restriction endonucleases can be used for studies on the genome of live organisms. Details of the biochemical cutting of DNA by means of type IIB restriction endonucleases were studied in a number of papers, including ours [6,53]. Type IIB enzymes were used in DNA-computing studies for developing a theoretical biomolecular push-down automaton model, that is, for a stack-memory computer. The main idea was based on using a circular double-stranded DNA and a single type IIB restriction endonuclease, *PsrI* [8], which enables cutting of the double-stranded DNA to the left and to the right of the restriction site. This approach is similar to the idea presented by Paul W.K. Rothemund in 1995, in which the symbols are encoded by means of the double-stranded DNA, and input data processing is affected by alternately cutting and ligating the double-stranded DNA. It should also be noted that our practical studies on the use of multiple restriction enzymes in a single reaction mixture also showed the applicability of type IIB restriction endonuclease for designing biomolecular computers [6].

The action of a typical type IIB restriction endonuclease (more specifically, *Bae*I) was studied in earlier works in a system of biomolecular computers using multiple restriction enzymes [6]. Those studies demonstrated how to design synthetic nucleotides with LITMUS 38i plasmids, and how to obtain the respective components of a biomolecular computer working in a system of multiple alternately functioning restriction enzymes. The biochemical reactions were optimized for two restriction enzymes acting in a single reaction mixture [5]. In those studies, we also investigated in detail the optimization of the reaction medium in which a biomolecular computer operates and identified problems that may occur in preparing the respective components of biomolecular computers. Moreover, we explained how to solve any problems that may occur in the practical functioning of the biomolecular computer comprising multiple restriction enzymes within a single reaction mixture.

It is worth mentioning that earlier experiments demonstrated the action of a single restriction enzyme in a biomolecular computer system [3,4,54]. The experimental conditions of the work of various restriction enzymes were also investigated as potentially useful in the construction of biomolecular computers [55].

Numerous research papers describe the development of biosensors, or small devices enabling detection of organic compounds, for instance DNA, by means of miniature physical detectors. Another concept is to design biochips, or devices that enable a number of biochemical reactions to take place in a single device, usually integrated with electronic components that constitute the hardware [56,57]. A compelling approach to designing diagnostic devices is the lab-on-a-chip (LOC), with a number of strategies to design actual devices that are based on the lab-on-a-chip idea [58] and have practical applications involving operations on DNA [59]. An interesting illustration of how the lab-on-a-chip idea may be coupled with DNA computing is the concept of a molecular inference system [60–62]. One more example of an innovative approach to using biomolecular computing is the idea of creating biosensors [63,64].

What is frequently required in the practical implementations of biomolecular computers is an advanced mathematical formal apparatus, the purpose of which is to organize state-of-the-art knowledge of various approaches to constructing biomolecular computers. A precursor formal apparatus, which enables computations performed with the use of restriction enzymes and a double-stranded DNA to be grasped, was described as the theory of tailor automata [7]. A uniform formal system helps to precisely define a formal model used for implementing biomolecular computers. This approach to DNA computing enables problems connected with the practical designing of biomolecular computers to be solved effectively. For instance, from the practical point of view, it is an important thing to increase the number of states of a biomolecular computer [6,54,65], and to correctly encode the symbols of the biomolecular computer, simply because their precise design is required for the optimum operation of a biomolecular computer in the conditions of a reaction medium [66,67].

In addition to that, a number of other concepts of building biomolecular computers as well as their applications are currently in the phase of theoretical considerations. As a proof of the principle, a computer can be used to identify and analyze mRNA of disease-related genes from in vivo cancer models. Theoretical studies on biomolecular computers include, as a leading topic, studies on the splicing system [68–71]. Another interesting approach to DNA computing is the reaction system [72,73]—the subject of numerous studies recently [74–76].

In this paper, we proposed an idea of biochips that can be constructed using DNA. Therefore, the natural target processed easily by our biochips is cell-free DNA (cfDNA) present in a wide variety of pathological conditions ranging from cancer to autoimmune diseases [77]. It is associated not only with disease occurrence, but also with the severity of symptoms and even treatment options. It is worth mentioning that cfDNA can easily be isolated using noninvasive methods and further processed. To date, cfDNA analysis has only been quantitative; however, it has recently been shown that cfDNA can be used to detect the sign of genomic instability. In other words, cfDNA profiling, defined as a common set of disease-specific mutations, can be a useful tool for screening healthy individuals for early symptoms of cancer and other diseases with the genomic instability background. Such a screening is time- and cost-consuming, as it requires sequencing followed by library preparation. Our conceptual biochips could be used instead of DNA sequencing. It is possible to configure our biochips in such a way that individual mutations would be scheduling by queue biomolecular automata and the signal is only emitted when the exact mutation is detected.

6. Conclusions

This paper presents a novel concept for building biochips of which the hardware and the software are based on biomolecular computers. Due to their unique properties, the biomolecular computers are of particular interest in building biochips. Among the various known theoretical models of computation, we selected the one that is exceptionally interesting regarding the aspect of PCR automation, namely, the deterministic input-driven queue automaton. We also indicated a group of restriction enzymes (type IIB restriction endonucleases), especially important for biomolecular computers. The use of such enzymes provides a foundation for designing biomolecular computers with memory, e.g., queue automata. It would also be interesting to pursue studies on the applicability of type IIB restriction endonucleases for designing various data structures known in computer science, e.g., tree data structure.

We also propose a new approach—Queue-PCR—for automation of the PCR method using the biomolecular computers. The Queue-PCR concept is important as a new idea of the use of biomolecular computers. It shows their applications and indicates the potential directions of study on new functionalities of programmable biomolecular nanodevices. This approach to PCR automation may be the beginning of new directions of study, focused on the automation of molecular genetics methods using biomolecular computers as the hardware. This provides fundamentals for creating biomolecular software for PCR solutions in their broad sense, thus enabling them to be programmed at the molecular level.

In the proposed approach, it is important to use machine-learning methods at the stage of designing biochips based on biomolecular computers, because the key element of the proposed solutions is knowledge on unique nucleotide sequences.

Author Contributions: Conceptualization, S.S.; investigation, S.S.; methodology, S.S., J.W. and T.P.; formal analysis, S.S. and J.W.; writing—original draft preparation, S.S., J.W., T.P. and I.M.; writing—review and editing, S.S., J.W., T.P. and I.M.; supervision, S.S.; project administration, S.S.; funding acquisition, I.M. All authors have read and agreed to the published version of the manuscript.

Funding: This research received no external funding.

Institutional Review Board Statement: Not applicable.

Informed Consent Statement: Not applicable.

Data Availability Statement: Not applicable.

Conflicts of Interest: The authors declare no conflict of interest.

Appendix A

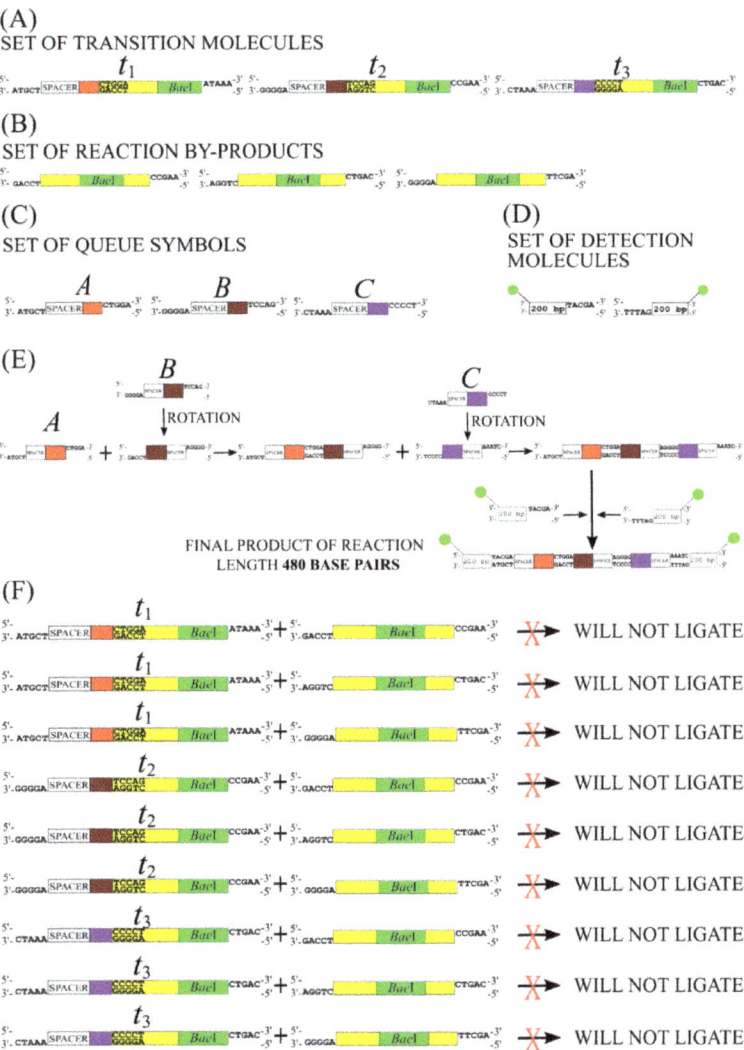

Figure A1. The list of DNA chains that are formed during the action of a biochip—an example: (**A**)—the set of all transition molecules; (**B**)—the set of all reaction by-products formed during the alternating action of type IIB restriction endonuclease (more specifically, *Bae*I); (**C**)—the set of all queue symbols. (**D**)—the set of all detection molecules; (**E**)—the process of biomolecular queue symbols ligation; (**F**)—the set of all reactions in which DNA molecules are not ligated together. Abbreviations: *A*, *B*, *C* (in italic text)—the queue symbols of a biomolecular computer; t_1, t_2, t_3, t_4, t_5—molecular software. The color markings are described in Figure 8.

Appendix B

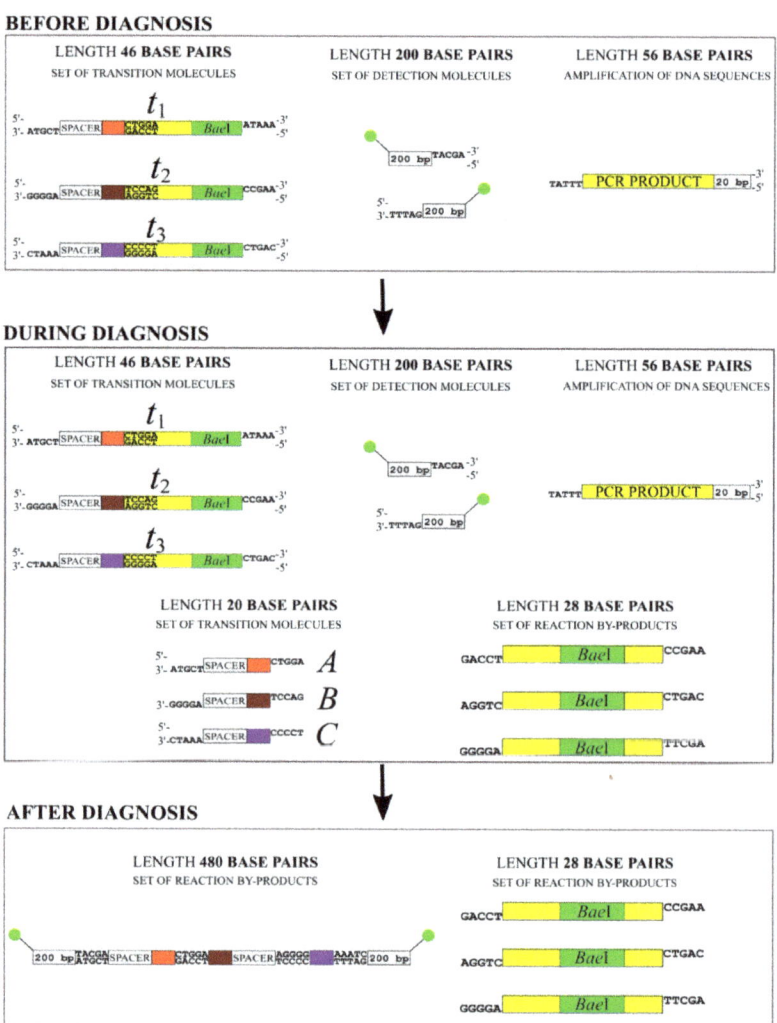

Figure A2. The list of DNA chain lengths before, during and after molecular diagnosis by means of a biochip based on a biomolecular computer. The length of DNA strands before the diagnosis is: 200 bp, 56 bp, and 46 bp, while after the molecular diagnosis it is: 480 bp, and 28 bp. The fluorescence mechanism is used, in which fluorescence occurs when a DNA chain of 480 appears in the solution. The color markings are described in Figure 8.

References

1. Bennett, C.H. The thermodynamics of computation—A review. *Int. J. Theoret. Phys.* **1982**, *21*, 905–940. [CrossRef]
2. Rothemund, P.W.K. A DNA and restriction enzyme implementation of Turing machines. In *DNA Based Computers. DIMACS Series in Discrete Mathematics and Theoretical Computer Science*; Lipton, R.J., Baum, E.B., Eds.; American Mathematical Society: Providence, RI, USA, 1995; pp. 75–120.
3. Benenson, Y.; Paz-Elizur, T.; Adar, R.; Keinan, E.; Livneh, Z.; Shapiro, E. Programmable and autonomous computing machine made of biomolecules. *Nature* **2001**, *414*, 430–434. [CrossRef] [PubMed]
4. Benenson, Y.; Adar, R.; Paz-Elizur, T.; Livneh, Z.; Shapiro, E. DNA molecule provides a computing machine with both data and fuel. *Proc. Natl. Acad. Sci. USA* **2003**, *100*, 2191–2196. [CrossRef] [PubMed]

5. Sakowski, S.; Krasiński, T.; Sarnik, J.; Blasiak, J.; Waldmajer, J.; Poplawski, T. A detailed experimental study of a DNA computer with two endonucleases. *Z. Naturforsch. C* **2017**, *72*, 303–313. [CrossRef]
6. Sakowski, S.; Krasiński, T.; Waldmajer, J.; Sarnik, J.; Blasiak, J.; Poplawski, T. Biomolecular computers with multiple restriction enzymes. *Genet. Mol. Biol.* **2017**, *40*, 860–870. [CrossRef]
7. Waldmajer, J.; Bonikowski, Z.; Sakowski, S. Theory of tailor automata. *Theor. Comput. Sci.* **2019**, *785*, 60–82. [CrossRef]
8. Cavaliere, M.; Jonoska, N.; Yogev, S.; Piran, R.; Keinan, E.; Seeman, N. Biomolecular implementation of computing devices with unbounded memory. *Lect. Notes Comput. Sci.* **2005**, *3384*, 35–49.
9. Agrawal, R.; Srikant, R. Mining sequential patterns. In Proceedings of the Eleventh International Conference on Data Engineering, Taipei, Taiwan, 6–10 March 1995; pp. 3–14.
10. Greener, J.G.; Kandathil, S.M.; Moffat, L.; Jones, D.T. A guide to machine learning for biologists. *Nat. Rev. Mol. Cell Biol.* **2022**, *23*, 40–55. [CrossRef]
11. Li, R.; Li, L.; Xu, Y.; Yang, J. Machine learning meets omics: Applications and perspectives. *Brief. Bioinform.* **2022**, *23*, bbab460. [CrossRef]
12. Eraslan, G.; Avsec, Ž.; Gagneur, J.; Theis, F.J. Deep learning: New computational modelling techniques for genomics. *Nat. Rev. Genet.* **2019**, *20*, 389–403. [CrossRef]
13. Bosco, G.L.; Di Gangi, M.A. Deep learning architectures for DNA sequence classification. In *International Workshop on Fuzzy Logic and Applications 2016*; Springer: Berlin/Heidelberg, Germany, 2017; pp. 162–171.
14. Nguyen, N.G.; Tran, V.A.; Phan, D.; Lumbanraja, F.R.; Faisal, M.R.; Abapihi, B.; Kubo, M.; Satou, K. DNA sequence classification by convolutional neural network. *J. Biomed. Sci. Eng.* **2016**, *9*, 280–286. [CrossRef]
15. Luedi, P.; Dietrich, F.; Weidman, J.; Bosko, J.; Jirtle, R.; Hartemink, A. Computational and experimental identification of novel human imprinted genes. *Genome Res.* **2007**, *17*, 1723–1730. [CrossRef] [PubMed]
16. Chen, L.; Cai, C.; Chen, V.; Lu, X. Learning a hierarchical representation of the yeast transcriptomic machinery using an autoencoder model. *BMC Bioinform.* **2016**, *17*, S9. [CrossRef] [PubMed]
17. Kelley, D.R.; Snoek, J.; Rinn, J.L. Basset: Learning the regulatory code of the accessible genome with deep convolutional neural networks. *Genome Res.* **2016**, *26*, 990–999. [CrossRef] [PubMed]
18. Amin, M.; Yurovsky, A.; Tian, Y.; Skiena, S. Deepannotator: Genome annotation with deep learning. In Proceedings of the 2018 ACM International Conference on Bioinformatics, Computational Biology, and Health Informatics, Online, 15 August 2018; pp. 254–259.
19. Zeng, W.; Wu, M.; Jiang, R. Prediction of enhancer-promoter interactions via natural language processing. *BMC Genom.* **2018**, *19*, 84. [CrossRef] [PubMed]
20. Yuan, Y.; Bar-Joseph, Z. Deep learning for inferring gene relationships from single-cell expression data. *Proc. Natl. Acad. Sci. USA* **2019**, *116*, 27151–27158. [CrossRef]
21. Fudenberg, G.; Kelley, D.R.; Pollard, K.S. Predicting 3D genome folding from DNA sequence with Akita. *Nat. Methods* **2020**, *17*, 1111–1117. [CrossRef]
22. Yang, A.; Zhang, W.; Wang, J.; Yang, K.; Han, Y.; Zhang, L. Review on the application of machine learning algorithms in the sequence data mining of DNA. *Front. Bioeng. Biotechnol.* **2020**, *8*, 1032. [CrossRef]
23. Srikant, R.; Agrawal, R. Mining sequential patterns: Generalizations and performance improvements. In Proceedings of the International Conference on Extending Database Technology, Avignon, France, 25–29 March 1996; Springer: Berlin/Heidelberg, Germany, 1996; pp. 1–17.
24. Pearson, W.R. An introduction to sequence similarity ("homology") searching. *Curr. Protoc. Bioinform.* **2013**, *42*, 3.1.1–3.1.8. [CrossRef]
25. Altschul, S.F.; Gish, W.; Miller, W.; Myers, E.W.; Lipman, D.J. Basic local alignment search tool. *J. Mol. Biol.* **1990**, *215*, 403–410. [CrossRef]
26. Wu, S.; Manber, U. Fast text searching: Allowing errors. *Commun. ACM* **1992**, *35*, 83–91. [CrossRef]
27. Vaswani, A.; Shazeer, N.; Parmar, N.; Uszkoreit, J.; Jones, L.; Gomez, A.N.; Kaiser, Ł.; Polosukhin, I. Attention is all you need. In *Advances in Neural Information Processing Systems*; Morgan Kaufmann Publishers Inc.: San Francisco, CA, USA, 2017; p. 30.
28. Clauwaert, J.; Menschaert, G.; Waegeman, W. Explainability in transformer models for functional genomics. *Brief. Bioinform.* **2021**, *22*, bbab060. [CrossRef] [PubMed]
29. Kutrib, M.; Malcher, A.; Wendlandt, M. Queue Automata: Foundations and Developments. In *Reversibility and Universality. Emergence, Complexity and Computation*; Adamatzky, A., Ed.; Springer: Cham, Switzerland, 2018; Volume 30, pp. 385–431.
30. Cormen, T.H.; Leiserson, C.E.; Rivest, R.L.; Stein, C. *Introduction to Algorithms*; MIT Press: Cambridge, MA, USA, 2009.
31. Kutrib, M.; Malcher, A.; Mereghetti, C.; Palano, B.; Wendlandt, M. Deterministic input-driven queue automata: Finite turns, decidability, and closure properties. *Theor. Comput. Sci.* **2015**, *578*, 58–71. [CrossRef]
32. Krasiński, T.; Sakowski, S.; Popławski, T. Autonomous push-down automaton built on DNA. *Informatica* **2012**, *36*, 263–276.
33. Brenner, S. DNA Sequencing by Stepwise Ligation and Cleavage. U.S. Patent Application No. 5599675, 4 February 1997.
34. Jones, D. Iterative and Regenerative DNA Sequencing Method. U.S. Patent Application No. 5858671, 12 January 1999.
35. Brandenburg, F.J. Multiple equality sets and post machines. *J. Comput. Syst. Sci.* **1980**, *21*, 292–316. [CrossRef]
36. Post, E.L. Formal reductions of the classical combinatorial decision problem. *Am. J. Math.* **1943**, *65*, 197–215. [CrossRef]
37. Brandenburg, F.J. On the intersection of stacks and queues. *Theor. Comput. Sci.* **1988**, *58*, 69–80. [CrossRef]

38. Allevi, E.; Cherubini, A.; Reghizzi, S.C. Breadth-first phrase structure grammars and queue automata. In *International Symposium on Mathematical Foundations of Computer Science*; Springer: Berlin/Heidelberg, Germany, 1988; pp. 162–170.
39. Cherubini, A.; Citrini, C.; Reghizzi, S.C.; Mandrioli, D. QRT FIFO automata, breadth-first grammars and their relations. *Theor. Comput. Sci.* **1991**, *85*, 171–203. [CrossRef]
40. Breveglieri, L.; Cherubini, A.; Crespi-Reghizzi, S. Real-time scheduling by queue automata. In *International Symposium on Formal Techniques in Real-Time and Fault-Tolerant Systems*; Springer: Berlin/Heidelberg, Germany, 1992; pp. 131–147.
41. Thomopoulos, N.T. *Fundamentals of Queuing Systems: Statistical Methods for Analyzing Queuing Models*; Springer Science & Business Media: New York, NY, USA, 2012.
42. Garrido, J.M. Queuing Networks. In *Performance Modeling of Operating Systems Using Object-Oriented Simulation: A Practical Introduction*; Springer: New York, NY, USA, 2000; pp. 61–83.
43. Arazi, A.; Ben-Jacob, E.; Yechiali, U. Bridging genetic networks and queueing theory. *Phys. A Stat. Mech. Its Appl.* **2004**, *332*, 585–616. [CrossRef]
44. Erlang, A.K. The theory of probabilities and telephone conversations. *Nyt. Tidsskr. Mat.* **1909**, *20*, 33–39.
45. Kleinrock, L. *Queueing Systems*; Wiley: New York, NY, USA, 1975.
46. Zimmermann, A. Queuing Models. In *Stochastic Discrete Event Systems: Modeling, Evaluation, Applications*; Springer: Berlin/Heidelberg, Germany, 2008; pp. 65–78.
47. Benenson, Y.; Gil, B.; Ben-Dor, U.; Adar, R.; Shapiro, E. An autonomous molecular computer for logical control of gene expression. *Nature* **2004**, *429*, 423–429. [CrossRef] [PubMed]
48. Grossi, G.; Jepsen, M.D.E.; Kjems, J.; Andersen, E.S. Control of enzyme reactions by a reconfigurable DNA nanovault. *Nat. Commun.* **2017**, *8*, 992. [CrossRef] [PubMed]
49. Sanger, F.; Nicklen, S.; Coulson, A.R. DNA sequencing with chain-terminating inhibitors. *Proc. Natl. Acad. Sci. USA* **1977**, *74*, 5463–5467. [CrossRef] [PubMed]
50. Brenner, S.; Livak, K.J. DNA fingerprinting by sampled sequencing. *Proc. Natl. Acad. Sci. USA* **1989**, *86*, 8902–8906. [CrossRef]
51. Jones, D.H. An iterative and regenerative method for DNA sequencing. *Biotechniques* **1997**, *22*, 938–946. [CrossRef]
52. Tengs, T.; LaFramboise, T.; Den, R.B.; Hayes, D.N.; Zhang, J.; DebRoy, S.; Gentleman, R.C.; O'Neill, K.; Birren, B.; Meyerson, M. Genomic representations using concatenates of Type IIB restriction endonuclease digestion fragments. *Nucleic Acids Res.* **2004**, *32*, e121. [CrossRef]
53. Marshall, J.J.; Gowers, D.M.; Halford, S.E. Restriction endonucleases that bridge and excise two recognition sites from DNA. *J. Mol. Biol.* **2007**, *367*, 419–431. [CrossRef]
54. Soreni, M.; Yogev, S.; Kossoy, E.; Shoham, Y.; Keinan, E. Parallel biomolecular computation on surfaces with advanced finite automata. *J. Am. Chem. Soc.* **2005**, *127*, 3935–3943. [CrossRef]
55. Chen, P.; Li, J.; Zhao, J.; He, L.; Zhang, Z. Differential dependence on DNA ligase of type II restriction enzymes: A practical way toward ligase-free DNA automaton. *Biochem. Biophys. Res. Commun.* **2007**, *353*, 733–737. [CrossRef]
56. Vo-Dinh, T.; Cullum, B. Biosensors and biochips: Advances in biological and medical diagnostics. *Fresenius J. Anal. Chem.* **2000**, *366*, 540–551. [CrossRef]
57. Vo-Dinh, T.; Cullum, B.; Stokes, D. Nanosensors and biochips: Frontiers in biomolecular diagnostics. *Sens. Actuators B Chem.* **2001**, *74*, 2–11. [CrossRef]
58. Temiz, Y.; Lovchik, R.D.; Kaigala, G.V.; Delamarche, E. Lab-on-a-chip devices: How to close and plug the lab? *Microelectron. Eng.* **2015**, *132*, 156–175. [CrossRef]
59. Lehmann, U.; Vandevyver, C.; Parashar, V.K.; Gijs, M.A. Droplet-based DNA purification in a magnetic lab-on-a-chip. *Angew. Chem. Int. Ed.* **2006**, *45*, 3062–3067. [CrossRef] [PubMed]
60. Wąsiewicz, P.; Mulawka, J. Lab-on-a-chip molecular inference system. In *Prace Naukowe Politechniki Warszawskiej. Elektronika*; Oficyna Wydawnicza Politechniki Warszawskiej: Warsaw, Poland, 2007; Volume 160, pp. 293–300.
61. Wąsiewicz, P.; Janczak, T.; Mulawka, J.J.; Płucienniczak, A. The inference based on molecular computing. *Cybernet. Syst.* **2000**, *31*, 283–315.
62. Wąsiewicz, P.; Malinowski, A.; Nowak, R.; Mulawka, J.J.; Borsuk, P.; Węgleński, P.; Płucienniczak, A. DNA computing: Implementation of data flow logical operations. *Future Gener. Comput. Syst.* **2001**, *17*, 361–378. [CrossRef]
63. de Murieta, I.S.; Rodríguez-Patón, A. DNA biosensors that reason. *Biosystems* **2012**, *109*, 91–104. [CrossRef]
64. Aiassa, S.; Terracciano, R.; Carrara, S.; Demarchi, D. Biosensors for Biomolecular Computing: A Review and Future Perspectives. *BioNanoScience* **2020**, *10*, 554–563. [CrossRef]
65. Unold, O.; Troć, M.; Dobosz, T.; Trusiewicz, A. Extended molecular computing model. *WSEAS Trans. Biol. Biomed.* **2004**, *1*, 15–19.
66. Krasiński, T.; Sakowski, S.; Waldmajer, J.; Popławski, T. Arithmetical analysis of biomolecular finite automaton. *Fundam. Inform.* **2013**, *128*, 463–474. [CrossRef]
67. Waldmajer, J.; Sakowski, S. A solution to the problem of the maximal number of symbols for biomolecular computer. *Informatica* **2019**, *43*, 485–494. [CrossRef]
68. Head, T. Formal language theory and DNA: An analysis of the generative capacity of specific recombinant behavior. *Bull. Math. Biol.* **1987**, *75*, 737–759. [CrossRef]
69. Paun, G. On the splicing operations. *Discret. Appl. Math.* **1996**, *70*, 57–79. [CrossRef]

70. Kari, L.; Kopecki, S. Deciding whether a regular language is generated by a splicing system. *J. Comput. Syst. Sci.* **2017**, *84*, 263–287. [CrossRef]
71. Kari, L.; Ng, T. Descriptional Complexity of Semi-Simple Splicing Systems. *Int. J. Found. Comput. Sci.* **2021**, *32*, 685–711. [CrossRef]
72. Ehrenfeucht, A.; Rozenberg, G. Basic Notions of Reaction Systems. *Lect. Notes Comput. Sci.* **2005**, *3340*, 27–29.
73. Ehrenfeucht, A.; Rozenberg, G. Reaction systems. *Fundam. Inform.* **2007**, *75*, 263–280.
74. Corolli, L.; Maj, C.; Marini, F.; Besozzi, D.; Mauri, G. An excursion in reaction systems: From computer science to biology. *Theor. Comput. Sci.* **2012**, *454*, 95–108. [CrossRef]
75. Męski, A.; Penczek, W.; Rozenberg, G. Model checking temporal properties of reaction systems. *Inf. Sci.* **2015**, *313*, 22–42. [CrossRef]
76. Bottoni, P.; Labella, A. Transactions and contracts based on reaction systems. *Theor. Comput. Sci.* **2021**, *881*, 25–61. [CrossRef]
77. Volik, S.; Alcaide, M.; Morin, R.D.; Collins, C. Cell-free DNA (cfDNA): Clinical significance and utility in cancer shaped by emerging technologies. *Mol. Cancer Res.* **2016**, *14*, 898–908. [CrossRef]

Article

Towards Machine Learning Algorithms in Predicting the Clinical Evolution of Patients Diagnosed with COVID-19

Evandro Carvalho de Andrade [1], Plácido Rogerio Pinheiro [1,2,*], Ana Luiza Bessa de Paula Barros [1,*], Luciano Comin Nunes [3], Luana Ibiapina C. C. Pinheiro [1,*], Pedro Gabriel Calíope Dantas Pinheiro [1] and Raimir Holanda Filho [2]

[1] Graduate Program in Computer Science-PPGCC, UECE State University of Ceará, Fortaleza 60714-903, CE, Brazil
[2] Graduate Program in Applied Informatics, PPGIA, University of Fortaleza, Fortaleza 60811-905, CE, Brazil
[3] University Center September 7, Fortaleza 60811-020, CE, Brazil
* Correspondence: placido@unifor.br (P.R.P.); analuiza.barros@uece.br (A.L.B.d.P.B.); luana.ibiapina@aluno.uece.br (L.I.C.C.P.)

Abstract: Predictive modelling strategies can optimise the clinical diagnostic process by identifying patterns among various symptoms and risk factors, such as those presented in cases of severe acute respiratory syndrome coronavirus 2 (SARS-CoV-2), also known as coronavirus (COVID-19). In this context, the present research proposes a comparative analysis using benchmarking techniques to evaluate and validate the performance of some classification algorithms applied to the same dataset, which contains information collected from patients diagnosed with COVID-19, registered in the Influenza Epidemiological Surveillance System (SIVEP). With this approach, 30,000 cases were analysed during the training and testing phase of the prediction models. This work proposes a comparative approach of machine learning algorithms (ML), working on the knowledge discovery task to predict clinical evolution in patients diagnosed with COVID-19. Our experiments show, through appropriate metrics, that the clinical evolution classification process of patients diagnosed with COVID-19 using the Multilayer Perceptron algorithm performs well against other ML algorithms. Its use has significant consequences for vital prognosis and agility in measures used in the first consultations in hospitals.

Keywords: machine learning; COVID-19; prediction; machine learning; medical diagnosis optimisation

Citation: Andrade, E.C.d.; Pinheiro, P.R.; Barros, A.L.B.d.P.; Nunes, L.C.; Pinheiro, L.I.C.C.; Pinheiro, P.G.C.D.; Holanda Filho, R. Towards Machine Learning Algorithms in Predicting the Clinical Evolution of Patients Diagnosed with COVID-19. Appl. Sci. 2022, 12, 8939. https://doi.org/10.3390/app12188939

Academic Editor: Grzegorz Dudek

Received: 7 August 2022
Accepted: 30 August 2022
Published: 6 September 2022

Publisher's Note: MDPI stays neutral with regard to jurisdictional claims in published maps and institutional affiliations.

Copyright: © 2022 by the authors. Licensee MDPI, Basel, Switzerland. This article is an open access article distributed under the terms and conditions of the Creative Commons Attribution (CC BY) license (https://creativecommons.org/licenses/by/4.0/).

1. Introduction

The COVID-19 pandemic has spread worldwide since the first cases were reported in China in December 2019 [1]. Since then, more than 546 million cases of COVID-19 have been reported, with features of severe acute respiratory syndrome due to SARS-CoV-2. Globally, the number of weekly COVID-19 cases increased for the third week, during 20–26 June 2022. COVID-19 variants such as Delta and Omicron are putting hundreds of thousands of people at risk, especially those with weakened immune systems. With the increasing spread of COVID-19, different ways to identify COVID-19 infection using deep learning (DL) methods are widely used to track the spread of the virus [2]. Symptom association activities and epidemiological and treatment recommendations for status alerts can utilise machine earning (ML) capabilities and deep learning (DL) approaches to optimise the correct interpretation of diagnoses, analysis of medical exam imaging treatments, and possible sequelae left by the infection [3].

Predictive models can identify and classify patterns and predict outcomes based on the analysed data. By applying its techniques to structured and unstructured data, a predictive model can lead to more realistic decision-making through relevant criteria and evaluation of various attributes (characteristics), such as the symptoms of a specific disease. According to Andrew Moore of Carnegie Mellon University School of Computer Science, artificial intelligence (AI) models look for computational devices to simulate the human ability to think and solve problems [4,5]. In addition, artificial intelligence can help guide medical analyses, aiming to assess and understand the characteristics of various symptoms such as those existing in COVID-19 cases. With the current crisis, the capacity of healthcare professionals has been challenged. The interpretation of tests to obtain diagnoses and prognoses during the waves of COVID-19 required hard work that was limited by experience, speed, and fatigue. In specific healthcare settings, such as intensive care services or in health crises such as COVID-19, professionals may experience high levels of compassion fatigue (CF), and their quality of work-life (ProQoL) may be impaired [6]. These healthcare workers exposed to COVID-19 are at high risk of developing mental health issues, including anxiety, depression, and stress, so may need psychological support or interventions to help them manage their situation [7]. Professionals who care for patients with COVID-19 have higher levels of HR and burnout (BO) than those who work in other healthcare settings [8,9].

The ability of machines to perform complex tasks and make decisions independently can help these professionals to be more efficient in investigating the case and implementing treatments in the first days of symptoms. Symptom association activities, epidemiological recommendations and status alert treatment can use AI resources to optimise the correct interpretation of diagnoses, treatments, and possible sequelae left by infection [10]. The AI-based methods employed to identify, classify, and diagnose medical images have significantly improved the screening, diagnosis, and prediction of COVID-19, resulting in superior scale-up, timely response, and more reliable and efficient results and occasionally outperforming humans in certain health activities [11]. Choosing the correct artificial intelligence (AI) algorithm for a specific problem is not a trivial task. The definition of which one will be applied to a dataset to perform a predictive analysis is decisive in the quality of forecasts and selecting strategies related to the desired objective. The health area requires the control of many stages, which are highly variable and depend on other stages of the patient's treatment. A predictive and centralised command and control system is needed to manage this variation, thus dealing with complex data, continuously learning from its experience, and improving the algorithms used in clinical predictions [12]. This study aims to evaluate the feasibility of using different ML techniques by applying predictive models to classify the clinical course of COVID-19 cases. Some metrics were used to measure the performance of the following algorithms: K-Nearest Neighbor (KNN), Naive Bayes (NB), Decision Trees (DT), Multilayer Perceptron (MLP), and Support Vector Machine (SVM). Once a comparative benchmark has been established between the different classification algorithms, showing which one has the best effectiveness, through the problem proposed in this study, the clinical evolution of patients with different symptoms of COVID-19 can be safely predicted.

For the learning process of the model, 129,475 cases of patients with COVID-19 were registered by the Epidemiological Surveillance of state and municipal bodies in the Epidemiological Surveillance System of the municipality (SIVEP-Influenza) were analysed until March 2021. The health area requires the control of many stages, which are highly variable and dependent on other stages of a patient's treatment. A predictive and centralised command and control system is needed to manage this variation, thus dealing with complex data, continuously learning from its experience, and improving the algorithms used in clinical predictions [4]. This study aims to evaluate the feasibility of using different ML techniques by applying predictive models to classify the clinical course of COVID-19 cases. Some metrics were used to measure the performance of the following algorithms: K-Nearest Neighbor (KNN), Naive Bayes, Decision Trees, Multilayer Perceptron (MLP), and Support Vector Machine (SVM). Once a comparative benchmark has been established between the different classification algorithms, showing which one has the best effectiveness, through the problem proposed in this study, the clinical evolution of patients with different symptoms of COVID-19 can be safely predicted.

This article is organised as follows. First, Section 2 highlights the concepts of COVID-19 and machine learning. Then, in Section 3, the methodology was used in this study.

In Section 4, the performance of the ML models is evaluated. Section 5 presents the comparative benchmark between the best values obtained from each prediction model. Finally, Section 6 exposes the target class prediction process. Section 6 summarises the conclusions, future work, and research limitations.

2. Background and Research

This research's theoretical framework and related work were structured into three topics: highlighted aspects of COVID-19, machine learning, and proposals for AI solutions used to diagnose and predict the disease's clinical evolution.

2.1. Highlights of COVID-19 Pandemic Concepts

COVID-19 has a wide spectrum, from superficial asymptomatic infection to severe pneumonia with acute respiratory distress syndrome (ARDS) and death. Anyone with consistent symptoms should be tested for SARS-CoV-2 infection [6]. Of 373,883 reported cases in the United States, 70% of the patients experienced fever, cough, and shortness of breath, 36% had muscle pain, and 34% reported headaches. Other reported symptoms include, but are not limited to, diarrhoea, dizziness, sore throat, abdominal pain, anorexia, and vomiting. SARS-CoV-2 was first identified in Wuhan, China, in December 2019. In Brazil, the first case was recorded in February 2020 in São Paulo [10]. COVID-19 has a significantly higher mortality rate than common influenza, and its transmission rate is higher than in recent epidemics such as SARS-CoV and H1N1 [11]. Sanitary measures to stop disease transmission have impacted the global socioeconomic scenario [12].

Brazil is currently the third country in the world in the total number of cases, behind only the United States and India. Furthermore, it ranks second in COVID-19 deaths [13].

2.2. Exposure of Healthcare Professionals to the COVID-19 Pandemic

The COVID-19 pandemic has exposed healthcare workers and new work-related problems [1]. Daily exposure to pandemic challenges can cause a risk described in the waiting context as a challenge (CF), such as burnout and secondary trauma (ST) [4,14].

Disease outbreaks provoke an intense response from the medical team, and fatigue, due to this challenge, has a significant impact on the mental health of health professionals, generally causing less vigilance and cognitive loss [15]. In the same way, stress with other psychological implications during the pandemic is considered to cause insomnia. Previous research on SARS identified poor sleep quality in nurses caring for patients with SARS [16].

In turn, isolation from loved ones, colleagues, and people with whom they used to have ties, the demand for long working hours, virus transmission in the workplace, and ethical concerns directly affect the physical and mental well-being of professionals [17]. Being in contact with the virus or feeling fear in day-to-day work can trigger more significant symptoms [18].

A systematic review found that many healthcare professionals experience significant anxiety, depression, and insomnia levels during the COVID-19 outbreak. A high proportion of healthcare professionals reported mild symptoms of both depression and anxiety [7,19].

Technology can reduce unnecessary visits, decrease healthcare workers' risk of infection, reduce their workload, and optimise their time to care for patients with acute conditions [20]. Artificial intelligence technology can also be applied to monitor the mental health of professionals, for example, to recognise people and medical teams at risk of suicide or other crises through psychological messages and necessary alarms [21,22].

It seeks to find patterns and make predictions [6]. Predictive models support the decision-making process, simplify the analysis of a problem and its alternatives, and, therefore, justify the choice of a particular action [7]. Another approach, from the point of view of decision-making based on verbal factors, is predictive ML models associated with a multi-criteria decision-support method of verbal decision analysis [8]. Based on machine learning algorithms and techniques, predictive models use mathematical calculations in datasets, according to a specific scenario and needs, to highlight patterns capable of highlighting trends or determining possible clinical diagnoses through statistics and probability [10,23] and, in short, extracting the valuable information stored in historical data to predict and decide the best actions. In addition to healthcare, other organisations are performing predictive analytics to solve complex problems and gain insights. One can mention the analysis of credit risk, finance, improvement in marketing actions, and supply and demand management.

AI predictive models can be supervised when the input data is known (labelled) or unsupervised when the ML algorithm is not telling the input data's meaning. The input data for this study are labelled. Thus, supervised models were applied to classify the data. The models aim to identify the class (target) an object (characteristics) belongs by mapping the input variables into distinct categories, such as the most important characteristics (clinical symptoms), thus determining the group or class to which the data belongs within the business context. Figure 1 presents the evaluation metrics used in the data classification task that are analysed in this study.

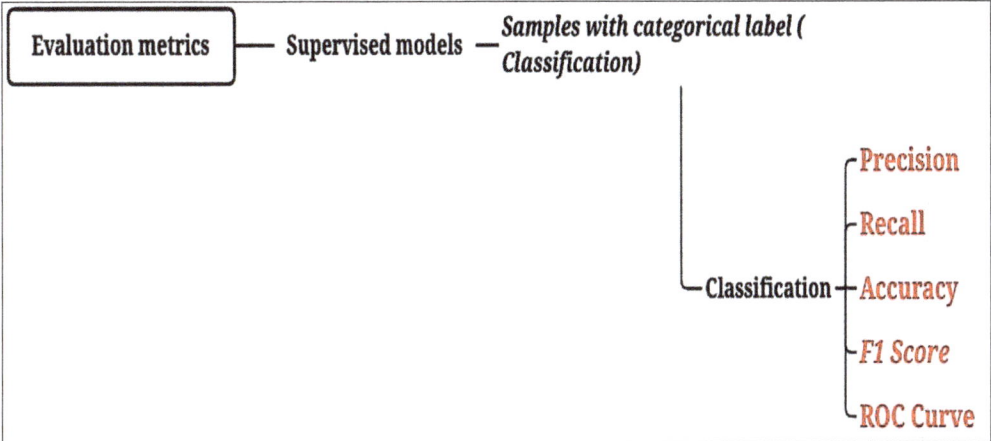

Figure 1. Measures for data classification.

2.3. Applying Artificial Intelligence to Pandemic Data

This section of the theoretical review describes the application of ML models used in data from patients diagnosed or suspected of having COVID-19, following a technological and practical approach to AI. ML models are applied to large amounts of data to obtain pattern detection of the information related to COVID-19 [24,25]. In this context, ML models played an important role in combating the COVID-19 pandemic [26]. Furthermore, studies propose a system with artificial intelligence to improve the ability to define the diagnosis more quickly in patients with COVID-19 [14,27]. Similarly, ML models are used to predict the prognosis of patients diagnosed with SARS-CoV-2 [2,28] and are used to analyse risk factors and predict mortality among patients in the ICU with COVID-19 [29]. In addition, the continuous development of AI is an effective tool for treating the COVID-19 pandemic and has reduced human intervention in medical practice [16]. Moreover, ML solutions can combat the chaos of the pandemic and help define the prognosis [17]. In a similar approach, deep learning is used in the initial screening of patients diagnosed with COVID-19 [18]. Some AI techniques are used to analyse blood tests and CT images to develop diagnostic and prognostic models of COVID-19 [19,30].

However, from the perspective of intelligent systems, ML algorithms have been used to predict intelligent physiological deterioration and death in patients diagnosed with COVID-19 [20]. ML models help analyse early mortality prediction in critically ill patients [31,32].

The K-means clustering method has also been used to provide input to the Indonesian government against the spread of COVID-19 [33].

Similarly, ML models are essential for clinical decision support to predict severity risk and the screening of patients with COVID-19 at hospital admission [34]. Studies have reported crucial symptoms such as dyspnea, cough, and fever to define the clinical course of patients with COVID-19. These resources are used as input to develop ML-based models and predict diagnostic results in patients with SARS-CoV-2 [35,36].

3. Methodology

The methodology used in this study is based on the execution of four steps, regardless of the ML method to be used.

- Step 01: Data collection and measurement (selection);
- Step 02: Data pre-processing;
- Step 03: Model execution (transformation/mining);
- Step 04: Validation of the results (interpretation/knowledge).

Figure 2 presents the execution flow to obtain knowledge through data and metrics collection, preprocessing, execution of the ML model, and final validation of the results.

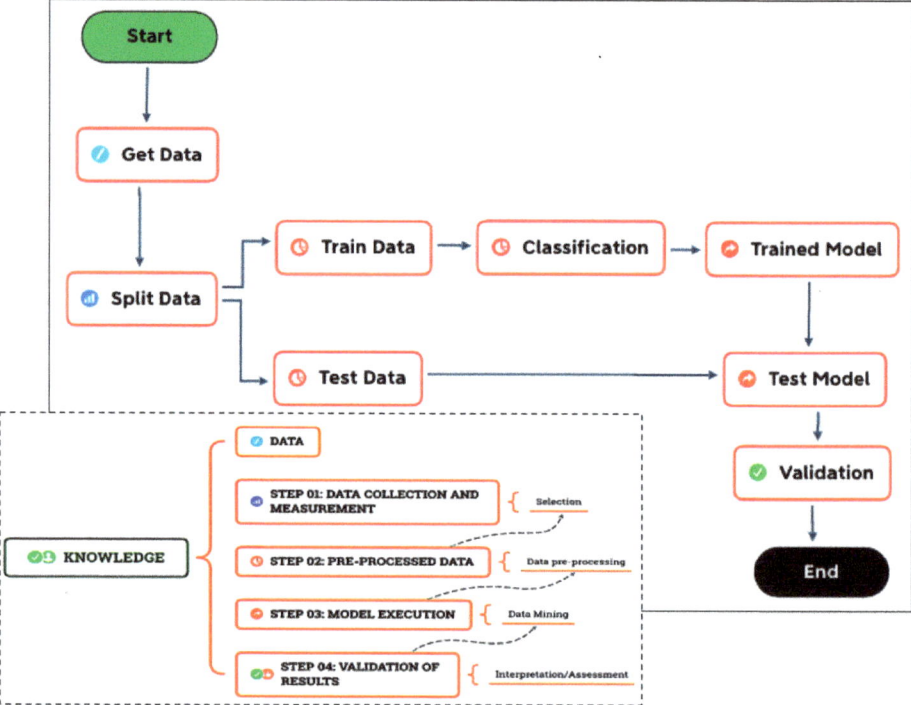

Figure 2. Get knowledge cycle.

This research used the collaborative environment, "Colab" (Collaboratory), a product of Google Research, based on the open-source project Jupyter. The sections used have access to a processor with two cores, 12 GBytes of RAM, and an L3 cache of 40–50 Mbytes. Furthermore, Google Colab is a free cloud service hosted by Google to encourage machine learning and artificial intelligence research. This environment is widely used to run Python code with machine learning libraries and tools.

In each of the four stages, the libraries NumPy, Pandas, Seaborn, and Scikit-learn were used to manipulate and analyse the data, generate calculations and statistical plot graphs, and apply the practice of ML methods. Specifically, NumPy is the foundational package for scientific computing in Python, and Pandas provides tools for data analysis and manipulation [37,38]. Seaborn is used for plotting statistics, and Scikit-learn is a machine learning library that supports supervised and unsupervised learning [39,40]. These are some of the main Python libraries [41].

3.1. Data Collection and Measurement

It is essential to obtain a satisfactory result, as the quality of the collected data affects how they will be processed and interpreted through the evaluation metrics.

3.1.1. Data Collection

Health data science, also known as the solution based on data science in health, can transform the reality of professionals in this area. The focus is on applying artificial intelligence and ML algorithms to interpret and understand patient data and generate clinical predictions [3,30].

The present study collected the data from 129,475 COVID-19 patients registered in the system developed by the Health Surveillance Secretariat (SVS) Ministry of Health of Brazil, SIVEP-Gripe. This system incorporated 2020-specific information about COVID-19 and, from there, information such as the date of onset of symptoms, date of death, date of hospitalisation, associated risk factors, age, sex, date of exam collection, and status of exams, among others, of hospitalised cases of a severe acute respiratory syndrome (SARS) by COVID-19. Therefore, improve the records of SARS deaths confirmed by COVID-19 in the SIVEP-Influenza system.

3.1.2. Data Dictionary

Table 1 describes the attributes used in this study.

Table 1. Data dictionary.

Individual Record Form—Hospitalised Severe Acute Respiratory Syndrome Cases			
Field Name	**Type**	**Allowed Values**	**Description**
FEVER	Varchar2 (1)		Did the patient have a fever?
COUGH	Varchar2 (1)		Did the patient cough?
DYSPNEA	Varchar2 (1)		Did the patient have dyspnea?
THROAT	Varchar2 (1)	1—Yes	Did the patient have a sore throat?
PAIN_ABD	Varchar2 (1)	2—No	Did the patient have abdominal pain?
FATIGUE	Varchar2 (1)	0—Ignored	Did the patient experience fatigue?
DIARRHEA	Varchar2 (1)	9—Ignored	Did the patient have diarrhoea?
SATURATION	Varchar2 (1)		Did the patient have O_2 saturation <95%?
VOMIT	Varchar2 (1)		Did the patient experience vomiting?
PERD_OLFT	Varchar2 (1)		Did the patient experience a loss of smell?
LOST_PALA	Varchar2 (1)		Did the patient experience taste loss?
RISC_FACTOR	Varchar2 (1)		Does the patient have risk factors?
OBESITY	Varchar2 (1)		Does the patient have obesity?
VACCINE	Varchar2 (1)		Was the patient vaccinated against influenza in the last campaign?

Table 1. Cont.

Field Name	Type	Allowed Values	Description
Individual Record Form—Hospitalised Severe Acute Respiratory Syndrome Cases			
SUPPORT_VEN	Varchar2 (1)	1—Yes, invasive 2—Yes, non-invasive 3—N 0—Ignored 9—Ignored	Did the patient use ventilatory support?
EVOLUTION	Varchar2 (1)	1—Cure 2—Death	Evolution of the case

The data fields FEVER, COUGH, DYSPNEA, THROAT, PAIN_ABD, FATIGUE, DIARRHEA, SATURATION, VOMIT, PERD_OLFT (loss of smell), and LOST_PALA (loss of taste) store the respective signs and symptoms of the patient, according to codes 1—Yes (if the patient presented the sign/symptom), 2—No (if the patient did not present the sign/symptom), or 0/9—Ignored (if the presence of the sign/symptom is unknown).

In addition, the RISC_FACTOR data field records the patient's risk factors for worsening the disease. It is filled with codes 1—Yes or 2—No, depending on the existence or not of the risk factor, and 0/9—Ignored (if the presence of the risk factor is unknown). The BMI must be specified for the risk factor Obesity registered in the OBESITY field if code 1—Yes is marked for "Obesity".

Information on the flu vaccine is registered in the VACCINE field. In this, data are obtained if the patient received the flu vaccine in the last flu vaccination campaign carried out in Brazil. It is filled in with the corresponding code, 1—Yes or 2—Patient's use of ventilatory support, which is recorded in the SUPPORT_VEN data field. It contains information on whether the patient used ventilatory support, with the corresponding code: 1—Yes, invasive (he used a ventilation technique with the patient with prostheses and endotracheal tubes that work as a patient/ventilatory support interface); 2—Yes, non-invasive (the patient used a ventilation technique in which a mask or similar device works as a patient/ventilatory support interface, without the use of prostheses and endotracheal tubes); and 3—No (the patient did not use ventilatory support).

Finally, recording the evolution of the case, the EVOLUTION data field, where the corresponding code of the patient's clinical evolution is found: 1—Cure, 2—Death, and 3—Death by causes. See the clinical evolution of the case for the unknown code 9—Ignored is used.

3.1.3. Data Measurement

At this stage, we seek to understand the collected data, identifying trends, and patterns to be mapped. A descriptive statistical analysis was used to understand, summarise, and describe the essential aspects of the set of observed characteristics of cases with the diagnosis of COVID-19.

Through the matrix presented in Figure 3, the correlation between attributes/symptoms is evaluated. Table 2 shows the highest correlation coefficients for the attribute pairs, demonstrating a linear relationship. The values indicate a moderately positive relationship. That is, as one attribute increases, the other attribute also increases. Taking as an example the pair with the highest correlation (0.96), when PERD_OLFT (loss of smell) increases from 1—Yes to 2—No, PERD_PALA (loss of taste) tends to increase. Furthermore, it is observed that when there is an improvement in the symptom of loss of smell, there may also be an improvement in the patient's taste.

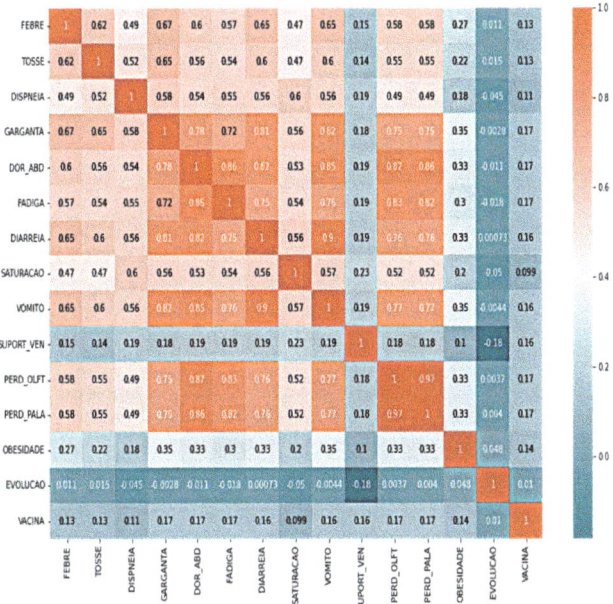

Figure 3. Correlation.

Table 2. Positive correlation.

Attribute 01	Attribute 02	Correlation Value
THROAT	VOMIT	0.81
PAIN_ABD	PERD_OLFT	0.85
FATIGUE	PAIN_ABD	0.86
DIARRHEA	PAIN_ABD	0.82
VOMIT	DIARRHEA	0.9
PERD_OLFT	LOST_PALA	0.96

Table 3 presents a negative linear relationship between the attributes EVOLUCAO and SUPPORT_VEN. Indeed, as the value of EVOLUTION goes from 1—Cure to 2—Death, the value of SUPPORT_VEN decreases from 2—Use of noninvasive ventilatory support) to 1—Use of invasive ventilatory support), thus demonstrating a relationship between invasive ventilatory support and death cases. In this study, attributes with high correlation were used, as they have the most significant predictive capacity (sign), and irrelevant variables (low correlation) were excluded.

Table 3. Negative correlation.

Attribute 01	Attribute 02	Correlation Value
EVOLUTION	SUPPORT_VEN	−0.19

3.2. Data Preprocessing

Data preprocessing is the process of preparing, organising, and structuring data. In this stage, techniques are used to extract knowledge, which is determined by the quality of the input data (collected data). Based on AI algorithms, data mining techniques can also help in data selection, preprocessing, and transformation, by discovering patterns and generating knowledge through their interpretations [21].

In this study, the values analysed for the EVOLUTION attribute are 1.0—Cure and 2.0—Death). The value "1.0—Cure" was considered "hospital discharge". Cases without clinical evolution records and records with death from other causes were excluded from the preprocessing, leaving 60,992 cases of patients with COVID-19.

3.2.1. Definition of Input Data

In this phase, the division between the desired attributes of the other features of the dataframe is carried out. Thus, the input data to be used by the prediction models are defined. The input data are denoted as X when determining the output class (target). The target class, y, is the attribute that wants to predict the output value. The prediction models will use the input data (X) to predict the clinical course (y) of the COVID-19 cases.

3.2.2. Training and Test Data

An ML prediction model is based on the observation of data. Once the learning is complete, it can perform complex tasks and make predictions with greater precision [3]. For this reason, we divide the input data into training and testing data. This segmentation aims to acquire knowledge to simulate forecasts and evaluate their performance. In this study, the Pareto proportion was used, where 80% (48,793 cases) were used for training and 20% (12,199 cases) were used for tests.

3.3. Model Execution

At this stage, the training base is submitted to the prediction models. Its parameters are optimised according to the data presented. In a second moment, the prediction of the target class was performed: the test data were applied to the trained models, and, finally, the predictions of the clinical evolution were obtained (1—Cure or 2—Death).

3.4. Validation of Results

The evaluation metric used to determine the best ML model depends on the analysed problem [42]. Metrics applied to health problems, such as the accuracy of a diagnosis, mean the ability of a prediction to discriminate between the target class and the patient's actual prognosis. For more critical qualifications in predicting clinical evolution, the diagnostic accuracy measures presented in Table 4 were used for the two models of this study.

Table 4. Evaluation metrics.

	Evaluation Metrics
Accuracy	Defines the overall performance of the model [43].
Precision	Indicates whether the model is accurate in its classifications [44].
Recall	Is the number of samples classified as belonging to a class divided by the total number of samples belonging to it, even if classified in another [44].
F1 score	Indicates the overall quality of the model [44].
Area Under the Curve (AUC)	Measures the area under the curve formed between the rate of positive examples and false positives [45].

4. Results and Discussion

Furthermore, the definition of the attributes to be used and the hyperparameters of each algorithm were adjusted to obtain the best behaviour for the proposed problem. Then, the performance of each one of them was evaluated through competitive benchmarking. Metrics indicative of performance and precision were used, thus obtaining the model's ability to learn by demonstrating a satisfactory result to perform in an authentic context.

4.1. KNN Results

The first model applied was K-Nearest Neighbor (KNN). For this method, analyses were performed, as shown in Table 5. The result obtained using three different K values (5, 25, and 45) is observed. The distance validation metrics were analysed for each K value: Euclidean, Manhattan, and Hamming.

Table 5. Benchmark for K-Nearest Neighbor—KNN.

Metrics/ Distance KNN	\multicolumn{4}{c}{K-Nearest Neighbor—KNN}								
	Accuracy	Precision	Recall That	F1 Score	Accuracy	Precision	Recall That	F1 Score	Accuracy	Precision	Recall That	F1 Score
Neighbor K	\multicolumn{4}{c}{5}	\multicolumn{4}{c}{25}	\multicolumn{4}{c}{45}
Euclidean	71.17%	74.31%	0.8518	0.79380	73.47%	74.25%	0.9073	0.81671	74.45%	75.04%	9107	0.82283
Manhattan	71.17%	74.32%	0.8516	0.79375	74.07%	74.62%	0.9122	0.82090	74.87%	75.09%	0.9191	0.82654
Hamming	71.87%	74.61%	0.8613	0.79957	74.65%	74.71%	0.9235	0.82599	**75.27%**	**74.93%**	**0.9322**	**0.83082**

The value of K equal to 45, as shown in Figure 4, using the Hamming distance measure, was the configuration with the best overall performance (accuracy), obtaining 75.27% confidence in the estimate. Its execution time was 69.995 s, the fastest execution using Euclidean distance and K equal to 5, taking 7.132 s, but it was the least accurate among the analysed K values.

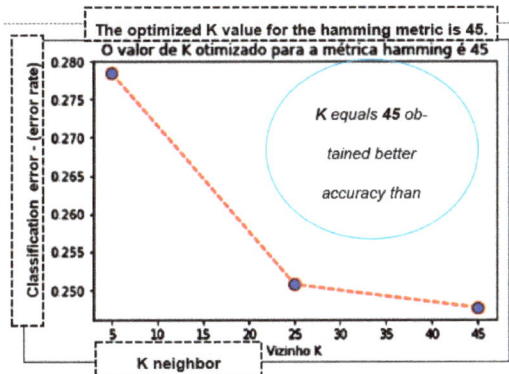

Figure 4. K optimized.

An accuracy of 74.93% was obtained according to the parameters, indicating the percentage of correct classification of clinical evolution. Recall (sensitivity), which indicates the frequency of the correct classification, obtained a value of 0.9322. KNN presents a good frequency of assertiveness (optimal value is equal to 1) when classifying the evolution of the clinical case as high: hospital or death. When combining the values obtained from precision and recall, we have an F1 score of 0.83082 (optimal value equal to 1). The value reached corroborates the information on the precision and recall values. AUC was performed for all K values, and the respective distances were investigated. Figure 5 shows the graph generated through the best parameters identified, reaching a value of 0.76 (ROC score). With this information, a patient chosen randomly is evaluated, with 76% assertiveness in classifying their clinical evolution, using the K-Nearest Neighbor (KNN) prediction model.

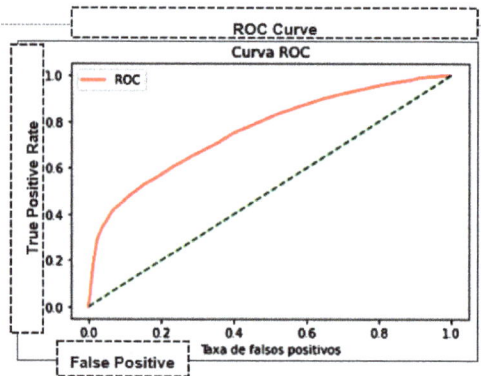

Figure 5. ROC curve—Hamming.

4.2. Naive Bayes Results

Then, the Naive Bayes model was applied to the training data sample. Table 6 presents the results obtained using the following distributions: Gaussian, Bernoulli, and Multinomial.

Table 6. Benchmark for Naive Bayes.

	Naive Bayes			
Metrics/Distribution	Accuracy	Precision	Recall That	F1 Score
Gaussian	65.13%	66.42%	0.9401	0.77843
Bernoulli	59.37%	66.93%	0.7439	0.70462
Multinomial	**66.62%**	**66.98%**	**0.9618**	**0.78966**

Moreover, with accuracy reaching 66.62%, the specific instance of the Naive Bayes classifier, using the Multinomial distribution, stood out from the others that were analysed. The Accuracy metric, used to investigate whether the model is accurate in its classifications, obtained 66.98%. Sensitivity or recall, indicative of assertiveness frequently in the classification of the patient's clinical evolution, obtained a value of 0.9618, considering the optimum equal to 1. This was a significant result. The harmonic means between precision and recall (F1 score) resulted in 0.78966 for the model's overall quality.

The area under the ROC curve or Area Under the ROC curve (AUC) was verified for all Naive Bayes distributions, as shown in Figure 6. The highest value reached was 0.64 for the multinomial distribution, which means a 64% chance of correctly classifying clinical evolution using the multinomial naive Bayes.

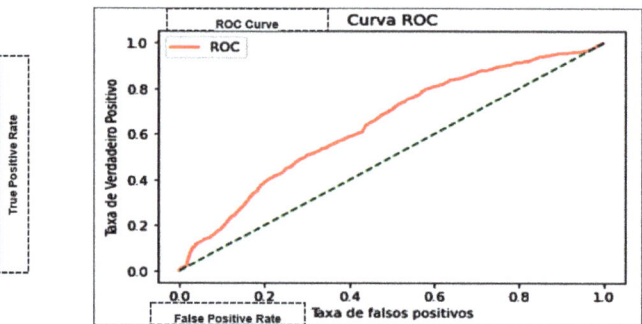

Figure 6. ROC curve—multinomial.

4.3. Results of the Decision Trees

The Decision Tree model was also applied to the same training data. Table 7 presents the result obtained. The parameters Gini and entropy index were used in its analysis.

Table 7. Benchmark for Decision Tree.

Metrics/Criteria	Accuracy	Precision	Recall That	F1 Score
Gini index	71.58%	74.61%	0.8546	0.79670
Entropy	**71.83%**	**74.87%**	**0.8544**	**0.79808**

The best accuracy of 71.83% was obtained using entropy. This parameter defines how to measure the purity of each subset in each decision tree. In other words, it measures the probability of obtaining an occurrence of a positive event (hospital discharge) from a random selection of the data subset. It is observed that the precision obtained was 74.87%, the sensitivity (recall) was 0.8544, and the harmonic mean between these two variables (F1 score) was 0.79808.

The value reached for the ROC curve analysis was 0.69 (with the entropy parameter), as shown in Figure 7. There is a 69% chance of correctly classifying the patient's clinical evolution using the Decision Tree model prediction.

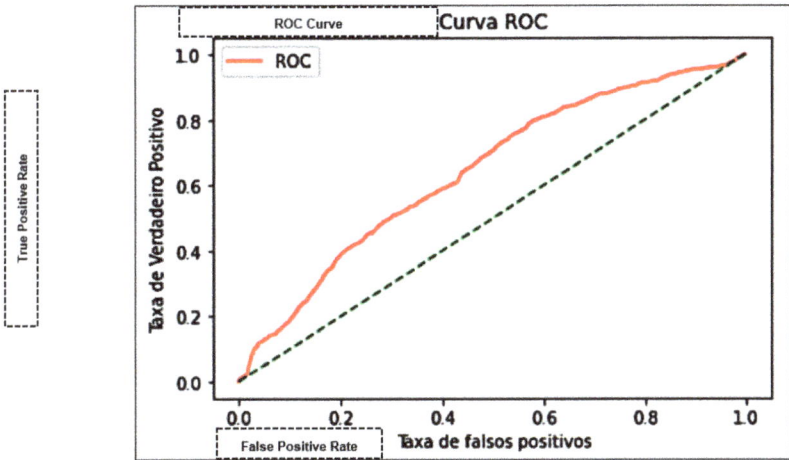

Figure 7. ROC curve—Decision Tree—entropy.

4.4. Multilayer Perceptron Results

Applying the Multilayer Perceptron (MLP) model, the values shown in Table 8 were obtained using different learning rates and momentum.

Table 8. Benchmark for Multilayer Perceptron (MLP).

Metrics/Learning Rate and Momentum	Accuracy	Precision	Recall That	F1 Score
learning_rate = constant momentum = 0.1	69.86%	70.48%	0.70633	0.70556
learning_rate = invscaling momentum = 0.9	61.1%	65.23%	0.64333	0.64781
learning_rate = adaptive momentum = 0.9	**76.3%**	**76.41%**	**0.76466**	**0.76441**

Using MLP, with learning rate parameters equal to adaptive and momentum equal to 0.9, an accuracy of 76.3% was obtained. The precision was 76.41%, and the sensitivity was 0.76466.

The F1 score reached the value of 0.76441, the general quality of the model. Following the ROC analysis, the best result was 0.84 (ROC score), with a hypothesis of an 84% correct classification in clinical evolution, using the Multilayer Perceptron—MLP model. Based on the hypothesis presented in this study, the results of the analysis of the behaviour of the MLP networks trained on the COVID-19 dataset proved to be entirely satisfactory, lacking in terms of time for model training.

4.5. Results of the Support Vector Machine

The results of the fifth and last applied model, Support Vector Machine (SVM), using different values for the Kernel parameters, width, and degree, are presented in Table 9.

Table 9. Benchmark for Support Vector Machine (SVM).

Metrics/Kernel	Support Vector Machine—SVM											
	Accuracy	Precision	Recall That	F1 Score	Accuracy	Precision	Recall That	F1 Score	Accuracy	Precision	Recall That	F1 Score
Cost	1				2				3			
kernel = linear Gamma = scale	66.25%	66.25%	1.0	0.79699	66.25%	66.25%	1.0	0.79699	66.25%	66.25%	1.0	0.79699
Kernel = Linear Gamma = auto	66.25%	66.25%	1.0	0.79699	66.25%	66.25%	1.0	0.79699	66.25%	66.25%	1.0	0.79699
Kernel = RBF Gamma = scale	72.08%	73.35%	0.9086	0.81173	72.80%	73.83%	0.91320	0.81646	73.28%	74.27%	0.91283	0.81902
Kernel = RBF Gamma = auto	74.92%	75.53%	0.91924	0.82927	75.58%	76.43%	0.91283	0.83198	**75.78%**	**76.61%**	**0.91320**	**0.83318**
Kernel = POLY Gamma = scale	66.25%	66.25%	1.0	0.79699	66.25%	66.25%	1.0	0.79699	-	-	-	-
Kernel = POLY Gamma = scale	66.25%	66.46%	0.99018	0.79539	66.27%	66.48%	0.99018	0.79551	66.33%	66.51%	0.99056	0.79581
Kernel = POLY Gamma = scale	66.95%	67.82%	0.95358	0.79265	-	-	-	-	-	-	-	-
Kernel = POLY Gamma = auto	66.25%	66.25%	1.0	0.79699	-	-	-	-	-	-	-	-
Kernel = POLY Gamma = auto	-	-	-	-	66.30%	66.51%	0.98981	0.79557	-	-	-	-

The parameters γ (gamma), C (cost), and degree were changed during the analysis of this algorithm, aiming for the best results for the learning of the model. During this exercise, it was noticed that as the values increased, the performance and complexity of the classifier increased.

An accuracy of 75.78% was obtained using Kernel RBF, with C equal to 3 and gamma equal to auto. This was the most performative result among the other configurations of this algorithm. A substantial compromise in the algorithm's performance is noticed when inserting new parameters in this configuration. Its precision was 76.61%, with a sensitivity of 0.91320 and 0.83318 as the harmonic mean (F1 score). The ROC curve analysis for the parameters Kernel linear, C equal to 1, and gamma equal to scale presented the best ROC score of 0.73772, as shown in Figure 8. Using these values, a patient has a 73% chance of being correctly classified using the Support Vector Machine.

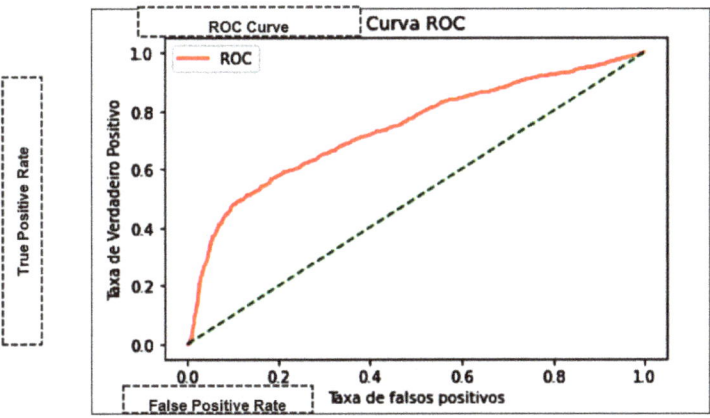

Figure 8. ROC curve—SVM.

4.6. Discussion

Among all the analysed characteristics of the five algorithms, it can be observed that, according to the parameters explicitly defined to control the learning process, different metrics were obtained that indicate the result of the performance of each one of them. The understanding of data was carried out in each case by testing different configurations at the beginning of the learning process of each model. As a result, the fastest algorithm in its execution was Decision Tree using entropy, with only 0.05444 s for performance. The best precision and F1 score were seen with the Support Vector Machine (SVM) algorithm, using Kernel RBF, C equal to 3, and gamma equal to auto. The multinomial naive Bayes algorithm has the best sensitivity or recall, and the K-Nearest Neighbor (KNN) also stands out in this metric. A comparative benchmark was created between the best values obtained from each forecast model, which was analysed to summarise the data obtained. Table 10 summarises the condensed results among the metrics obtained.

Table 10. Benchmark for prediction models.

Comparative Benchmark between Prediction Models						
Metric/Prediction Model	Accuracy	Precision	Recall That	F1 Score	ROC	Time (s)
K-Nearest Neighbor—KNN	75.27%	74.93%	0.9322	0.83082	0.76202	69.995
Naive Bayes	66.62%	66.98%	0.9618	0.78966	0.64363	0.0826
Decision trees	71.83%	74.87%	0.8544	0.79808	0.69686	0.5455
Multilayer Perceptron—MLP	76.3%	76.41%	0.7646	0.76441	0.84300	286.023
Support Vector Machine—SVM	75.78%	76.61%	0.91320	0.83318	0.73772	0.00101

Accuracy and reliability are essential in studies carried out in health [22,46]. According to the no free lunch theorem, if an algorithm outperforms another in one metric, it may lose in a different metric, depending on the problem. So, in general, there is no certainty about which algorithm is the best. However, the Multilayer Perceptron (MLP) algorithm, which is extremely fast when performing predictions, obtained the best results for the present study. Training MLP networks with backpropagation took considerable time, despite using the term momentum. Analysing the cost of recognising bold patterns in predicting clinical evolution was prioritised to obtain the best precision at the speed of diagnosis. Next, the predictions made with the winning MLP prediction model are presented.

5. Experimental Evaluation

Through the definition of an experimental process, the ability to predict the target class is analysed, based on random tests, with different attributes (symptoms) applied to the MLP model. The following parameters were used in the prediction activity of the target class (clinical evolution):

- Model: Multilayer Perceptron (MLP):
- Parameter 01: Learning rate = adaptive;
- Parameter 02: Momentum = 0.9;
- Parameter 03: Solver = SGD.

5.1. Definition of Values

Table 11 presents the questionnaire on the symptoms of COVID-19. Randomly, responses were defined for five clinical cases.

Table 11. Clinical questionnaire.

Individual Record Form—Hospitalised Severe Acute Respiratory Syndrome Cases	
1. Did the patient have a fever?	9. Did the patient experience vomiting?
2. Did the patient have a cough?	10. Did the patient use ventilatory support?
3. Did the patient have dyspnea?	11. Did the patient experience a loss of smell?
4. Did the patient have a sore throat?	12. Did the patient experience a loss of taste?
5. Did the patient have abdominal pain?	13. Does the patient have any risk factors?
6. Did the patient experience fatigue?	14. Does the patient have obesity?
7. Did the patient have diarrhoea?	15. Was the patient vaccinated against influenza in the last campaign?
8. Did the patient have O_2 saturation <95%?	

5.2. Prediction of Clinical Evolution

By applying the scikit-learn, *predict (X)*, and *predict_proba (X)* methods, the prediction of the clinical evolution of the patient diagnosed with COVID-19 was obtained, as was the percentage perspective of assertiveness of this class.

The percentage of precision of 76.3% (accuracy) and 76.41% accuracy in the classification of the target class (hospital discharge or death) to obtain the prediction results is shown in Table 12. It is close between accuracy and precision, thus indicating the absence of systematic errors.

Table 12. Prediction of clinical evolution.

Questions/Patients	Patient 01	Patient 02	Patient 03	Patient 04	Patient 05
1. Did the patient have a fever?	1—Yes	2—No	1—Yes	1—Yes	1—Yes
2. Did the patient have a cough?	1—Yes	2—No	1—Yes	1—Yes	1—Yes
3. Did the patient have dyspnea?	1—Yes	1—Yes	1—Yes	2—No	2—No
4. Did the patient have a sore throat?	0—Ignored	2—No	2—No	2—No	2—No
5. Did the patient have abdominal pain?	0—Ignored	2—No	2—No	2—No	2—No
6. Did the patient experience fatigue?	1—Yes	2—No	1—Yes	1—Yes	1—Yes
7. Did the patient have diarrhoea?	1—Yes	2—No	1—Yes	2—No	2—No
8. Did the patient have O_2 saturation < 95%?	0—Ignored	2—No	1—Yes	2—No	2—No
9. Did the patient experience vomiting?	1—Yes	2—No	2—No	2—No	2—No
10. Did the patient use ventilatory support?	0—Ignored	1—Yes	1—Yes	1—Yes	2—No

Table 12. *Cont.*

Questions/Patients	Patient 01	Patient 02	Patient 03	Patient 04	Patient 05
11. Did the patient experience a loss of smell?	0—Ignored	2—No	1—Yes	1—Yes	1—Yes
12. Did the patient experience a loss of taste?	0—Ignored	2—No	1—Yes	1—Yes	1—Yes
13. Does the patient have any risk factors?	1—Yes	1—Yes	2—No	2—No	1—Yes
14. Does the patient have obesity?	1—Yes	2—No	2—No	1—Yes	2—No
15. Was the patient vaccinated against influenza in the last campaign?	0—Ignored	1—Yes	1—Yes	1—Yes	1—Yes
Clinical Case Evolution	73%—the case progressed to the cure (1) of the patient	84%—the case progressed to death (2) of the patient	92%—the case progressed to death (2) of the patient	86%—the case progressed to death (2) of the patient	85%—the case progressed to the cure (1) of the patient

Through the symptoms of the five patients as input data not observed in the training and testing phase of the MLP model, the prediction results are observed:

- In general, the model obtains a probability above 70% in the classification of the target class (hospital discharge or death);
- Patient 01 has a 73% probability of being discharged from the hospital;
- Patient 02 has an 84% probability of clinical evolution to death;
- Patient 03 obtained a chance of 92% that their clinical case would evolve to an end;
- Patient 04 has an 86% probability of clinical evolution to an end;
- Patient 05 reaches an 85% probability of discharge from the hospital.

6. Conclusions and Future Works

In this step, the purpose of this study is analysed with the application of a machine learning model optimised to predict the clinical evolution in patients diagnosed with COVID-19. A case study was carried out with ML techniques to classify the clinical evolution in cases of COVID-19. Through a historical base of patients, 30,000 cases were analysed during the training and testing phase of the prediction models. A competitive benchmark was obtained, comparing the metrics aiming at a behaviour closer to reality. Among the K-Nearest Neighbor (KNN), Naive Bayes, Decision Trees, and Support Vector Machine (SVM) algorithms, the Multilayer Perceptron (MLP) obtained a more specific behaviour for this study approach, which helped with the recognition of patterns in the data not observed in the model preprocessing phase [15]. This way, the proposed objective was achieved by classifying the clinical evolution of patients diagnosed with COVID-19, by analysing their symptoms and classifying the clinical development through an optimised prediction model. The implication of the conclusion obtained by this study is to indicate, among the analysed algorithms, the one with the highest performance. In this case, the MLP has specific parameters, classifying the clinical evolution of patients diagnosed with COVID-19 through the symptoms identified in the SIVEP database. Furthermore, it was necessary to analyse different characteristics of each concurrent algorithm (K-Nearest Neighbor, Naive Bayes, Decision Trees, and Support Vector Machine), demonstrating their details and where each stands out using the same database.

Some future work suggestions are clinical data analysis using bootstrap and temporary aeries analysis for prognosis classification of COVID-19 patients; using ensemble learning to obtain the result via various ML algorithms and perform a comparative benchmark with COVID-19 patient data from other countries; and analysing the performance of some convolutional neural network algorithms as well as the Farmland Fertility algorithm [46,47], African Vultures Optimization Algorithm [48], and Artificial Gorilla Troops Optimizer [49] for the same COVID-19 datasets.

This study has potential limitations. The effect estimates in the model are based on the interventional and prospective observational studies of five predictive models of ML, to build a benchmark with the analysed data from patients diagnosed with COVID-19. For the construction of this comparative model, only the classification of evolution to death or not was analysed, without analysis of the other clinical conclusions. Overall, there are other critical limitations of machine learning models in medical applications stemming from the quality of the data, as it can mean the difference in diagnosing patients to the risk of intentional manipulation, so that the algorithm can introduce a particular bias leading doctors to wrong conclusions.

Author Contributions: Conceptualization, E.C.d.A.; Investigation, P.G.C.D.P.; Methodology, P.R.P. and A.L.B.d.P.B.; Project administration, L.C.N.; Supervision, R.H.F.; Validation, L.I.C.C.P. All authors have read and agreed to the published version of the manuscript.

Funding: This research was funded by the National Scientific and Technological Development Council (CNPq) Grants Nos. 304272/2020-5 and 306389/2020-7.

Institutional Review Board Statement: Not applicable.

Informed Consent Statement: Not applicable.

Data Availability Statement: No datasets are generated during the current study. The datasets analysed during this work are publicly available in this published article.

Acknowledgments: The authors Placido Rogerio Pinheiro and Raimir Holanda Filho would like to thank Fundação Edson Queiroz/Universidade de Fortaleza.

Conflicts of Interest: The authors have no competing interest to declare relevant to this article's content.

References

1. WHO. Coronavirus Disease (COVID-19) Weekly Epidemiological Update and Weekly Operational Update. Available online: https://www.who.int/emergencies/diseases/novel-coronavirus-2019/situation-reports (accessed on 9 December 2020).
2. Heidari, A.; Navimipour, N.J.; Unal, M.; Toumaj, S. Machine learning applications for COVID-19 outbreak management. *Neural Comput. Appl.* **2022**, *34*, 15313–15348. [CrossRef] [PubMed]
3. Heidari, A.; Toumaj, S.; Navimipour, N.J.; Unal, M. A privacy-aware method for COVID-19 detection in chest CT images using lightweight deep conventional neural network and blockchain. *Comput. Biol. Med.* **2022**, *145*, 105461. [CrossRef] [PubMed]
4. Andrade, E.A. Hybrid Model in Machine Learning and Verbal Decision Analysis Applied to the Diagnosis of Master. Master's Thesis, University of Fortaleza, Fortaleza, Brazil, 2020.
5. Souza, R.W.R.; Silva, D.S.; Passos, L.A.; Roder, M.; Santana, M.C.; Pinheiro, P.R.; Albuquerque, V.H.C. Computer-Assisted Parkinson's Disease Diagnosis Using Fuzzy Optimum-Path Forest, and Restricted Boltzmann Machines. *Comput. Biol. Med.* **2021**, *131*, 104260. [CrossRef]
6. Andrade, E.C.; Pinheiro, P.R.; Filho, R.H.; Nunes, L.C.; Pinheiro, M.C.D.; Abreu, W.C.; Filho, M.S.; Pinheiro, L.I.C.C.; Pereira, M.L.D.; Pinheiro, P.G.C.D.; et al. Application of Machine Learning to Infer Symptoms and Risk Factors of COVID-19. In *The International Research & Innovation Forum*; Springer: Cham, Switzerland, 2022; pp. 13–24.
7. Pinheiro, P.R.; Tamanini, I.; Pinheiro, M.C.D.; Albuquerque, V.H.C. Evaluation of Alzheimer's Disease Clinical Stages under the Optics of Hybrid Approaches in Verbal Decision Analysis. *Telemat. Inform.* **2018**, *35*, 776–789. [CrossRef]
8. Andrade, E.; Portela, S.; Pinheiro, P.R.; Comin, L.N.; Filho, M.S.; Costa, W.; Pinheiro, M.C.D. A Protocol for the Diagnosis of Autism Spectrum Disorder Structured in Machine Learning and Verbal Decision Analysis. *Comput. Math. Methods Med.* **2021**, *2021*, 1628959. [CrossRef]
9. Ruiz-Fernández, M.D.; Pérez-García, E.; Ortega-Galán, M. Quality of Life in Nursing Professionals: Burnout, Fatigue, and Compassion Satisfaction. *Int. J. Environ. Res. Public Health* **2020**, *17*, 1253. [CrossRef]
10. Shereen, M.A.; Khan, S.; Kazmi, A.; Bashir, N.; Siddique, R. COVID-19 infection: Origin, transmission, and characteristics of human coronaviruses. *J. Adv. Res.* **2020**, *24*, 91–98. [CrossRef]
11. Heidari, A.; Navimipour, N.J.; Unal, M.; Toumaj, S. The COVID-19 epidemic analysis and diagnosis using deep learning: A systematic literature review and future directions. *Comput. Biol. Med.* **2021**, *141*, 105141. [CrossRef]
12. Matos, P.; Costa, A.; Silva, C. COVID-19, stock market and sectoral contagion in the U.S.: A time-frequency analysis. *Res. Int. Bus. Financ.* **2021**, *57*, 101400. [CrossRef]
13. Vizheh, M.; Qorbani, M.; Arzaghi, S.M.; Muhidin, S.; Javanmard, Z.; Esmaeili, M. The mental health of healthcare workers in the COVID-19 pandemic: A systematic review. *J. Diabetes Metab. Disord.* **2020**, *19*, 1967–1978. [CrossRef]
14. Jin, C.; Chen, W.; Cao, Y.; Xu, Z.; Tan, Z.; Zhang, X.; Deng, L.; Zheng, C.; Zhou, J.; Shi, H.; et al. Development and evaluation of an artificial intelligence system for COVID-19 diagnosis. *Nat. Commun.* **2020**, *11*, 5088. [CrossRef] [PubMed]
15. Carvalho, D.; Pinheiro, P.R.; Pinheiro, M.C.D. A Hybrid Model to Support the Early Diagnosis of Breast Cancer. *Procedia Comput. Sci.* **2016**, *91*, 927–934. [CrossRef]
16. Lalmuanawma, S.; Hussain, J.; Chhakchhuak, L. Applications of machine learning and artificial intelligence for the covid-19 (SARS-COV-2) pandemic: A review. *Chaos Solitons Fractals* **2020**, *139*, 110059. [CrossRef]

17. Booth, A.L.; Abels, E.; McCaffrey, P. Development of a prognostic model for mortality in covid-19 infection using machine learning. *Mod. Pathol.* **2021**, *34*, 522–531. [CrossRef] [PubMed]
18. Liang, W.; Yao, J.; Chen, A.; Lv, Q.; Zanin, M.; Liu, J.; Wong, S.; Li, Y.; Lu, J.; Liang, H.; et al. Early triage of critically ill COVID-19 patients using deep learning. *Nat. Commun.* **2020**, *11*, 3543. [CrossRef] [PubMed]
19. Yang, P.; Xie, Y.; Rao, X.; Frix, A.N.; Moutschen, M.; Li, J.; Du, D.; Zhao, S.; Ding, Y.; Liu, B.; et al. Development of a clinical decision support system for severity risk prediction and triage of COVID-19 patients at hospital admission: An international multicenter study. *Eur. Respir. J.* **2020**, *56*, 2001104.
20. Gao, Y.; Cai, G.-Y.; Fang, W.; Li, H.-Y.; Wang, S.-Y.; Chen, L.; Yu, Y.; Liu, D.; Xu, S.; Cui, P.-F.; et al. Machine learning based early warning system enables accurate mortality risk prediction for COVID-19. *Nat. Commun.* **2020**, *11*, 5033. [CrossRef]
21. Pinheiro, L.I.C.C.; Pereira, M.L.D.; Andrade, E.C.; Nunes, L.C.; Abreu, W.C.; Pinheiro, P.G.C.D.; Filho, R.H.; Pinheiro, P.R. An Intelligent Multicriteria Model for Diagnosing Dementia in People Infected with Human Immunodeficiency Virus. *Appl. Sci.* **2021**, *11*, 10457. [CrossRef]
22. Castro, A.K.A.; Pinheiro, P.R.; Pinheiro, M.C.D.; Tamanini, I. Towards the Applied Hybrid Model in Decision Making: A Neuropsychological Diagnosis of Alzheimer's Disease Study Case. *Int. J. Comput. Intell. Syst.* **2011**, *4*, 89–99. [CrossRef]
23. Russell, J.; Norvig, P. *Artificial Intelligence: A Modern Approach*, 3rd ed.; Prentice-Hall: Hoboke, NJ, USA, 2010.
24. Shilo, S.; Rossman, H.; Segal, E. Axes of a revolution challenges and promises big data in healthcare. *Nat. Med.* **2020**, *26*, 29–38. [CrossRef]
25. Yu, K.H.; Beam, L.A.; Kohane, I.S. Artificial intelligence in healthcare. *Nat. Biomed. Eng.* **2018**, *2*, 719–731. [CrossRef]
26. Alimadadi, A.; Aryal, S.; Manandhar, I.; Munroe, P.B.; Joe, B.; Cheng, X. Artificial intelligence and machine learning to fight COVID-19. *Physiol. Genom.* **2020**, *52*, 200–202. [CrossRef] [PubMed]
27. Mei, X.; Lee, H.C.; Diao, K.Y.; Huang, M.; Lin, B.; Liu, C.; Xie, Z.; Ma, Y.; Robson, P.M.; Chung, M.; et al. Artificial intelligence-enabled rapid diagnosis of patients with COVID-19. *Nat. Med.* **2020**, *26*, 1224–1228. [CrossRef] [PubMed]
28. Yan, L.; Zhang, H.-T.; Goncalves, J.; Xiao, Y.; Wang, M.; Guo, Y.; Sun, C.; Tang, X.; Jing, L.; Zhang, M.; et al. An interpretable mortality prediction model for COVID-19 patients. *Nat. Mach. Intell.* **2020**, *2*, 283–288. [CrossRef]
29. Pan, P.; Li, Y.; Xiao, Y.; Han, B.; Su, L.; Su, M.; Li, Y.; Zhang, S.; Jiang, D.; Chen, X.; et al. Prognostic assessment of COVID-19 in the intensive care unit by machine learning methods: Model development and validation. *J. Med. Internet Res.* **2020**, *22*, e23128. [CrossRef]
30. Waheed, A.; Goyal, M.; Gupta, D.; Khanna, A.; Al-Turjman, F.; Pinheiro, P.R. CovidGAN: Data Augmentation Using Auxiliary Classifier GAN for Improved COVID-19 Detection. *IEEE Access* **2020**, *8*, 91916–91923. [CrossRef]
31. Bai, T.; Zhu, X.; Zhou, X.; Grathwohl, D.; Yang, P.; Zha, Y.; Jin, Y.; Chong, H.; Yu, Q.; Isberner, N.; et al. Reliable and Interpretable Mortality Prediction With Strong Foresight in COVID-19 Patients: An International Study From China and Germany. *Front. Artif. Intell.* **2021**, *4*, 672050. [CrossRef]
32. Heldt, F.S.; Vizcaychipi, M.P.; Peacock, S.; Cinelli, M.; McLachlan, L.; Andreotti, F.; Jovanović, S.; Dürichen, R.; Lipunova, N.; Fletcher, R.A.; et al. Early risk assessment for COVID-19 patients from emergency department data using machine learning. *Sci. Rep.* **2021**, *11*, 4200. [CrossRef]
33. Abdullah, D.; Susilo, S.; Ahmar, A.S.; Rusli, R.; Hidayat, R. The application of K-means clustering for province clustering in Indonesia of the risk of the COD-19 pandemic based on COVID-19 data. *Qual. Quant.* **2021**, *56*, 1283–1291. [CrossRef]
34. Ryan, L.; Lam, C.; Mataraso, S.; Allen, A.; Green-Saxen, A.; Pellegrini, E.; Hoffman, J.; Barton, C.; McCoy, A.; Das, R. A Mortality prediction model for the triage of COVID-19, pneumonia, and mechanically ventilated ICU patients: A retrospective study. *Ann. Med. Surg.* **2020**, *59*, 207–216. [CrossRef]
35. Assaf, D.; Gutman, Y.; Neuman, Y.; Segal, G.; Amit, S.; Gefen-Halevi, S.; Shilo, N.; Epstein, A.; Mor-Cohen, R.; Biber, A.; et al. Utilization of machine-learning models to accurately predict the risk for critical COVID-19. *Intern. Emerg. Med.* **2020**, *15*, 1435–1443. [CrossRef] [PubMed]
36. Fernandes, F.T.; de Oliveira, T.A.; Teixeira, C.E.; Batista, A.F.D.M.; Costa, G.D.; Filho, A.D.P.C. A multipurpose machine learning approach to predict COVID-19 negative prognosis in São Paulo, Brazil. *Sci. Rep.* **2021**, *11*, 3343. [CrossRef] [PubMed]
37. Numpy. Available online: https://numpy.org/ (accessed on 5 January 2022).
38. Pandas. Available online: https://pandas.pydata.org/ (accessed on 15 January 2022).
39. Seaborn. Available online: https://seaborn.pydata.org/ (accessed on 12 January 2022).
40. Scikit-Learn. Available online: https://scikit-learn.org/stable/ (accessed on 7 January 2022).
41. Python. Available online: https://www.python.org/ (accessed on 11 January 2022).
42. Korbut, D. Machine Learning Algorithms: Which to Choose for Your Problem. Available online: https://blog.statsbot.co/machine-learning-algorithms-183cc73197c (accessed on 7 January 2022).
43. Presesti, E.; Gosmaro, F. Trueness, Precision and Accuracy: A Critical Overview of the Concepts and Proposals for revision. *Accredit. Qual. Assur.* **2015**, *20*, 33–40. [CrossRef]
44. Powers, D.M. Evaluation: From precision, recall, and f-measure to roc, informedness, markedness, and correlation. *ArXiv* **2020**, arXiv:2010.16061.
45. Fawcett, T. Roc graphs: Notes and practical considerations for researchers. *Mach. Learn.* **2004**, *31*, 1–38.
46. Zrigat, E.; Altamimi, A.; Azzeh, M. A Comparative Study for Predicting Heart Diseases Using Data Mining Classification Methods. *Int. J. Comput. Sci. Inf. Secur.* **2016**, *14*, 868–879.

47. Shayanfar, H.; Gharehchopogh, F.S. Farmland fertility: A new metaheuristic algorithm for solving continuous optimization problems. *Appl. Soft Comput.* **2018**, *71*, 728–746. [CrossRef]
48. Abdollahzadeh, B.; Gharehchopogh, F.S.; Mirjalili, S. African vultures optimization algorithm: A new nature-inspired metaheuristic algorithm for global optimization problems. *Comput. Ind. Eng.* **2021**, *158*, 107408. [CrossRef]
49. Abdollahzadeh, B.; Gharehchopogh, F.S.; Mirjalili, S. Artificial gorilla troops optimizer: A new nature-inspired metaheuristic algorithm for global optimization problems. *Int. J. Intell. Syst.* **2021**, *36*, 5887–5958. [CrossRef]

Article

Multi-Output Regression with Generative Adversarial Networks (MOR-GANs)

Toby R. F. Phillips [1,*], Claire E. Heaney [1,2], Ellyess Benmoufok [3], Qingyang Li [3], Lily Hua [4], Alexandra E. Porter [5], Kian Fan Chung [6] and Christopher C. Pain [1,2]

1. Applied Modelling and Computation Group, Department of Earth Science and Engineering, Imperial College London, London SW7 2AZ, UK
2. Centre for AI-Physics Modelling, Imperial-X, Imperial College London, London W12 7SL, UK
3. Department of Earth Science and Engineering, Imperial College London, London SW7 2AZ, UK
4. Department of Chemistry, Imperial College London, London SW7 2AZ, UK
5. Department of Materials, Imperial College London, London SW7 2AZ, UK
6. Faculty of Medicine, National Heart & Lung Institute, Imperial College London, London SW3 6LY, UK
* Correspondence: t.phillips18@imperial.ac.uk

Abstract: Regression modelling has always been a key process in unlocking the relationships between independent and dependent variables that are held within data. In recent years, machine learning has uncovered new insights in many fields, providing predictions to previously unsolved problems. Generative Adversarial Networks (GANs) have been widely applied to image processing producing good results, however, these methods have not often been applied to non-image data. Seeing the powerful generative capabilities of the GANs, we explore their use, here, as a regression method. In particular, we explore the use of the Wasserstein GAN (WGAN) as a multi-output regression method. The resulting method we call Multi-Output Regression GANs (MOR-GANs) and its performance is compared to a Gaussian Process Regression method (GPR)—a commonly used non-parametric regression method that has been well tested on small datasets with noisy responses. The WGAN regression model performs well for all types of datasets and exhibits substantial improvements over the performance of the GPR for certain types of datasets, demonstrating the flexibility of the GAN as a model for regression.

Keywords: Generative Adversarial Networks; Wasserstein GAN; regression; multi-output regression; multi-modal distributions

1. Introduction

Regression is a statistical technique which aims to find and describe relationships that exist between inputs (the independent variables also known as predictors, covariates, features) and outputs (dependent variables also known as responses, targets, outcomes). An abundance of data has enabled machine learning techniques to be successfully applied to regression modelling. Data from observations or experiments often comes from complex nonlinear systems that are challenging to model, therefore, a regression model that is able to model uni- or multi-modal distributions, single or multi-output regression problems and quantify uncertainty is highly desirable. Borchani et al. [1] highlight two challenges for regression: (1) modelling uncertainty, both handling the uncertainty in the data itself, but also in quantifying the uncertainty in the responses; and (2) identifying co-dependencies between response variables (for multi-output regression problems). Two approaches are commonly used for multi-output regression problems: transforming the problem and applying single-output methods, and developing extensions to single-output regression methods (such as kernel methods, regression trees and support vector regression) so they are capable of analysing multi-output distributions [2]. Although the former is more straightforward, the latter, when possible, gives better results. In this paper, we propose a generative model for performing regression. This model is flexible as it can be applied (without modification other than hyperparameter tuning) to uni- and multi-modal data; multiple regression problems; single- and multi-output regression tasks (including co-varying responses); and to data with uncertainty or noise. It can also be used to calculate the uncertainty associated with a prediction. We compare this method to Gaussian Process Regression (GPR) which has performed well for regression problems. GPR is a machine learning technique based on Gaussian Processes introduced by Rasmussen and Williams in 1996 [3]. A probability distribution is defined, rather than a single-valued function, which can be applied to data where a range of responses can come from a single point in the regression phase space. Feed-forward neural networks give a single response for a given input, whereas, both GPR and the method proposed here can give multiple responses for a single input enabling the uncertainty in the response to be quantified. This is a highly desirable feature for a regression method.

1.1. Related Work

Generative models were originally developed with the aim of creating a network that could generate realistic examples, that is examples that appear to be drawn from the distribution which was used to train the model. A powerful generative model is the Generative Adversarial Network (GAN) introduced in 2014 by Goodfellow et al. [4]. GANs have quickly become one of the most popular generative models and are widely used in image processing [5] where they are well known for generating images that are capable of tricking the human eye into believing that it is seeing genuine data [6]. Instead of learning a mapping between an input and output determined by training data, these models attempt to learn the distribution underlying the training data (in fact, they learn a mapping from a simple distribution to the more complex distribution which describes the training data). This property is desirable as we would like to avoid extrapolating because it can lead to unreliable results. A GAN consists of two neural networks, a generator and a discriminator that are trained simultaneously according to a min-max game. The generator and discriminator adopt the structure of popular neural networks [7–9]. Although many studies have explored the idea of using GANs when manipulating or identifying images, little research currently exists around implementing GANs to generate non-image data with targeted distributions. One exception is Jolaade et al. [10] who apply GANs to the time series prediction of fluid flow. Furthermore, GANs have shown to be able to perform well even with small samples of data [11], making them a reliable technique and suitable for regression in these circumstances. Since their introduction in 2014, a number of variants have been developed, including the Wasserstein GAN (WGAN) [12,13]. This particular flavour of GAN was introduced to address the problems of mode collapse and vanishing gradients [14] from which the GAN [4] and DCGAN [7] are known to suffer.

GAN methods are not widely used for regression in the literature, with the exception of Aggarwal et al. [15] and McDermott et al. [16]. Aggarwal et al. [15] apply Conditional GAN (CGAN) to a number of datasets, including one which predicted property prices in California and another which predicted the control action on the ailerons given the status of the aeroplane. McDermott et al. [16] apply a semi-supervised Cycle Wasserstein Regression GAN (CWR-GAN) to biomedical applications such as predicting a patient's response to treatment. Both articles showed good results, but both commented on the additional training time and training complexity exhibited by the GAN models in comparison with other methods. The CGAN and the CWR-GAN both have a different structure to the WGAN implemented here. Our WGAN (as with a standard GAN) generates a sample from random values (the input to the WGAN), whereas the CGAN and CWR-GAN have inputs and outputs of the same dimension, although the input can have additional variables corresponding to noise or constraints. Therefore CGANs and the CWR-GAN can be more straightforward to use for regression and time series modelling.

We compare our GAN approach with regression performed by Gaussian Process Regression (GPR). GPR has become an effective, non-parametric Bayesian approach that can be applied to regression problems and can be utilised in exploration and exploitation scenarios [17]. Instead of inferring the distribution of parameters, non-parametric methods can directly predict the distribution of functions. Gaussian Process Regression starts with a set of prior functions based on a specified kernel. After incorporating some known function values (from the training dataset), a posterior distribution is obtained. The posterior can then be evaluated at points of interest (from the test dataset) [18].

1.2. Contributions and Outline

Due to the structure of GANs, the independent and dependent variables appear in the output of the generator (whereas for feedforward networks, the independent variables would be more likely to appear in the input, and the dependent variables in the output). The input of a GAN is a set of random variables, and it generates a realistic sample from these random variables. For regression problems, although sampling the latent space will give a good idea of the distribution learned by the generator, it can also be desirable to be able to obtain a response at a particular value of the independent variable. In order to do this, we propose a prediction algorithm which involves minimising the difference between the output of the GAN for the independent variable and its desired value. This prediction algorithm has been used previously to enable a GAN to make time series predictions [10,19]. It is somewhat similar to an algorithm presented by Wang et al. [20], which searches the latent space in order to match a given image with an image produced by the generator. The necessity for these algorithms comes about because the output of the GAN contains both the independent and dependent variables. In this paper, we develop a new regression method based on GANs and show how it compares to a state-of-the-art GPR regression method by testing both methods on a range of datasets. We apply the same model (a GAN) to all the datasets in the paper and compare with a standard GPR model. Although specific types of GPR have been developed for particular datasets (for example, Heteroscedastic GPR [21], and GPR for clustered data [22]), here we choose a single type of GPR model as we do not tailor the GAN to the specific datasets (other than optimising the architecture and other hyperparameters as is usual). This enables us to demonstrate the flexibility of the single GAN model.

The contributions of this article are the use of a WGAN to perform regression; the ability to apply this model to multi-modal data and multi-output regression (MOR-GAN) tasks with no modifications required to the GAN; the presentation of a prediction algorithm to be used with the trained GAN in order to predict a response for a given independent variable; the exploitation of the WGAN's critic to provide a confidence level or assessment of reliability for the predictions made by the WGAN's generator.

The remainder of the paper is organised as follows: Section 2 describes the methods used in this paper, Section 3 presents results from the synthetic example problems and Section 4 shows results from an in vitro study. Section 5 gives an overview of the speed of the proposed method. Conclusions are drawn and indications given as to future work in the final section. The notation used in this paper is summarised in Table A1 in the Appendix A.

2. Methods
2.1. Data Generation

We investigate the performance of Gaussian Process Regression (GPR) and Wasserstein GAN (WGAN) models for regression using a number of datasets. Simple functions were used to generate all but one of the datasets, which have different properties, including with and without additive Gaussian noise (which here, represents uncertainty in the data); one- or two-dimensional examples; uni- and multi-modal distributions; single or multi-output regression; and, for the WGAN model, we explore both random inputs and constrained inputs (where input refers to the independent variable or input of the regression problem not the input of the WGAN). The final dataset is taken from an in vitro study and explores the influence of silver nanoparticles on cells taken from the lungs. Following standard practice, preprocessing was applied to all the datasets to ensure that no bias is introduced due to different variables having different ranges of values. This was done by applying a linear mapping to normalise the values so they were in the range $[-1, 1]$.

2.2. Gaussian Process Regression

GPR is a machine learning technique, based on Bayesian theory and statistical learning which has wide applicability to complex regression problems with multiple dimensions and non-linearity [18]. The basic theory of prediction with Gaussian processes dates back to the 1940s [23,24], and, since then, there have been many developments and insights gained into using Gaussian Processes as a regression technique. For example, Jerome Sacks and Wynn [25] introduced GPR for computer experiments and used parameter optimisation in the covariance function and also applied it to experimental design, i.e., the choice of input that provides the most information. Moreover, Rasmussen and Williams [18] described GPR in a machine learning context, and expressed the optimisation of the GPR parameters in terms of co-variance functions.

A python library GPy was used to perform the GPR [26]. Important to the performance of the GPR is the choice of kernel. Here we use a radial basis function (RBF) kernel which has three hyperparameters; length, kernel variance, and the standard deviation of the Gaussian noise. These hyperparameters are automatically tuned via GPy.

2.3. Generative Adversarial Networks

A Generative Adversarial Network (GAN) consists of two neural networks: a generative model or generator, G, and a discriminative model or discriminator, D. The models are trained simultaneously resulting in a generator that can produce samples which appear to be taken from the same distribution as the training data. During training, the generator tries to fool the discriminator that it is generating real data, see [4]. For each data point the following combined loss function is defined for G and D:

$$L = \min_G \max_D [\log(D(x)) + \log(1 - D(G(\alpha)))] \tag{1}$$

where $x \in \mathbb{P}_r$ is a sample from the real data and α represents the latent variables. The generator and discriminator are essentially playing a two-player min-max game through the corresponding function $V(G, D)$ [4]:

$$\min_G \max_D V(D, G) = \mathbb{E}_{x \sim \mathbb{P}_r(x)}[\log D(x)] + \mathbb{E}_{z \sim p_\alpha(\alpha)}[\log(1 - D(G(\alpha)))]. \tag{2}$$

GANs are notoriously difficult to train, often reported to suffer from mode collapse and the vanishing gradient problem [14]. Mode collapse occurs when the generator G produces only one solution, or a limited set of solutions, which is/are able to fool the discriminator, and the vanishing gradient problem is described below (Section 2.4).

2.4. Wasserstein Generative Adversarial Networks

The WGAN [12] was developed in order to alleviate the issue of the vanishing gradient problem. To measure the distance between probability distributions, rather than use the Jensen-Shannon (JS) divergence (expressed by Equation (1)) as in the GAN, Arjovsky et al proposed the Earth-Mover (EM) or Wasserstein-1 distance:

$$W(\mathbb{P}_r, \mathbb{P}_g) = \inf_{\gamma \in \Pi(\mathbb{P}_r, \mathbb{P}_g)} \mathbb{E}_{(x,y) \sim \gamma}[\|x - y\|], \tag{3}$$

where $\Pi(\mathbb{P}_r, \mathbb{P}_g)$ denotes the set of all joint distributions $\gamma(x, y)$ whose marginals are respectively $\mathbb{P}_r$ (real data) and $\mathbb{P}_g$ (generated data) [12]. The Wasserstein-1 distance is able to provide a similarity measure between two probability distributions, even when the two probability distributions have no overlap, making it a more sensible cost function. The discriminative model is renamed the **critic** in the WGAN, as it is not explicitly attempting to classify inputs as real or fake, but rather to determine how real an input is. The WGAN value function is constructed via the Kantorovich-Rubinstein duality as Equation (3) is computationally intractable [12]:

$$\min_G \max_{D \in \mathcal{D}} \mathbb{E}_{x \sim \mathbb{P}_r}[D(x)] - \mathbb{E}_{\tilde{x} \sim \mathbb{P}_g}[D(\tilde{x})] \quad (4)$$

where $\mathcal{D}$ is the set of 1-Lipschitz functions. To enforce the Lipschitz constraint, weight clipping was originally used by Arjovsky et al. [12], who stated that this method of enforcement was terrible, despite it working well for the examples shown in their paper and was, at least, simple. Gulrajani et al. [13] introduced an improvement to weight clipping, by enforcing the Lipschitz constraint with a **Gradient Penalty (GP)** method. By enforcing a soft version of the constraint with a penalty, the new loss function becomes:

$$L = \underbrace{\mathbb{E}_{\tilde{x} \sim \mathbb{P}_g}[D(\tilde{x})] - \mathbb{E}_{x \sim \mathbb{P}_r}[D(x)]}_{\text{loss of the critic}} + \underbrace{\lambda \mathbb{E}_{\hat{x} \sim \mathbb{P}_{\hat{x}}}\left[(\|\nabla_{\hat{x}} D(\hat{x})\|_2 - 1)^2\right]}_{\text{gradient penalty}}. \quad (5)$$

Throughout this study we enforce the Lipschitz constraint by using the GP method in our WGAN models.

2.5. Regression with WGAN

GANs are a type of generative network, the aim of which is to generate realistic looking samples that appear to have been drawn from the same distribution as the training data. The input to a WGAN (and GANs in general) is a set of random numbers (not related to the data) and the output contains the generated sample. Consider simple regression, where a relationship is sought between an independent variable x (also known as covariate or feature) and a dependent variable y (also known as a response). The WGAN is trained to produce both the independent and dependent variables of the regression problem (x, y) as its output. In contrast, for feed-forward networks, the input of the network often takes the independent variable and the output, the dependent variable. Therefore, in order to specify a particular value for the independent variable, a prediction algorithm is introduced to the WGAN.

Suppose we have trained the WGAN and wish to use it to predict the output at a given value of the independent variable x_p. First, the latent variables (α) are set to random numbers. The generator is evaluated at these values, $G(\alpha)$, producing a pair of values (x, y)—the input and output or response in our regression problem. The difference between x and x_p is then minimised with respect to the latent variables. Once this is done, we assume that the output of the generator closely approximates (x_p, y_p). The minimisation can be done efficiently by using the same software libraries that are used for back-propagation during training. This procedure means that we can generate multiple outputs for one input, x_p, by starting from different random states for the latent variables, and we can therefore produce a distribution of values which reflect the uncertainty in the output y_p. This procedure is detailed in Algorithm 1 and introduces a projection operator, Proj, which projects the output of the WGAN onto a space that contains only the variables that are to be constrained. For the example described in this paragraph, the projection operator would be represented by the matrix [1 0] for an output of the generator in the form $(x, y)^T$.

Simple regression (for a single independent variable), multiple regression (for more than one independent variable) and multi-output or multi-variate regression (for more than one dependent variable) can all be performed by the WGAN and demonstrated by the results in this paper. Due to the generative nature of the WGAN, both independent and dependent variables are contained in the output of the generator which means that, when randomly sampling the latent space of the generator to produce an output, we have no control over the particular value of independent variable. In order to specify particular values of independent variable(s), a prediction algorithm is used, described in Algorithm 1. So there are two ways of using the WGAN, either with random values for the independent variable or with constrained values:

- **Random input:** Random variables are assigned to the latent space from which the generator of the WGAN yields a realistic output of a n-tuple of the independent and dependent variables associated with regression problem. By sampling the generator many times, this can be used to assess the probability density function learned by the generator. The value of the independent variable(s) cannot be controlled, however, as they are an output of the generator. Although random inputs allow us to see the distribution learned by the generator, having the facility to constrain the independent variables is an important feature.
- **Constrained input:** An algorithm is used in conjunction with the (trained) WGAN to find predictions for given value(s) of the dependent variable(s). This results in a property similar to a GPR, where, for example, the independent variables are inputs of the GPR (and can be prescribed) and the outputs are dependent variables. An inherent property of a trained WGAN is that both independent and dependent variables are contained within the output the generator. Using the constrained input method described here, a WGAN can therefore make a prediction for any combination of known and unknown variables, with the independent variables being treated in the same way as dependent variables. A GPR, however, can only make predictions for the particular set of dependent variables that it was trained on, given the set of independent variables that it was trained on.

Algorithm 1 Prediction Function. Built to be used in conjunction with the trained WGAN, to constrain the independent variable of the regression problem.

Require: The desired value of the independent variable x_p, initial values of the latent variables $\alpha^{(1)} \sim \mathcal{N}(0,1)$, trained generator G, number of iterations N.
   for i=1,...,N **do**
     $\tilde{x}^i = G(\alpha^{(i)})$ ▷ Output of GAN from latent space of iteration i
     $\varepsilon = \text{Proj}(\tilde{x}^i - x_p)$ ▷ Work out mismatch between GAN output and desired value
     $\alpha^{i+1} \leftarrow BackPropagation(\alpha^i, \varepsilon)$ ▷ Adjust latent space by backpropagating mistmatch
   end for

2.6. WGAN Architectures

The WGAN models were constructed using `Keras` [27]. The generator is a four-layered network, as displayed in the top orange box in Figure 1, which takes Gaussian distributed noise from the latent space as an input, and outputs the x and y coordinates in a 1D regression problem. The first dense layer employs batch normalisation and the leaky rectified linear activation functions (LeakyReLU) followed by fully-connected dense layers. The last layer applies the non-linear *tanh* activation function. The structure of the critic is also a four-layered network, with a reduced number of neurons. Its input is data from the training set and data generated from the generator. To reduce the likelihood of overfitting, dropout with a probability of 0.2 is applied to the critic. Layer normalisation is employed for the critic as opposed to batch normalisation, as the latter inhibits the performance of the gradient penalty term in Equation (5).

The MOR-GAN used in Section 3.4 for the co-varying spiral dataset follows the same architecture described in the previous paragraph but with certain fully-connected layers replaced by convolutional layers. In fully-connected or dense layers, every neuron in the input is connected to every neuron in the output. Instead, convolutional layers apply filters to the input where only neurons close to each other are connected to the output.

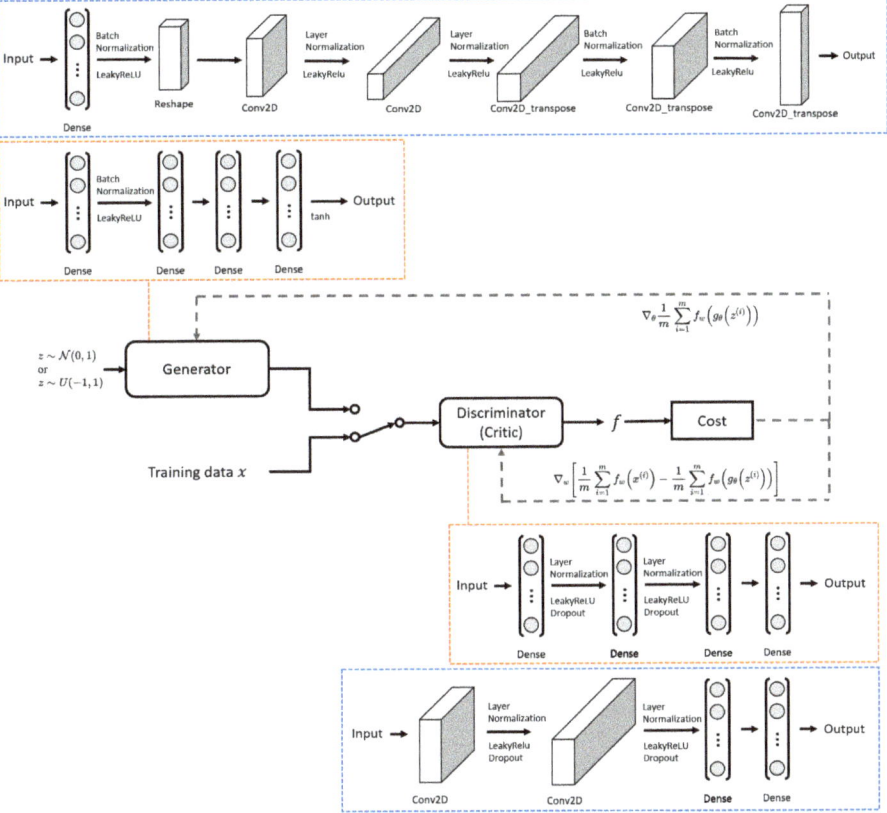

Figure 1. WGAN Structure. The architectures of the Generator and Critic are shown above and below the WGAN structure respectively. The equations displayed are the losses used to update each component. The orange-boxed structure used for the **single-output regression** problems is a multilayer perceptron network. The blue-boxed structure used for **multi-output regression** has convolutional layers.

2.7. Visualisation

To compare the models, the predictions of a test set are visualised. Assuming we have a regression problem in which x is on the horizontal axis and y on the vertical axis and a point on the graph is represented by (x, y). The GPR outputs are the randomly sampled x values and the associated y values from the GPR posterior distribution. On the other hand the WGAN outputs a prediction of both the x and y values. After training, the generator will produce an output of (x, y) when given a value(s) of the latent variable(s) α.

2.8. Statistical Analysis

To assess the accuracy of the regression method some statistical analysis is performed on the results. The 1D synthetic datasets have the Kolmogorov-Smirnov (KS) test applied to them [28]. A number of specific coordinates (x_i) are chosen with which to perform the KS test. Within the real and generated data there exists a range where the x-coordinate satisfies the condition $x_i - 0.01 < x < x_i + 0.01$. The corresponding y-coordinates form a distribution in the real dataset ($\mathbb{P}_{r,i}$) and a distribution in the generated dataset ($\mathbb{P}_{g,i}$). The average p-value is then determined by:

$$\bar{p} = \frac{\sum_{i=1}^{I} KS(\mathbb{P}_{r,i}, \mathbb{P}_{g,i})}{I}, \tag{6}$$

where KS is the Kolmogorov-Smirnov test.

The silver data is assessed by using the Mann-Whitney U test [29]. The test is performed on the real data and generated data that corresponds with a given time level (x_i), concentration level (y_j) and surface area (z_k). A number of responses ($r_{i,j,k}$) exists for these three measurements and they form a distribution in the real dataset ($\mathbb{P}_{r,i,j,k}$) and a distribution in the generated dataset ($\mathbb{P}_{r,i,j,k}$). The average p-value is then determined by:

$$\bar{p} = \frac{\sum_{i=1}^{I} \sum_{j=1}^{J} \sum_{k=1}^{K} MW(\mathbb{P}_{r,i,j,k}, \mathbb{P}_{g,i,j,k})}{IJK}, \tag{7}$$

where MW is the Mann-Whitney U test. Both metrics are implemented using the `SciPy` package [30].

3. Results from Synthetic Datasets

In this section we present results for the performance of the GPR and WGAN approaches for regression on a number of synthetic datasets. We would like our model to perform well on different types of dataset, so datasets with different properties are used here, including uni- and multi-modal distributions, one- or two-dimensional inputs (or independent variables), single- or multi-output. The WGAN can also be used in two ways: with a random input or a constrained input. These combinations are given in Table 1. For the datasets with noise, 500 samples are taken. All the models here follow the general architecture in the orange box of Figure 1 with slight variations on the number of nodes in each dense layer.

Table 1. Properties of the synthetic datasets.

Dataset	Dimension	Distribution of Dataset			Input Type	Section
		Noise	Type	Output		
sine wave	1D	✓	uni-modal	single output	random	3.2.1
heteroscedastic	1D	✓	uni-modal	single output	random	3.2.1
circle	1D	✓	multi-modal	single output	random	3.2.2
sine wave with lines	1D	✓	multi-modal	single output	random	3.2.2
distance	2D	✗	uni-modal	single output	random	3.2.4
helix	2D	✓	multi-modal	single output	random	3.2.4
sine wave	1D	✓	uni-modal	single output	constrained	3.3
heteroscedastic	1D	✓	uni-modal	single output	constrained	3.3
circle	1D	✓	multi-modal	single output	constrained	3.3
eye	1D	✗	multi-modal	multi-output	constrained	3.4.1
spiral	2D	✗	uni-modal	multi-output	constrained	3.4.2

3.1. Training

The training process of the WGAN is described in Algorithm 2. Training a WGAN can be easier than training a GAN, due to the former's removal of the issues associated with mode collapse and weight clipping. Nonetheless, there are still many factors (neural network architecture and training hyperparameters) that can be optimised during training. See Table 2 for the set of hyperparameters that we use for WGAN training. Some values were found by hyperparameter optimisation; others were informed by the literature. For example, $\lambda = 10$ and $n_{\text{critic}} = 5$ are commonly used settings and have been shown to work well across a range of datasets and architectures [12,31].

Algorithm 2 WGAN with gradient penalty and sample-wise optimisation. All experiments in the paper used the default values $\lambda = 10, n_{\text{critic}} = 5, \alpha^\ell = 0.0001, \beta_1 = 0.5, \beta_2 = 0.9$. This algorithm is a modified version of the one displayed in the paper by Gulrajani et al. [13]

Require: The gradient penalty coefficient λ, the number of critic iterations per generator iteration n_{critic}, the batch size m, Adam hyperparameters $\alpha^\ell, \beta_1, \beta_2$.
Require: initial critic parameters ω_0, initial generator parameters θ_0.
    while θ has not converged **do**
        for $t = 1, \ldots, n_{\text{critic}}$ **do**
            for i = 1, ..., m **do**
                real data $x \sim \mathbb{P}_r$, latent variable $\alpha \sim p(\alpha)$, a random number $\epsilon \sim \mathcal{U}[0,1]$.
                $\tilde{x} \leftarrow G_\theta(\alpha)$
                $\hat{x} \leftarrow \epsilon x + (1 - \epsilon)\tilde{x}$
                $L^{(i)} \leftarrow D_\omega(\tilde{x}) - D_\omega(x) + \lambda(||\nabla_{\hat{x}} D_\omega(\hat{x})||_2 - 1)^2$
            end for
        $\omega \leftarrow \text{Adam}(\nabla_\omega \frac{1}{m}\sum_{i=1}^m L^{(i)}, \omega, \alpha^\ell, \beta_1, \beta_2)$
        end for
        Sample a batch of latent variables $\{\alpha^{(i)}\}_{i=1}^m \sim p(\alpha)$.
        $\theta \leftarrow \text{Adam}(\nabla_\theta \frac{1}{m}\sum_{i=1}^m -D_\omega(G_\theta(\alpha)), \theta, \alpha^\ell, \beta_1, \beta_2)$
    end while

Table 2. Hyperparameters used in the construction and training of our WGANs for both the single-output and multi-output distributions.

Hyperparameters	Single-Output	Multi-Output
Learning rate	10^{-3}	10^{-4}
Number of Critic iterations per Generator iterations	5	5
Batch size	100	32
Latent Space Dimension	3	3 (3, 6, 12 used for spiral problem)
Adam optimiser hyperparameters (decay rates of moving averages)	0.5 & 0.9	0.5 & 0.9
Gradient penalty hyperparameter λ	10	10

3.2. Single-Output Regression with Random Input Values

In this section, we sample the posterior of the GPR at random points. For the WGAN, we randomly sample points in the latent space which leads to outputs of n-tuples which are the inputs and responses of the regression problem. We do not control which values are taken by the independent variables(s) or inputs when using regression with randomly generated inputs. The test or sample data is generated by evaluating the functions used to create the training data with randomly generated independent variables. Therefore, the three sets of results have different values of the independent variable(s).

3.2.1. 1D Uni-Modal Examples

To generate a sinusoidal dataset with uncertainty, we use the function

$$y = \sin(x) + \eta\phi \quad \text{where} \quad \phi \sim \mathcal{N}(\mu, \sigma) \tag{8}$$

where $\mathcal{N}$ is a Gaussian distribution with mean $\mu = 0$ and standard deviation $\sigma = 1$. The uncertainty is represented by Gaussian noise through the term ϕ and its magnitude is adjusted by a scalar $\eta \in [0, 1]$. We can see from Figure 2 that the random sampling from WGAN and GPR both match well to the test data. For the sinusoidal dataset, the WGAN structure shown in Figure 3 is used, and for the remaining problems in this section, we increase the number of neurons, see Figure 4.

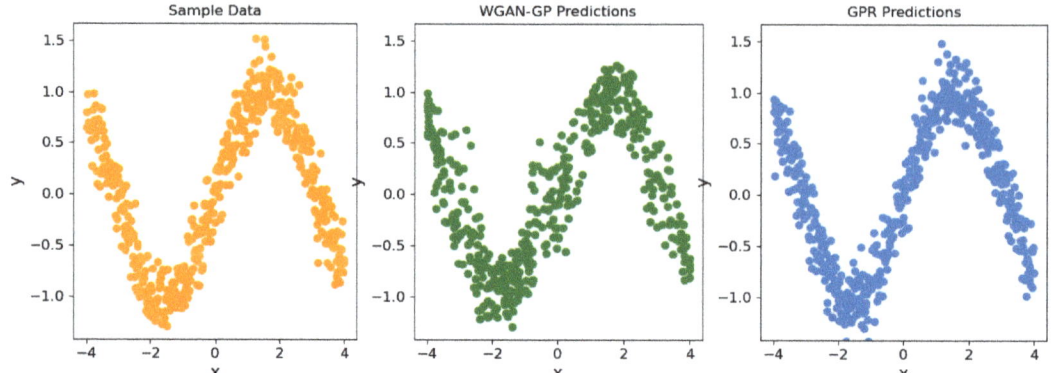

Figure 2. Sinusoidal dataset with added noise ($\eta = 0.2$, see Equation (8)). The test data is shown on the left, sampled points from the WGAN are shown in the middle and sampled points from the GPR posterior are shown on the right.

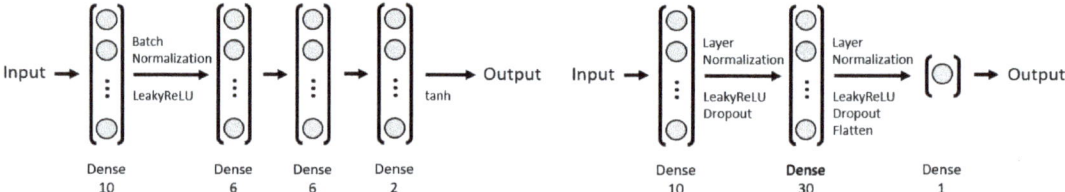

Figure 3. The structure of the generator (**left**) and critic (**right**) for the sinusoidal datasets.

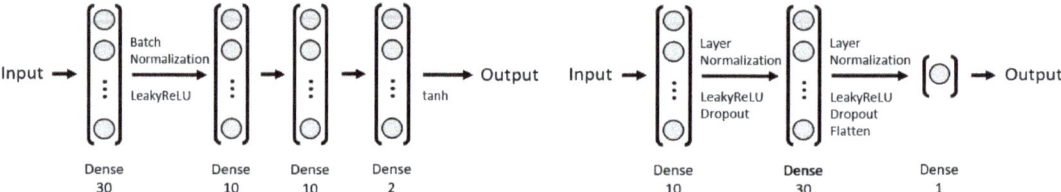

Figure 4. The structure of the generator (**left**) and critic (**right**) for the majority of the problems in this section.

The previous example modelled uncertainty by using noise that was independent of x. To test the WGAN model more thoroughly, a heteroscedastic dataset is used where the noise increases with increasing x. Figure 5 shows that the WGAN model is capable of modelling the variation in noise accurately, whereas the GPR, with a single kernel size representing the probability density function, is unable to do so. We note that there is a variant of GPR called Heteroscedastic GPR [21], which has been designed to handle intricate changes in noise. Implementing this method would result in a better performance of the GPR. However, here we aim to avoid tailoring methods to different datasets, so that we can demonstrate the flexibility of the single WGAN model.

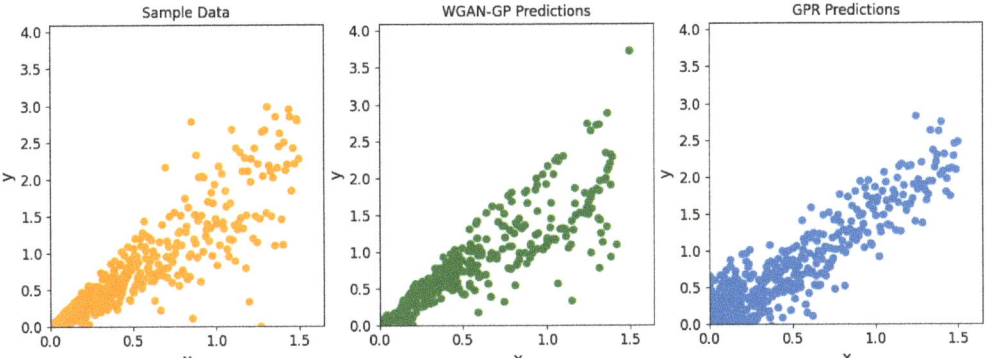

Figure 5. Heteroscedastic dataset. The test data is shown on the left, sampled points from the WGAN are shown in the middle and sampled points from the GPR posterior are shown on the right.

3.2.2. 1D Multi-Modal Examples

Here we explore the use of WGAN and GPR to perform regression of multi-modal distributions. The WGAN models in this section use the architecture displayed in Figure 4. For the first multi-modal distribution, a uniform distribution of data points is generated within an annulus (i.e. between two concentric circles) as shown in Figure 6 (left). There is a significant difference in the performance of the GPR and WGAN. Whilst the WGAN captures the distribution very well (see Figure 6 (middle)), the GPR is unable to represent it (see Figure 6 (right)), predicting an almost uniform distribution of points.

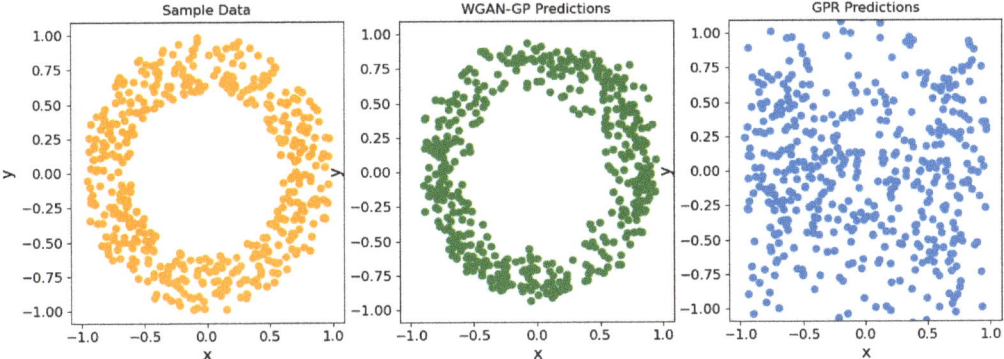

Figure 6. Annulus dataset. The test data is shown on the left, sampled points from the WGAN are shown in the middle and sampled points from the GPR posterior are shown on the right.

The second multi-modal distribution is a sinusoidal wave with several intersecting lines. The same trends appear as seen when using the annulus dataset: the WGAN outperforms the GPR, which is unable to detect the gaps that exist in the dataset, see Figure 7. The overall profile of the data is visible, but within the bounds of the minimum and maximum y values there is no gap. Although GPR struggles with these complex functions, it has been used and built upon to work on clustering complex functions [22], so there is the capability of modelling these types of complex functions. However, we wish to compare the WGAN against one model, without tailoring it for different types of data.

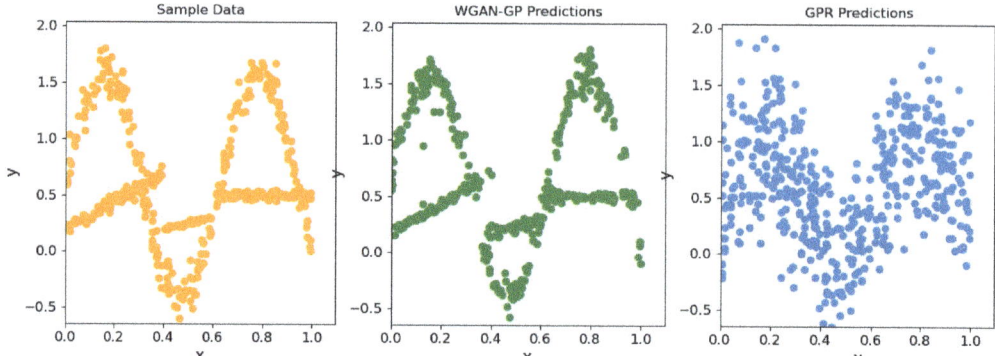

Figure 7. A sine wave intersected by several lines. The test data is shown on the left, sampled points from the WGAN are shown in the middle and sampled points from the GPR posterior are shown on the right.

3.2.3. Confidence of Solutions from the Critic

Sections 3.2.1 and 3.2.2 show how sampled points produced by the generator of the WGAN match the distribution seen in the test data (or sample data). During the training of the WGAN, the critic learns to determine how real an sample is. This section demonstrates how the critic can be used to determine the confidence in a sample produced by the generator, which is an indication of how reliable the method's predictions are.

Figure 8 shows the value taken by the critic for predictions or responses made throughout domain for both the sinusoidal and annulus datasets. These are produced by finding the value of the critic for each point on a 100×100 grid that covers the same domain as the original data. As previously stated, the critic of a WGAN does not explicitly determine whether a sample is real or fake, but instead, how real a sample is. Therefore the larger the value produced by the critic, the more confidence the model has in the prediction. The critic values shown here are normalised to be between 0 and 1.

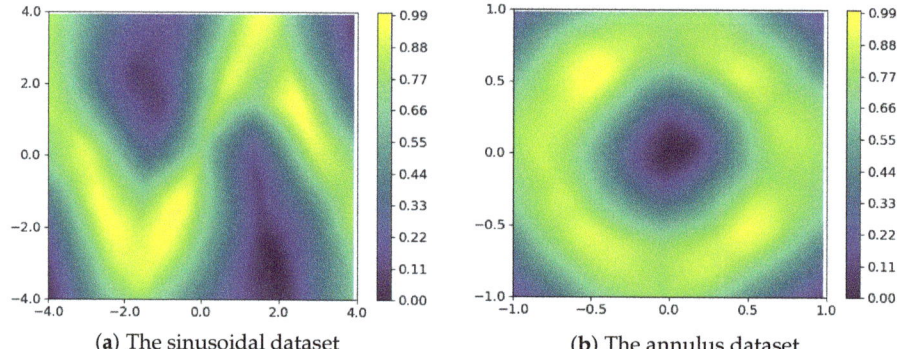

(a) The sinusoidal dataset   (b) The annulus dataset

Figure 8. Contour plots showing the values of the two critics for the sinusoidal and annulus datasets. These indicate the confidence in or reliability of the predictions and also indicate where extra training data may be required.

Figure 8a shows the values of the critic produced for the sinusoidal dataset. It can be observed that the values of the critic are higher where the data of the noisy sine curve occurs (see Figure 2), which corresponds to the region mostly occupied by the training data. These values are higher where there is a higher concentration of data points, particularly around $x = -2.0$ and $x = 2.0$. Outside of where the sine wave is located the critic value sharply decreases, therefore confidence in any prediction made here is low.

Figure 8b shows the values of the critic produced by the annulus dataset. It can be observed that the values are higher within the annulus, which corresponds to the region occupied by the training data (see Figure 6). We can see that the critic produces lower values for coordinates predicted outside of the annulus, meaning that the confidence in predictions or responses that occur here is low.

Figure 8a,b demonstrate how the critic can be used in conjunction with the generator to produce a confidence level in the predictions made by the generator. A lower critic value, and therefore a lower confidence, in a prediction made may indicate that extra training data is required there. A possible location requiring extra data for the sinusoidal dataset is $x = 0.5$ and for the annulus dataset is $x = 0.0$. The critic value can be used to remove solutions generated that are not realistic, thereby improving the results. The solutions shown in Figures 2 and 6 had their average p-value improved from <0.2 to <0.1 by removing the 10% of solutions generated that had the lowest value after being passed through the critic.

Thus, the confidence level might help us to determine where to collect more experimental data or where to observe the system. It also suggests where the neural network is not predicting well, which might not be because of lack of data. Ultimately, this confidence level should be combined with the importance of the region where the confidence is being determined. This importance could be set according to how much or little influence this region may be have on the final results. If applying the GAN approach to regression to optimisation, importance could, for example, be determined from sensitivities (or adjoints) of what is important with respect to the independent variables.

3.2.4. 2D Uni- and Multi-Modal Examples

Increasing the dimensions in the inputs of the regression problem means the need for a larger neural network, thus the following problems use the structure displayed in Figure 9.

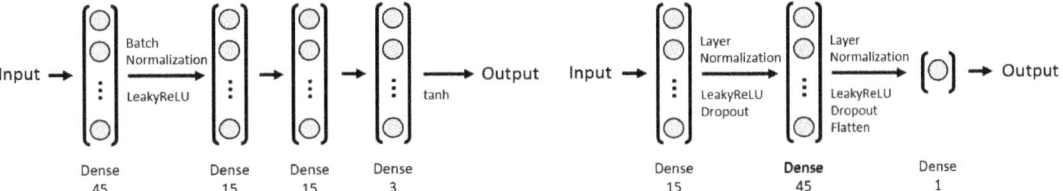

Figure 9. The structure of the generator (**left**) and critic (**right**) for the two-dimensional problems.

The performance of the WGAN regression method for data with a single input has been shown to be very reliable. We now test the GPR and WGAN methods on two-dimensional data with a distance function $h = \sqrt{x^2 + y^2}$. The GPR performs exceptionally well, outputting predictions very close to the true model, see Figure 10. The WGAN also performs well, although some deviation from the distance function can be seen.

Having demonstrated that both models are capable of performing regression on datasets with multiple intputs, a more complicated problem is defined as a 2D multi-modal function in the form of a helix with additive Gaussian noise. Figure 11 shows that WGAN is capable of generating data similar to the true model, whereas the GPR struggles to recognise the variation in h (on the z axis) and fills the hole in the circle, looking at the xy plane.

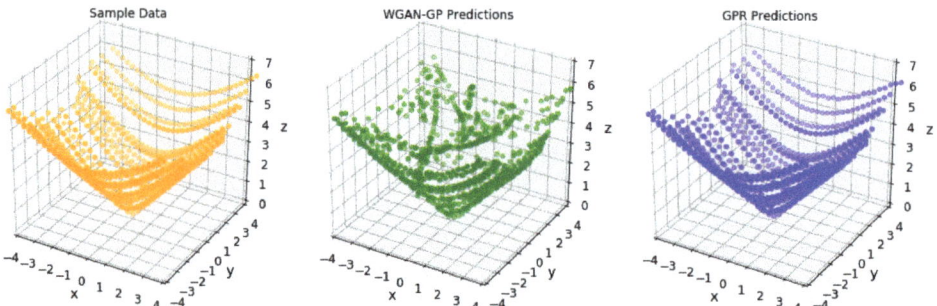

Figure 10. 2D distance function. The test data is shown on the left, sampled points from the WGAN are shown in the middle and sampled points from the GPR posterior are shown on the right.

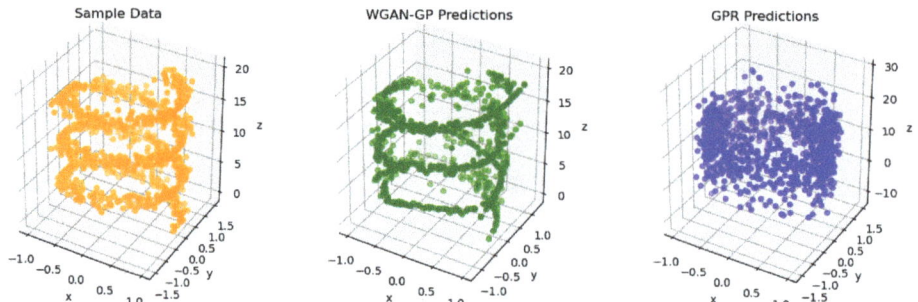

Figure 11. The helix dataset. The test data is shown on the left, sampled points from the WGAN are shown in the middle and sampled points from the GPR posterior are shown on the right.

3.3. Single-Output Regression with Constrained Input Values

A key benefit of using the WGAN for regression is its capability of producing a latent space that with a constrained input, can be optimised to produce multi-modal responses. In Figure 12 we can see the function displaying a few of the potential responses y, at differing fixed x. The WGANs used for the constrained input regression are the same ones used in Sections 3.2.1 and 3.2.2 for their respective datasets.

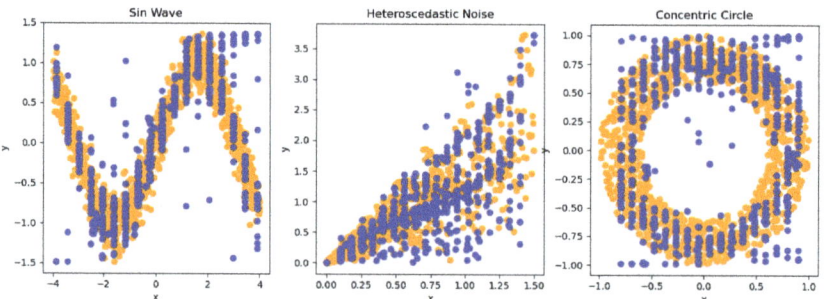

Figure 12. The sinusoidal wave dataset, heteroscedastic noise dataset and annulus dataset predicted at a given values of the x coordinate using the WGAN prediction method. Prediction displays potential responses at the given x coordinates.

The way this optimisation is performed is to first randomly generate a latent input vector of the generator. Then from this initial condition point in latent space we apply our optimiser to minimise the least squares functional, see Algorithm 1, which aims to match the latent space with the specified x coordinate. We repeat this multiple times in order to obtain a probability density function for this fixed x coordinate but with differing initial latent space inputs. The average p-value for all three solutions generated this way is <0.05.

3.4. Multi-Output Regression with MOR-GAN

3.4.1. 1D Eye Dataset with Covariance

By taking a digitised, hand-drawn eye and adding a second eye which is obtained by a rotation of 90° and a reflection of the first eye, we produce a distribution which is multi-modal and multi-output or multivariate, see Figure 13. This forms the dataset for the first multi-output regression test. The WGAN is trained to produce two pairs of coordinates, (x_1, y_1) and (x_2, y_2).

Figures 14 and 15 contains the structure of the generator and discriminator respectively used for the WGAN model in this section.

To provide a challenge for the algorithm which enables the WGAN to make predictions a particular values for the independent variable (Algorithm 1), we constrain the value of x_1 (for the non-rotated eye) and predict the corresponding values for y_1 (non-rotated eye), x_2 and y_2 (rotated eye). We repeat this process for every point in the eye dataset to form the image shown in Figure 16. Similarly, we constrain the value of x_2 (for the rotated eye) and predict the corresponding values for y_2 (rotated eye), x_1 and y_1 (non-rotated eye). This is done for every point in the dataset and the result can be seen in Figure 17. The predictions using the MOR-GAN method take into account the known or learned covariance information between the images, enabling the model to determine the second image from all the points in the first image and vice versa. The agreement between the real data and the predicted data using the constrained input is excellent.

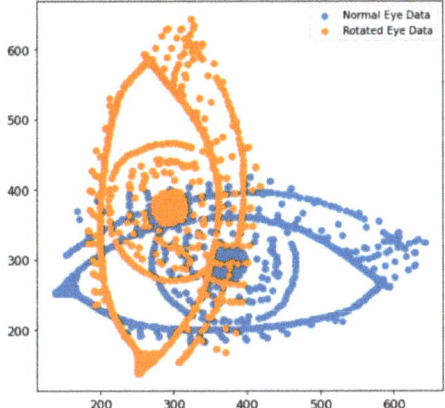

Figure 13. The eye dataset which contains two eyes. One eye is rotated and reflected to produce a second eye.

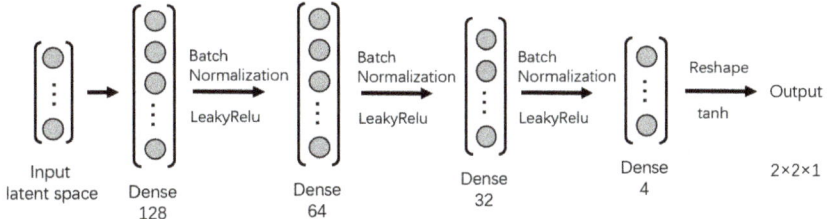

Figure 14. The structure of the generator for the eye dataset.

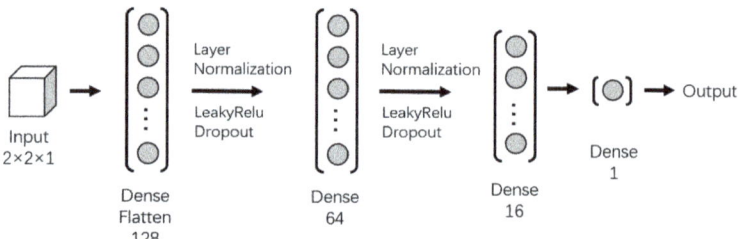

Figure 15. The structure of the discriminator for the eye dataset.

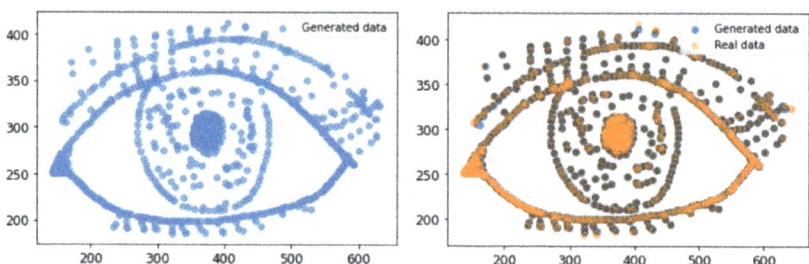

Figure 16. The eye generated by the WGAN (**left**) and the comparison between the real data and the generated data (**right**) using the constrained input method described in Algorithm 1.

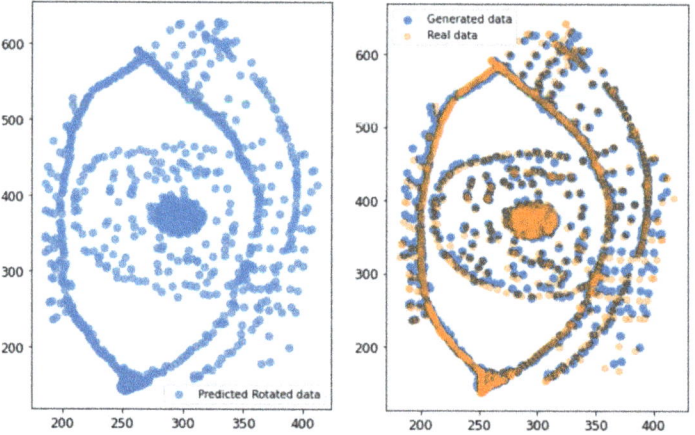

Figure 17. The rotated eye predicted using Algorithm 1 (**left**) and the comparison between the real rotated data and the predicted data (**right**).

3.4.2. Co-Varying Spiral Dataset

In many applications, variables often co-vary, in other words, a change in one variable is typically reflected by a change in another variable. In this work, we use a two dimensional spirals dataset as a benchmark to compare the capability of both GAN and WGAN. x and y are the variables that define the spiral at 20 different z levels which are equally spaced with $z \in [0, 4]$. Thus there are 20 pairs of x, y coordinates as the output of the MOR-GAN.

The structure of the model and the hyperparameters of each layer used in this section are displayed in Figures 18 and 19, and Table 3.

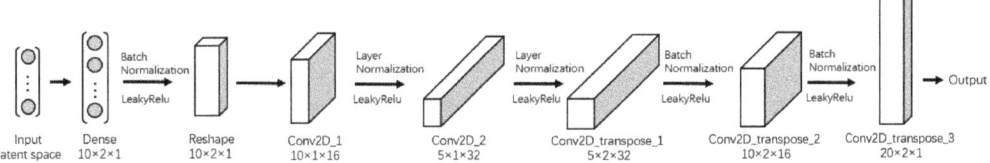

Figure 18. The structure of the generator for the Co-Varying Spiral problem.

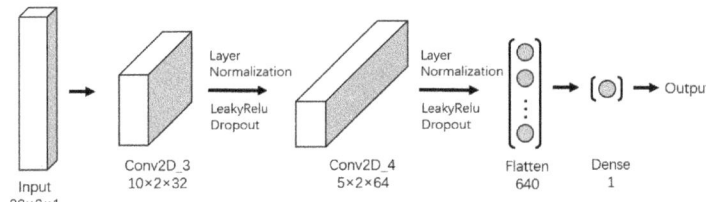

Figure 19. The structure of the discriminator for the Co-Varying Spiral problem.

Table 3. Hyperparameters used in the construction of the convolutional neural network.

Layer	Kernel Size	Strides	Padding	Use Bias
Conv2D_1	(8, 2)	(1, 2)	same	True
Conv2D_2	(8, 2)	(2, 1)	same	True
Conv2D_transpose_1	(8, 2)	(1, 2)	same	False
Conv2D_transpose_2	(8, 2)	(2, 1)	same	False
Conv2D_transpose_3	(8, 2)	(2, 1)	same	False
Conv2D_3	(8, 2)	(2, 1)	same	True
Conv2D_4	(8, 2)	(2, 1)	same	True

The three-dimensional spiral curves dataset is generated based on the equations below:

$$x = r \sin \theta, \qquad (9)$$
$$y = r \cos \theta, \qquad (10)$$
$$z = 4\left(\frac{\theta - a}{b - a}\right), \qquad (11)$$

where $\theta \in [a, b]$, $a = 4\pi x_1 - 2\pi$ and $b = 4\pi x_2 + 2\pi$ for x_1, x_2 chosen randomly from the unit interval, and the radius r is chosen randomly from the interval $[0.6, 1]$. For each spiral, r, x_1 and x_2 are chosen at random, and 20 equally-spaced values for θ are chosen from the interval $[a, b]$ to generate the curves shown in Figure 20.

Figure 20 shows the predictions made by the MOR-GAN. The first 10 data points in the spiral, shown as solid blue dots, are used to predict the next 10 data points in the spiral, produced by constraining the output using Algorithm 1. The real spiral is given by the blue line and the spiral generated by the algorithm constraining the first 10 samples is given by the red line. Three different sizes of latent spaces are used and it can be observed that all latent spaces give reasonable reconstructions of the real spirals, therefore demonstrating that the reconstruction reliability of the shape of the curve does not vary much with the increasing dimension of latent space. Figure 20 also shows that the MOR-GAN can learn the structure of the input data and can recreate the shapes (which are spirals in this case) with approximate distributions (which are annular distributions representing the start of the spirals in this case).

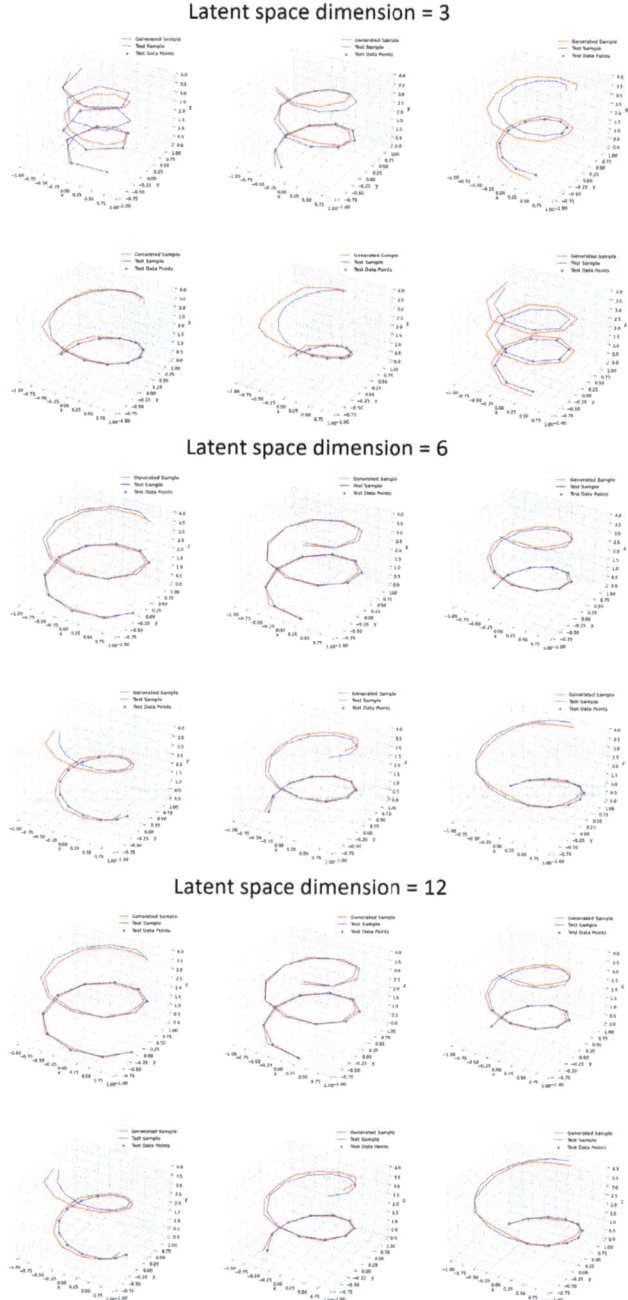

Figure 20. The figures above show the generated data using the prediction function on real samples (rows 1, 3, 5) and test samples (rows 2, 4, 6) when the size of the latent space is 3, 6 and 12 respectively. The blue lines indicate the real spiral, the solid blue dots show the 10 data points that are constrained using Algorithm 1 and the red lines show the spiral produced by the generator for these 10 constrained points.

4. Silver Nanoparticle Data

We now explore the application of WGAN to real-world data regression. Reference [32] explores the effects on cells from the lungs of four types of silver nanoparticles (AgNPs): silver nanospheres (AgNS) of diameter 20 nm and 50 nm; short silver nanowires (s-AgNWs) of length 1.5 μm and diameter 72 nm; and long silver nanowires (l-AgNWs) of length 10 μm and diameter 72 nm. Silver nanoparticles are increasingly used in consumer products and reports state that up to 14% of products containing AgNPs will release these nanoparticles into ambient air [33,34] where they can be inhaled into the lungs of workers and consumers. The work in [32] explores the influence of the nanoparticles on airway smooth muscle (ASM) cells, which are an important component of the airways in the lungs, being responsible for narrowing the airways in conditions such as asthma. Bronchi and tracheas from transplant donor lungs were dissected to obtain the cells. These cells were serum-starved overnight and then incubated with 20 nm or 50 nm AgNSs, or s-AgNWs (5 μg mL^{-1} or 25 μg mL^{-1}) or Ag$^+$ ions (0.25 μg mL^{-1} or 25 μg mL^{-1}) for 24 or 72 h. Change in cell viability assessed by a reduction assay and change in cell proliferation assessed by the rate of DNA synthesis were both measured, and the results are reproduced in Figure 21. Cell viability is defined as the number of live, healthy cells in a sample.

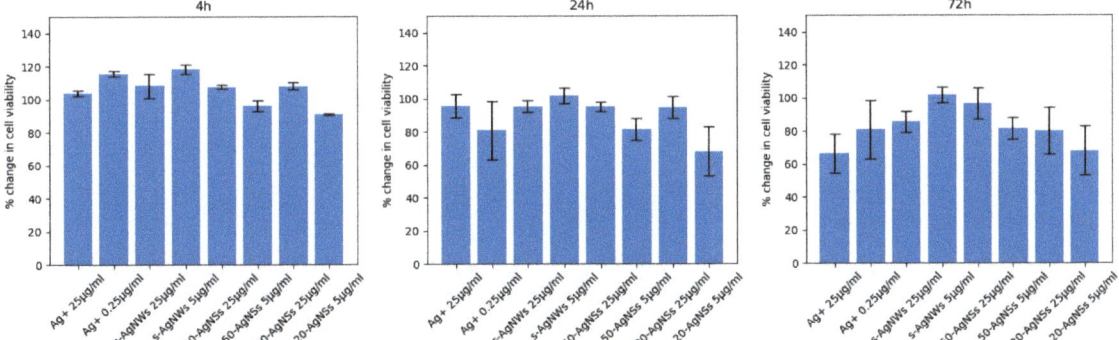

Figure 21. Concentration and time-dependent effect of AgNSs and AgNWs, and Ag$^+$ ions on ASM cell viability after 4 h, 24 h and 72 h. The bars represent mean values of 3 ASM cell donors and the whiskers indicate standard error of the mean (SEM). The data is expressed as percentage change with respect to the untreated control. This plot was formed from the dataset also reported in [32].

The data from [32] contains four different molecules analysed at two concentrations at three different times. The molecules were given numerical values based on their specific surface area, defined as the total surface area of a material per unit of mass. This can be seen in Table 4:

Table 4. Specific surface area of the particles formed from different molecules which form independent variables for the WGAN regression.

Molecule	Specific Surface Area m^2 g^{-1}
Ag$^+$	4.4
s-AgNWs	4.6
50 nm AgNSs	6
20 nm AgNSs	40.4

The generator part of the WGAN was trained to produce four outputs: the specific surface area of the particles containing a specific molecule, the concentration level, the time level (we sample the response at 3 time levels: 4 h, 24 h and 72 h) and the response (change in cell viability). All four outputs were scaled to be between 0 and 1. The WGAN architecture can be seen in Figure 22.

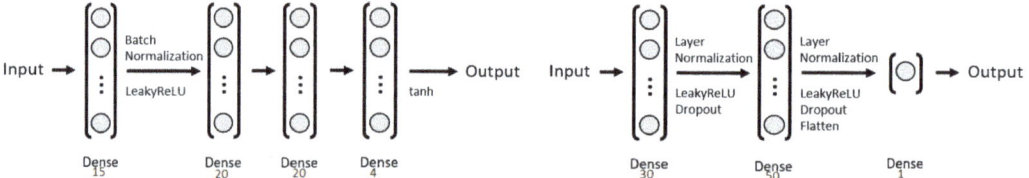

Figure 22. The structure of the generator (**left**) and critic (**right**) for modelling the silver data in this section.

Figure 23 contains the predictions made by the WGAN for cell viability, given time level, concentration level and surface area taken from the original study. For each combination of parameters (time level, concentration level and surface area), 10 predictions are made using the prediction Algorithm 1, minimising the error in the numerical value associated with a molecule, the concentration level and the time of interest. It can be observed that the mean of the predictions is close to the mean of the assessment. The average p-value for these predictions made is <0.2.

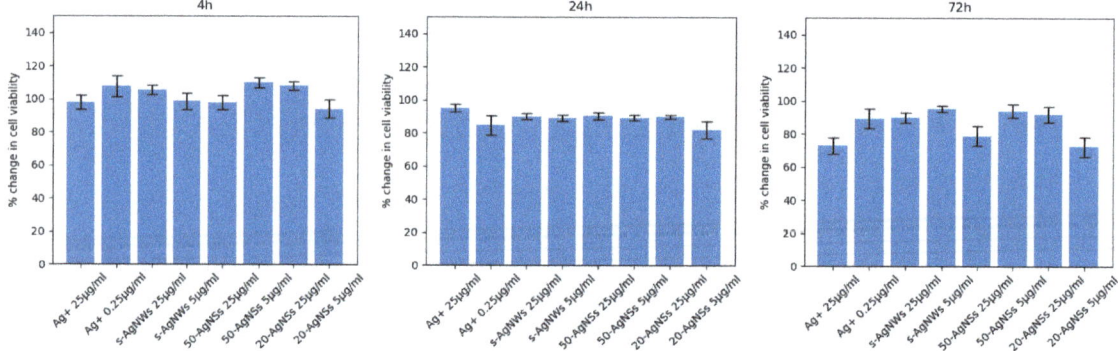

Figure 23. Concentration and time-dependent predictions of AgNSs and AgNWs, and Ag$^+$ ions on ASM cell viability after 4 h, 24 h and 72 h. The bars represent mean values of 10 predictions made using a WGAN and the whiskers indicate standard error of the mean (SEM).

5. Execution Time of Method

Presented in Table 5 is an overview of the execution time of the method.

Table 5. First column contains the type of dataset, second column contains how long randomly sampling 4000 of the posterior of the GPR took in seconds, third column contains how long it took to randomly sample 4000 points of the latent space of the WGAN took in seconds and fourth column is how long the WGAN took to run the prediction Algorithm 1 for 1000 iterations.

Dataset	GPR	WGAN—Random	WGAN—Constrained
sine wave	0.0325 s	0.328 s	2.412 s
heteroscedastic	0.0642 s	0.144 s	2.737 s
circle	0.0444 s	0.198 s	2.543 s
helix	0.0774 s	0.231 s	3.528 s
silver nanoparticle	0.0623 s	0.261 s	4.601 s

Table 5 contains the time taken, in seconds, for randomly sampling 4000 points of the GPR posterior and the WGAN latent space for different datasets. It can be observed that the time taken to randomly sample does not increase significantly as the number of input parameters increases but sampling the GPR posterior is an order of magnitude faster than sampling the WGAN latent space.

The third column of Table 5 contains the time taken to run the prediction algorithm 1 for 1000 iterations. The values here are meant as a form of comparison, Algorithm 1 incorporating a convergence criteria would could reduce the amount of iterations but would make comparison less clear. There is a notable increase in time taken for the algorithm to be applied to the datasets with a larger number of independent variables.

6. Conclusions and Future Work

In this paper, we demonstrate that Generative Adversarial Networks (GANs) can perform well for a number of regression tasks, sometimes outperforming a model based on state-of-the-art Gaussian Process Regression (GPR). The particular model used is a Wasserstein GAN (WGAN), which can be easier to train than a standard GAN. For simple regression and multiple regression tasks, both GAN and GPR perform well, although for the dataset which has variable uncertainty (modelled as heteroscedastic noise), the GPR fails to learn any variation in uncertainty, whereas the GAN captures this variation well. Also, for the more challenging problem of multi-modal distributions, the GPR struggles to learn the distribution whereas the GAN is able to reproduce the distribution very well. Furthermore, for multi-output regression, the WGAN also demonstrated good performance, showing that the GAN is able to capture the covariance information between all the output variables (which includes the independent and dependent variables of the regression problem).

Although the GPR can be modified for improved performance on specific types of data (such as heteroscedastic noise and multi-output regression), we wanted to highlight, here, that the WGAN needs no modification for these problems: one single WGAN model can perform well for all the datasets with which we tested the models.

Novelties of the work include using a GAN for regression; being able to apply this model to multi-modal data and multi-output regression (MOR-GAN) tasks with no fundamental modifications; the presentation of a prediction algorithm to be used with the trained GAN in order to predict a response for a given independent variable; using the critic to provide a confidence level of the predictions made by the generator, which could ultimately be used to help determine where more data is needed.

In the future, the methods developed here could be applied to imaging, for example, where, when there is missing data from an image or video, we could attempt to re-construct the missing parts. Being able to reconstruct this image with specified uncertainties would be useful. In modelling, the approach could be applied in high-dimensional space (with applications across computational physics e.g. Computational Fluid Dynamics) to perform data assimilation and analyse remaining uncertainties in the modelling, see Silva et al. [35]. Using the confidence level provided by the discriminator in such applications could determine where better models are needed or where coarser models (that are faster) can be used. Performing a sensitivity analysis of the discriminator could also indicate where the model is most error prone and thus where it needs to be improved.

Author Contributions: Conceptualisation, C.C.P., A.E.P. and K.F.C.; methodology, C.C.P., T.R.F.P. and C.E.H.; software, T.R.F.P., E.B., Q.L. and L.H.; data curation, A.E.P.; writing—original draft preparation, T.R.F.P., E.B. and C.E.H.; writing—review and editing, C.C.P., C.E.H. and K.F.C.; funding acquisition, C.C.P. and K.F.C. All authors read and agreed to the published version of the manuscript.

Funding: The authors would like to acknowledge the following EPSRC grants: INHALE, Health assessment across biological length scales (EP/T003189/1); RELIANT, Risk EvaLuatIon fAst iNtelligent Tool for COVID19 (EP/V036777/1); MUFFINS, MUltiphase Flow-induced Fluid-flexible structure InteractioN in Subsea applications (EP/P033180/1); the PREMIERE programme grant (EP/T000414/1) and MAGIC, Managing Air for Green Inner Cities (EP/N010221/1).

Institutional Review Board Statement: Not applicable.

Informed Consent Statement: Not applicable.

Data Availability Statement: Not applicable.

Acknowledgments: We would like to thank the reviewers for their comments which have improved the article.

Conflicts of Interest: The authors declare no conflict of interest.

Appendix A. Nomenclature

See Table A1 for a description of the nomenclature used in this article.

Table A1. Nomenclature used in the paper.

Section 2 and Algorithm 2 from Section 3	
G, D	generator and discriminator (or critic) networks (for GANs, D is referred to as the discriminator, for WGANs it is referred to as the critic)
α	latent variables
L, V	the loss function and function describing the two player min-max game
$x, \tilde{x}$	samples from real and generated data
$\mathbb{P}_r, \mathbb{P}_g$	distributions for the real data and the generated data
p_α	distribution of the latent variables
W	Wasserstein distance between distributions
$\gamma(x, y)$	a joint distribution
$\mathcal{D}$	set of 1-Lipschitz functions
$\hat{x}$	a linear combination of a real sample and a generated sample (at which the gradient penalty will be imposed)
λ	gradient penalty
ε	mismatch between desired (partial) output of GAN and actual (partial) output of GAN
x, y	independent and dependent variables
x_p, y_p	particular values of the independent and dependent variables
ϵ	random number
$\mathcal{U}$	Uniform probability distribution
α^ℓ	learning rate
β_1, β_2	optimiser hyperparameters
n_{critic}	number of iterations of the critic
m	batch size
N	number of iterations
Section 3	
x, y, z	independent and dependent variables
x_1, x_2, y_1, y_2	independent and dependent variables
θ	angle
η	a scalar controlling the amount of noise
$\phi \sim \mathcal{N}(\mu, \sigma)$	random variable (noise) sampled from a Gaussian distribution $\mathcal{N}$ with mean μ and standard deviation σ
h	distance function

References

1. Borchani, H.; Varando, G.; Bielza, C.; Larrañaga, P. A survey on multi-output regression. *WIREs Data Min. Knowl. Discov.* **2015**, *5*, 216–233. [CrossRef]
2. Xu, D.; Shi, Y.; Tsang, I.W.; Ong, Y.S.; Gong, C.; Shen, X. Survey on Multi-Output Learning. *IEEE Trans. Neural Netw. Learn. Syst.* **2020**, *31*, 2409–2429. [CrossRef] [PubMed]
3. Rasmussen, C.E. Gaussian Processes in machine learning. In *Advanced Lectures on Machine Learning*; Springer: Berlin/Heidelberg, Germany, 2004; Volume 3176, pp. 63–71. [CrossRef]
4. Goodfellow, I.J.; Pouget-Abadie, J.; Mirza, M.; Xu, B.; Warde-Farley, D.; Ozair, S.; Courville, A.; Bengio, Y. Generative Adversarial Nets. Technical report. *arXiv* **2014**, arXiv:1406.2661v1.

5. Kazeminia, S.; Baur, C.; Kuijper, A.; van Ginneken, B.; Navab, N.; Albarqouni, S.; Mukhopadhyay, A. GANs for Medical Image Analysis. *Artif. Intell. Med.* **2020**, *109*, 101938, [CrossRef] [PubMed]
6. Wang, K.; Gou, C.; Duan, Y.; Lin, Y.; Zheng, X.; Wang, F.Y. Generative adversarial networks: Introduction and outlook. *IEEE/CAA J. Autom. Sin.* **2017**, *4*, 588–598. [CrossRef]
7. Radford, A.; Metz, L.; Chintala, S. Unsupervised Representation Learning with Deep Convolutional Generative Adversarial Networks. *arXiv* **2015**, arXiv:1511.06434. [CrossRef]
8. Kunfeng, W.; Yue, L.; Yutong, W.; Fei-Yue, W. Parallel imaging: A unified theoretical framework for image generation. In Proceedings of the 2017 Chinese Automation Congress, CAC 2017, Jinan, China, 20–22 October 2017; pp. 7687–7692. [CrossRef]
9. Zhang, K.; Kang, Q.; Wang, X.; Zhou, M.; Li, S. A visual domain adaptation method based on enhanced subspace distribution matching. In Proceedings of the ICNSC 2018—15th IEEE International Conference on Networking, Sensing and Control, Zhuhai, China, 27–29 March 2018; pp. 1–6. [CrossRef]
10. Jolaade, M.; Silva, V.L.; Heaney, C.E.; Pain, C.C. Generative Networks Applied to Model Fluid Flows. In Proceedings of the International Conference on Computational Science, London, UK, 21–23 June 2022; Springer: Berlin/Heidelberg, Germany, 2022; pp. 742–755. [CrossRef]
11. Salimans, T.; Goodfellow, I.; Zaremba, W.; Cheung, V.; Radford, A.; Chen, X. Improved Techniques for Training GANs. Technical report. *arXiv* **2017**, arXiv:1606.03498.
12. Arjovsky, M.; Chintala, S.; Bottou, L. Wasserstein GAN. Technical report. *arXiv* **2017**, arXiv:1701.07875
13. Gulrajani, I.; Ahmed, F.; Arjovsky, M.; Dumoulin, V.; Courville, A. Improved Training of Wasserstein GANs Montreal Institute for Learning Algorithms. Technical report. *arXiv* **2017**, arXiv:1704.00028
14. Barnett, S.A. Convergence Problems with Generative Adversarial Networks (GANs) A dissertation presented for CCD Dissertations on a Mathematical Topic. Technical report. *arXiv* **2018**, arXiv:1806.11382
15. Aggarwal, K.; Kirchmeyer, M.; Yadav, P.; Keerthi, S.S.; Gallinari, P. Regression with Conditional GAN. Technical report. *arXiv* **2019**, arXiv:1905.12868. [CrossRef]
16. McDermott, M.B.A.; Yan, T.; Naumann, T.; Hunt, N.; Suresh, H.; Szolovits, P.; Ghassemi, M. Semi-Supervised Biomedical Translation with Cycle Wasserstein Regression GANs. In Proceedings of the Thirty-Second AAAI Conference on Artificial Intelligence and Thirtieth Innovative Applications of Artificial Intelligence Conference and Eighth AAAI Symposium on Educational Advances in Artificial Intelligence, New Orleans, LA, USA, 2–7 February 2018.
17. Schulz, E.; Speekenbrink, M.; Krause, A. A tutorial on Gaussian process regression: Modelling, exploring, and exploiting functions. *J. Math. Psychol.* **2018**, *85*, 1–16. [CrossRef]
18. Rasmussen, C.; Williams, C. *Gaussian Process for Machine Learning*; MIT Press: Cambridge, MA, USA, 2006.
19. Silva, V.L.; Heaney, C.E.; Li, Y.; Pain, C.C. Data Assimilation Predictive GAN (DA-PredGAN): Applied to determine the spread of COVID-19. *arXiv* **2021**, arXiv:2105.07729.
20. Wang, S.; Tarroni, G.; Qin, C.; Mo, Y.; Dai, C.; Chen, C.; Glocker, B.; Guo, Y.; Rueckert, D.; Bai, W. Deep generative model-based quality control for cardiac MRI segmentation. In Proceedings of the International Conference on Medical Image Computing and Computer-Assisted Intervention, Lima, Peru, 4–8 October 2020; Springer: Berlin/Heidelberg, Germany, 2020; pp. 88–97.
21. Le, Q.V.; Smola, A.J.; Canu, S. Heteroscedastic Gaussian process regression. In Proceedings of the ICML 2005—The 22nd International Conference on Machine Learning, Bonn, Germany, 7–11 August 2005; ACM Press: New York, NY, USA, 2005; pp. 489–496. [CrossRef]
22. Kim, H.C.; Lee, J. Clustering based on Gaussian processes. *Neural Comput.* **2007**, *19*, 3088–3107. [CrossRef]
23. Kolmogorov, A.N. Interpolation and extrapolation of stationary random sequences. In *Selected Works of A. N. Kolmogorov*; Springer: Dordrecht, The Netherlands, 1992.
24. Wiener, N. *Extrapolation, Interpolation and Smoothing of Stationary Time Series*; MIT Press: Cambridge, MA, USA, 1949.
25. Sacks, J.; William, J.; Welch, T.J.M.; Wynn, H.P. *Design and Analysis of Computer Experiments*; Institute of Mathematical Statistics: Hayward, CA, USA, 1989. [CrossRef]
26. GPy. GPy: A Gaussian Process Framework in Python. 2012. Available online: http://github.com/SheffieldML/GPy (accessed on 20 December 2020).
27. Chollet, F. Keras. 2015. Available online: https://github.com/fchollet/keras (accessed on 20 December 2020).
28. Smirnov, N.V. On the estimation of the discrepancy between empirical curves of distribution for two independent samples. *Bull. Math. Univ. Moscou* **1939**, *2*, 3–14.
29. Mann, H.B.; Whitney, D.R. On a test of whether one of two random variables is stochastically larger than the other. *Ann. Math. Stat.* **1947**, *18*, 50–60. [CrossRef]
30. Virtanen, P.; Gommers, R.; Oliphant, T.E.; Haberland, M.; Reddy, T.; Cournapeau, D.; Burovski, E.; Peterson, P.; Weckesser, W.; Bright, J.; et al. SciPy 1.0: Fundamental Algorithms for Scientific Computing in Python. *Nat. Methods* **2020**, *17*, 261–272. [CrossRef]
31. Gulrajani, I.; Ahmed, F.; Arjovsky, M.; Dumoulin, V.; Courville, A.C. Improved Training of Wasserstein GANs. In *Advances in Neural Information Processing Systems 30*; Guyon, I., Luxburg, U.V., Bengio, S., Wallach, H., Fergus, R., Vishwanathan, S., Garnett, R., Eds.; Curran Associates, Inc.: Nice, France, 2017; pp. 5767–5775.
32. Michaeloudes, C.; Seiffert, J.; Chen, S.; Ruenraroengsak, P.; Bey, L.; Theodorou, I.G.; Ryan, M.; Cui, X.; Zhang, J.; Shaffer, M.; et al. Effect of silver nanospheres and nanowires on human airway smooth muscle cells: Role of sulfidatio. *Nanoscale Adv.* **2020**, *2*, 5635–5647. [CrossRef]

33. Quadros, M.E.; Marr, L.C. Silver nanoparticles and total aerosols emitted by nanotechnology-related consumer spray products. *Environ. Sci. Technol.* **2011**, *45*, 10713–10719. [CrossRef]
34. Benn, T.; Cavanagh, B.; Hristovski, K.; Posner, J.D.; Westerhoff, P. The Release of Nanosilver from Consumer Products Used in the Home. *J. Environ. Qual.* **2010**, *39*, 1875–1882. [CrossRef]
35. Silva, V.L.S.; Heaney, C.E.; Pain, C.C. GAN for time series prediction, data assimilation and uncertainty quantification. *arXiv* **2021**, arXiv:2105.13859. [CrossRef]

Article

ReSTiNet: On Improving the Performance of Tiny-YOLO-Based CNN Architecture for Applications in Human Detection

Shahriar Shakir Sumit [1,*], Dayang Rohaya Awang Rambli [1], Seyedali Mirjalili [2,3], Muhammad Mudassir Ejaz [4] and M. Saef Ullah Miah [5]

1. Department of Computer & Information Sciences, Universiti Teknologi PETRONAS (UTP), Seri Iskandar 32610, Perak, Malaysia
2. Centre for Artificial Intelligence Research and Optimization, Torrens University Australia, Brisbane, QLD 4006, Australia
3. Yonsei Frontier Lab, Yonsei University, 50 Yonsei-ro Seodaemun-gu, Seoul 03722, Korea
4. Electrical & Electronics Engineering, Universiti Teknologi PETRONAS (UTP), Seri Iskandar 32610, Perak, Malaysia
5. Faculty of Computing, College of Computing and Applied Sciences, Universiti Malaysia Pahang, Pekan 26600, Pahang, Malaysia
* Correspondence: shahriar9121@gmail.com

Abstract: Human detection is a special application of object recognition and is considered one of the greatest challenges in computer vision. It is the starting point of a number of applications, including public safety and security surveillance around the world. Human detection technologies have advanced significantly in recent years due to the rapid development of deep learning techniques. Despite recent advances, we still need to adopt the best network-design practices that enable compact sizes, deep designs, and fast training times while maintaining high accuracies. In this article, we propose ReSTiNet, a novel compressed convolutional neural network that addresses the issues of size, detection speed, and accuracy. Following SqueezeNet, ReSTiNet adopts the fire modules by examining the number of fire modules and their placement within the model to reduce the number of parameters and thus the model size. The residual connections within the fire modules in ReSTiNet are interpolated and finely constructed to improve feature propagation and ensure the largest possible information flow in the model, with the goal of further improving the proposed ReSTiNet in terms of detection speed and accuracy. The proposed algorithm downsizes the previously popular Tiny-YOLO model and improves the following features: (1) faster detection speed; (2) compact model size; (3) solving the overfitting problems; and (4) superior performance than other lightweight models such as MobileNet and SqueezeNet in terms of mAP. The proposed model was trained and tested using MS COCO and Pascal VOC datasets. The resulting ReSTiNet model is 10.7 MB in size (almost five times smaller than Tiny-YOLO), but it achieves an mAP of 63.74% on PASCAL VOC and 27.3% on MS COCO datasets using Tesla k80 GPU.

Keywords: computer vision; object detection; human detection; convolutional neural networks

1. Introduction

Human beings possess an inherent ability to perceive surrounding objects in static images or image sequences almost flawlessly. They can also sense emotions and interactions among persons and notice the total persons present in images by making mere observations. The computer vision field is expected to provide the required technological assistance for this human aptitude in order to improve the quality of life of humans. Hence, the aim of this field is to explore methods for effectively teaching machines or computers to observe and understand characteristics in images or videos using digital cameras [1].

A precise detection of objects in an image is essential in computer vision in order to suit the demands of various applications involving vision-based approaches. For instance, object detection includes the identification of specific details in an image, and localizing its coordinates is considered to be a problem in vision technology. Identifying objects is not the only task that requires performance but categorizing them accordingly across various classes in an appropriate manner is also required [2]. A classic example of this includes visual object detection [2]. Figure 1 illustrates the basic operation of a machine learning (ML) model for detecting objects. For example, consider the goal of classifying three dissimilar objects: a bird, a human being, and a lion. Initially, training images are collected with labeled data in preparation for training an ML framework. Secondly, the desired features are extracted and then added to the classifier's architecture.

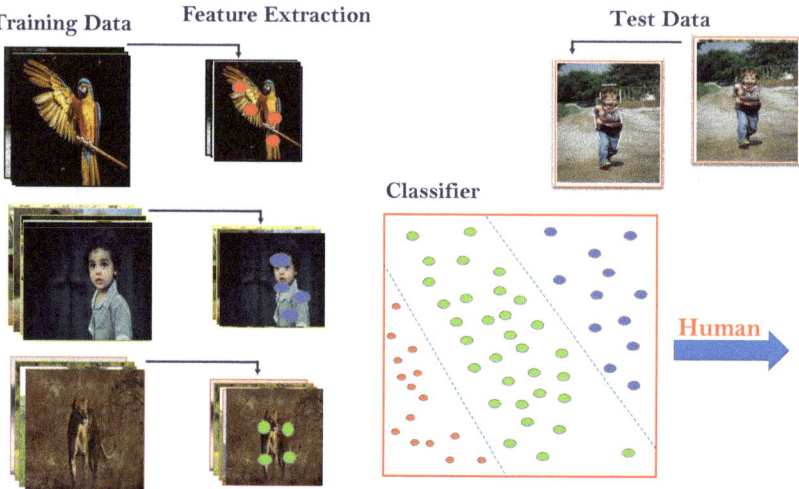

Figure 1. Example of machine learning work flow for object classification across three different classes (bird, human, and lion).

Certain features can be best expressed by utilizing various object characteristics that include colors, corners, edges, ridges, and regions or blobs [3]. The success achieved from training is directly proportional to several factors that include feature extraction, classifier selection, and the training procedure. The first task is important as it not only enhances the accuracy of trained networks but also eliminates redundant features in the image. It involves reducing the dimensionality of data by extracting redundant information, which in turn improves the quality of inference while simultaneously improving the training rate. An ideological view is to expect features to be invariable in the control of dynamic and illuminated conditions while possessing the capability to cope with any randomized variations during either scaling or rotational motions. Features are appended to the training framework after all feasible features from the image samples have been extracted. They are then supplied to an appropriate sort of classifier based on accuracy and speed. Some normally used classifiers exist, which include the Support Vector Machines (SVM), Nearest Neighbor (NN), Random Forest (RF), and Decision Tree (DT). Once the training framework is ready, removing alike features from the test image samples and, as a consequence, predicting the proper class from features using the trained framework for each provided test image are feasible.

Several techniques were proposed in light of the efficient extraction of features as well as classification to detect arbitrary objects in images [4]. Over the past two decades, the focus had been on the design of efficient hand-crafted features to improve detection robustness and accuracy. A diverse set of extraction techniques was provided by the vision research community such as Scale Invariant Feature Transform (SIFT), Viola Jones

(VJ), Histogram of Oriented Gradients (HoG), Speeded Up Robust Features (SURF), and Deformable Part-Based Models (DPM) [5,6].

Deep learning techniques have effectively combined the task of extracting the features and classification in an end-to-end way [4]. Convolutional neural networks (CNNs) have become quite popular for tackling various problems, among which includes object detection. Subsequently, the performance of such architectures has led to a proliferation in both achievable speed and accuracy. The object detection methods using deep CNN such as Spatial Pyramid Pooling Networks (SPPNets), Region-based CNN (R-CNN), Feature Pyramid Networks (FPNs), fast RCNN, You Only Look Once (YOLO), faster R-CNN, Single-Shot Multibox Detector (SSD), and Region-based Fully Convolutional Networks (R-FCNs) have shown excellent benefits relative to state-of-the-art ML methods [7,8]. This article focuses on a specific sub-domain of detection, which is the human detection.

In a year, over a billion people lost their lives and around 20–50 million people experienced fatal complications as a result of traffic accidents [9]. In 2015, more than 5000 pedestrians died in traffic accidents, while about 130,000 pedestrians required medical care for non-fatal problems in the United States. However, the ratio of traffic fatality can be reduced or even eliminated by utilizing various detection techniques in autonomous vehicles that use sensors to interact with other neighboring vehicles in the vicinity [10].

With increases in crime and public fear of terrorism, public security has become an unavoidable concern, and human detection techniques can be employed to monitor and control public spaces remotely. Approximately 21,000 people lose their lives because of terrorist activities every year and 0.05% of the total deaths in 2017 occurred due to terrorism [11]. The necessity to install a sufficient number of human-detecting devices has spiked in public locations following tragedies in London, New York, and other cities across the globe. Such incidents are critical enough and demand a robust design and global deployment of such systems. Hence, human-detection systems are observed as a viable answer for ensuring public safety and have become one of the most significant study fields today.

The detection of human beings is one of the key responsibilities in the field of computer vision. It is indeed difficult to identify human in pictures because of several background effects such as occlusions [12], illuminated conditions and background clutters [13]. Previous techniques have been unsuccessful in real-world scenarios for detecting humans, as they took a longer period of time for detection and yielded outcomes that were not sufficiently accurate due to distance as well as changes in appearance [6]. Therefore, a universal representation of objects still continues to remain an open challenge in midst of such factors. Human detection is currently being utilized for many applications. Human detection is in the early stages in a number of use cases including pedestrian detection, e-health systems, abnormal behavior, person re-identification, driving assistance systems, crowd analysis, gender categorization, smart-video surveillance, human-pose estimation, human tracking, intelligent digital content management, and, finally, human-activity recognition [6,14–17].

The deep CNN is a dense computing framework in and of itself. With a large number of parameters and higher processing loads, followed by high memory access, energy consumption increases rapidly, thereby making it impossible to adopt the method for compact devices with minimal hardware resources. A feasible approach is a compressive, deep CNN technique for real-time applications and compact low-memory devices, which reduces the number of parameters, the cost of calculation, and power usage by compressing deep CNNs [18].

Over the past few years, the construction of tiny and effective network techniques to detect objects has become a point of discussion in the field of computer vision research. Acceleration and compression techniques are related primarily to the compact configuration of network architecture [19], knowledge distillation [20], network sparsity and pruning [21], and network quantization [22]. Various studies on network compression have advanced network models: for instance, SqueezeNet [23], which is a fire module based architecture; MobileNets [24], a depthwise separable filters based architecture; and, finally, the ShuffleNet [25], a residual structure based network in which channel shuffle strategy and group pointwise convolution were incorporated.

Motivated by lightweight architectures, a novel compact model was proposed to detect humans for the portable devices that were absent in the current literature. Tiny-YOLO, which is the tiny version of the YOLO model, is used as the base architecture of this proposed model. YOLO is a faster and more accurate technique compared to other object detection models, and it has been enhanced since its first implementation, which includes v1-YOLO, v2-YOLO, and v3-YOLO. However, these architectures are not suitable for portable devices because of their large sizes and inability to maintain real-time performance in constrained environments. As mentioned, Tiny-YOLO is smaller than these models. However, it failed to achieve high accuracy, and speed remained unsatisfactory for low-memory devices.

This article proposes a model called ReSTiNet that is based on Tiny-YOLO. This model reduces the size of the model while simultaneously achieving higher accuracy and boosting detection speeds. The ultimate goal of this article is to develop a more capable human detection model for portable devices. Intelligent surveillance systems that use portable devices with less processing power can easily take advantages of this smaller and lighter model. This improves the performance and capabilities of the system without increasing the cost of the hardware or the amount of processing power it needs. Furthermore, lighter and faster models can be used in low-latency real-time human detection applications. The inspiration for ReSTiNet came from SqueezeNet, which use the fire module in order to decrease the total model parameter numbers and therefore compressed the overall size of the model. Determining the number of fire modules and where in the network they should be placed is one of the parts of integrating the fire module in Tiny-YOLO that presents one of the greatest challenges. The investigation of the residual connection between fire modules is still another key issue that needs to be addressed in order to improve detection accuracies and speeds even more. The useful feature of residual connections in Resnet [26] served as an inspiration for the implementation of residual connections within the fire modules of ReSTiNet. This was performed to ensure that the maximum amount of information flowed and to improve feature propagation throughout the architecture. In the end, dropout was used in ReSTiNet in order to circumvent the overfitting issue, attain an overall satisfactory level of performance, and lower the amount of computing effort required.

Prior to delving into the details of the study, it is essential to discuss the scope of the current effort. The following sections are the contents of this paper: Section 2 discusses the recent literature on human detection. In Section 3, the proposed ReSTiNet model for portable devices is explained. The experimental results are reported step-by-step in Section 4: system specification, dataset Specification, mAP, model training, ablation experiments of the proposed ReSTiNet, comparison with other lightweight models, and performance analysis of the proposed ReSTiNet. Finally, Section 6 concludes the article.

2. Related Literature: State-of-the-Art Methods

Human detection is the process of identifying each object in a static image or image sequences that are regarded to be human. Human detection is widely acknowledged to have advanced through two different historical periods in recent decades: "conventional human detection period (before 2012)" and "deep learning-based detection period (after 2012)", as illustrated in Figure 2.

Human detection is typically accomplished by extracting regions of interest (ROI) from an arbitrary image sample, illustrating the regions using descriptors, and then categorizing the regions as non-human or human, accompanied by post-processing processes [27].

In conventional techniques, human descriptors are generally designed by locally removing the features. A few examples include "edge-based shape features (e.g., [28])", "appearance features (e.g., color [29], texture [30])", "motion features (e.g., temporal differences [31])", "optical flows [32]", and their combinations [33]. Most of their functions are manually designed, which benefit from the ease of description and intuitively comprehending them. In addition, they were shown to perform well with limited collections of training datasets.

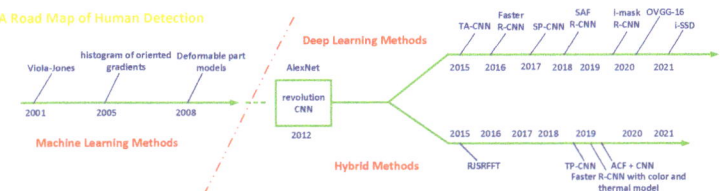

Figure 2. Human-detection milestones.

The Deformable Part-based Model (DPM) is the earlier state-of-the-art approach for detection process [34]. DPM is considered an extension of the histograms of the oriented gradients (HOG) model. The projected object is scored using the entire image's coarse global template as well as the six higher-resolution portions of the object. HOG is used to characterize every single input. Following this approach, HOG's multi-model can address the varying viewpoint problem. In the training phase, a latent support vector machine (latent SVM) was employed to decrease the detection drawback relative to the classification area. The coordinates of the component are considered as the latent element. This approach resulted in a massive impact due to its robustness.

Manually described features on the other hand, are unable to present more detailed information about the objects. In particular, they were challenged by the background, occlusion, motion blur, and illumination conditions. Hence, deep learning algorithms are regarded as relatively more efficient in human detection because they can learn more sophisticated features from images [35–37]. Although these initial deep algorithms have demonstrated some improvements over the classical models, these functions are still constructed manually, and the key concept is to expand the earlier models. Deep CNNs are also applied for the feature extraction in a few studies, for example [38]. A complexity perception cascade training for human detection was performed followed by the extraction of features.

Deep learning approaches are currently being used to address many identification problems in several ways. One of the most promising architectures is the Convolutional Neural Network (CNN). Deep CNNs can learn object features on their own; thus, they depend less on the object's classes. Training a class-independent method, contrastingly, means that more data will be used for learning as deep learning requires a significant volume of data relative to training a domain-specific method. Only a few articles have been published in the field of human detection using the CNNs method. Tian et al. [39] employed a CNN to learn human segmentation characteristics (e.g., hats and backpacks), but the network component leads to boosting the prediction accuracy by re-classifying the prediction item as negative or positive, rather than making predictions directly. Li et al. [40] included a sub-network relative to a novel network built on Fast R-CNN to deal with small-scale objects. Zhang et al. [41] straightforwardly examined a cross-class detection method (CNN), which involved faster R-CNNs performances on independent pedestrian detection, and came up with good findings. Among the three techniques, besides [39], which does not directly deal with detection, refs. [40,41] performed various experiments based on cross-class detection techniques. In [42], the authors suggested a system based on the combination of "Faster R-CNN" and "skip pooling" to deal with human detection issues. The architecture of "Faster R-CNN's region proposal network" is generalized to a multi-layer structure and finally combined with skip pooling. The skip pooling structure removes several interest regions from the lower layer and is fed to the higher layer, without considering the middle layer. In [43], the authors had suggested an enhanced mask R-CNN approach for real-time human detection that achieved 88% accuracy.

In [44], a deep convolutional neural network-based human detection technique was proposed using images that were used as input data to classify pedestrians and humans. The authors used the VGG-16 network as a backbone and the model had provided better accuracy on the "INRIA dataset". In [45], the authors combined a deep learning model with machine learning technique to achieve high accuracies with less computational time for human detection and tracking in real time. However, the model had a lower speed. In [46], the authors suggested a sparse network-based approach for removing irregular features and the developed approach was applied to a kernel-based architecture to reduce nonlinear resemblance across different features. This model, on the other hand, cannot be used for real-time detection and tracking.

H. Jeon et al. [47] resolved the human detection problem in extreme conditions by applying a deep learning-based triangle pattern integration approach. Triangular patterns are employed to derive more precise and reliable attributes from the local region. The extracted attributes are fed into a deep neural architecture, which uses them to detect humans in dense and occluded situation. In [48], K.N.Renu et al. proposed a deep learning-based brightness aware method to detect human in various illuminated conditions for both day and night scenarios. In [49], the authors cascaded aggregate channel features (ACF) with the deep convolutional neural network for quicker pedestrian and human detection. Then, a hybrid Gaussian asymmetric function was proposed to define the constraints of human perception. In [50], the authors proposed a single-shot multibox detector (SSD) to detect pedestrians. The SSD convolutional neural architecture extracts low features and then combines them with deep semantic information in the convolutional layer. Finally, humans are identified in still images. In the suggested technique, pre-selection boxes with different ratios are used, which increased the detection capability of the entire model.

In [51], the authors proposed a multi-stage cascade framework for coarse-to-fine human-object interaction (HOI) recognition understanding. The introduced method achieved first position in ICCV2019 Person Context Challenge (PIC-19) and also showed the excellent outcomes on V-COCO dataset. In [52], the authors developed a compressed, powerful, and effective architecture to resolve the instance-aware human part parsing issue. In the proposed method, structural information are used across a variety of human granularities, which makes the challenging task of person-partitioning easier.

3. The Proposed ReSTiNet for Low-Memory Devices

3.1. Motivation

The network structure of Tiny-YOLO is shown in Figure 3. This architecture consists of a total of nine convolutional layers followed by six max-pooling layers that are used to remove features of images along with one detection layer. This method uses convolutional layers containing 512 and 1024 filters that provide a large parameter density, large memory storage, and a lower detection speed. Another issue with Tiny-YOLO is its low detection accuracy. The network's irrational compression techniques may further decrease detection accuracies.

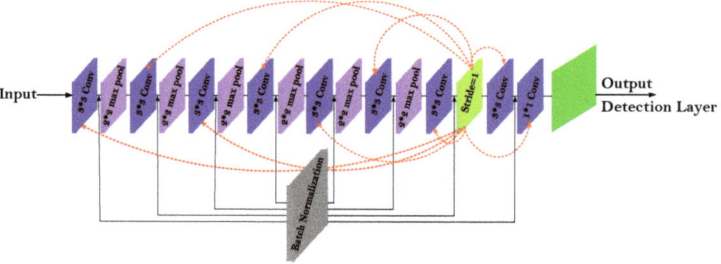

Figure 3. The structure of Tiny-YOLO.

Hence, in order to address such issues, ReSTiNet is introduced in this research, which directs towards the performance of the model's size as well as its accuracy. Algorithm 1 details the proposed ReSTiNet model.

Algorithm 1 ReSTiNet pseudocode

    Input: Input(shape= (input_size, input_size,3))
    Input: learning_ rate, epoch, batch_size
    Input: iou_ threshold, score_ threshold
    Output: output_shape, mAP
    def fire_module(model, fire_id, squeeze, expand)
    def maxpooling (pool_size, stride)
    def resnet_block (model, filters, reps, stride)
    def mAP (model):
        map = model.evaluate (generator, iou_threshold,
        score_threshold, average_precisions)
      return map
    def layer(conv, batchnorm, activation, maxpooling, dropout)
    def main (){
    create layer1: ([16,3,1], norm_1, leakyReLU[.1], 2, null)
    x ← layer1
      for i in range(2,3,4,5):
        create layer(i): ([32*(2**i), 3, 1], norm_ + str(i+2),
        leakyReLU[.1], 2, [0.20])
        x ← (x) (layer(i))
    //return x
    create fire_module1: (x, 2, 16, 64)
    create fire_module2: (x, 3, 16, 64)
    create maxpooling1: (3, 2)
    create resnet_block1: (x, 64, 3, 1)
    create fire_module3: (x, 4, 32, 128)
    create fire_module4: (x, 5, 32, 128)
    create maxpooling2: (3, 2)
    create resnet_block1: (x, 128, 4, 2)
    create fire_module5: (x, 6, 48, 192)
    create fire_module6: (x, 7, 48, 192)
    create fire_module7: (x, 8, 64, 256)
    create fire_module8: (x, 9, 64, 256)
    dropout ← 0.50
    return mAP(x), output_shape(x)}

The goal of ReSTiNet is to develop a model that is smaller, swifter, and more capable at detecting humans on lightweight devices. The network's optimization is carried out by performing a reduction in parameters to an acceptable level rather than blindly decimating the convolution layers. SqueezeNet's fire module compresses the framework using a bottleneck network layer and widens the network module without significantly sacrificing detection accuracy. As a result, the introduction of fire module was carried out to achieve the performance of a faster as well as a smaller network structure. ReSTiNet then seeks achieve a higher accuracy in detection while simultaneously minimizing the parameters. Study [53] achieved a higher accuracy with a smaller number of parameters in which residual blocks were integrated between fire modules in the VGG-16 network. Thus, in between the fire modules lies the residual block, which is used in ReSTiNet to maximize the detection accuracy.

3.2. Construction of ReSTiNet

The structure of ReSTiNet is shown in Figure 4. The first five convolutional layers of Tiny-YOLO are retained in ReSTiNet. Layers with 512 and 1024 filters in the Tiny-YOLO are replaced with the fire modules, which shrink the model. Then, residual connections from Resnet-50 network inside the fire modules are integrated, which help the proposed model achieve a higher mAP. This article synthesizes three widely used approaches: Tiny-YOLO, ResNet, and the SqueezeNet method. The details of the implementations are as follows.

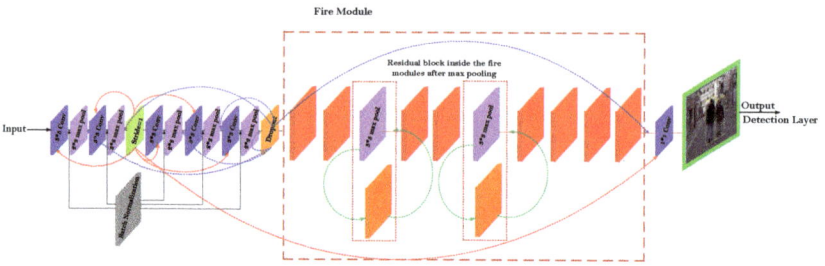

Figure 4. The structure of ReSTiNet. Fire modules are adopted from SqueezeNet, which shrinks the model. Then, residual connections are integrated from ResNet-50 network inside the fire modules to enhance the proposed ReSTiNet's efficiency.

3.2.1. Tiny-YOLO

A popular technique called "Tiny-YOLO", which is the smaller version of "You Only Look Once (YOLO)", was formulated to create a single step procedure that involved both the detection as well as the classification process. Upon a single appraisal of the input image, both the bounding box and class predictions are produced.

The distinguishing feature of this technique as opposed to the conventional models is that the class as well as bounding box predictions are performed at the same time. The procedure is as follows: Firstly, the image that is considered as the input is split across the $S \times S$ grid. Secondly, every single grid cell is assigned with a confidence score, which contains the respective bounding box. The probability or chances that the object is present in every bounding box is referred to as the confidence score and is mathematically given by the following:

$$C = \Pr(Object) * IOU_{pred}^{truth} \qquad (1)$$

where term IOU ("intersection over union") is defined to be a fraction that numerically lies within the limits of [0, 1]. The overlapped area in between the ground truth as well as the bounding box predictor is termed as the intersection. The entire region between the ground truth and the predictor is known as the union. In ideal terms, the IOU must be closer to 1, which implies that the ground truth is approximately equal to the bounding-box predictor.

Similarly, the conditional class probability C is also predicted by individual grid cells while the bounding boxes are created. Thus, for every cell, the class-specific probability function is expressed as follows.

$$\Pr(Class_i|Object) * \Pr(Object) * IOU_{pred}^{truth} \\ = \Pr(Class_i) * IOU_{pred}^{truth}. \qquad (2)$$

3.2.2. Fire Module of ReSTiNet

The introduction of the fire module under ReSTiNet was to decrease the number of parameters as well as escalate the width and depth of the entire network. This was performed in order to ensure the accuracy of detection. This model consists of both expand as well as the squeeze components so that the model's network tends to expand and compress. The compress or squeeze component utilizes the convolutional layer with a size of 1 × 1 introduced by NIN as a substitute for the usual layer with the size 3 × 3. In order to decrease the number of parameters, the model that follows the 1 × 1 technique was found to be more efficient. Additionally, the accuracy of detection does not reduce significantly as the training parameter is only a single variable that should be learnt. During the expansion, both the models with sizes 1 × 1 as well as 3 × 3 are typically used. Finally, the arrived outputs from the respective convolutional layers are concatenated at the concatenation layer.

For a convolutional layer, the parameters are given as c_i, the number of channel input variables, k as the kernel size, and c_o as the number of channel output variables. Using Equation (3), the value of the number of parameters for the convolutional layer is then calculated. The number of channel inputs is c_i for the fire module; k_{s_1} is the kernel size of the squeeze component, and s_1 is the number of channel output variables. If the value of k_{s_1} is assigned to 1, a reduction in a large number of model parameters for the squeeze component is possible. The number of channel input variables is s_1 followed by the kernel sizes k_{e_1} and k_{e_3} for the expanded component. The total number of channel output variables is the sum of e_1 and e_3. Using Equation (4), the number of model parameters is calculated. Figure 5 illustrates the structure of the fire modules in ReSTiNet.

$$P_{conv} = (c_i \times k^2 + 1) \times c_o \tag{3}$$

$$\begin{aligned}P_{fire} = (c_i \times k_{s_1}^2 + 1) \times s_1 + (s_1 \times k_{e_1}^2 + 1) \\ \times e_1 + (s_1 \times k_{e_3}^2 + 1) \times e_3\end{aligned} \tag{4}$$

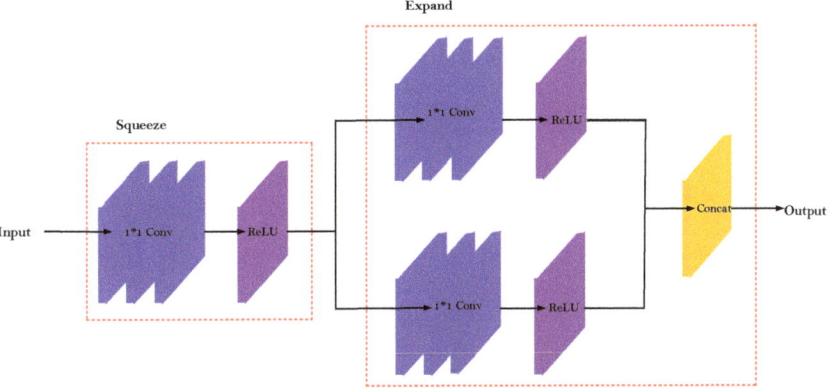

Figure 5. The structure of Fire Module. It is made up of two layers: squeeze and expand. The squeeze layer consists of a small number 1 × 1 filters, and the expand layer consists of a small number of 3 × 3 and 1 × 1 filters.

The ability with which the fire can be utilized more effectively depends on the appropriateness of the position of the fire module within the network. ReSTiNet architecture comprises a total of eight fire modules. In the ReSTiNet network, the sixth layer is replaced with the initial four fire modules where the former contains 512 filters followed by downsampling technique. Layers seventh and eighth containing 1024 filters are replaced with four other fire modules, and this is carried out before the 1 × 1 convolutional layer and detection layer. However, the choice of the number of channel inputs c_i is not bounded, while choosing a large number of channel inputs would lead to reduction in parameters.

3.2.3. Residual Block between Fire Modules

The optimization trajectory will follow a negative slope due to degradation when it is expected of depth to provide an enhanced detection accuracy. Relative to the conclusions derived from other neural networks, it is observed that the error is typically higher in deep CNN architectures [53]. In study [26], the authors developed a degradation resolution that enables a subset of stacked layers to accept the existing residual mapping. This is the area where the degradation typically halts the layers in order to be congruent with the standard subsidiary mapping. Formula (6) represents the subsidiary mapping rather than Formula (5), where $H(x)$ is the desired mapping, and $F(x)$ is the learned residual mapping. The actual mapping is modified into $F(x) + x$. In study [26], the authors found that optimization is relatively easier in a residual-based mapping than the primary one.

$$F(x) = H(x) \tag{5}$$

$$F(x) := H(x) - x \tag{6}$$

$$H(x) = F(x) + x \tag{7}$$

However, one or more layers were ignored during "shortcut connections", as mentioned in studies [26,53]. "Shortcut connections" are expressed in Equation (7) [26]. Study [26] utilized "shortcut connections" in order to conduct identity mappings. The fusing of stacked layer outputs is performed with that of the "shortcut connections" output values. The latter possesses the advantage of being parameter-free, thereby using minor values during the computational process. Paper [54] developed highway-based networks by merging "shortcut connections" and "gating functions" along with their parameters. The possibility of optimization using a "stochastic gradient descent (SGD)" is another benefit of "shortcut connections" [26]. It is easier to integrate "identity shortcut connections" using deep learning open-source libraries [26,53].

We integrated "residual learning" from ResNet-50 within ReSTiNet architecture followed by a down-sampling technique after the 2nd and 4th fire modules. The building residual block is expressed in Equation (8).

$$y = F(x, W_i) + x \tag{8}$$

Terms y and x represent the output and input vectors of the layers, respectively. The mentioned function, $F(x, W_i)$, is nothing but the residual mapping to be learnt. As in Figure 2, there are 2 layers, $F = W_{2\sigma}(W_1 x)$, in which the term σ represents the ReLU functionl; for reducing the complexity of notations, many biases were appropriately removed. The process, $F + x$, was carried out by the use of a "shortcut connection" and "elemental-wise addition" operation upon which the second ReLU (non-linearity) function was made use of. The "shortcut connections" in Equation (8) add neither more parameters nor complexity to the computation [26].

3.2.4. Dropout in ReSTiNet

The mask that neutralizes the effects caused by neurons in the succeeding layer is termed as the dropout layer. This mask tends to stabilize the neurons and keeps the others unchanged. This layer is important while training CNNs since they counteract the effects of overfitting on the data that needs to be trained. Otherwise, an influence from the initial batch of samples will be present on the learning and causes disproportionate results in the performance. Thus, the efficiency in learning the features will be deeply affected; it further delays the arrival of such results in later batches [55]. The common practice of a dropout is to use a small value within the range of 20–50% of neurons, with 20% being a decent starting point. A probability that is too low has no impact, whereas a value that is too large results in the network's under-learning [56]. In the convolutional layers (2nd–5th), 0.2 and, after the fire module, 0.5 dropouts are used in the proposed ReSTiNet network to overcome the overfitting problem.

3.2.5. Loss Function of ReSTiNet

The custom loss function is utilized in this study, unlike Tiny-YOLO, which consists of three parts: error in prediction coordinate, error in IOU, and classification error.

The error in coordinate prediction is described as follows:

$$Error_{coord} = \lambda_{coord} \sum_{i=0}^{s^2} \sum_{j=0}^{B} L_{ij}^{obj} \left[(x_i - \hat{x}_i)^2 + (y_i - \hat{y}_i)^2 \right] \\ + \lambda_{coord} \sum_{i=0}^{s^2} \sum_{j=0}^{B} L_{ij}^{obj} \left[(\sqrt{w_i} - \sqrt{\hat{w}_i})^2 + \left(\sqrt{h_i} - \sqrt{\hat{h}_i}\right)^2 \right] \quad (9)$$

where s^2 denotes the grid cell number of all scale. B represents the bounding-box number for every grid. L_{ij}^{obj} defines target of the i-th grid cell, which falls in the j-th bounding box. $(\hat{x}_i, \hat{y}_i, \hat{w}_i, \hat{h}_i)$ and (x_i, y_i, w_i, h_i) represent the center coordinate, height, and width of the predicted box and the ground truth, respectively.

The IOU error is described as follows:

$$Error_{IOU} = \sum_{i=0}^{s^2} \sum_{j=0}^{B} L_{ij}^{obj} (C_i - \hat{C}_i)^2 \\ + \lambda_{noobj} \sum_{i=0}^{s^2} \sum_{j=0}^{B} L_{ij}^{noobj} (C_i - \hat{C}_i)^2 \quad (10)$$

where $\hat{C}_i$ and C_i define the predicted and true confidence, correspondingly.

The classification error is defined as follows:

$$Error_{cls} = \sum_{i=0}^{s^2} L_i^{obj} \sum_{c \in classes} (p_i(c) - \hat{p}(c))^2. \quad (11)$$

where $\hat{p}_i(c)$ denotes the predicted value, while $p_i(c)$ denotes the target's true probability. From the above, the final loss function is shown in Equation (12).

$$Loss = Error_{coord} + Error_{IOU} + Error_{cls} \\ = \lambda_{coord} \sum_{i=0}^{s^2} \sum_{j=0}^{B} L_{ij}^{obj} \left[(x_i - \hat{x}_i)^2 + (y_i - \hat{y}_i)^2 \right] \\ + \lambda_{coord} \sum_{i=0}^{s^2} \sum_{j=0}^{B} L_{ij}^{obj} \left[(\sqrt{w_i} - \sqrt{\hat{w}_i})^2 + \left(\sqrt{h_i} - \sqrt{\hat{h}_i}\right)^2 \right] \\ + \sum_{i=0}^{s^2} \sum_{j=0}^{B} L_{ij}^{obj} (C_i - \hat{C}_i)^2 \\ + \lambda_{noobj} \sum_{i=0}^{s^2} \sum_{j=0}^{B} L_{ij}^{noobj} (C_i - \hat{C}_i)^2 \\ + \sum_{i=0}^{s^2} L_i^{obj} \sum_{c \in classes} (p_i(c) - \hat{p}(c))^2. \quad (12)$$

3.3. Time Complexity, Success, and Challenge of ReSTiNet

In this section, time complexities of the proposed ReSTiNet with its success and challenge are described.

3.3.1. Time Complexity

In the proposed algorithm, some operations occur only once and their time complexity is $O(1)$. However, in ReSTiNet, different methods have iteration, and their time complexity is $O(n^2)$. Therefore, the time complexity of our proposed algorithm is as follows: $O(1) + O(n^2) = O(n^2)$. Therefore, we define this algorithm as having a Quadratic Time

Complexity to indicate that as the size of the input increases, the amount of time needed to run it increases accordingly. Informally, Quadratic Time Complexity represents an algorithm for which its performance is directly proportional to the squared size of the input data set.

3.3.2. Advantage of the Model

This proposed method is easily adaptable; therefore, this process can be applied to compress various current deep CNN models. As human detection is the first phase of many applications, this developed method can be used for pedestrian detection and pose estimation with low-memory devices.

3.3.3. Challenge of the Model

ReSTiNet employs fire modules that reduce the model's parameter and, thus, the computational cost. However, the procedure still requires a significant amount of processing to be performed on a portable device. As a result, the architecture is still trained on a machine (i.e., remote server) capable of handling this computationally intensive method.

4. Experimental Results

Initially, the experimental environment setups, datasets, and evaluation criteria (mAP) are described in this segment of the article. The performance is then compared based on training time, mAP, and model size metrics. Moreover, to validate the advantage of ReSTiNet performance over alternative lightweight networks, we conducted comprehensive experiments to verify the findings of the performance comparison.

4.1. System Specification

The Tesla K80 is used to train the ReSTiNet model and also to evaluate the detection speed of the architecture. The Tesla K80 is a pro graphics card launched by NVIDIA. Tesla K80 is built on the GK210 GPU and manufactured using 28 nm technology. The GK210 GPU has a 561 mm² die area with 7100 million transistors. The Tesla K80 integrates two GPUs to boost the performance. The configuration of the Tesla K80 is provided in Table 1.

Table 1. Configuration of Tesla K80.

Computing Platform	Graphics Processor	Memory
Tesla K80	GK210 × 2, 2496 × 2 shading units, 208 × 2 TUMs, 48 × 2 ROPs	12 GB × 2, 384 bit × 2, GDDR5, 240.6 GB/s × 2

Ubuntu-16.04 LTS is used as base operating system with 62 GB RAM, NVIDIA CUDA v10.2, NVIDIA cuDNN v7.6.5. The script is written in python v2.7 with TensorFlow v1.14.0, Keras v2.2.2, cv2, NumPy v1.16.4.

4.2. Data-Set Specification

This study makes use of the "MS COCO" [57] and "Pascal VOC" [2] datasets. Generally, object detection, image classification, and segmentation are performed with these two datasets. The "Pascal VOC" dataset consists of "Pascal VOC 2007" and "Pascal VOC 2012". There are 8540 images of human beings from the "Pascal VOC" dataset used for this experiment. "MS COCO" is more challenging while "Pascal VOC" is easier to train. Generally, the performance on the MS COCO dataset of a method for object detection models is more inclined. There are 45,174 images of human beings used from the "MS COCO-train2014" dataset for accomplishing this study. Both datasets are split 80/20 for training and validation, respectively. The IOU ("intersection over union") is set 0.5 by default for both datasets while calculating mAP values. The "INRIA" dataset [6] (1208 images) is used to test the proposed ReSTiNet model's detection speed.

4.3. Evaluation Criteria (mAP)

The mean average precision (mAP) metric is utilized to estimate the performance of the introduced ReSTiNet and the baseline architectures. The mAP scores are reported for both "MS COCO" and "Pascal VOC".

Average Precision (AP): The recall/precision curve is used to assess the output performance for a specific class and task. Precision is the ratio between the relevant and retrieved examples explained in Equation (13).

$$precision = \frac{|\{relevant\ instances\} \cap \{retrieved\ instances\}|}{|\{retrieved\ instances\}|} \quad (13)$$

The rate of recall is described as the ratio of the total number of relevant examples to the total positive instances. The average precision is utilized for evaluating precision over multiple equidistant recall levels:

$$AP = \sum_{k=0}^{k=n-1}[Recalls(k) - Recalls(k+1)] * Precisions(k) \quad (14)$$

where n defines the number of the threshold.

The mAP ("mean average precision") is employed to calculate the C class's average precision:

$$mAP = \frac{1}{C}\sum_{i \in \{0,1,2,\ldots,C\}} AP(c_i) \quad (15)$$

where $AP(c_i)$ defines the average precision for the class of c_i.

4.4. Model Training

The pre-trained weight daraknet19.conv model is imported into ReSTiNet before the training started on both "MS COCO" and "Pascal VOC" datasets. ReSTiNet takes 416*416 as the size of the input. The learning rate of ReSTiNet is 0.001, and the batch size is 16 with 50 epochs. MS COCO has a max iteration batch number of 504K, whereas Pascal VOC has a max iteration batch number of 129 K. Table 2 represents the model's trained hyperparameters.

Table 2. Hyperparameters used in the ReSTiNet.

Hyperparameter	Range
input size	416 × 416
learning rate	0.001
activation	Leaky ReLU ($\alpha = 0.1$), ReLU
batchsize	16
no. of epoch	50
optimizer	adam ($\beta_1 = 0.9$, $\beta_2 = 0.999$, $\epsilon = 1 \times 10^{-8}$)
loss function	custom loss
dropout	0.2, 0.5
iou_threshold	0.5
score_threshold	0.5

4.5. Ablation Experiments of the Proposed ReSTiNet

We have conducted ablation experiments in the ReSTiNet network by sequentially adding fire modules, residual connections, and dropout layers to demonstrate the impact of these methods on ReSTiNet's performance. Table 3 shows the results (mAP) of the proposed model, ReSTiNet, and the original Tiny-YOLO on the "Pascal VOC" and the "MS COCO" dataset.

Table 3. Ablation experiments: Tiny-YOLO vs. ReSTiNet.

	Tiny-YOLO		ReSTiNet
fire module		✓	✓
residual learning			✓
dropout		✓	✓
MS COCO mAP(%)	19.0	24.37	27.31
Pascal VOC mAP(%)	42.21	55.67	63.79

Detection accuracy is commonly evaluated using the mAP. The new proposed model achieved 27.31% mAP on the MS COCO dataset, whereas Tiny-YOLO obtained 19% mAP. The dropout layer and residual connections helps the ReSTiNet model in achieving higher accuracies than Tiny-YOLO. ReSTiNet achieves 63.79% mAP on the Pascal VOC dataset; on the other hand, Tiny-YOLO reaches 42.21% mAP. The use of residual connections between the fire modules and the dropout layer significantly contributes to the increase in mAP without requiring an excessive number of parameters. Utilizing residual connections and dropout improves mAP by 12.06% on "MS COCO" and 14.59% on "Pascal VOC" based on adding fire modules. In addition, employing the dropout layer helps reduce the training time and helps the model from the over-fitting problem. ReSTiNet outperforms Tiny-YOLO, showing 43.74% and 51.09% improvements on the "MS COCO" and "Pascal VOC" datasets, respectively.

Detection Time, Parameter, and FLOPs Comparison between Tiny-YOLO and ReSTiNet

The entire testing time is calculated for 1208 images from the "INRIA Person" dataset using the Tesla K80. Table 4 shows the average test time, total parameter, and FLOPs for both Tiny-YOLO and ReSTiNet models. As observed, the overall time needed to detect 1208 images using the ReSTiNet is less than 40 s. ReSTiNet outperforms Tiny-YOLO in terms of detection speeds. Tiny-YOLO completes the detection in more than 74 s. When compared to Tiny-YOLO, the detection speed of ReSTiNet is improved by 49.2%. On the other hand, it has been observed that ReSTiNet has 80.90% less parameters than Tiny-YOLO, and the FLOP's amount is also reduced by 34.47%.

Table 4. Detection time, parameter, and FLOP comparison.

	Tiny-YOLO	ReSTiNet	Dataset
Avg. test time	74.486 (s)	37.514 (s)	INRIA
Model parameters	11.043 (m)	2.109 (m)	-
FLOPs	11.552 (bn)	7.570 (bn)	-

4.6. ReSTiNet Performance Comparison with Other Lightweight Methods

ReSTiNet is compared with the other lightweight state-of the-art networks, such as MobileNet, SqueezeNet, and Tiny-YOLO in order to analyze the proposed model's further improvement. The "Pascal VOC" customized dataset is used to train the MobileNet and SqueezeNet models. The training operation is performed on the Tesla k80, which operates in similar experimental settings as ReSTiNet.

The comparative findings of the four models are summarized in Table 5. As shown in Table 5, ReSTiNet outperforms Tiny-YOLO and MobileNet in terms of model size and achieves higher mAP compared with all three models. The model size of SqueezeNet is very impressive, while resulting in very low mAP. The proposed model is 10.7 MB, which is larger than SqueezeNet yet smaller than MobileNet and TinyYOLO. Compared with Tiny-YOLO, ReSTiNet reduces the model size of 82.31%, which is suitable for portable devices. ReSTiNet shows 51.09%, 35.38%, and 53.67% improvements in terms of mAP on Tiny-YOLO, MobileNet, and SqueezeNet, respectively.

Table 5. ReSTiNet vs. other lightweight models.

Network	mAP (%)	Model Size (MB)
MobileNet	47.12	13.5
SqueezeNet	41.51	3.0
Tiny-YOLO	42.21	60.50
ReSTiNet	63.79	10.7

5. Performance Analysis of ReSTiNet

Tiny-YOLO is used as the backbone architecture for the proposed ReSTiNet model. As Tiny-YOLO has several layers with 512 and 1024 filters, it has a large number of parameters, its speed is slow, and its model size is large. A replacement is carried out, thereby using the fire module instead of the sixth, seventh, and eighth layer present in the Tiny-YOLO method as the fire module contains far lower numbers of parameters as opposed to its counterpart filter of size 3×3.

The input channels also decreased to the filters with a size of 3×3. Then, by multiplying the number of filters as well as the input channel values, the net parameters present in the fire module can be calculated. By reducing the input channel and filter count, a deep CNN network can be designed containing only fewer number of parameters. Table 6 shows that the parameters that are reduced in the layer containing 256 filters are numerically lower relative to the layer with 512 filters.

Table 6. Parameter numbers comparison between fire modules and convolutional layers.

Conv. Layer	Input Channel	Output Channel	Kernel Size	Conv. Layer (Parameters)	Fire Module (Parameters)
1	3	16	3	448	184
2	16	32	3	4680	740
3	32	64	3	18,496	2888
4	64	128	3	73,856	11,408
5	128	256	3	295,168	45,344
6	256	512	3	1,180,160	180,800
7	512	1024	3	4,719,616	722,048
8	1024	512	3	4,719,616	722,048

If the goal is to further decrease the number of model parameters, a replacement with a larger number of channel inputs in the convolutional layer is required while distributing such layers in the middle and the end components of the ReSTiNet module.

It was found that the accuracy of detection becomes poor if fire modules substitute the total convolutional layers since fire modules replace certain convolutional layers with a limited number of filters. If the convolutional layers (first five) with a fewer number (less than 256) of convolution filters are retained instead of being substituted by fire modules, the rate of accuracy can improve by 6.2 percent and the size of model can increase by 1.6 megabyte. Thus, ReSTiNet retains the frontal (first five) convolutional layers while replacing the convolutional layers (three) with eight fire modules at the end of Tiny-YOLO.

A simplistic method to compress the network is to decrease the number of layers in the network, network scaling factor, and to utilize networks that are considered shallow. However, the degree of freedom to efficiently compress such networks is limited and more distant from existing DNN models [58]. Ba et al. [59] suggested a training procedure of shallow neural networks that best simulates the deep models, but there has been an increase in the number of parameters. In study [60], the authors had shown that the degree of expansion possesses the capability to be exponentially grown as a function of increasing depth. However, networks that are too shallow do not play the role of substitution for deeper networks. As illustrated in Figure 4, there are five pooling layers after the five convolutional layers. It contains a total of eight fire modules with a depth value of 2 followed by convolutional layer with a kernel size 1×1 in the ReSTiNets architecture.

The above mentioned eight fire modules in ReSTiNets replaced the three convolutional layers from the last layer in Tiny-YOLO. As a result, the net depth attains a value of 29, which is exactly twelve layers deeper in physical depth compared to Tiny-YOLO thereby raising the network's accuracy.

All max-poolings are set to 3×3 in size followed by the down-sampling technique later within the architecture. This in turn yields several layers with large activation maps [61]. Such layers provide activation maps with a minimum of 1×1 spatial resolution and typically in higher orders at other times.

Activation maps' width and height can be determined using a set of variables, namely the input data size and various choices of layers in which down-sampling more likely tends to occur. The down-sampling strategy has been accomplished in studies [62–64] using a stride that is larger than one during a choice of convolutional or pooling layers. It was concluded that a large number of layers contain smaller activation maps when the initial layers are set to larger stride parameters. The authors in [65] detected improved classification accuracies after implementing down-sampling strategies into four distinct CNN networks [53].

Then, residual connections are integrated to examine whether it can increase the efficacy of the Tiny-YOLO network while making the model quicker and smaller at the same time. The concept of the fire module [23] is modified by adding residual connections at strategic locations across the network. The model does not experience an increase in complexity apart from a bit of computation associated with the collection operation as the residual connections do not have any parameters. This model employs the dropout layer to handle the over-fitting issue and speed up data processing. The dropout method disregards the randomly chosen neurons during the training period.

Figures 6 and 7 show the detection results for both proposed ReSTiNet and Tiny-YOLO models. From all figures, it can be seen that the proposed model detects human objects with a higher accuracy, while Tiny-YOLO can sometimes miss objects and recognize non-human objects as human. These scenarios are shown in Figures 6c and 7b . The proposed ReSTiNet sometimes misses people in a dense scenario shown in Figure 7a. In this scenario, there are five people on the wall. Of these five people, ReSTiNet detected only four. However, the detection rate is still better than that of Tiny-YOLO, which detected only two out of the five people, but the proposed method can still be improved. The images showing the results of the detection are available in full size at the following URLs: Figure 6: https://i.ibb.co/6FhDYf5/P1-comp.png (accessed on 4 September 2022); Figure 7: https://i.ibb.co/tDs6xPB/P2-comp.png (accessed on 4 September 2022).

The ReSTiNet architecture that has been suggested has a significantly reduced number of parameters while also preserving a greater amount of information flow throughout the model. It detects humans more quickly than other lightweight models, and its performance in terms of detection time and mAP score is superior to that of those models. This is despite the fact that the model itself is quite compact.

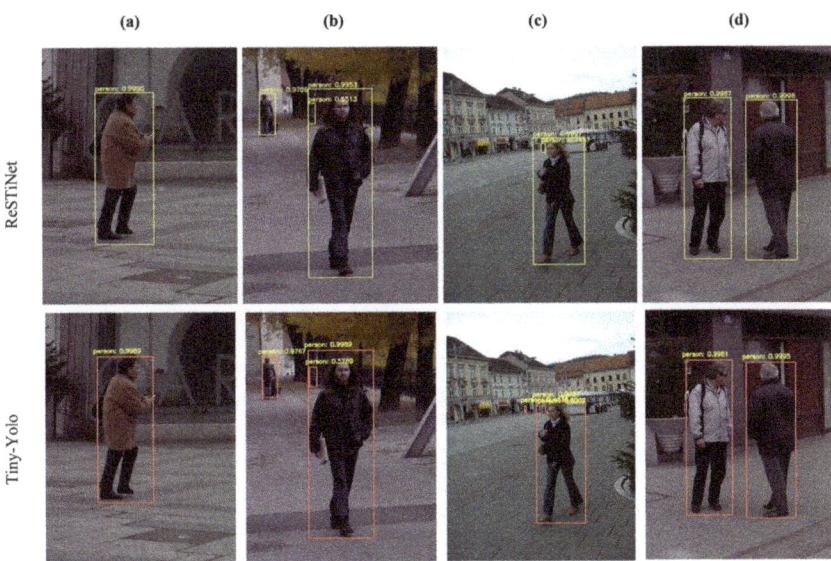

Figure 6. Detection results with confidence values for the proposed ReSTiNet and Tiny-YOLO model in a sparse scenario. (**a**–**d**) presents comparison for four images for the models.

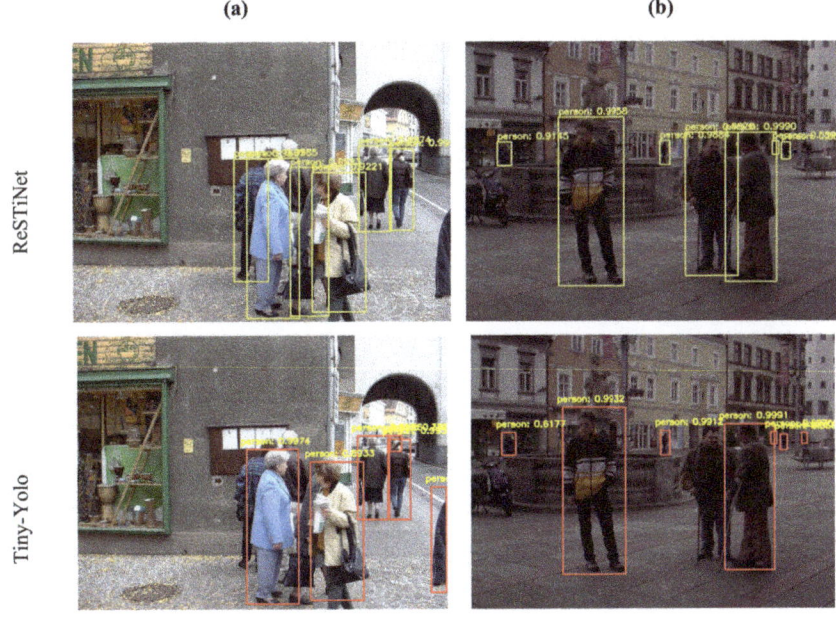

Figure 7. Detection results with confidence values for proposed ReSTiNet and Tiny-YOLO model in a dense scenario. (**a**,**b**) presents comparison for two images for the models.

6. Conclusions

In this article, ReSTiNet, a compact human-detection method, is proposed for portable devices, and it focuses on issues related to size, speed, and accuracy. The suggested method reduces the size of the previously popular Tiny-YOLO algorithm while improving the following characteristics: improving detection performance, reducing model size, resolving overfitting issues, and outperforming existing lightweight models in terms of mAP. ReSTiNet is constructed by first incorporating the fire modules from SqueezeNet inside the Tiny-YOLO with the aim of minimizing the model's size. Following that, the fire module numbers and their placement have been investigated in the model's architecture. The residual connection inside the fire modules in Tiny-YOLO is integrated from the Resnet model. The residual connection helps maximize feature propagation and information flow within the network, with the aim of further improving the developed ReSTiNet's detection speed and accuracy. Using the dropout layer in the convolutional layer and at the end of the fire module helps resolve the overfitting problem in ReSTiNet. The experimental results show that ReSTiNet outperforms Tiny-YOLO in terms of efficiency. ReSTiNet also exhibits comparable performances when compared to lightweight models such as MobileNet and SqueezeNet with respect to the model's size and mAP. The findings show the effectiveness of ReSTiNet for portable devices. The developed algorithm can be simply modified and completely incorporated into a variety of different deep convolutional neural networks for compression. The performance of ReSTiNet will be further optimized in future for high-resolution images, particularly for the EuroCity Persons dataset.

Author Contributions: Conceptualization, S.S.S., D.R.A.R. and S.M.; methodology, S.S.S., D.R.A.R. and S.M.; software, S.S.S., M.M.E. and M.S.U.M.; validation, D.R.A.R., S.M., M.M.E. and M.S.U.M.; investigation, S.S.S., D.R.A.R., S.M., M.M.E. and M.S.U.M.; writing—original draft preparation, S.S.S.; writing—review and editing, S.S.S., D.R.A.R., S.M., M.M.E. and M.S.U.M.; supervision, D.R.A.R. and S.M.; funding acquisition, D.R.A.R. All authors have read and agreed to the published version of the manuscript.

Funding: YUTP-FRG (Cost Centre 015LCO-242), Universiti Teknologi PETRONAS (UTP), funded this work.

Institutional Review Board Statement: Not applicable.

Informed Consent Statement: Not applicable.

Data Availability Statement: Not applicable.

Acknowledgments: The authors would like to extend their gratitude to the High Performance Computing Centre (HPCC), Department of Computer and Information Sciences, Universiti Teknologi PETRONAS, Malaysia, for providing opportunities in the use of resources.

Conflicts of Interest: The authors declare no conflict of interest.

References

1. Ansari, M.; Singh, D.K. Human detection techniques for real time surveillance: A comprehensive survey. *Multimed. Tools Appl.* **2021**, *80*, 8759–8808. [CrossRef]
2. Everingham, M.; Van Gool, L.; Williams, C.K.; Winn, J.; Zisserman, A. The pascal visual object classes (voc) challenge. *Int. J. Comput. Vis.* **2010**, *88*, 303–338. [CrossRef]
3. Mahmmod, B.M.; Abdul-Hadi, A.M.; Abdulhussain, S.H.; Hussien, A. On computational aspects of Krawtchouk polynomials for high orders. *J. Imaging* **2020**, *6*, 81. [CrossRef] [PubMed]
4. Haq, E.U.; Jianjun, H.; Li, K.; Haq, H.U. Human detection and tracking with deep convolutional neural networks under the constrained of noise and occluded scenes. *Multimed. Tools Appl.* **2020**, *79*, 30685–30708. [CrossRef]
5. Kim, K.; Oh, C.; Sohn, K. Personness estimation for real-time human detection on mobile devices. *Expert Syst. Appl.* **2017**, *72*, 130–138. [CrossRef]
6. Sumit, S.S.; Rambli, D.R.A.; Mirjalili, S. Vision-Based Human Detection Techniques: A Descriptive Review. *IEEE Access* **2021**, *9*, 42724–42761. [CrossRef]
7. Zhao, Z.Q.; Zheng, P.; Xu, S.T.; Wu, X. Object detection with deep learning: A review. *IEEE Trans. Neural Netw. Learn. Syst.* **2019**, *30*, 3212–3232. [CrossRef]
8. Shao, Y.; Zhang, X.; Chu, H.; Zhang, X.; Zhang, D.; Rao, Y. AIR-YOLOv3: Aerial Infrared Pedestrian Detection via an Improved YOLOv3 with Network Pruning. *Appl. Sci.* **2022**, *12*, 3627. [CrossRef]
9. Road Traffic Injuries. 2022. Available online: https://www.who.int/news-room/fact-sheets/detail/road-traffic-injuries (accessed on 2 March 2022).
10. García, F.; García, J.; Ponz, A.; De La Escalera, A.; Armingol, J.M. Context aided pedestrian detection for danger estimation based on laser scanner and computer vision. *Expert Syst. Appl.* **2014**, *41*, 6646–6661. [CrossRef]

11. Ritchie, H.; Hasell, J.; Mathieu, E.; Appel, C.; Roser, M. Terrorism. *Our World in Data.* 2019. Available online: https://ourworldindata.org/terrorism (accessed on 2 March 2022).
12. Idrees, H.; Soomro, K.; Shah, M. Detecting humans in dense crowds using locally-consistent scale prior and global occlusion reasoning. *IEEE Trans. Pattern Anal. Mach. Intell.* 2015, *37*, 1986–1998. [CrossRef]
13. Kalayeh, M.M.; Basaran, E.; Gökmen, M.; Kamasak, M.E.; Shah, M. Human semantic parsing for person re-identification. In Proceedings of the IEEE Conference on Computer Vision and Pattern Recognition, Salt Lake City, UT, USA, 18–22 June 2018; pp. 1062–1071.
14. Sumit, S.S.; Watada, J.; Roy, A.; Rambli, D. In object detection deep learning methods, YOLO shows supremum to Mask R-CNN. *J. Phys. Conf. Ser.* 2020, *1529*, 042086. [CrossRef]
15. Luna, C.A.; Losada-Gutiérrez, C.; Fuentes-Jiménez, D.; Mazo, M. Fast heuristic method to detect people in frontal depth images. *Expert Syst. Appl.* 2021, *168*, 114483. [CrossRef]
16. Fuentes-Jimenez, D.; Martin-Lopez, R.; Losada-Gutierrez, C.; Casillas-Perez, D.; Macias-Guarasa, J.; Luna, C.A.; Pizarro, D. DPDnet: A robust people detector using deep learning with an overhead depth camera. *Expert Syst. Appl.* 2020, *146*, 113168. [CrossRef]
17. Kim, D.; Kim, H.; Mok, Y.; Paik, J. Real-Time Surveillance System for Analyzing Abnormal Behavior of Pedestrians. *Appl. Sci.* 2021, *11*, 6153. [CrossRef]
18. Wang, W.; Li, Y.; Zou, T.; Wang, X.; You, J.; Luo, Y. A novel image classification approach via dense-MobileNet models. *Mob. Inf. Syst.* 2020, *2020*, 7602384. [CrossRef]
19. Fang, W.; Wang, L.; Ren, P. Tinier-YOLO: A real-time object detection method for constrained environments. *IEEE Access* 2019, *8*, 1935–1944. [CrossRef]
20. Yim, J.; Joo, D.; Bae, J.; Kim, J. A gift from knowledge distillation: Fast optimization, network minimization and transfer learning. In Proceedings of the IEEE Conference on Computer Vision and Pattern Recognition, Honolulu, HI, USA, 21–26 July 2017; pp. 4133–4141.
21. Han, S.; Mao, H.; Dally, W.J. Deep compression: Compressing deep neural networks with pruning, trained quantization and huffman coding. *arXiv* 2015, arXiv:1510.00149.
22. Hubara, I.; Courbariaux, M.; Soudry, D.; El-Yaniv, R.; Bengio, Y. Quantized neural networks: Training neural networks with low precision weights and activations. *J. Mach. Learn. Res.* 2017, *18*, 6869–6898.
23. Iandola, F.N.; Han, S.; Moskewicz, M.W.; Ashraf, K.; Dally, W.J.; Keutzer, K. SqueezeNet: AlexNet-level accuracy with 50x fewer parameters and< 0.5 MB model size. *arXiv* 2016, arXiv:1602.07360.
24. Howard, A.G.; Zhu, M.; Chen, B.; Kalenichenko, D.; Wang, W.; Weyand, T.; Andreetto, M.; Adam, H. Mobilenets: Efficient convolutional neural networks for mobile vision applications. *arXiv* 2017, arXiv:1704.04861.
25. Zhang, X.; Zhou, X.; Lin, M.; Sun, J. Shufflenet: An extremely efficient convolutional neural network for mobile devices. In Proceedings of the IEEE Conference on Computer Vision and Pattern Recognition, Salt Lake City, UT, USA, 18–22 June 2018; pp. 6848–6856.
26. He, K.; Zhang, X.; Ren, S.; Sun, J. Deep residual learning for image recognition. In Proceedings of the IEEE Conference on Computer Vision and Pattern Recognition, Las Vegas, NV, USA, 27–30 June 2016; pp. 770–778.
27. Nguyen, D.T.; Li, W.; Ogunbona, P.O. Human detection from images and videos: A survey. *Pattern Recognit.* 2016, *51*, 148–175. [CrossRef]
28. Sabzmeydani, P.; Mori, G. Detecting pedestrians by learning shapelet features. In Proceedings of the 2007 IEEE Conference on Computer Vision and Pattern Recognition, Minneapolis, MN, USA, 17–22 June 2007; pp. 1–8.
29. Dalal, N.; Triggs, B. Histograms of oriented gradients for human detection. In Proceedings of the International Conference on Computer Vision & Pattern Recognition (CVPR'05), San Diego, CA, USA, 20–26 June 2005; IEEE Computer Society: Washington, DC, USA, 2005; Volume 1, pp. 886–893.
30. Mu, Y.; Yan, S.; Liu, Y.; Huang, T.; Zhou, B. Discriminative local binary patterns for human detection in personal album. In Proceedings of the 2008 IEEE Conference on Computer Vision and Pattern Recognition, Anchorage, AK, USA, 23–28 June 2008; pp. 1–8.
31. Viola, P.; Jones, M.J.; Snow, D. Detecting pedestrians using patterns of motion and appearance. *Int. J. Comput. Vis.* 2005, *63*, 153–161. [CrossRef]
32. Dalal, N.; Triggs, B.; Schmid, C. Human detection using oriented histograms of flow and appearance. In Proceedings of the European Conference on Computer Vision, Graz, Austria, 7–13 May 2006; pp. 428–441.
33. Xu, Y.; Xu, D.; Lin, S.; Han, T.X.; Cao, X.; Li, X. Detection of sudden pedestrian crossings for driving assistance systems. *IEEE Trans. Syst. Man Cybern. Part B (Cybern.)* 2011, *42*, 729–739.
34. Felzenszwalb, P.; McAllester, D.; Ramanan, D. A discriminatively trained, multiscale, deformable part model. In Proceedings of the 2008 IEEE Conference on Computer Vision And Pattern Recognition, Anchorage, AK, USA, 23–28 June 2008; pp. 1–8.
35. Ouyang, W.; Wang, X. Joint deep learning for pedestrian detection. In Proceedings of the IEEE International Conference on Computer Vision, Sydney, Australia, 1–8 December 2013; pp. 2056–2063.
36. Zeng, X.; Ouyang, W.; Wang, X. Multi-stage contextual deep learning for pedestrian detection. In Proceedings of the IEEE International Conference on Computer Vision, Sydney, Australia, 1–8 December 2013; pp. 121–128.

37. Luo, P.; Tian, Y.; Wang, X.; Tang, X. Switchable deep network for pedestrian detection. In Proceedings of the IEEE Conference on Computer Vision and Pattern Recognition, Columbus, OH, USA, 23–28 June 2014; pp. 899–906.
38. Cai, Z.; Saberian, M.; Vasconcelos, N. Learning complexity-aware cascades for deep pedestrian detection. In Proceedings of the IEEE International Conference on Computer Vision, Santiago, Chile, 7–13 December 2015; pp. 3361–3369.
39. Tian, Y.; Luo, P.; Wang, X.; Tang, X. Pedestrian detection aided by deep learning semantic tasks. In Proceedings of the IEEE Conference on Computer Vision and Pattern Recognition, Boston, MA, USA, 7–12 June 2015; pp. 5079–5087.
40. Li, J.; Liang, X.; Shen, S.; Xu, T.; Feng, J.; Yan, S. Scale-aware fast R-CNN for pedestrian detection. *IEEE Trans. Multimed.* **2017**, *20*, 985–996. [CrossRef]
41. Zhang, L.; Lin, L.; Liang, X.; He, K. Is faster R-CNN doing well for pedestrian detection? In Proceedings of the European Conference on Computer Vision, Graz, Austria, 7–13 May 2016; pp. 443–457.
42. Liu, J.; Gao, X.; Bao, N.; Tang, J.; Wu, G. Deep convolutional neural networks for pedestrian detection with skip pooling. In Proceedings of the 2017 International Joint Conference on Neural Networks (IJCNN), Anchorage, AK, USA, 14–19 May 2017; pp. 2056–2063.
43. Xu, C.; Wang, G.; Yan, S.; Yu, J.; Zhang, B.; Dai, S.; Li, Y.; Xu, L. Fast Vehicle and Pedestrian Detection Using Improved Mask R-CNN. *Math. Probl. Eng.* **2020**, *2020*, 5761414. [CrossRef]
44. Kim, B.; Yuvaraj, N.; Sri Preethaa, K.; Santhosh, R.; Sabari, A. Enhanced pedestrian detection using optimized deep convolution neural network for smart building surveillance. *Soft Comput.* **2020**, *24*, 17081–17092. [CrossRef]
45. Brunetti, A.; Buongiorno, D.; Trotta, G.F.; Bevilacqua, V. Computer vision and deep learning techniques for pedestrian detection and tracking: A survey. *Neurocomputing* **2018**, *300*, 17–33. [CrossRef]
46. Lan, X.; Ma, A.J.; Yuen, P.C.; Chellappa, R. Joint sparse representation and robust feature-level fusion for multi-cue visual tracking. *IEEE Trans. Image Process.* **2015**, *24*, 5826–5841. [CrossRef]
47. Jeon, H.M.; Nguyen, V.D.; Jeon, J.W. Pedestrian detection based on deep learning. In Proceedings of the IECON 2019-45th Annual Conference of the IEEE Industrial Electronics Society, Lisbon, Portugal, 14–17 October 2019; Volume 1, pp. 144–151.
48. Chebrolu, K.N.R.; Kumar, P. Deep learning based pedestrian detection at all light conditions. In Proceedings of the 2019 International Conference on Communication and Signal Processing (ICCSP), Chennai, India, 4–6 April 2019; pp. 0838–0842.
49. Mateus, A.; Ribeiro, D.; Miraldo, P.; Nascimento, J.C. Efficient and robust pedestrian detection using deep learning for human-aware navigation. *Robot. Auton. Syst.* **2019**, *113*, 23–37.
50. Liu, S.a.; Lv, S.; Zhang, H.; Gong, J. Pedestrian detection algorithm based on the improved ssd. In Proceedings of the 2019 Chinese Control And Decision Conference (CCDC), Nanchang, China, 3–5 June 2019; pp. 3559–3563.
51. Zhou, T.; Wang, W.; Qi, S.; Ling, H.; Shen, J. Cascaded human-object interaction recognition. In Proceedings of the IEEE/CVF Conference on Computer Vision and Pattern Recognition, Seattle, WA, USA, 14–19 June 2020; pp. 4263–4272.
52. Zhou, T.; Wang, W.; Liu, S.; Yang, Y.; Van Gool, L. Differentiable multi-granularity human representation learning for instance-aware human semantic parsing. In Proceedings of the IEEE/CVF Conference on Computer Vision and Pattern Recognition, Nashville, TN, USA, 19–25 June 2021; pp. 1622–1631.
53. Qassim, H.; Verma, A.; Feinzimer, D. Compressed residual-VGG16 CNN model for big data places image recognition. In Proceedings of the 2018 IEEE 8th Annual Computing and Communication Workshop and Conference (CCWC), Las Vegas, NV, USA, 8–10 January 2018; pp. 169–175.
54. Hochreiter, S.; Schmidhuber, J. Long short-term memory. *Neural Comput.* **1997**, *9*, 1735–1780. [CrossRef]
55. Srivastava, N.; Hinton, G.; Krizhevsky, A.; Sutskever, I.; Salakhutdinov, R. Dropout: A simple way to prevent neural networks from overfitting. *J. Mach. Learn. Res.* **2014**, *15*, 1929–1958.
56. Rennie, S.J.; Goel, V.; Thomas, S. Annealed dropout training of deep networks. In Proceedings of the 2014 IEEE Spoken Language Technology Workshop (SLT), South Lake Tahoe, NV, USA, 7–10 December 2014; pp. 159–164.
57. Lin, T.Y.; Maire, M.; Belongie, S.; Hays, J.; Perona, P.; Ramanan, D.; Dollár, P.; Zitnick, C.L. Microsoft coco: Common objects in context. In Proceedings of the European Conference on Computer Vision, Zurich, Switzerland, 6–12 September 2014; pp. 740–755.
58. Dauphin, Y.N.; Bengio, Y. Big neural networks waste capacity. *arXiv* **2013**, arXiv:1301.3583.
59. Ba, L.J.; Caruana, R. Do deep nets really need to be deep? *arXiv* **2013**, arXiv:1312.6184.
60. Poole, B.; Lahiri, S.; Raghu, M.; Sohl-Dickstein, J.; Ganguli, S. Exponential expressivity in deep neural networks through transient chaos. *Adv. Neural Inf. Process. Syst.* **2016**, *29*, 3360–3368.
61. Dean, J.; Corrado, G.; Monga, R.; Chen, K.; Devin, M.; Mao, M.; Ranzato, M.; Senior, A.; Tucker, P.; Yang, K.; et al. Large scale distributed deep networks. *Adv. Neural Inf. Process. Syst.* **2012**, *25*, 1223–1231.
62. Krizhevsky, A.; Sutskever, I.; Hinton, G.E. Imagenet classification with deep convolutional neural networks. In Proceedings of the Advances in Neural Information Processing Systems, Lake Tahoe, NV, USA, 3–6 December 2012; pp. 1097–1105.
63. Simonyan, K.; Zisserman, A. Very deep convolutional networks for large-scale image recognition. *arXiv* **2014**, arXiv:1409.1556.
64. Ioffe, S.; Szegedy, C. Batch normalization: Accelerating deep network training by reducing internal covariate shift. In Proceedings of the International Conference on Machine Learning, PMLR, Lille, France, 6–11 July 2015; pp. 448–456.
65. He, K.; Sun, J. Convolutional neural networks at constrained time cost. In Proceedings of the IEEE Conference on Computer Vision and Pattern Recognition, Boston, MA, USA, 7–12 June 2015; pp. 5353–5360.

Article

Systematic Machine Translation of Social Network Data Privacy Policies [†]

Irfan Khan Tanoli [1,*,‡,§], Imran Amin [1,§], Faraz Junejo [1,§] and Nukman Yusoff [2,*,§]

1 Departement of Computer Science, SZABIST, Karachi 75600, Sindh, Pakistan
2 Department of Engineering Design and Manufacture, Faculty of Engineering, University of Malaya, Kuala Lumpur 50603, Malaysia
* Correspondence: dr.irfankhan@szabist.pk (I.K.T.); nukman@um.edu.my (N.Y.)
† This paper is extended version of the paper "*Towards automatic translation of social network policies into controlled natural language*" published in *2018*, *12th International Conference on Research Challenges in Information Science (RCIS)*.
‡ Current address: SZABIST, Karachi 75600, Sindh, Pakistan.
§ These authors contributed equally to this work.

Citation: Tanoli, I.K.; Amin, I.; Junejo, F.; Yusoff, N. Systematic Machine Translation of Social Network Data Privacy Policies. *Appl. Sci.* **2022**, *12*, 10499. https://doi.org/10.3390/app122010499

Academic Editor: Valentino Santucci

Received: 6 September 2022
Accepted: 11 October 2022
Published: 18 October 2022

Publisher's Note: MDPI stays neutral with regard to jurisdictional claims in published maps and institutional affiliations.

Copyright: © 2022 by the authors. Licensee MDPI, Basel, Switzerland. This article is an open access article distributed under the terms and conditions of the Creative Commons Attribution (CC BY) license (https://creativecommons.org/licenses/by/4.0/).

Abstract: With the growing popularity of online social networks, one common desire of people is to use of social networking services for establishing social relations with others. The boom of social networking has transformed common users into content (data) contributors. People highly rely on social sites to share their ideas and interests and express opinions. Social network sites store all such activities in a data form and exploit the data for various purposes, e.g., marketing, advertisements, product delivery, product research, and even sentiment analysis, etc. Privacy policies primarily defined in Natural Language (NL) specify storage, usage, and sharing of the user's data and describe authorization, obligation, or denial of specific actions under specific contextual conditions. Although these policies expressed in Natural Language (NL) allow users to read and understand the allowed (or obliged or denied) operations on their data, the described policies cannot undergo automatic control of the actual use of the data by the entities that operate on them. This paper proposes an approach to systematically translate privacy statements related to data from NL into a controlled natural one, i.e., CNL4DSA to improve the machine processing. The methodology discussed in this work is based on a combination of standard Natural Language Processing (NLP) techniques, logic programming, and ontologies. The proposed technique is demonstrated with a prototype implementation and tested with policy examples. The system is tested with a number of data privacy policies from five different social network service providers. Predominantly, this work primarily takes into account two key aspects: (i) The translation of social networks' data privacy policy and (ii) the effectiveness and efficiency of the developed system. It is concluded that the proposed system can successfully and efficiently translate any common data policy based on an empirical analysis performed of the obtained results.

Keywords: natural language; controlled natural language; natural language processing; privacy policies; social networks; machine learning

1. Introduction

The advent of Online Social Networks (OSNs) allows users to establish and maintain interpersonal relations among people without any boundaries [1]. OSN interactions usually require exchanging users' data for numerous purposes, including the provisioning of services. However, by offering such services for virtual social interaction and data sharing, OSNs also raised user privacy issues by having access to personal data and exposing it, such as blogs, videos, images, or user profile information, e.g., name, date of birth, phone number, email, etc. This shared data leaves traces that may disclose users' activities and their opinions, norms, consent, and beliefs. OSNs usually regulate the collection, usage, and sharing of users' data (e.g., Facebook [2], Twitter [3], Google [4]), etc. in terms of privacy policies. Usually, the policies [5] published in English describe the terms and conditions under which the provider will manage the data in terms of, e.g., authorization, obligation, or denial. Although the use of English as a natural language enables end-users to read and understand the operations allowed (or obliged, or denied) on their data, a key fact exists that a plain Natural Language (NL) cannot be used as the input language for a policy-based software infrastructure dedicated to automatic policy management and machine readability [6]. Both automated policy analysis (the process to assure the lack of conflicting data policies, see, e.g., [7]) and policy enforcement (the actual application of the data policies, whenever a data access request takes place) require machine-readable language as inputs, such as the standard XACML [8].

An approach proposed for translating Natural Language (NL) data privacy policies [6] as they appear on an OSN website into a Controlled Natural Language (CNL) is the so-called *Controlled Natural Language for Data Sharing Agreements (CNL4DSA)* [9–11]. The system refers to 'Natural Language Policy Translator (Natural Language Policy Translator (NLPT) 1.0)', which outlined the policy translation on a small set of Facebook data privacy policies [6].

This paper presents the extended prototype version of *'Natural Language Policy Translator (NLPT) 1.0'*, [6] the so-called *'Natural Language Policy Translator (NLPT) 2.0'*, with improvements from the previous version. The system (*NLPT 2.0*) is equipped with a user-friendly Graphical User Interface (GUI), and it is composed of different components, i.e., *Policy Parser (PP), Policy Processor (PR), Ontology Builder (OB), Fragment Extractor (FE), Context Extractor (CE),* and *Controlled Natural Language (CNLT)* (details of each component is discussed in Section 5). The system (*NLPT 2.0*) simply allows non-expert users to write or input policies in Natural Language (NL) sentences, and the system automatically translates it into CNL4DSA. To validate the system's performance, it is tested with five popular social network platforms' data privacy policies, i.e., Twitter [3], Facebook [2], Google [4], Instagram [12] and LinkedIn [13]. Moreover, the system is also designed to assist researchers in evaluating the specification of social networks' data privacy policies but can also be utilized for the other application domains (e.g., e-health, e-commerce, etc.).

The rest of the paper is outlined as follows: Section 2 gives an overview of the Controlled Natural Languages (CNLs). Section 3 explores the previous literature work. Section 4 describes the proposed methodology. Section 5 depicts the overall architecture of the system. Section 6 presents the experimental setup. Section 7 explains the results and analysis. Finally, Section 8 concludes the work with possible future directions.

2. Controlled Natural Language

Generally, formal languages have been proposed and used as knowledge representation languages as they are designed with proper well-defined syntax and unambiguous semantics and support automated reasoning [14]. However, their syntaxes and semantics are quite complex for domain experts to understand and recognize and cause a cognitive distance to the application domain that is not inherent in the Natural Language (NL). One approach to bridge the gap between natural and formal ones is the utilization of Controlled Natural Language (CNL) and full Natural Languages (NLs), developed with well-defined grammar and vocabulary to make statements more understandable and unambigious [15,16]. CNLs have certain writing rules that are, in general, easier for humans to understand and easier for machines to process [14]. CNLs are generally defined in the literature with attributes such as *processable, human-readable, structured* and *simplified* [17]. Controlled Natural Language (CNL) approaches has evolved in different environments based on the requirements, i.e., different specifications in the context of industry, academia, and government, as well as in different disciplines, i.e., artificial intelligence, computer science, linguistics, biology, literature, etc., since 1930 till today [17].

CNLs have been classified into two broad categories: human-oriented and machine-oriented [18]. Both are built for different purposes and have various applications. Human-oriented CNLs are designed to help humans read and understand technical documents, e.g., ASD Simplified Technical English [19], and to make human-to-human interactions simpler in certain situations, for instance, air traffic control [20]. Machine-oriented CNLs are designed for the Semantic Web to improve the translation of technical documents and enhance knowledge representation and processing [14]. These languages facilitate the technical document's translatability, e.g., [21], and the acquisition, representation, and processing of knowledge (e.g., for knowledge systems [22] and, in particular, for the Semantic Web [16].

2.1. CNL4DSA

CNL4DSA, *Controlled Natural Language for Data Sharing Agreements*, is chosen as a target language. This language was introduced in [9,23], within the EU projects Consequence (Consequence: http://www.consequence-project.eu/) and Coco Cloud (Coco Cloud: http://www.coco-cloud.eu/) and successfully applied to the pilots of the two projects. It is equipped with analytic tools, i.e., a policy authoring tool, a policy analyzer, and conflict solver, and a policy mapper of enforceable language. CNL4DSA was originally developed for editing so-called *data sharing agreements* (formal contracts regulating data sharing), allowing a simple and readable, yet formal, specification of different classes of privacy policies, as listed below:

- **Authorizations**, referring to permission for subjects to perform actions on object under a specific context.
- **Prohibitions**, expressing the fact that a subject cannot perform actions on an object under a specific context.
- **Obligations**, referring to subjects obliged to perform actions on objects under a specific context.

CNL4DSA relies on the notion of *fragments*, tuples of the form $f = \langle s, a, o \rangle$, where s is the subject, a is the action, o is the object. A fragment simply says that 'subject s performs action a on object o'. By adding *can/must/cannot* constructs to the basic fragment, a fragment becomes either an authorization, obligation, or prohibition. In the scenario of social networks, subjects are usually physical or legal entities (e.g., users and service providers), actions are, e.g., collect, login, etc., while objects consist of any data published on the social network or stored on its servers, e.g., the personal details of a Facebook account, content created by the social network users, or the data policies themselves.

Fragments are assessed in a certain *context*. A context is assessed as a Boolean value (true/false) in CNL4DSA. It makes claims about the characteristics of subjects and objects in words such as user's roles, data categories, date, and location. Simple context examples are 'subject hasRole Facebook_admin', or 'object hasCategory user_post'. It predicates the constructs that connect subjects and objects to their values, such as hasRole and hasCategory in the examples above. Contexts must be mixed to define complicated policies. Therefore, the Boolean connectors *and*, *or*, and *not* are used to indicate a composite context C, which is defined inductively as follows :

$$C := c \mid C \text{ and } C \mid C \text{ or } C \mid \text{not } c$$

The syntax of a *composite fragment* denoted as F_A is as follows:

$$F := nil \mid can, must, cannot\ f \mid F; F \mid if\ C\ then\ F \mid after\ f\ then\ F$$

- *nil* can do nothing.
- *can, must, cannot f* is the atomic fragment that expresses that f is allowed/require/not permitted, where $f = \langle s, a, o \rangle$. Its informal meaning is *the subject s can perform action a on the object o*.
- *F; F* is a list of composite fragments (i.e., a list of authorizations, obligations, or prohibitions).
- *if C then F* expresses the logical implication between a context C and a composite fragment: if C holds, then F is allowed/required/not allowed.
- *after f then F* is a temporal sequence of fragments. Informally, after f has happened, then the composite fragment F is allowed/required/not allowed.

Additionally, the syntax used by CNL4DSA to represent composite obligation and prohibition fragments are unique. The obligation fragment, such as the authorizations, states that *the subject s must perform action a on the object o*, whereas *the subject s cannot execute action a on the object o* is stated for the prohibition.

2.2. Scenario Examples

Consider the example of an emergency situation in which many cars are engaged in a collision, including a tanker [23]. Firefighters, Red Cross paramedics, and toxicologists all rush to help the wounded. Firefighters and Red Cross volunteers are referred to as 'rescuers' or 'Rescuers' in a general sense (complete details available in [23]).

Consider the following sample cases:

1. P1: Firefighters can access the victim's personal and medical information.
2. O1: Once the alert states of the accidents have been determined by the Red Cross members, if it is larger than five, they must then inform the local community of the alert level.
3. PT1: Non-firemen cannot access tanker delivery notes that are currently in progress.

The expression of P1 in CNL4DSA are as follows:

$$\text{IF c THEN CAN f}$$

where:

- c = hasRole(user1, fireman) and hasDataCategory(data, personal) and hasDataCategory(data, medical) and isReferredTo(data, user2) and isInvolvedIn(user2, accident) is a composite context.
- f = can access(user1, data) is a composite authorization fragment.

The expression of O1 in CNL4DSA are as follows:

$$\text{IF c THEN MUST f}$$

where:

- c = hasRole(user1, RedCross) and hasDataCategory(data, alertState) then after that access(user1, data) then if isGreaterThan(alertState,five).
- f = must communicate(user1,data) is a composite obligation fragment.

The expression of PT1 in CNL4DSA are as follows:

$$\text{IF c THEN CANNOT f}$$

where:

- c = not hasRole(user1,fireman) and hasDataCategory(data, deliveryNote) and isReferredTo(data,truck) then cannot access(user1, data) where not hasRole(user1, fireman) and hasDataCategory(data,deliveryNote) and isReferredTo(data,truck) is a composite context.
- f = cannot access(user1, data) is a composite prohibition fragment.

The impetus for selecting CNL4DSA as the aim translation's language is due to the following facts: first, as proposed in [9], composite fragments have formal semantics that are described by *modal transition systems*. Because of this, the language may be formally analyzed, even using already available tools such as *Maude* [24]; for instance, the authors of [7,25] show the automated analysis of data sharing and privacy policies completely; second, the CNL4DSA is equipped with an editor with a dedicated authoring tool, having preloaded domain-specific vocabularies in the form of ontologies, understandable for machine translation, and can be automatically mapped into a low-level language, namely XACML [8], which enables seamless policy enforcement.

3. Related Work

Controlled Natural Languages (CNLs) are generally discussed in the literature with characteristics such as *easy to process*, *human-readable*, *structured* and *simplified* [17]. Controlled Natural Languages (CNLs) are more contrived subsets of Natural Languages (NLs), whose representation—including grammar, syntax, semantics, and vocabulary—have been developed in a simple but more efficient way to reduce and mitigate the ambiguity and complexity of natural language and make it feasible for machine processing [14]. A variety of CNLs have been proposed for different purposes by researchers of diverse expertise and background [17], e.g., Tateish et al. [26] propose an approach to automatically generate a smart contract from a Natural Language (NL) contract document that is defined using a document template and a Controlled Natural Language (CNL). The system is based on the mapping of the document template and the Controlled Natural Language (CNL) to a formal model that can describe the terms and conditions in a contract, including temporal constraints and procedures. The formal model is translated into an executable smart contract. A framework for tax fraud detection was developed by Calafato et al. [27], where the fraud expert is empowered to design tax fraud patterns through a Controlled Natural Language (CNL) independently. Colombo et al. [28] suggested a Controlled Natural Language (CNL) that maintains machine readability while allowing non-technical users to make queries that are simple to comprehend.

The automatic and unambiguous translation from a Controlled Natural Language (CNL) to first-order logic is demonstrated by Fuchs et al. [22]. Originally intended to be a specification language, the language has evolved to focus on knowledge representation and applications for working with the Semantic Web [17]. A tool known as 'RuleCNL (a CNL for creating business rules) incorporates formal syntax and semantics to enable business professionals to formalize their business rules in a business-friendly manner that machines can understand [29]. The key feature of 'RuleCNL' is the business rule definition alignment with the business vocabulary that assures consistency and traceability in this domain.

Brodie et al. [30] developed a policy workbench called 'SPARCLE' for parsing privacy policy rules in Natural Language (NL). 'SPARCLE' enables organizational users to enter policies in Natural Language (NL), parse the policies to identify policy elements, and then generate a machine-readable Extensible Markup Language (XML) version of the policy. The work is empirically evaluated from the usability perspective by targeting organizational privacy policies. This results in the successful implementation of the parsing capabilities to provide a usable and effective method for an organization to map the natural language version of privacy policies to their implementation and subsequent verification through compliance auditing of the enforcement records.

Fisler et al. [31] provided an authoring language based on Datalog-like formats as input for the policy editor. The work emphasizes the social and environmental aspects that can influence the interpretation and specification of trust and privacy policies. Kiyavitskaya et al. [32] proposed a methodology that delivered the transformation of natural language into semi-structured specifications. The approach suggests a mechanism to support designers during requirements elicitation, modeling, and analysis.

Fantechi et al. [33] provided a tool that formalizes the behavioral needs of reactive systems into a process algebra and converts natural language phrases into ACTL (Action-based Temporal Logic). A logic-based framework for policy analysis was developed by Craven et al. [34] that enables the expression of responsibilities and authorizations offers practical diagnostic data and allows for dynamic system modeling. Fockle et al. [35] created a model-driven development-based methodology for requirements engineering. For documentation, elicitation, and requirements negotiation, the system depends on requirements models and a controlled natural language. Through a bidirectional, multi-step model transformation between two documentation forms, the methodology combines the advantages of model-based and natural language documentation.

A graphical visual interface with an adequate level of abstraction was developed by Mousas et al. [36] to allow users to specify fundamental ideas for privacy protection, such as values for roles, activities, data kinds, rules, and contextual information. Ruiz et al. [37] developed a software infrastructure to handle data sharing agreements (DSA), which govern data access, usage, and sharing. The framework permits DSA editing, analysis, and enforcement. The input language used by the authoring tool to edit the DSA is 'CNL4DSA' [9]. The CNL4DSA provides easy yet explicit specifications for many privacy policy kinds, including authorizations, obligations, and prohibitions. The language can be automatically mapped into a low-level language, XACML [8], thus enabling seamless policy enforcement.

The approach proposed by Tanoli et al. [6] is one of the few initiatives to bridge the gap between modifying and processing a Controlled Natural Language (CNL), such as CNL4DSA, and maintaining complete readability of privacy policies by expressing them in a natural language. The approach relies on standard and well-established Natural language Processing (NLP) techniques, e.g., Crossley et al. [38], the Natural Language Toolkit [39], the Stanford CoreNLP [40], Spacy [41] and the adoption of ontologies [42].

4. Design Approach

This section highlights an overview of the design approach for semi-automatically translating natural language data privacy policies into CNL4DSA. A prototype console-based system referred to as 'Natural Language Policy Translator (NLPT) 1.0' is designed to translate the data policy into CNL4DSA [6]. The core of the approach relies upon three phases: (i) Natural Language Processing (NLP); (ii) building ontologies; (iii) translation into CNL4DS using logic programming. The various steps are depicted in Figure 1. (The complete details following step-by-step policy translation, as shown in Figure 1, are discussed in [6]).

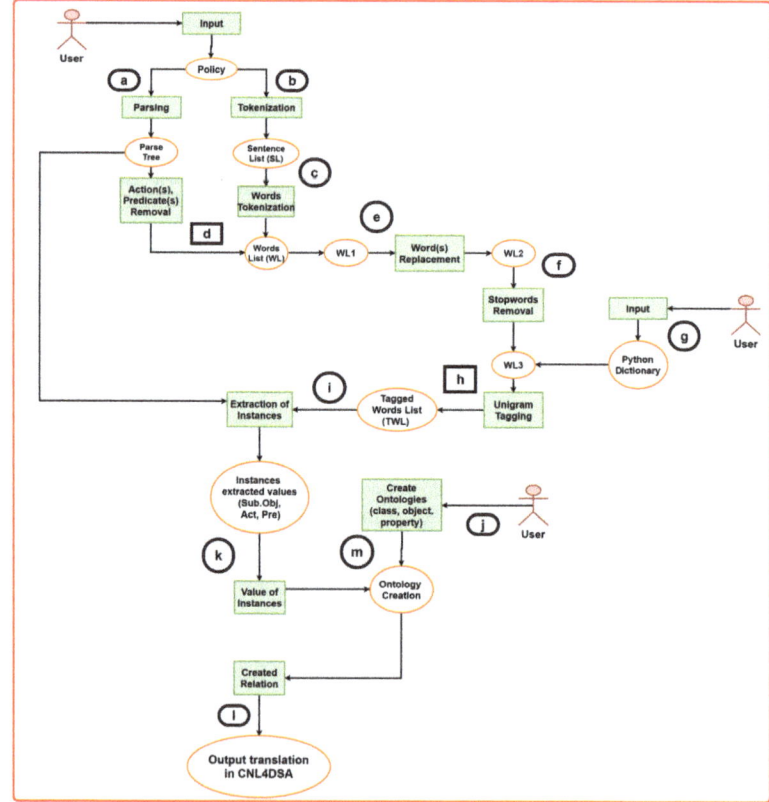

Figure 1. Pictorial representation of the system operations.

4.1. Policy Translation Using Natural Language Policy Translator (NLPT) 1.0

To explain the process of three phases, consider the following subset of the Facebook data privacy policy as a case example—available at [43].

P1: *"We collect the content and other information you provide when you use our Services [...]"*

Policy P1 is an authorization policy, allowing the social networking service provider to collect information provided by the user when the user interacts with the platform services.

P1 as an authorization policy in CNL4DSA:

The CNL4DSA representation of the policy P1:

IF c1 THEN CAN f1

where:

- c1 = subject1 hasRole *'social_networking_service_provider'* AND (object1 hasCategory *'content'* OR object1 hasCategory *'other_information'*) AND (subject2 provides object1 OR subject2 provides object1) AND subject2 hasRole *'user'* AND subject2 uses *'social_networking_service'* is a composite context.
- f1 = subject1 collect object1 is an atomic fragment.

In the above translation, for the sake of a more direct understanding, the term *'we'* of the original policy is substituted with *'social_networking_service_provider'*, the term *'you'* with *'user'*, and the term *'service'* with *'social_networking_service'*.

4.1.1. Natural Language Processing

The first phase of the translation process is the application of Natural Language Processing (NLP) techniques to policy P1. The goal of this phase is to automatically derive, from the sentences in Natural Language (NL), the standard elements of a data policy (i.e., subject, object, and action), as well as the typical constructs of CNL4DSA (i.e., fragments and contexts).

Following standard NLP approaches, a data policy is first parsed and then represented in a tree form, using a syntactic dependency parser (step (a) in Figure 1). A dependency parser shows syntactical dependencies among individual words in a sentence, as well as among the main sub-sentence and its subordinates. For our goals, the dependency parser is used to discriminate among actions and predicates for those cases in which the predicate in the sentence is under a verbal form. Such concepts are illustrated with the following example.

Considering P1, it is needed to automatically verify whether 'collect' is the action element of the policy (as it is, see fragment f1 defined in the CNL4DSA representation of P1) or part of a context. To meet the goal, the dependency parser is used. This enables picking up the verb(s) of the main sentence and labeling them as action(s), while the verb(s) in the subordinate's sentences will be tagged as predicates. In this case, the system recognizes the terms 'provide' and 'use' as predicates. Finally, it is worth noting that other predicates, e.g., 'hasRole' and 'hasCategory', will be defined in a subsequent phase during the definition of ontologies (Section 4.1.2).

Upon considering different parsers, i.e., the Stanford parser [44], the one provided by the NLTK toolkit [39], and the one provided by the SpaCy Python package [41], the latter is found to be fast and accurate enough to parse the sentences. Figure 2 shows the resulting tree after applying the SpaCy dependency parser to P1.

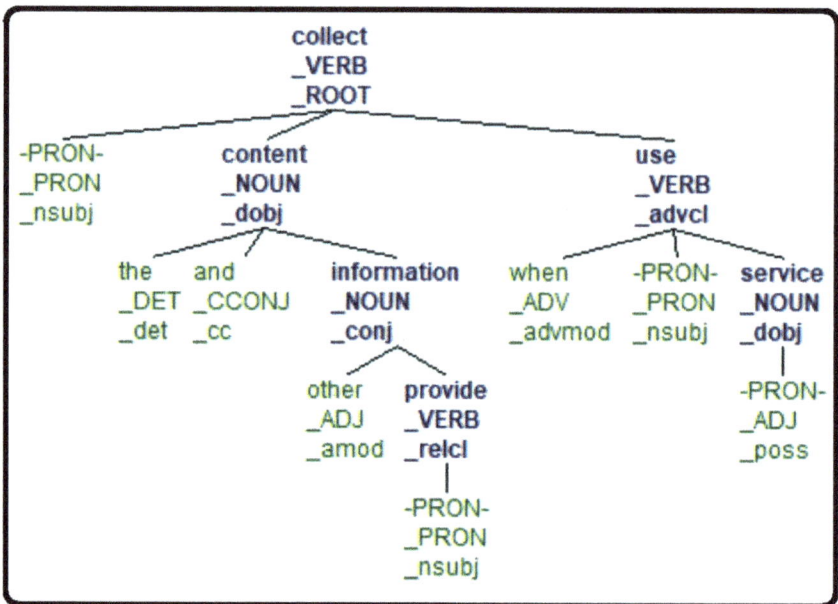

Figure 2. P1 upon dependency parser processing.

Referring to Figure 1, the data policy is also split into single sentences, using a sentence tokenizer—step (b). Each sentence is further divided into words, using a word tokenizer—step (c). Plurals are substituted with their singular forms, and different forms of verbs are led back to their first form using the NLTK lemmatizer [39]. Upon step (c), a word list WL is obtained.

In the specific case of P1, the NLTK word tokenizer and the SpaCy dependency parser treat the two terms 'other and information' as two separate words (see, e.g., Figure 2). For the sake of the next processing phase, the two terms have been then manually replaced with a single one *'other_information'* by relying on the Python string replace method [45].

```
Sentences are tokenized:
['we collect the content and other_information
you provide when you use our services]

Words are tokenized:
['we', 'collect', 'the', 'content', 'and',
'other_information', 'you', 'provide','when',
'you', 'use', 'our', 'service']
```

From WL, the terms that constitute the actions and the predicates are removed, as identified by the dependency parsing operations, as well as duplicate items if there are any in a list. The actions and predicates removal corresponds to step (d) in Figure 1. In the second list of words, WL1 is obtained.

```
Action and Predicates removal:
['we', 'the', 'content', 'and','other_information',
'you', 'when', 'our', 'service']
```

In next phase of word replacement, in which in WL1 is replaced with a few ambiguous words with a more precise meaning. In P1, for example, the term 'service' is replaced with 'social_networking_service', 'we' with 'social_networking_ service_provider', 'you' with 'user'. The replacement happens according to a manually pre-defined list of words: the tool replaces such words accordingly. It is worth noting that, in the prototype implementation presented in the work [6], automatic co-reference detection is not considered. Although a current limitation of the approach, it is argued that this necessary refinement can be applied in future work, possibly using existing tools for automatic co-reference detection. A modified list of WL2 is obtained.

```
Words replacement with meaningful words:
['social_networking_service_provider','the',
'content', 'and', 'other_information','user',
'when', 'our', 'social_networking_service']
```

Then, a list of stop words is used to remove words, such as articles *an*, *a*, *the*, etc., prepositions, e.g., *in*, *on*, etc., and adverbs, e.g., *before* (step f). As words for removal, the pre-defined NLTK stop words list [39] is applied. The modified list WL3 is obtained.

```
Stop words removal:
['social_networking_service_provider','content',
'other_information','user','social_networking_
service']
```

As already discussed at the beginning of Section 4.1.1, it is required to identify each data policy:

1. The subjects, the objects, and the actions;
2. The contexts and fragments, as required by the CNL4DSA language.

It is worth mentioning that actions and (part of) predicates are already identified during the application of the dependency parser. The Unigram Tagger [46] is exploited to label the tokenized words in WL3 as subjects or objects. The UnigramTagger class implements a simple statistical tagging algorithm: for each token, it sets the most likely label for that type of token. For example, it assigns the 'JJ' (adjective) tag to any occurrence of the word 'frequent' since it is mostly used as an adjective (e.g., *a frequent word*) rather than as a verb (e.g., *I often frequent this place*).

Before actually using the Unigram Tagger to tag the data, it must be trained on the tagged Python dictionary. The creation of the training dictionary happens once, on a set of initial words. For subsequent words, the user will update the dictionary with the possibly encountered new terms, which are not in the original set of terms, until no major update is needed. The tool prompts a message for the user to define a Python dictionary tagged according to a privacy policies terminology—step (g). The user can define as many terms as possible so that the tagging machine can automatically label the words that will appear in subsequent data policies. The use of the Unigram Tagger in this work is specific to tag terms as either subject or object. In addition, the tagger also considers the terms expressing authorizations, prohibitions, and obligations (such as *can*, *must*, and *cannot*).

```
##############################################
Do you want to define a training dictionary?
'Y' or 'N' => Y
Please define a Python dictionary, e.g.,
'user':'subject', 'data':'object'
##############################################
Please proceed with dictionary (subject, object,
as keys) => 'social_networking_service_provider':
'subject','user':'subject','other_user':'subject'
Dictionary Data =>
{'social_networking_service_provider':'subject',
'user':'subject','other_user':'subject'}
##############################################

##############################################
Updated Dictionary =>{'other_information':'object',
'device':'object','data':'object', 'information':
'object','user':'subject','must':'obligation',
'content': 'object','can_not': 'prohibition',
'can':'authorization',
'social_networking_service':'object',
'other_user': 'subject',
'social_networking_service_provider':'subject'}
```

After running the Unigram Tagger on P1—step (h), the following list of tagged words (TWL) is obtained:

```
Words tagged according to policy elements:
[[('social_networking_service_provider','subject'),
('content', 'object'),('user', 'subject'),
('other_information','object'),
('social_networking_service', 'object')]]
```

Regarding the distinction among authorizations, prohibitions, and obligations, the following simple procedure is adopted. The keywords *can, should, may* in the original Natural Language (NL) statement lead to considering the policy an authorization. The keywords *can not, should not, shall not, must not* (and relative contracted forms) lead to considering the policy a prohibition. Finally, the keywords *must, shall, will* characterize obligations. The choice is made following the interpretation given in RFC2119 [47].

Additionally, terms *should* and *may* are replaced with *can* during the replacement phase. Similarly, *shall not should not, must not* are replaced with *cannot*, while *shall* and *will* are replaced with *must*. Whenever such keywords appear in the original policy statement, the tool labels them accordingly. However, a current limitation of the approach is that, if such keywords do not appear in the natural language statement, the tool treats the statement as an authorization policy. This is exactly what happens in the case of P1.

Finally, to handle incorrect tagging, when the user defines the Python dictionary, the allowed keys for tags are only: subject, object, authorization, prohibition, and obligation. When more than one term is tagged as subject (resp., as object), the labels are subject1, subject2, ..., subjectn (resp., object1, ..., objectn). The same holds for actions and predicates when applying the dependency parser.

Regarding the formation of the CNL4DSA contexts, the next Section 4.1.2 will show how to link objects and subjects to predicates employing ontologies.

4.1.2. Building Ontologies

An ontology is a explicit formal description of a domain of interest [48]. A specific ontology-based vocabulary is defined, inherent to the scenario of privacy policies, which defines terms representing, e.g., categories for objects (such as posts, content, picture, etc.), roles for subjects (such as the user, social networking service providers, Facebook provider, etc.), identifiers for subjects and objects (e.g., John Doe, pic12345) and terms for actions (such as read, send, access, store). Then, the ontology defines the relations between all the terms in the vocabulary. Relations are established using predicates, e.g., hasRole, hasCategory, isTime, hasLocation, etc. Owl ontologies [49] and Owl ready [42], a Python module, are used to load them.

The classes: subject, object, action, category, and role are defined. Below is an example of class declaration—step (j) in Figure 1.

```
class Category(ObjVocabItem):
ontology=onto
```

The predicates are hasRole, hasCategory, provide and use. In Owl ready, these predicates are called object properties. The object properties create relations between the classes. Examples of object properties are:

```
class hasCategory(ObjectProperty):
domain=[Object], range=[Category]
```

or

```
class hasRole(ObjectProperty):
domain=[Subject], range=[Role]
```

As an example, hasCategory is an object property with the domain class Object and range class Category. Moreover, the predicates hasRole and hasCategory are created manually through ontologies, while the predicates use and provide are obtained by the application of the dependency parser. As a remark, hasCategory and hasRole are object properties of the ontology classes. In Owlready, they are declared with the following syntax: 'class hasCategory (ObjectProperty)', where ObjectProperty syntax refers to the predicate as object property [42]. 'Collect' is defined as a functional property; it has only one value, and it is created by inheriting the FunctionalProperty class [42]:

```
class collect(FunctionalProperty):
domain=[Collect], range = [str]
```

The relations are defined as follows: subject1 hasRole: 'subject1', subject2 hasRole: 'subject2', object1 hasCategory: 'object1','subject2' provide 'object1', 'subject2' provide 'object1', and subject2 use 'object3'.

Figure 3 shows the ontology representation of P1, created using Protégé [50], where Thing is the main ontology class and Term, Action, and ObjVocabitem are the ontology subclasses. Furthermore, Term has Subject and Object as subclasses and Objvocabitem has Category, Subject, Object, Role, etc. To establish relations between subject and object, object properties are used. As an example, to establish a relation between subject and role class, the hasRole object property is used.

To conclude this step, the actual values of subject1, subject2, object1, object2, and object3, as well as the values for action(s) and predicate(s), are required: the subject and object values are extracted from the policy tagged-tokens and create the instances—step (i). Actions and predicates values are extracted from the dependency parsing tree, as follows:

```
Extracted Values for Subject, Action, Object,
Predicate: Subject1 is:  ['social_networking_service_provider']
Subject2 is: ['user'], Object1 is: ['content'] Object2 is:
['other_information'],
Object3 is: ['social_networking_service']
Action1 is: ['collect'], Predicate1 is: ['provide']
Predicate2 is: ['use']
```

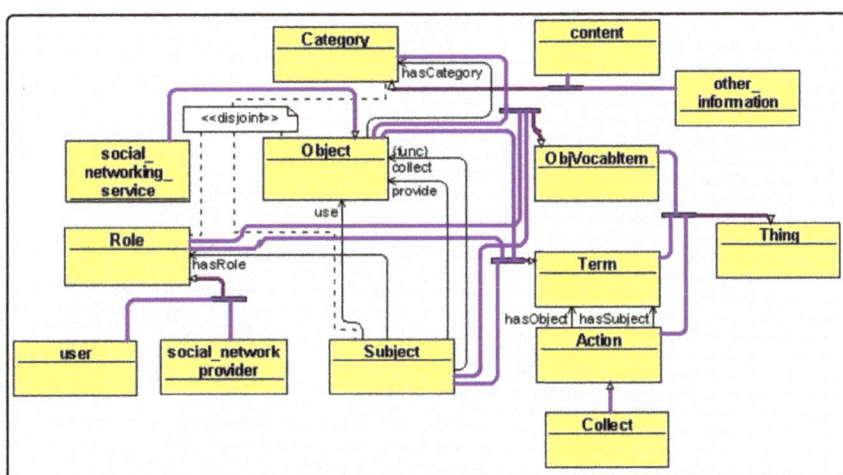

Figure 3. Ontology representation for P1.

4.1.3. Translation into CNL4DSA

In the final phase, the extracted values for the various instances of subject and object are passed as arguments to the ontology classes previously defined—steps (k), (l), (m). As an example, subject1, with value *'social_networking_service_provider'*, is passed to the Role class, and the relation between the subject and the Role class is established through *has_Role*; object1, with value *content*, is passed to the Category class, and the relation between the object and the Category class is established through *has_Category*.

```
print ('IF subject1 hasRole:',Subject1.hasRole)
output: IF subject1 hasRole: [onto.'social_networking_service_provider']
```

Similarly, the action 'collect' is passed as an argument to the Action class. The printed output represents the translation of the natural language data policy into CNL4DSA. The outputs are stored in variables c1 and f1:

IF c1 THEN CAN f1

where:

```
c1 = subject1 hasRole: [onto.social_networking_service_provider]
AND (object1 hasCategory: [onto.content] OR object2 hasCategory:
[onto.other_information]) AND subject2 hasRole: [onto.user] AND
(subject2 [onto.user] provide object1:[onto.content] OR
subject2 [onto.user] provide object2 [onto.other_information])
AND subject2 [onto.user] use [onto.social_networking_service]
is a composite context.
f1 = subject1 (action): [collect] object1 is an atomic fragment.
```

onto is the Python variable that is used to modify, save, and load ontologies, for example: onto = *get_ontology* [42]. The example of obligation and prohibition policy is presented and discussed in the work [6].

5. Architecture and Graphical User Interface

In Section 4, the mechanism of the social network data privacy policy translation into CNL4DSA is demonstrated. Initially, the system was designed to translate only a limited set of Facebook data privacy policies [2]. Here, an improved new prototypical version of *Natural Language Policy Translator (NLPT) 1.0* is referred to as *Natural Language Policy Translator (Natural Language Policy Translator (NLPT) 2.0)*. The major development in the *NLPT 2.0* is that it is equipped with a user-friendly graphical interface to directly input the policy, and the system is capable enough to translate any common social network data privacy policies defined in Natural Language (NL) into CNL4DSA.

Natural Language Policy Translator (NLPT) 2.0 is composed of the following components:

- *Policy Parser (PP)*
- *Policy Processor (PR)*
- *Ontology Builder (OB)*
- *Fragment Extractor (FE)*
- *Context Extractor (CE)*
- *Controlled Natural Language Translator (CNLT)*

The translation of the policy is split among these components to ease the user into understanding the translation process, which was not possible in the previous version ('Natural Language Policy Translator (NLPT) 1.0').

The high-level architecture of the system '*(Natural Language Policy Translator (NLPT)) 2.0*' is presented in Figure 4.

The detailed working of each component is as follows:

Policy Writer: A person or entity who properly enters the policy is known as the "Policy Writer". To prevent potential incorrect/wrong tagging performed by the policy parser, a policy writer is essential. The *Policy Writer* just needs to be an end-user who is aware of the proper way to write/enter the policy in the system. They do not need to be a Controlled Natural Language (CNL) expert or a domain specialist. A *Policy Manual* with all essential instructions on how to write/input the policy is provided to train the *Policy Manual*. The *Policy Manual* is a document that outlines a process for properly combining Subject, Verb, and Object (SVO) in an original policy by giving various policy examples [51].

The introduction of the *Policy Writer* role is diverse since writing styles are used by online service providers to describe the policies, and if a privacy statement is lengthy and complex, it is possible that it may contain several distinct predicates. As a result, it is possible that the dependency parser incorrectly tags some policy terms or fails to appropriately parse the statement. These problems also directly affect the translation of policy, especially in terms of the extraction of actions and predicates.

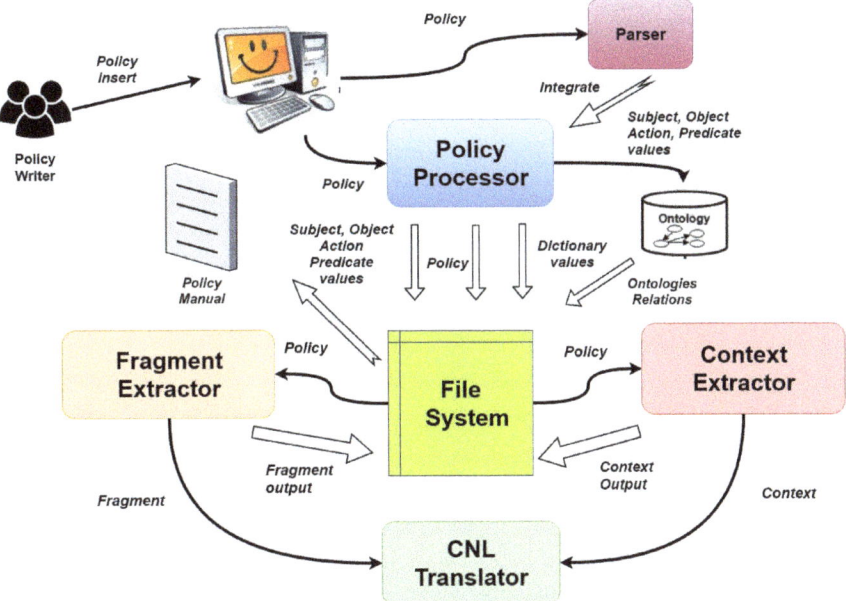

Figure 4. System architecture *Natural Language Policy Translator (NLPT) 2.0*.

Consider the following Facebook policy example:

Policy M1: 'We also collect contact information if you choose to upload, sync, or import it from a device [...]' [43]. .

When the *Policy Writer* inputs M1 in *Natural Language Policy Translator (NLPT) 2.0*, and upon processing M1 using the policy parser, the following output is generated, as shown in Figure 5.

The Policy Parser (PP) labels 'sync' as a noun, but this should be tagged as a verb. However, the policy writer can rephrase the policy following policy manual guidelines to specify it properly, i.e., the parser tags the words properly with the right combination of Subject, Verb, and Object (SVO).

An adequate rephrasing is:

Rephrase M1: 'We also collect data if you choose_to _upload data or you sync data, or you import data from a device.

When using the system once on M1, it is apparent that with the right rephrasing, the parser correctly tags 'sync' as a verb, as demonstrated in Figure 6. It is important to note that for better and more precise tagging, words such as 'information', 'content', 'contact information, 'content and information', etc., are replaced with the general term 'data'. An infinitive form verb, e.g., 'decide to signup', (_) is introduced, i.e., 'choose_to _upload', which makes the *Natural Language Policy Translator (NLPT) 2.0* consider infinitive verb(s) as a single word.

Policy Parser (PP): The policy parser simply parses the policy using the Spacy dependency parser [41] to obtain action and predicate(s), as already properly explained in Section 4.

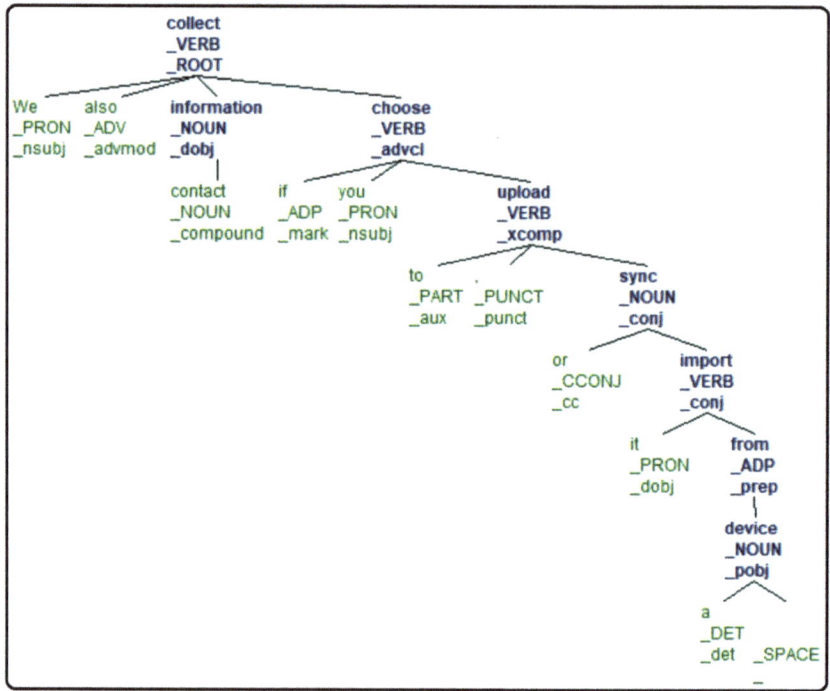

Figure 5. Policy (M1) upon dependency parser processing.

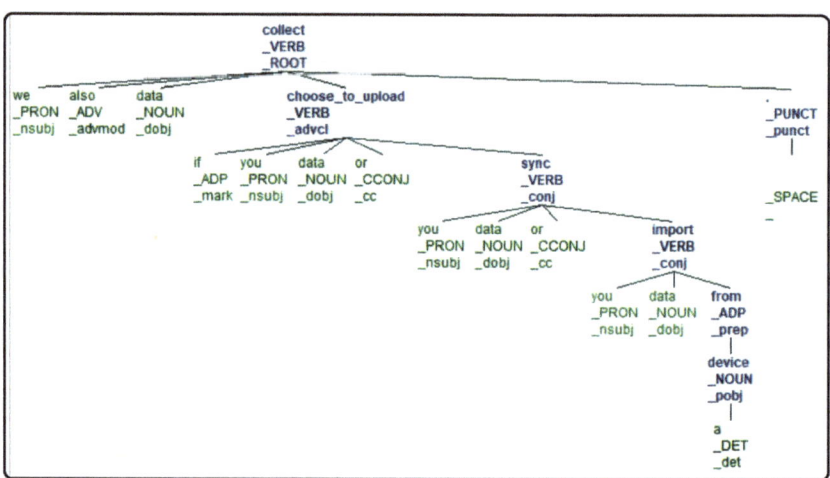

Figure 6. Rephrase-policy (M1) upon dependency parser processing—3.

Policy Processor (PR): Policy processor (PR) applies sentence and word tokenization, removes stop-words, and creates a dictionary for extra stop-words. For uni-gram tagging, it allows creating the dictionary containing subject(s) and object(s) in the policy. *PR* is entirely developed with the combination of NLTK [39], and Spacy [41]. The results of this processing are then saved in a file using the Python OS.System function.

Ontology Builder (OB): The identified subjects, objects, actions, and predicates are provided as input to the *Ontology Builder*, which is already furnished with some pre-defined predicates, such as 'object/subject isRelatedto', 'object/subject isPartof', and 'object/subject hasCategory', for objects, and 'subject hasRole, hasID', and "object hasOwner'. The subject, object, action, category, predicate, id, owner, and role classes are all specified. Owlready, a python package to load ontologies is utilized to implement the *Ontology Builder*. Each time a new predicate is needed to process the policy, the ontology vocabulary is manually updated. The *Context Extractor (CE)* will use the result after storing it in a file.

Fragment Extractor (FE): 'Subject Action Object' is a policy fragment that is extracted by *Fragment Extractor (FE)*. For fragment recognition, this component is implemented in a policy using logic programming; specifically, it translates the subject, action, and object to the values determined by *Policy Processor (PR)*. For instance, the *FE* extracts the fragment *'we collect data'*: *'subject action object'*. The result is once more recorded in a separate file, saved to the file system, and utilized by the *Controlled Natural Language Translator (CNLT)* afterward.

Context Extractor (CE): The CNL4DSA context is extracted from the policy by *Context Extractor (CFE)*. The output of the *Ontology Builder* is also recalled to obtain any contexts with the predicates 'hasRole' and 'hasCategory'. *Fragment Extractor (FE)* and *Context Extractor (CFE)* are created using logic programming. Concerning policy M1, the anticipated output is:

subject hasRole: 'we' AND subject hasRole: 'you' AND object hasCategory: 'data' AND subject (you) predicate (choose_to_upload) object (data) AND subject (you) predicate (sync) object (data) AND subject (you) predicate (import) object (data) is a composite context.

The acquired output is saved once more in a different file and utilized later by the *Controlled Natural Language Translator (CNLT)*.

Controlled Natural Language Translator (CNLT): The outputs of *Fragment Extractor (FE)* and *Context Extractor (CFE)* are simply retrieved from the file system by *Controlled Natural Language Translator (CNLT)*, which then displays the policy translation in CNL4DSA. *Controlled Natural Language Translator (CNLT)* can also categorize the obtained output as authorization, obligation, and prohibition fragments.

Complete Translation into Controlled Natural Language (CTCNL) is developed with a mechanism that orchestrates the components to process the translation all at once. It does this by first calling the *Policy Parser (PP)*, then the *Policy Processor (PR)*, *Ontology Builder (OB)*, *Fragment Extractor (FE)*, *Context Extractor (CFE)*, and *Controlled Natural Language Translator (CNLT)*. The full process flow of the translation is depicted in Figure 7 as a single iteration.

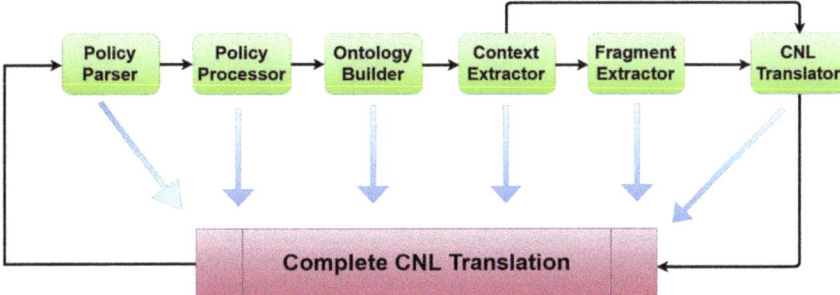

Figure 7. Complete Controlled Natural Language (CNL) translation process.

Figure 8 display the Graphical User Interface of*Natural Language Policy Translator (NLPT) 2.0*. The *Graphical User Interface (GUI)* is developed with Python GUI Generator (PAGE) [52]. The are shown on the window's right and bottom sides (in the form of buttons).

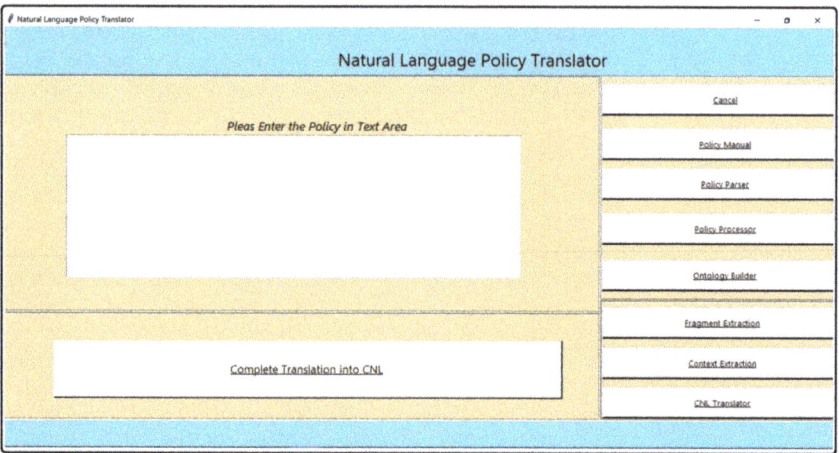

Figure 8. *NLPT 2.0* graphical user interface.

6. Experimental Social Networks Policies

The experimental setup was established based on the evaluation criteria to analyze the overall system performance. The components of the *Natural Language Policy Translator (CNLT) 2.0* are tested with five social networks' data privacy policies. The objective of the experiment is simply to check whether *Natural Language Policy Translator (NLPT) 2.0* is efficient enough to translate any common data privacy policy in the social network domain. To carry out the experiments, the subset of five different popular social network services' data privacy policies are gathered, i.e., Facebook [2], Twitter [3], Google [4], Instagram [12], and LinkedIn [13].

6.1. Experimental Setup

On social networking sites, there are different policy categories listed, e.g., Facebook (https://www.facebook.com/policies_center), Twitter (https://help.twitter.com/en), Google (https://policies.google.com/?hl=en-US), LinkedIn (https://www.linkedin.com/legal/user-agreement), Instagram (https://help.instagram.com/). The policies are manually skimmed, and only such policies that deal with user data management are considered. The choice of the policies is also determined by the fact that the policies are presented in full text, even if two different policies are defined in one paragraph. The subset of a data privacy policy from sets of policies is considered. In total, 100 different data privacy policies [53] that are related to user data regulation were chosen for the experiment.

The 'one output per input' evaluation paradigm is adopted to analyze components' accuracy using the following formula [54]:

$$A = \frac{\sum_{i=1..n,agr_i}}{n} = \frac{numbercount}{n} \quad (1)$$

where agr_i is 1 if $l_i = t_i$ and 0 otherwise. Sometimes the inverse of accuracy, or error rate, is reported instead: $1 - A$. To determine the performances, the following evaluation criteria are established.

6.2. Evaluation Criteria

- How many policies are accurately parsed by *Policy Parser (PP)*, i.e., extracting action(s) and predicate(s) in a policy?
- How many times is a dictionary update required in terms of subject(s) and object(s) while processing the policy with *Policy Processor (PR)* until no update is required?

- How many times does an existing ontology have to be updated, or be created, while processing with *Ontology Builder (OB)* until no update is required?
- Can the *Fragment Extractor (FE)* accurately extract the fragment from the given policy?
- Can the *Context Extractor (CFE)* properly extract the context(s) from the input policy?
- Can the *Controlled Natural Language Translator (CNLT)* correctly classify the policy as authorization, obligation, and prohibition fragment?
- What is the success rate of *Policy Parser (PP)*, *Fragment Extractor (FE)*, *Context Extractor (CFE)* and *Controlled Natural Language Translator (CNLT)* over the total number of policies?

6.3. Experimental Operations

To maintain uniformity for components testing, the policies are processed in the following manner:

1. **Run Policy Parser**
   - Count the number of policies parsed correctly in a single iteration.
2. **Run Policy Processor**
   - Count the number of policies where it is required to update the vocabulary, with new subjects, objects, and predicates until no update is required.
3. **Run Ontology Builder**
   - Count the number of policies where it is required to create or update the ontology dictionary until no update is required.
4. **Run Fragment Extractor**
   - Count the number of fragments correctly extracted in a single iteration.
5. **Run Context Extractor**
   - Count the number of contexts correctly extracted in a single iteration.
6. **Run Controlled Natural Language (CNL) Translator**
   - Count the number of policies where a *Controlled Natural Language Translator (CNLT)* successfully identifies fragments as authorizations, obligations, and prohibitions in a single iteration.

Considering the experimental operations (Section 6.3), for example, the policy writer inputs a policy into the system and runs the policy parser in a single iteration. The obtained result from *Policy Parser (PP)* is analyzed to validate whether verbs and predicates are correctly identified, and the result is noted. Similarly, the same is performed for all other components. All *100* policies are processed according to the above-defined operations, and the obtained results for each component are stored, evaluated against the criteria defined in Section 6.2 and reported in Section 7.

The success rate of the following components, i.e., *Policy Parser (PP)*, *Fragment Extractor (FE)*, *Context Extractor (CFE)*, and *Controlled Natural Language Translator (CNLT)*, is calculated using the following formula:

Success rate formula:

$$\text{Success Rate} = \frac{X}{T} * 100$$

where:

T = Total number of policies.

X = Number of policies correctly parsed by *Policy Parser (PP)* or number of policies accurately extracted by *Fragment Extractor (FE)* and *Context Extractor (CFE)* in a single iteration or number of policies correctly recognized as authorization, obligation, and prohibition fragment by *Controlled Natural Language Translator (CNLT)*.

6.4. Performance Evaluation Criteria

Referring to the 'summarizing and comparing performance' evaluation paradigm [54], the performance metric scale for for Policy Parser (PP), Fragment Extractor (FE), Context Extractor (CFE) and Controlled Natural Language Translator (CNLT) is defined as reported in Table 1. The upper bound is set if the component's success rate is above or equal to 80% and the lower bound is above or equal to 20%.

Table 1. Performance evaluation against success rate.

Success Rate	80% >=	80% < and >=60%	60% < and >=40%	40% < and >=20%	20% <
Rating	Excellent	Above Average	Average	Below Average	Low

7. Results and Discussion

Tables 2 and 3 show the results of each component's performance with respect to the evaluation criteria described in Section 6, where the first row denotes the evaluation criteria, the first column identifies the targeted social network domain, and the other columns offer information about the evaluation. The complete results of all *100* policy translations are available at [53].

Success Rate: For Google, *Policy Parser (PP)*, *Fragment Extractor (FE)*, *Context Extractor (CFE)* and *Controlled Natural Language Translator (CNLT)* success rates are calculated as follows:

$$PP \text{ Success Rate} = (14/20) * 100 = 70\%$$

$$FE \text{ Success Rate} = (16/20) * 100 = 80\%$$

$$CE \text{ Success Rate} = (13/20) * 100 = 65\%$$

$$CNLT \text{ Success Rate} = (18/20) * 100 = 90\%$$

The computation of the success rate for the rest of the social network policies is depicted in Figure 9.

The analysis of the obtained results is as follows:

- **Google:** Out of 20 policies, 14 *(70%)* are accurately parsed by the *Policy Parser (PP)*, identifying terms either as the main action or predicate(s). Initially, the dictionary has been updated 11 times *(55%)* with new terms for subjects and objects (including seven times *(35%)* with predicates due to the wrong parser tagging). The vocabulary for ontologies required an update eight times *(40%)* manually by the *Policy Writer*. It is hypothesized as if the percentage for dictionary and ontology updates is becoming low, as the system becomes more efficient at classifying subject(s), object(s), or predicates within a policy with less human intervention.
  In total, 16 fragments *(80%)* and 13 contexts *(65%)* have been properly extracted, while for 18 policies *(90%)*, the *Controlled Natural Language Translator (CNLT)* classified terms as either authorization, obligation, or prohibition fragments.

- **Facebook:** 13 policies *(65%)* are correctly parsed by *Policy Parser (PP)*, and the dictionary and ontology are updated by the *Policy Writer* 7 *(35%)* and 4 *(20%)* times. *Fragment Extractor (FE)* classifies 17 *(85%)* fragments and *Context Extractor (CFE)* 11 *(55%)* contexts correctly. *Controlled Natural Language Translator (CNLT)* validates 16 *(80%)* policy fragments as authorizations, obligations, or prohibitions accurately.

- **Twitter:** The obtained results of Twitter appear to be quite promising. In total, 16 *(80%)* policies are correctly parsed, while there was no need to update vocabularies for ontology and terms. *Fragment Extractor (FE)* obtains 20 *(100%)* fragments accurately. A total of 16 *(80%)* contexts are correctly extracted by *Context Extractor (CFE)*. *Controlled Natural Language Translator (CNLT)* recognizes all 20 *(100%)* policies as authorization, obligation, or prohibition.

- **LinkedIn and Instagram:** For LinkedIn and Instagram, 17 *(85%)* and 16 *80* are properly parsed. The dictionary terms and ontologies are required to update only 1–2 times. *Fragment Extractor (FE)* and *Context Extractor (CFE)* obtained 18 *(90%)* fragments and 15 *(75%)* contexts for the premier, 20 *(100%)* and 15 *(75%)* for later. The performance of *Controlled Natural Language Translator (CNLT)* is *(95%)* for LinkedIn and *(100%)* for Instagram.

Table 2. Experiment results of social network data policies.

Social Network Site	Total Policies	Correct Parsing	Accurate FE	Accurate CE	Distinction by CNLT
Google	20	14 ($\approx$70%)	16 ($\approx$80%)	13 ($\approx$65%)	18 ($\approx$90%)
Facebook	20	13 ($\approx$65%)	17 ($\approx$85%)	11 ($\approx$55%)	16 ($\approx$80%)
Twitter	20	16 ($\approx$80%)	20 ($\approx$100%)	16 ($\approx$80%)	20 ($\approx$100%)
LinkedIn	20	17 ($\approx$85%)	18 ($\approx$90%)	15 ($\approx$75%)	19 ($\approx$95%)
Instagram	20	16 ($\approx$80%)	20 ($\approx$100%)	15 ($\approx$75%)	20 ($\approx$100%)
Total	100	76 ($\approx$76%)	91 ($\approx$91%)	71 ($\approx$70%)	93 ($\approx$93%)

Table 3. Experimental results of social network data policies.

Social Network Site	Number of Policies	Dictionary Update	Ontology Update
Google	20	11 ($\approx$55%)	08 ($\approx$40%)
Facebook	20	07 ($\approx$35%)	04 ($\approx$20%)
Twitter	20	0 ($\approx$0%)	0 ($\approx$0%)
LinkedIn	20	02 ($\approx$1%)	01 ($\approx$1%)
Instagram	20	01 ($\approx$1%)	0 ($\approx$0%)
Total	100	21 ($\approx$21%)	13 ($\approx$12%)

Initially, the *Natural Language Policy Translator (NLPT) 2.0* did not perform well parsing Google and Facebook policies, which also affected *Context Extractor (CFE)*'s performance. It is due to the *Policy Writer* finding difficulty in rephrasing policies. However, it is hypothesised that *Policy Writer* may gain the appropriate experience to input the policies correctly, which later happened in the case of Twitter, LinkedIn, and Instagram. This also reveals that the parser performance is relatively dependent on how the *Policy Writer* inputs policy.

The complete experimental results show that the whole performance of *Natural Language Policy Translator (NLPT) 2.0's* components is really good. In total, 76% of the policies are parsed precisely. Initially, the vocabulary for terms and ontology relations needs to be created or updated frequently by the *Policy Writer* due to new terms appearing in the policies. Once the dictionary is enriched enough with unique vocabularies and an ontologies relations lexicon, the human intervention decreases, and the system is trained enough to automatically tag the words as subject(s) and object(s) more accurately and produce proper ontology relations as in the case of Twitter, LinkedIn, and Instagram. The total accuracy of the *Fragment Extractor (FE)* and *Context Extractor (CFE)* is (91%) and (71%), respectively. The overall accuracy achieved by the *Controlled Natural Language Translator (CNLT)* is (93%).

The classification of *Policy Parser (PP)*, *Fragment Extractor (FE)*, *Context Extractor (CFE)*, and *Controlled Natural Language Translator (CNLT)* performance based on the established evaluation criterion in Table 1 is shown in Table 4. The performance of *Policy Parser (PP)* in the case of Google and Facebook is categorized as 'Above Average', while for other three, the performance appeared as 'Excellent'. The performance of *Fragment Extractor (FE)* and *Controlled Natural Language Translator (CNLT)* for all five social network policies is classified as 'Excellent'. For *Context Extractor (CFE)*, in the case of Google, LinkedIn and Instagram, the performance appeared as 'Above Average', while for Facebook, 'Average', and 'Excellent' for Twitter. The complete performance of the *Fragment Extractor (FE)* and *Controlled Natural Language Translator (CNLT)* emerged as 'Excellent' for all five social network policies and 'Above average' for *Policy Parser (PP)* and *Context Extractor (CFE)*.

Table 4. Policy Parser (PP), Fragment Extractor (FE), Context Extractor (CFE) and Controlled Natural Language Translator (CNLT) performance evaluation against success rate.

Case Study	PP Performance	FE Performance	CE Performance	CNLT Performance
Google	Above Average	Excellent	Above Average	Excellent
Facebook	Above Average	Excellent	Average	Excellent
Twitter	Excellent	Excellent	Excellent	Excellent
LinkedIn	Excellent	Excellent	Above Average	Excellent
Instagram	Excellent	Excellent	Above Average	Excellent
Total	Above Average	Excellent	Above Average	Excellent

Fragment Extractor (FE); Context Extractor (CE); Controlled Natural Language Translator (CNLT).

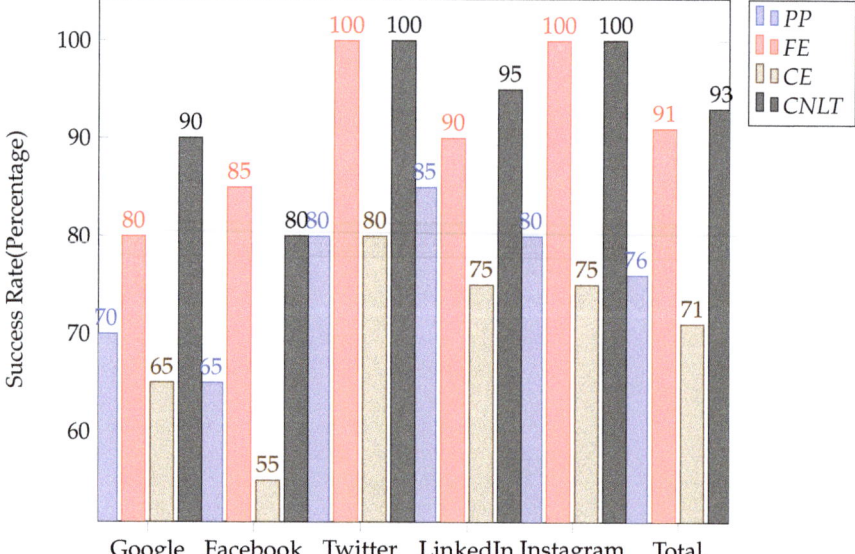

Figure 9. Performance of Policy Parser (PP), Fragment Extractor (FE), Context Extractor (CFE) and Controlled Natural Language Translator (CNLT) with respect to success rates.

During the experimentation, certain limitations and issues were observed. The policy writer found it quite difficult to rephrase the policy, which also impacts the performance of the *Policy Parser (PP)*. However, after gaining experience and the following instruction from the policy manual, it became easy to rephrase, and the *Policy Parsers (PP)* performance also improved, which can be observed in the case of Twitter, Instagram and LinkedIn, as shown in Table 2. The creation and updating of ontologies are currently manual, and we aim to make it automatic or semi-automatic in future work. The dependency parser tagging is based on how the policy is inputted. Wrong parsing may occur if the policies are composed of many complex sentences. The wrong parsing has a direct impact on the performance of

Fragment Extractor (FE) and *Context Extractor (CFE)*. The *Policy Writer* role has mitigated this issue at a certain level.

Moreover, automatic co-reference detection is not considered, and it will be assailed in future work. In addition, the complete process of translation is semi-automatic since it requires human intervention at different stages. However, it is argued that once the system is trained enough on upgraded lexicons with unique terms and ontology relations, the human interventione intervention lessens. In general, the overall performance indicators of the system's components indicate that *Natural Language Policy Translator (NLPT) 2.0* is capable of automatically translating any social network data privacy policy into a CNL4DSA.

8. Conclusions

The data management regulations on social media platforms are defined using Natural Language (NL). These policies are not machine-checkable and are mostly vague and imprecise. The tight lexicon(s), vocabulary, syntax(es), grammatical structure, and pragmatics of Controlled Natural Languages CNLs make them more suitable for machine processing. This study proposes a unique technique for handling data privacy policies by introducing the translation of their natural language descriptions into phrases that are easier for non-experts in terms of readability and usability. The goal of this work is to provide an effective and efficient approach for the formal analysis of privacy rules. The aimed language for translation is Controlled Natural Language for Data Sharing Agreement [55], which is more similar to a pure Natural Language (NL) and is easier for non-experts in terms of understandability and usability [51].

The proposed methodology is based on processing the data policies through Natural Language Processing (NLP) techniques, logic programming and ontologies, recognising—and appropriately relating—the typical elements of a privacy policy in the original natural language statements. The prototype system that translates the data privacy policies is presented and is referred to as 'Natural Language Policy Translator (NLPT) 2.0', an extended version of the system 'Natural Language Policy Translator (NLPT) 1.0' [6]. *Natural Language Policy Translator (NLPT) 2.0* is composed of different components that allow the end-user to analyze the functionality and operations required for policy translation. The system is equipped with a user-friendly GUI that supports end-users entering the policies, and the system translates it into CNL4DSA.

In conclusion, *Natural Language Policy Translator (NLPT) 2.0* provides the following functionalities:

- Parses the policy to extract action(s) and predicate(s).
- Processes policy by means of tokenization of sentences, words, stop-words, unigram tagging to label subject(s) and object(s) and extract subject(s), object(s), action(s) and predicate(s).
- Identifies and produces ontologies with respect to subject hasRole, the object hasCategory, the object hasPurpose, relation as subject predicate object, etc.
- Extracts the fragment from the original policy.
- Extracts the context from the original policy.
- Classifies between authorization, obligation, and prohibition fragments.
- Performs all the above tasks separately and together.

For experimentation, *NLPT 2.0* is tested with five popular social network data privacy policies. To analyze the components' performance, a criterion is defined for evaluation. The obtained results of various components' performances are between 70% and 95%. The performance indicators of the system components appeared relatively encouraging and satisfactory. Initially, the work aims to provide complete automatic machine translation without human intervention. However, due to certain limitations found during experimentation, there is a need for human intervention to define the vocabulary for unigram tagging and ontologies at the initial stage. It is argued that once the system is fully trained with unique terms for the vocabulary and ontology lexicon, human intervention becomes minimal, and the system can automatically tag the words as subject(s) and object(s) more accurately and produce proper ontology relations.

As discussed in Section 7, the policy cannot simply be input in its original form since the dependency parser [41] may not be able to correctly parse too complicated phrases. Of course, improper parsing also has a direct influence on Fragment Extractor (FE) and Context Extractor (CFE) performance. This issue has been dealt with by introducing the role of a *Policy Writer* to enter the policy following the manual's guidelines. The approach is currently not fully automatic because it needs human involvement at certain points, yet it is close to fully automatic translation. All these issues will be addressed in future work.

Author Contributions: Conceptualization, I.K.T.; methodology, I.K.T.; software, I.K.T. and I.A.; validation, F.J. and N.Y.; writing—original draft preparation, I.K.T.; writing—review and editing, I.A. and F.J.; visualization, N.Y.; supervision, I.A.; funding acquisition, N.Y. All authors have read and agreed to the published version of the manuscript.

Funding: This research received no external funding.

Institutional Review Board Statement: Not applicable.

Informed Consent Statement: Not applicable.

Data Availability Statement: The complete translation of all 100 policies is available here [53].

Acknowledgments: The authors would like to extend their gratitude to Marinella Petrochhi, Asif Khalid, Khalid Rasheed and Yaseen Khan Tanoli who helped in this study.

Conflicts of Interest: The authors declare no conflict of interest.

References

1. Ali, S.; Islam, N.; Rauf, A.; Din, I.U.; Guizani, M.; Rodrigues, J.J. Privacy and security issues in online social networks. *Future Internet* **2018**, *10*, 114. [CrossRef]
2. Facebook Privacy Policy, 2022. Available online: https://m.facebook.com/privacy/explanation/ (accessed on 20 June 2022).
3. Twitter Privay Policy, 2022. Available online: https://twitter.com/en/privacy (accessed on 20 June 2022).
4. Google Privacy and Terms, 2022. Available online: https://policies.google.com/privacy (accessed on 20 June 2022).
5. Cambridge Dictionary. 1999. Available online: https://dictionary.cambridge.org/dictionary/english/policy (accessed on 20 June 2021).
6. Tanoli, I.K.; Petrocchi, M.; De Nicola, R. Towards automatic translation of social network policies into controlled natural language. In Proceedings of the 2018 12th International Conference on Research Challenges in Information Science (RCIS), Nantes, France, 29–31 May 2018.
7. Costantino, G.; Martinelli, F.; Matteucci, I.; Petrocchi, M. Analysis of Data Sharing Agreements. In Proceedings of the Information Systems Security and Privacy, Porto, Portugal, 19–21 February 2017; pp. 167–178.
8. Standard, O. Extensible Access Control Markup Language (Xacml) Version 3.0. 2013. Available online: http://docs.oasis-open.org/xacml/3.0/xacml-3.0-core-spec-os-en.html (accessed on 22 January 2018).
9. Matteucci, I.; Petrocchi, M.; Sbodio, M.L. CNL4DSA: A controlled natural language for data sharing agreements. In Proceedings of the Symposium on Applied Computing, Sierre, Switzerland, 22–26 March 2010; pp. 616–620.
10. Costantino, G.; Martinelli, F.; Matteucci, I.; Petrocchi, M. Efficient Detection of Conflicts in Data Sharing Agreements. In Proceedings of the Information Systems Security and Privacy—Revised Selected Papers, Porto, Portugal, 19–21 February 2017; pp. 148–172.
11. Lenzini, G.; Petrocchi, M. Modelling of Railway Signalling System Requirements by Controlled Natural Languages: A Case Study. In *From Software Engineering to Formal Methods and Tools, and Back*; Springer: Berlin, Germany, 2019; pp. 502–518.
12. Instagram Data Policy, 2021. Available online: https://help.instagram.com/519522125107875 (accessed on 20 June 2021).
13. LinkedIn Privacy Policy, 2021. Available online: https://www.linkedin.com/legal/privacy-policy (accessed on 20 June 2021).
14. Schwitter, R. Controlled natural languages for knowledge representation. In Proceedings of the Coling 2010: Posters, Beijing, China, 23–27 August 2010; pp. 1113–1121.
15. Gao, T. Controlled natural languages for knowledge representation and reasoning. In Proceedings of the Technical Communications of the 32nd International Conference on Logic Programming (ICLP 2016), New York, NY, USA, 16–21 October 2016.
16. Schwitter, R.; Kaljurand, K.; Cregan, A.; Dolbear, C.; Hart, G. *A Comparison of Three Controlled Natural Languages for OWL 1.1*; 2008. Available online: https://www.researchgate.net/publication/228635222_A_comparison_of_three_controlled_natural_languages_for_OWL_11 (accessed on 20 June 2022).
17. Kuhn, T. A survey and classification of controlled natural languages. *Comput. Linguist.* **2014**, *40*, 121–170. [CrossRef]

18. Hujisen, W.O. Controlled language: An introduction. In Proceedings of the 2nd International Workshop on Controlled Language Applications (CLAW), Pittsburgh, PA, USA, 21–22 May 1998; pp. 1–15.
19. ASD Simplified Technical English, 2017. Available online: http://www.asd-ste100.org/ (accessed on 20 June 2021).
20. Civil Aviation Authority. CAP 722 Unmanned Aircraft System Operations in UK Airspace—Guidance. *Dir. Airsp. Policy* **2010**, *8*, 1–238.
21. Nyberg, E.; Mitamura, T. The KANTOO machine translation environment. In Proceedings of the Conference of the Association for Machine Translation in the Americas, Cuernavaca, Mexico, 10–14 October 2000; pp. 192–195.
22. Fuchs, N.; Kaljurand, K.; Kuhn, T. Attempto Controlled English for knowledge representation. In *Reasoning Web*; Springer: Berlin/Heidelberg, Germany, 2008; pp. 104–124.
23. Martinelli, F.; Matteucci, I.; Petrocchi, M.; Wiegand, L. A formal support for collaborative data sharing. In Proceedings of the Availability, Reliability, and Security, Prague, Czech Republic, 20–24 August 2012; pp. 547–561.
24. Clavel, M.; Durán, F.; Eker, S.; Lincoln, P.; Martí-Oliet, N.; Meseguer, J.; Talcott, C. *All About Maude—A High-Performance Logical Framework: How to Specify, Program and Verify Systems in Rewriting Logic*; Springer: Berlin/Heidelberg, Germany, 2007.
25. Matteucci, I.; Mori, P.; Petrocchi, M.; Wiegand, L. Controlled data sharing in E-health. In Proceedings of the Socio-Technical Aspects in Security and Trust (STAST), Milan, Italy, 8 September 2011; pp. 17–23.
26. Tateishi, T.; Yoshihama, S.; Sato, N.; Saito, S. Automatic smart contract generation using controlled natural language and template. *IBM J. Res. Dev.* **2019**, *63*, 6:1–6:12. [CrossRef]
27. Calafato, A.; Colombo, C.; Pace, G.J. A Controlled Natural Language for Tax Fraud Detection. In Proceedings of the International Workshop on Controlled Natural Language, Aberdeen, UK, 25–27 July 2016; pp. 1–12.
28. Colombo, C.; Grech, J.P.; Pace, G.J. A controlled natural language for business intelligence monitoring. In Proceedings of the Applications of Natural Language to Information Systems, Passau, Germany, 17–19 June 2015; pp. 300–306.
29. Feuto Njonko, P.B.; Cardey, S.; Greenfield, P.; El Abed, W. RuleCNL: A controlled natural language for business rule specifications. In Proceedings of the International Workshop on Controlled Natural Language, Galway, Ireland, 20–22 August 2014; pp. 66–77.
30. Brodie, C.A.; Karat, C.M.; Karat, J. An empirical study of natural language parsing of privacy policy rules using the SPARCLE policy workbench. In Proceedings of the Usable Privacy and Security, Pittsburgh, PA, USA, 12–14 July 2006; pp. 8–19.
31. Fisler, K.; Krishnamurthi, S. A model of triangulating environments for policy authoring. In Proceedings of the Access Control Models and Technologies, Pittsburgh, PA, USA, 9–11 June 2010; pp. 3–12.
32. Kiyavitskaya, N.; Zannone, N. Requirements model generation to support requirements elicitation: The Secure Tropos experience. *Autom. Softw. Eng.* **2008**, *15*, 149–173. [CrossRef]
33. Fantechi, A.; Gnesi, S.; Ristori, G.; Carenini, M.; Vanocchi, M.; Moreschini, P. Assisting requirement formalization by means of natural language translation. *Form. Methods Syst. Des.* **1994**, *4*, 243–263. [CrossRef]
34. Craven, R.; Lobo, J.; Ma, J.; Russo, A.; Lupu, E.; Bandara, A. Expressive policy analysis with enhanced system dynamicity. In Proceedings of the Information, Computer, and Communications Security, Sydney, Australia, 10–12 March 2009; pp. 239–250.
35. Fockel, M.; Holtmann, J. A requirements engineering methodology combining models and controlled natural language. In Proceedings of the 2014 IEEE 4th International Model-Driven Requirements Engineering Workshop (MoDRE), Karlskrona, Sweden, 25 August 2014; pp. 67–76.
36. Mousas, A.S.; Antonakopoulou, A.; Gogoulos, F.; Lioudakis, G.V.; Kaklamani, D.I.; Venieris, I.S. Visualising access control: The PRISM approach. In Proceedings of the Panellenic Conference on Informatics (PCI), Tripoli, Greece, 10–12 September 2010; pp. 107–111.
37. Ruiz, J.F.; Petrocchi, M.; Matteucci, I.; Costantino, G.; Gambardella, C.; Manea, M.; Ozdeniz, A. A lifecycle for data sharing agreements: How it works out. In Proceedings of the Annual Privacy Forum, Frankfurt am Main, Germany, 7–8 September 2016; pp. 3–20.
38. Crossley, S.A.; Allen, L.K.; Kyle, K.; McNamara, D.S. Analyzing discourse processing using a simple natural language processing tool. *Discourse Process.* **2014**, *51*, 511–534. [CrossRef]
39. Bird, S. NLTK: The natural language toolkit. In Proceedings of the COLING, Sydney, Australia, 17–21 July 2006; pp. 69–72.
40. Manning, C.D.; Surdeanu, M.; Bauer, J.; Finkel, J.R.; Bethard, S.; McClosky, D. The Stanford CoreNLP natural language processing toolkit. In Proceedings of the 52nd Annual Meeting of the Association for Computational Linguistics: System Demonstrations, Baltimore, MD, USA, 23–24 June 2014; pp. 55–60.
41. Matthew Honnibal, Ines Montani. spaCy 101: Everything You Need to Know. 2017. Available online: https://spacy.io/ (accessed on 20 June 2022)
42. Lamy, J.B. Owlready: Ontology-oriented programming in Python with automatic classification and high level constructs for biomedical ontologies. *Artif. Intell. Med.* **2017**, *80*, 11–28. [CrossRef] [PubMed]
43. Facebook Data Policy, 2022. Available online: https://www.facebook.com/policy.php (accessed on 20 June 2022).
44. Chen, D.; Manning, C. A fast and accurate dependency parser using neural networks. In Proceedings of the 2014 Conference on Empirical Methods in Natural Language Processing (EMNLP), Doha, Qatar, 25–29 October 2014; pp. 740–750.
45. Maruch, S.; Maruch, A. *Python for Dummies*; John Wiley & Sons: Hoboken, NJ, USA, 2006.
46. Bird, S.; Klein, E.; Loper, E. *Natural Language Processing with Python: Analyzing Text with the Natural Language Toolkit*; O'Reilly Media: Newton, MA, USA, 2009.

47. Bradner, S. RFC 2119: Keywords for Use in RFCs to Indicate Requirement Levels. 1997. Available online: https://www.ietf.org/rfc/rfc2119.txt (accessed on 20 June 2022)
48. Noy, N.F.; McGuinness, D.L. Ontology Development 101: A Guide to Creating Your First Ontology. 2001. Available online: https://protege.stanford.edu/ (accessed on 20 June 2022)
49. Hitzler, P.; Krötzsch, M.; Parsia, B.; Patel-Schneider, P.F.; Rudolph, S. OWL 2 web ontology language primer. *W3C Recomm.* **2009**, *27*, 123.
50. Musen, M.A. The protégé project: A look back and a look forward. *AI Matters* **2015**, *1*, 4–12. [CrossRef] [PubMed]
51. Tanoli, I.K.; Tanoli, Y.K.; Qureshi, A.K. Semi-automatic Translations of Data Privacy Policies into Controlled Natural Languages. *J. Indep. Stud. Res. Comput.* **2021**, *17*. [CrossRef]
52. Don Rozenberg. PAGE PYTHON. Available online: http://page.sourceforge.net/ (accessed on 20 June 2022).
53. Tanoli, I.K. Policies Dataset Result. 2022. Available online: https://www.dropbox.com/sh/prkfyizeaxe3mmg/AAAiFOkFbPDPXr22B1crnvIba?dl=0 (accessed on 20 June 2022).
54. Resnik, P.; Lin, J. 11 evaluation of NLP systems. In *The Handbook of Computational Linguistics and Natural Language Processing*; Wiley: Hoboken, NJ, USA, 2010; Volume 57.
55. Matteucci, I.; Petrocchi, M.; Sbodio, M.L.; Wiegand, L. A design phase for data sharing agreements. In *Data Privacy Management and Autonomous Spontaneus Security*; Springer: Berlin, Germany, 2012; pp. 25–41.

MDPI
St. Alban-Anlage 66
4052 Basel
Switzerland
www.mdpi.com

Applied Sciences Editorial Office
E-mail: applsci@mdpi.com
www.mdpi.com/journal/applsci

Disclaimer/Publisher's Note: The statements, opinions and data contained in all publications are solely those of the individual author(s) and contributor(s) and not of MDPI and/or the editor(s). MDPI and/or the editor(s) disclaim responsibility for any injury to people or property resulting from any ideas, methods, instructions or products referred to in the content.

www.ingramcontent.com/pod-product-compliance
Lightning Source LLC
LaVergne TN
LVHW070436100526
838202LV00014B/1612